D0129261

Eric J. Sharpe

NOT TO DESTROY

BUT TO FULFIL

BV
3269
.F23
S53
1965

STUDIA MISSIONALIA UPSALIENSIA V

Eric J. Sharpe

NOT TO DESTROY
BUT TO FULFIL

The Contribution of J. N. Farquhar
to Protestant Missionary Thought
in India before 1914

GLEERUP

33627

HIEBERT LIBRARY
WITHDRAWN
Fresno Pacific College - M. B. Seminary
Fresno, Calit 93702

© 1965 · ERIC J. SHARPE

SWEDISH INSTITUTE OF MISSIONARY RESEARCH

UPPSALA

Printed in Sweden by

Almqvist & Wiksells Boktryckeri AB

Uppsala 1965

For
A. S.
J. S.
A.-L. B. S.

Contents

Introduction

John Nicol Farquhar, Professor of Comparative Religion in the University of Manchester, died on July 17, 1929, at the age of sixty-eight. Only six years earlier he had retired from missionary work in India, in which he had been engaged since 1891.

Most obituary notices drew attention to his position as an authority on Indian religion. *The Times* wrote that he "did more than any contemporary writer to interpret to English readers the religious culture of India".[1] And *The Statesman* (Calcutta) called him "... one of the most illustrious interpreters of Indian religious thought among recent European writers".[2] It was pointed out that his reputation as an authority on Hinduism rested on three books, *A Primer of Hinduism* (1911), *Modern Religious Movements in India* (1915) and *An Outline of the Religious Literature of India* (1920), and that he had written important articles for Hastings' *Encyclopaedia of Religion and Ethics* and *Encyclopaedia Britannica*. At the time of his death he was Wilde Lecturer in Natural and Comparative Religion in the University of Oxford, and an Elector to the Boden Professorship of Sanskrit in the same University; and his widow later received official recognition of the services rendered by him "in the study of Comparative Religion".[3]

But writers drew attention to more than his purely scholarly attainments. *The Scotsman* (Edinburgh) wrote that he "led the way in building up a new [missionary] apologetic", and stated that "Dr. Farquhar's work has left its mark on Christian thought in India and beyond its borders".[4] Similar judgments were expressed privately. A. J. Appasamy told of the indebtedness of the Indian peoples to him for inaugurating "a new attitude towards Indian culture in all its aspects".[5] A fellow-missionary, H. A. Popley, spoke of his work "as a pioneer in a new approach to the great religions of India",[6]

---

[1] *The Times,* 19.7.1929 (Material in notes 1–7 from Farquhar collection).

[2] *The Statesman,* 20.7.1929.

[3] Mrs. Farquhar was awarded a Civil List Pension: Prime Minister to Mrs. E. N. M. Farquhar, 7.3.1931.

[4] *The Scotsman,* 19.7.1929.

[5] A. J. Appasamy to Mrs. E. N. M. Farquhar, 7.8.1929.

[6] H. A. Popley to Mrs. E. N. M. Farquhar, undated.

and John R. Mott referred to his "great creative and undying work".[7]

It might perhaps be argued that these are in some measure expressions of conventional politeness and sympathy. But their very unanimity suggests that Farquhar had made some noteworthy contribution to the study of Indian religions on the one hand, and to the Christian (in this case Protestant or Evangelical Christian) attitude to those same religions on the other. One aspect of his work was scholarly; the other missionary. On this at least Farquhar's contemporaries were agreed: that his was no ordinary missionary career, and that his contribution was outstanding of its kind. Nicol Macnicol even went so far as to suggest that the name of Farquhar symbolized the first quarter of the twentieth century, much as the name of Alexander Duff had symbolized the second quarter of the nineteenth century in Indian missions. Macnicol's estimate of Farquhar's contribution was generous:

We owe to him two things—first, a new orientation of the whole missionary outlook as over against the non-Christian systems; and second, a re-birth of Christian literature, the initiation of a movement of active and awakened thought in the service of the Christian enterprise. Rightly understood these two facts, so important in the missionary history of our time and so closely linked with J. N. Farquhar's name, are not two but one, for the second issues from the first. Others may have discovered simultaneously with him, or even before him, the implications for missionary method of the facts that "comparative religion" was disclosing; the significance of his name and work consists in the fact that he translated this discovery into action and summoned others to unite with him in a new adventure of the mind.[8]

Elsewhere Macnicol wrote that

It may be claimed for Farquhar that he, more than any other individual, brought about a new orientation of the whole missionary outlook towards the non-Christian religions.[9]

And E. C. Dewick, referring to Farquhar's book *The Crown of Hinduism* (1913), claimed that it "marked a definite milestone in the history of missionary thought and ideals in India".[1]

---

[7] Telegram: J. R. Mott to Mrs. E. N. M. Farquhar, 24.7.1929.

[8] Macnicol, "Dr. J. N. Farquhar", in *YMI* XLI: 9 (Sept. 1929), p. 681.

[9] *Dict. Nat. Biogr. 1922–1930* (1937), p. 296. Cf. the description of Farquhar as "the inaugurator of a new era in the study of Indian religious thought and practice", in *Report of the Commission on Christian Higher Education in India* (1931), p. 117, cf. p. 129.

[1] Dewick, "Dr. J. N. Farquhar", in *YMI* XLI: 10 (Oct. 1929), p. 753.

If these are accurate judgments—and we have no reason to doubt the sincerity with which they are written—then Farquhar's position in the history of Christian missions in India ought to be secure. It is all the more surprising, then, to find that his name is scarcely mentioned in modern missionary literature. The latest histories—for example those of Neill, Firth and Westman-von Sicard[2]—omit Farquhar altogether; while even Latourette limits himself to one single mention. Yet this one brief statement is substantially in line with what Macnicol had written: that

J. N. Farquhar as a secretary of the Young Men's Christian Associations inaugurated a new era in the production of Christian literature and helped to bring about a reorientation of the Protestant missions towards non-Christian religions.[3]

This is tantalizing in its brevity, recognizing as it does Farquhar's importance without making any attempt to expand or explain. Otherwise, Farquhar is mentioned in E. C. Dewick's valuable Hulsean Lectures,[4] in books by the Swedish writers Estborn and Diehl,[5] and occasionally by Indian authors,[6] but none of these makes any claim to be a specialist study.

One of the main reasons for this apparent neglect is the profound change in theological climate which has come about since Farquhar's time. As far as missions are concerned, this is best exemplified in the work of Hendrik Kraemer, whose book *The Christian Message in a Non-Christian World* (1938) has been responsible for setting a new trend in missionary thought, but at the same time for obscur-

---

[2] Neill, *A History of Christian Missions* (1964), Firth, *An Introduction to Indian Church History* (1961), Westman-von Sicard, *Den kristna missionens historia* (1960). Westman has however mentioned Farquhar in another context, see n. 5 below.

[3] *A History of the Expansion of Christianity* VI (1944), p. 191. The reference is to the Lindsay Report (cf. n. 9 above).

[4] Dewick, *The Christian Attitude to Other Religions* (1953), pp. 49, 51. Cf. the same writer's earlier book *The Gospel and Other Faiths* (1948), p. 96 f.

[5] Estborn, *Indiens nydaning och kristendomen* (1945), p. 25 f., Diehl, *Kristendomens möte med religionerna* (1961), p. 59 f.; cf. Westman, "Missionens uppgift i Indien", in *Religion och Bibel* IV (1945), p. 24.

[6] D. G. Moses has significantly entitled a recent article "Apologetic Literature since Farquhar" [*NCCR* LXXXIII: 8 (August 1963), pp. 276–286], which recalls Macnicol's thesis that Farquhar in a sense symbolized his generation. Moses writes that Farquhar was "one of the greatest apologists of the Christian faith in the first two decades of this century" (p. 278). See also S. Kulendran, "The Significance of Theological Thinking for Evangelism among Hindus", in *IRM* XXXIII: 32 (Oct. 1944), pp. 390 ff.

ing much of the distinctive contribution made by the preceding generation of missionary scholars.

Kraemer's estimate of Farquhar is interesting. Though the first impression is almost entirely negative, there proves on closer examination to be a striking ambivalence in Kraemer's attitude. At an early date Kraemer had recognized the positive value of Farquhar's contribution to Christian literature in India, and he had been appreciative of his sympathetic approach to Hinduism—an approach based on careful and detailed study.[7] But Farquhar's theology, and particularly his use of the concept of "fulfilment" to characterize the relationship between Christianity and Hinduism, he expressly rejected, not because he wished to deny altogether the possibility of some kind of divine revelation having taken place in the non-Christian religions, but because he wished to guard against relativism in respect of the unique revelation in Christ.[8]

Kraemer has since sharpened his criticism, labelling Farquhar's work (or rather the theology behind it) as "too facile and ... too complacent", and has dismissed his attempt to formulate a theory of Christian-Hindu relationships as "benevolent superiority intending to be gracious modesty".[9] The tone and the intention of this judgment are both symptomatic of the post-Barthian attitude to the "liberal" period.

It would however be wrong to assume that further *historical* study of the earlier period is thereby rendered superfluous. In this case, theological polemic, whether justified or not, has been allowed to encroach on the field of the historian. The need is obviously for historical research: for a type of research, moreover, which is prepared to set aside theological presuppositions and examine the "liberal" period as far as possible dispassionately.

A further reason for careful historical study of this period is provided by the generalizations and inaccuracies of a modern Indian

---

[7] In 1923 Kraemer spoke of "the excellent Dr. Farquhar" (*den vortreffelijken Dr. Farquhar*) in this connexion: H. Kraemer to J. W. Gunning, 28.5.1923 (Zendingshogeschool, N. H. Kerk, Oegstgeest, Holland). For this observation I am indebted to Teol. Lic. Carl F. Hallencreutz.

[8] *The Christian Message in a Non-Christian World* (1938), p. 123. That Kraemer even at this date regarded Farquhar as the main representative of the "fulfilment" school is clear from his earlier book *De Outmoeting van het Christendom en de Wereldsgodsdiensten* (1936), p. 49 f.

[9] *Religion and the Christian Faith* (1956), p. 215. A similar view has been expressed by Radhakrishnan, *East and West in Religion* (1933), p. 24.

historian such as K. M. Panikkar. Panikkar's main contention is that Christian missions have failed to make any appreciable impression on India. He is clearly entitled to his opinion, and his book *Asia and Western Dominance* (1954) must be treated with respect. But unless his sweeping statements can be shown to proceed from adequate knowledge of the facts, their value must be slight.[1]

The object of this present study is, then, historical: to trace Farquhar's background, and his religious and intellectual development in the total context of the Indian missionary situation up to the outbreak of the first world war, and to the publication of his most notable work of "apologetics" (as distinct from the history of religions), *The Crown of Hinduism*. Its overall aim will be to indicate the nature and extent of Farquhar's contribution to the debate surrounding the question of the Christian attitude to Hinduism before 1914. The boundary is not merely arbitrary. The appearance of *The Crown of Hinduism* marks the climax of Farquhar's work as a missionary apologist; when he is mentioned or criticized today, it is commonly as the author of that one book. Further, after 1913 his own work came to be centred more and more on the problem of interpreting the history, structure and ethos of Indian religion to Western readers; the actual writing of distinctively Christian missionary literature he left to others, his own contribution being the onerous one of recruiting and encouraging writers, and seeing their work through the press. The first world war of course marked the end of an epoch: in theology, in politics, and in the Indian national movement. In a sense it is true to say that the culmination of the particular Christian literary movement launched by Farquhar, and the theories on which it was based, was not reached until the Jerusalem conference of 1928; but a detailed study of the period from 1914 to 1928 and beyond must await some future occasion.

---

[1] Panikkar entitles a chapter of *Asia and Western Dominance* "The Failure of Christian Missions" (pp. 454 ff.), and points to the too-close connexion between missions and imperialism as one of the factors involved. But pp. 445–448, dealing with "The Decline of Missionary Effort in India", are full of inaccuracies. There is no evidence that early 20th-century missionaries "felt the ground under them slipping" (p. 445); the names of two of the three nationalist leaders mentioned on the same page are misspelt; to date Christian interest in Indian culture from the first world war is plainly incorrect (p. 446); to classify Stanley Jones and John Mott together as " 'progressive' missionaries" is misleading (p. 447). Such criticisms might be multiplied.

Something must now be said about the principles on which this study is based. First of all, it must be emphasized that the primary object of this investigation is not biographical; it is true that it follows the early part of Farquhar's missionary career rather closely, but only in so far as the events described illustrate the development of a concept—the concept of "Christ (or Christianity) the fulfilment of Hinduism"—and the increasing application of that concept in the missionary debate of the period. It would of course have been possible to have dealt with the same problem thematically, but this alternative was dismissed as inadequate. First, because a knowledge of the course of events in the years before 1914 is vital to an understanding of the missionary debate of the time; and secondly, because it was felt that such a working knowledge is not easily obtained from the existing literature. This being so, Farquhar's career offers a convenient framework on which to build. The division into chapters, corresponding to the various stages of his career, was again made as a matter of convenience; however, this has proved to have decided advantages, not least since such a scheme can be departed from where necessary. A further point which must be stressed is that this study attempts to illustrate the development of *a missionary attitude,* and does not purport to describe the total missionary situation of the pre-1914 period in India. Thus while it has been found necessary to summarize various aspects of that total situation, for example the Hindu renaissance and its alliance with Indian nationalism, these are always subservient to the main end in view—the interpretation of how a representative Evangelical missionary reacted to the challenge of Hinduism in that situation.[2]

Certain rigid limitations have had to be imposed. Thus little mention has been made of the Continental debate on the subject of the Christian approach to the non-Christian religions. This is of course not to say that this debate is uninteresting or unimportant. On the contrary: it was felt that to do adequate justice to the various schools of thought involved would have caused this study to expand to an inordinate size. A further factor to be taken into consideration is that the main Continental missionary contribution before 1914 was not made in India, where British (and to a lesser extent

---

[2] For an example of an alternative approach, from the side of the Hindu rather than the Christian material, see Krämer, *Christus und Christentum im Denken des modernen Hinduismus* (1958).

American) missions had a privileged position, where the official language was English, and where much of the development with which we shall be concerned took place in the context of higher education, with which the Continental missions were not concerned, and of which they were later openly critical.[3]

Another omission is—with one exception, the Oxford Mission to Calcutta—the missions of the Catholic tradition, Roman and Anglican; again, their theology was distinctive, and calls for much fuller treatment than could be given it here. The Anglican school of theology which Richardson characterizes as "liberal orthodoxy",[4] although it had its own small mission (the Cambridge Mission to Delhi), is also passed over for the most past, as lying to one side of the dominant Evangelical stream of missionary thought.

In Part One of this present study an attempt will be made to describe the conditions obtaining in Evangelical missions in India prior to Farquhar's arrival, some of the significant movements in missionary thought during the later part of the nineteenth century, and the climate of missionary opinion at that time with regard to Hinduism. This will involve an examination, first, of the theoretical background of Evangelical missions; and secondly, of the practical situation within which the need for a new approach to Hinduism first came to be appreciated—the developing situation of Christian higher education. This study has been made necessary by the lack of up-to-date literature dealing with the problems of the period in question. Part One ends with a sketch of Farquhar's religious and intellectual background. Part Two follows Farquhar's career from 1891 to 1913, with special reference to the various formative elements which gave rise to his own distinctive contribution—particularly the Hindu renaissance, the Indian political crisis, student work, and

[3] See e.g. Schomerus, *Indien und das Christentum* II (1932), p. 143 f., idem, *Kan kristendomen erövra Indien?* (1923), p. 15. For a brief characterization of German missionary ideals, see Richter, in *Evangelism for the World Today*, ed. Mott (1938), p. 266.

[4] Richardson, *The Bible in the Age of Science* (1961), p. 65. The foremost representatives of this school were the Cambridge theologians B. F. Westcott, J. B. Lightfoot and F. J. A. Hort. We may note in passing that although Westcott's published lectures on Hebrews bear the title *Christus Consummator* (1886), he later wrote that the Christian revelation is "absolutely unique, essentially different in kind from all other religions ... Of this Gospel there is no anticipation in the noblest utterances of prae-Christian Gentile teachers, though their speculations and their hopes cannot find satisfaction without it." *Christian Aspects of Life* (1897), p. 170 f.

the missionary debate of the period, centring on the concept of "fulfilment".

We have already had occasion to use the word "apologetics" (or "apologetic"), and even a cursory examination of the missionary literature of the period shows that the term had a wide, if rather vague, currency. It may be well, in order to avoid undue misunderstanding at a later stage, to say a few words about this ambiguous term. Missionary theologians in recent years have tended to reject the idea of "apologetics" outright, as being incompatible with the Christian Gospel.[5] The implication here is that "apologetics", since it indicates the holding of a defensive attitude, cannot be equated with the Christian proclamation, which is dynamic and not defensive. But it must be recognized that the difficulty is, in part at least, semantic: in short, that "apologetics" in the missionary thought of the pre-1914 period is not necessarily identical with "apologetics" in the classical sense of "the defensive statement of Christianity". This is not a subject we can discuss in detail here, but some comment is called for.[6]

Evangelical missionaries of the late nineteenth and early twentieth centuries tended to look upon "apologetic" or "apologetics" as being simply "the communication of the Gospel". This involved, on the one hand, the pedagogical principle of the removal of hindrances to the Christian faith, and on the other, the proclamation of the Gospel itself. Secondly, it was recognized that the practice of "apologetics" was partly—but only partly—defensive. The criterion was

---

[5] Again, this is best illustrated by reference to Kraemer, whose article "Christianity and Secularism", in *IRM* XIX: 73 (Jan. 1930), pp. 195–208, is an uncompromising rejection of the "apologetic attitude", particularly in its unconscious assumptions. "Christianity in the sense of the revelation of God in Jesus Christ, the Incarnate Word, the Truth and the Life claims as such to be the only tenable view of life when the stern realities of life and the world are fully taken into account. In this sense Christianity cannot and may not be a matter of apologetics" (p. 205). The crux is that Christianity must be made, not "acceptable" but "inescapable" (p. 205 f.). See also Hartenstein, *Was hat die Theologie Karl Barths der Mission zu sagen?* (2. Aufl., 1928).

[6] Cf. Richardson, *Christian Apologetics* (1947), p. 19 f.: "Apologetics, as distinct from apology, is the study of ways and means of defending Christian truth ... Hence, also, apologetics is primarily a study undertaken by Christians for Christians; and in this respect it is to be distinguished from the task of apology, since an apology is addressed to non-Christians." This distinction may be useful in the present-day debate, but it does not correspond to the use of the term "apologetics" with which we are concerned.

normally empirical, rather than theoretical; in India, the Christian faith was subject to attack from many quarters, and had to be defended, almost as a condition of survival. Misunderstanding and misrepresentation was rife, and could not be ignored. But "apologetics" did not cease when the missionary passed over to direct proclamation. And thirdly, "apologetics" came to be closely linked with the idea of the proclamation of the Gospel to adherents of other religions (in this case Hinduism), and with the problem of the "relationship" between Christianity and Hinduism. It thus involved close and detailed study, both of the non-Christian religion itself, and of the essence of the Christian faith.[7] A further facet must be borne in mind: from 1905 on, "apologetics" came to be used in the special sense of "the intellectual approach", particularly to students.[8] The term must therefore be judged on its merits, and as far as possible understood in the sense in which the missionaries understood it. Farquhar used the word in a very wide sense indeed, and it may be of value to have his definition. At the Oxford W.S.C.F. conference of 1909 he said:

The process of bringing the Hindu to faith in Christ implies so much and usually depends on so many elements that, in order to make myself intelligible, I am compelled to use the word apologetic in a very wide sense, so as to cover everything that helps to produce faith as well as formal arguments to that end.[9]

When I began this investigation, no biography of Farquhar existed, apart from a short entry in the *Dictionary of National Biography*.[1] In 1963, however, I published in India a short popular biographical sketch, *J. N. Farquhar: A Memoir*,[2] in which will be found a number of personal details not included in this account. But as this book is not as yet generally available outside India, I have restricted references to a minimum.

---

[7] Cairns, "The Need for Apologists", in the *Student World* IV (April 1911), pp. 53, 56; cf. Mott's use of the term in connexion with the Edinburgh conference, below, p. 277; Mott, *The Decisive Hour of Christian Missions* (1910), p. 76.

[8] Below, pp. 231 ff.

[9] *Report of the Conference of the World's Student Christian Federation held at Oxford, England* (1909), p. 72. Cf. below, pp. 254 ff.

[1] *Dict. Nat. Biogr. 1922–1930* (1937), p. 296.

[2] Sharpe, *J. N. Farquhar: A Memoir*, with an Introduction by A. J. Appasamy (Association Press, Calcutta, 1963). Cf. idem, "Ett missionens dilemma", in *SMT* 48: 4 (1960), pp. 244–248, and idem, "John Nicol Farquhar", in *Association Men* XIII: 8 (Oct. 1961).

The sources on which this study is based may be divided into two categories: published and unpublished. Of published sources there has been an *embarras de richesse,* modified in practice by considerable difficulty of access. Farquhar himself was a prolific writer, and his published works (both in India and Europe) run into many hundreds of thousands of words. These, together with the large number of other books, pamphlets, conference reports, periodicals and the like, which have been consulted, have been found in many libraries and in a number of private collections in Great Britain and the United States. At the same time the absence of a fully adequate missionary bibliography makes oversight and omission virtually inevitable. The principal unpublished sources which have been utilized have been Farquhar's and T. E. Slater's letters to the London Missionary Society, Farquhar's and other secretaries' letters and reports to the International Committee of the Y.M.C.A., preserved in the Y.M.C.A. Historical Library, New York, and private letters and papers, together with annotated copies of some of Farquhar's own works, in the possession of Mrs. M. I. G. Dibben (née Farquhar). The manuscript answers sent by missionary correspondents to Commissions I and IV of the Edinburgh conference of 1910 were consulted in the Missionary Research Library, New York, and a second copy of some (but not all) of the Commission IV papers was later placed at my disposal by the Rev. Professor David Cairns of Aberdeen. Letters and papers relating to Professor A. G. Hogg, including a series of letters from Principal D. S. Cairns, were made available by Mrs. A. G. Hogg, the late Mr. L. A. Hogg of Edinburgh, and Professor Cairns.

I should finally like to thank those who have contributed in any way to the production of this study. First of all I must thank the Rt. Rev. Professor Bengt Sundkler, on whose suggestion it was begun and by whose unfailing encouragement its progress has been sustained. I thank Teol. Lic. Carl F. Hallencreutz, for many hours of stimulating discussion; the Rt. Rev. Professor Stephen Neill, the Rev. Dr. Sigfrid Estborn, the Rev. Professor David Cairns and the Rev. Principal S. C. Duthie for much valuable criticism and many suggestions; Dr. Paul Anderson of the American Y.M.C.A.; the late Mr. L. A. Hogg and Mrs. A. G. Hogg; and Mrs. M. I. G. Dibben for making available so many of her Father's papers and books. I should also like to thank the librarians of the London Missionary Society, the Church Missionary Society, the Society for the Propagation of the Gospel, the Cambridge Mission to Delhi and the India Office Library in London; the Indian Institute, Mansfield College and Pusey House in Oxford; New College Edinburgh; Christ's College Aberdeen; the Y.M.C.A. Historical Library and the Missionary Research Library in New York; and Uppsala University Library, for invaluable assistance. Much of this archive work was made possible by grants from the funds administered by the Faculty of Theology in the University of Uppsala, for which my thanks are also due.

The dedication of this book is a sign of a debt of gratitude which cannot be expressed in words.

PART ONE

The Nineteenth-Century Background

CHAPTER I

Protestant Missionary Attitudes to Hinduism
after 1858

WHEN J. N. Farquhar adopted, in the years between 1902 and 1913, the "fulfilment hypothesis" as an explanation of the relationship he believed to exist between Christianity and Hinduism, he was making use of an idea (and a formula) which had emerged in late nineteenth-century Britain, in the work of Max Müller and Monier Monier-Williams, and which had been introduced into the Indian missionary debate by T. E. Slater and F. W. Kellett. It follows, therefore, that before we can appreciate the nature and extent of Farquhar's contribution to early twentieth-century missionary thought, we must have some picture of the foundations on which he built. We must take note of the climate of missionary opinion which called forth this new departure; and trends of nineteenth-century theological thought, in so far as they serve to cast light on this particular missionary theory. This chapter will be concerned with the theoretical background; in Chapters Two and Three we consider something of the practical background of the "fulfilment" idea.

It will be clear that to attempt a full-scale account of every attitude, theory and doctrine having a bearing on this problem is out of the question here. The history of nineteenth-century ideas is notoriously complex; and the result would inevitably be disproportionate. We therefore restrict this survey to the most significant features of the situation. For the same reason we restrict this introductory account to Britain and (to a lesser extent) America, since the idea of "fulfilment" in this form was developed in Britain, expressed in English, and applied in the context of British and American Evangelical missions in India; German and other Continental missions stood rather to one side of this particular stream of development, and language difficulties hampered debate across the frontiers.[1] A further principle of selection must be mentioned. J. N. Farquhar's contribution was made in the field of Christian-*Hindu* relations; we shall therefore concentrate on missionary attitudes to *Hinduism* in this account, to the exclusion of parallel developments in other fields.

The risk of undue generalization in a survey of this kind is of course considerable, particularly in view of the rapid and many-sided development of thought during the late nineteenth century. Nevertheless an attempt must be made. In this chapter we have taken 1858 as our starting-point, for two reasons: first, because the transfer of rule over India from the East India Company to the British Crown provides a convenient *terminus a quo;* and secondly, because the attitudes of the earlier period have been adequately dealt with by G. D. Bearce, in a study which, while not specifically missionary, gives valuable insights into the missionary thought of the East India Company period.[2] Further, the years immediately following the Mutiny witnessed, in Great Britain, the first stages in the emergence of the attitude this study sets out to describe. In America, with its cosmopolitan structure and its internal problems, parallel development occurred much later, after the turn of the century.[3] The rise of the doctrine of evolution, the coming of Biblical criticism to the popular attention, and the new "science of religion" all made a notable impact on late nineteenth-century thought, missionary thought not excepted. But before we go on to consider these, and other trends, we must briefly consider the traditional attitudes with which these new departures came into conflict.

---

[1] It is important that these factors should be kept in mind during the whole of the discussion that follows: (i) that Continental missions, by reason of the confessional background, were less susceptible than their British and American counterparts to new departures in doctrine; (ii) that their work was almost exclusively among lower-caste Hindus and outcastes; and (iii) that their contribution to the higher educational enterprise was slight [see *Report of the Commission on Christian Higher Education in India* (1931), p. 373]. So while there were isolated attempts made outside the English-language area to apply the concept of "fulfilment" to Indian missions [as for example by Windisch, *Die altindischen Religionsurkunden und die christliche Mission* (1897), pp. 6–9], these seem hardly to have touched the missionaries themselves, who were usually suspicious of syncretism. These points were stressed by the late Bishop Johannes Sandegren in conversation with the present writer.

[2] Bearce, *British Attitudes towards India, 1784–1858* (1961).

[3] Below, p. 40.

The Traditional Protestant Missionary Attitude
to Hinduism

Nineteenth-century Protestant missions were mainly the product of what has been called the Evangelical Awakening.[4] This late eighteenth and early nineteenth-century movement was, as is well known, derived historically from European Pietism. Like Pietism, it concentrated on the salvation of the individual, effected by the substitutionary Atonement of Jesus Christ, and on his personal relationship with the Deity, rather than on the institutional aspect of religion. Its sole authority was the Bible, interpreted for the most part literally. And while it took on various aspects, not all "fundamental" doctrines being interpreted identically by the various groups,[5] its main features were consistent. Evangelicalism as a whole held mankind to be fallen, to be in a state of sin and rebellion, and hence under the condemnation of God. Its main authorities were the third chapter of Genesis and the first chapter of Romans. The Evangelical missionary held "the conversion of individual souls to Christ by the preaching of the Gospel" to be the true end of all his work.[6] He also attempted to draw them away from contact with the corruption of "this world" into societies of the faithful, regenerate churches.

Non-Christian religions (in this case Hinduism) were of a piece with the corrupt world, and were summed up as "heathenism" or "idolatry". Early Evangelical missionaries were normally convinced as a matter of theological fact that the individual "heathen" in his darkness was doomed, unless he turned in faith to the sole remedy for his sin, the atoning death of Jesus Christ.[7] The position of the "heathen Hindu" was one not merely of misfortune, but of sin; and his undoubted condemnation, though grievous, was just. "The heathen are under condemnation, and to them a dark and hopeless

---

[4] Rouse and Neill (ed.), *A History of the Ecumenical Movement, 1517–1948* (1954), pp. 309 ff., Latourette, *A History of the Expansion of Christianity* III (1939).

[5] The main doctrinal divergence was between Calvinist and Arminian views of the extent of the Atonement, the Calvinists holding that Christ had made propitiation for the sins of the elect only, while the Arminians held the theory of universal atonement; for an illustration of this conflict in practice, see below, pp. 111 ff.

[6] *CMI* IX N.S. (1884), p. 415.

[7] This is perhaps best illustrated by the missionary hymnody of the period. See Routley, *Hymns and Human Life* (1952), pp. 91–98, for examples.

one; they know of no escape ... the wrath of God is abiding on them."[8] Some went to such lengths as to claim that if the heathen were not lost, and did not perish, then there would be no need whatever for missionary work.[9]

Hinduism was a "false religion" *a priori,* the work of the prince of this world, not of God. Thus it was typical that Alexander Duff should call Hinduism "an old, pestilent religion"[1] and that his fellow-Scotsman John Wilson should characterize Hinduism as "the grandest embodiment of Gentile error".[2] Such terms of opprobrium might be multiplied almost indefinitely from the missionary literature of the period.

The Evangelical missionary's unfavourable impression was strengthened in practice by what he regarded as being a fatal cleavage in Hinduism between religion and moral behaviour. Part of the eighteenth-century heritage in the Evangelical Awakening was of course the emphasis on morals: Christianity must be known by its fruits, and not merely by its preaching. Hinduism fell far short of the missionaries' ethical ideal. Much of what they saw disgusted them. The caste system, with its hard-and-fast barriers between man and man; the practice of *satī*; the zenana; infant marriage; hook-swinging and Hindu ascetic practices generally—all this, and more, seemed incommensurate with what they understood as being the purpose of religion. God, they felt, could not have spoken in such a religion. A religion which countenanced, and even recommended such practices degraded its adherents, rather than uplifting them;[3] they spoke of "the loathsome link between Indian piety and Indian impurity".[4] It is perhaps not surprising that they reacted so sharply, or that they concentrated whenever possible on eradicating both cause and symptom; commonly the latter, for some held—and continued to

---

[8] An unsigned article in the *Biblical Repository* (1860), p. 448.

[9] The Rev. H. Shepheard, in correspondence with the Rev. C. C. Lowndes. The letter in which this expression occurs is dated 3.11.1865 (Mansfield College Library, Oxford).

[1] Duff, *Missionary Addresses* (1850), p. 33.

[2] *Report of the General Missionary Conference held at Allahabad, 1872–1873* (1873), p. 14 f.

[3] Early Western observers of Hinduism "speak with almost unanimous abhorrence of a religion which sanctioned and even sanctified burning women alive, throwing young children to crocodiles, suffocating sick old people with mud and marrying little girls to old men ... They did not inquire into philosophy; they judged by what they saw." Woodruff, *The Men who Ruled India* I (1953), p. 242.

[4] G. Ensor, writing in *CMI* XVII N.S. (1892), p. 328.

hold—that to concentrate on philosophical argument in face of the fact of widow-burning, or to discuss the Vedas and do nothing for the outcaste, was both irrelevant and dangerous.[5] The only valid standard of measurement for most missionaries was, as Bishop Caldwell expressed it, "the forms in which it [Hinduism] manifests itself in daily life among the masses, and the tone of mind and style of character it produces".[6] The argument advanced by an Anglican writer in 1855 was typical of the traditional attitude. Hindu inhabitants of India, he claimed, were morally unhealthy;

nor can we be surprised that they are so when the deteriorating influences to which, under the name of religion, they are subjected, are brought to remembrance. Of that fearful system it may with truth be said, that the corrupt heart of man, under Satanic influence, elaborated it out of the depths of its own depravity, and set up as objects of worship the personifications of its own vices.[7]

It was to say the least unfortunate, in the eyes of the missionaries, that the East India Company had long observed a policy of religious tolerance towards Hinduism. The Company, concerned to foster a feeling of security among its Indian "subjects", had, on assuming administrative responsibility, recognized wherever possible existing rights and privileges, religious as well as civil.[8] Both Hinduism and Mohammedanism had benefited. State endowments of non-Christian religions had continued: money had been provided for the support of mosques and temples.[9] The Company thus found itself in the position of patron and protector of much active Hinduism;[1] which

---

[5] This view persisted throughout the period; see Whitehead, "The New Movement in India and the Old Gospel", in *The East and the West* IX: 33 (1911), pp. 1 ff.

[6] Caldwell, *The Relation of Christianity to Hinduism* (1874), p. 8. It is interesting to note that Bishop Caldwell advocates the study of "the Hindu philosophies", "... but only for the sake of self-defence", *ibid.*, p. 11.

[7] *CMI* VI (1855), p. 76. Cf. *The Indian Empire Reader* (1898), p. 151: "Truly Hinduism is a mixture of sin and folly."

[8] The Government "believed it to be necessary, for the stability of their position, not merely to recognize the religions of the people of India, but to support and patronize them as the native rulers had done". Farquhar, *Modern Religious Movements in India* (1915), p. 9. Cf. Richter, *Indische Missionsgeschichte* (2 Aufl. 1924), pp. 199 ff., Mayhew, *Christianity and the Government of India* (1929), p. 145.

[9] Mayhew, *op. cit.*, p. 146.

[1] This went to surprising lengths: Brahmins were employed as weather forecasters; Government offices were kept open on Sundays, but closed on Hindu festivals; and Government records were dedicated to Ganesh. These and other examples are given by Mayhew, *op. cit.*, p. 146 f.

was doubly unfortunate, since its official attitude to Christian missions was not enthusiastic. This official patronage of "idolatry" not unnaturally aroused bitter opposition among the missionaries: some sincerely believed the Mutiny of 1857–58 to have been an expression of the wrath of God, brought about by British dallying with heathenism.[2] In 1858 the Bombay Missionary Conference had sent a sharp reminder to Parliament, to the effect that considerations of "policy" must not be allowed to lead to a compromise with the work of the devil.[3] These and similar objections had their desired result; the process of transference had already begun in 1858, and the last temple was handed over to the Hindu authorities in 1862.[4]

It is evident, reading the literature of the period, that the majority of Evangelical missionaries at work in India in the 1850's and later tended to regard Hinduism in its least favourable aspect, and to contrast it in their own minds with Christianity at its best. Attempts to describe Hinduism in more favourable terms could be coolly received. As late as 1880 a reviewer criticized Monier-Williams' book *Indian Wisdom* on the grounds that

... a student wholly ignorant of India would with difficulty gather that the religion of India is, and has been for many centuries, naked idolatry of the most gross and vulgar description, little superior to that of savages in Central Africa.[5]

But missionaries sincerely desired the betterment of the Indian; his conversion, they were sure, would lead to moral and social improvement as well as the salvation of his soul—issues closely connected in the eyes of nineteenth-century Evangelicalism.[6] First remove the "withering influence" of Hinduism, wrote Dr. Murdoch, then India may perhaps attain happiness and prosperity in the strength of the Christian Gospel.[7] It was not the "quietism" of the *Bhagavad Gītā*, claimed Bishop Caldwell, that was covering India with a network

---

[2] *CMI* VIII (1857), p. 249 f.

[3] The full text will be found in *CMI* IX (1858), pp. 129–132. See also *Report of the Wesleyan Methodist Missionary Society* (1858), pp. 144, 152 ff.

[4] Farquhar, *Modern Religious Movements*, p. 9.

[5] *CMI* V N.S. (1880), p. 220. The same journal later criticized Max Müller and the World's Parliament of Religions in Chicago in most immoderate terms: XLV N.S. (1894), pp. 161–175.

[6] The classical statement of this attitude is to be found in Dennis, *Christian Missions and Social Progress* (1897).

[7] *The Indian Students' Manual* (1887), p. 285.

of railways and telegraphs.[8] Only the Christian Gospel, preached by men having their roots in the progressive and industrialized West, could meet India's needs in the modern age.[9] These tones were echoed by early Indian reformers.[1]

It must further be borne in mind when evaluating traditional attitudes to Hinduism that India was part of the British Empire, and as such subject to imperialist judgments. Too much prominence must not be given to this aspect of the situation: it is impossible to generalize over the extent to which missionaries shared the mental attitudes of the rest of the "Anglo-Indian" community, with its too-common contempt for everything Indian, Hinduism included. That many believed in the reality of "the White Man's Burden" cannot be questioned; but most were not prepared to look down on the Indian as "half devil and half child". Some sense of superiority there undoubtedly was, yet it was generally held in check, and in later years came to be very considerably modified.[2] And the missionary was constantly attempting, by means of education, to "improve" the India: this topic we discuss at length in Chapter Two.

The perpetuation of the traditional Protestant attitude to Hinduism was due to a number of factors, acting in conjunction. The first of these will again be discussed in detail in our next chapter, and a bare mention will suffice here. From the 1830's on, thanks to the pioneer work of Alexander Duff and the reforms inagurated by Bentinck and Macaulay, English came to be the medium of education in missionary and government colleges. At the same time Western patterns were imposed on the educational system as a whole, particularly at its higher levels. This implied a total rejection of traditional Hindu culture; it had the effect of separating "educated India" from its traditional cultural roots, and created a new class of "deracinated" Hindu. It further ensured that most Western mis-

---

[8] *Bishop Caldwell on Krishna and the Bhagavad Gita* (1894), p. 27.

[9] Cf. Mott, "The Christian Ministry in Relation to the Non-Christian World", in *The Report of the British Theological Students' Conference, Birmingham* (1898), p. 50 f. See also below, p. 343.

[1] Keshub Chunder Sen spoke of the "mischief and misery" caused by Hinduism, and asked his countrymen: "Have you not often wept bitterly in solitude for your hard lot?" *An Appeal to Young India* (1897 ed.), p. 5.

[2] On this subject generally, see Bodelsen, *Studies in Mid-Victorian Imperialism* (1924), Hinden, *Empire and After: A Study of British Imperial Attitudes* (1949), Woodruff, *The Men who Ruled India* I, p. 291, II, pp. 172 ff.

sionaries continued to think, and teach, in Western terms. Most important, it severely restricted the areas of contact between the best missionary thought and traditional Indian culture. The demand was for Western education; and Western education was closely bound up with Western religious attitudes. Adaptation and assimilation could not take place under such conditions as these.

Secondly must be mentioned the "mission compound". We have said that the "gathered church" was part of the Pietist and Evangelical heritage. This ideal—of the small, self-contained Christian community, presided over by the missionary—soon proved indispensable in the Indian situation. The Indian convert, particularly if he were a member of one of the highest castes, was forced, when he accepted baptism, to leave the society in which he had grown up. He automatically lost caste, was frequently disowned and disinherited by his family, and had henceforth either to fend for himself or to join the Christian community in the mission compound. Some of the consequences have been pointed out by Miss I. L. Sircar:

> The missionary, not wanting to see the new convert stranded in life, sheltered him in the mission compound. Thus, through force of circumstance, segregated and isolated from the rest of India, the Indian Christian developed what is sometimes contemptuously referred to as "the mission compound mentality".[3]

As part of this "mentality" consisted in the perpetuation of the ways of worship, thought-forms and attitudes which the missionary had brought with him from the West, it is not surprising that the Indian convert commonly shared the missionary's attitude to Hinduism.[4] Conversion to Christianity could—and often did—bring with it a desire to disassociate himself altogether from his heathen past in all its aspects.[5]

A third factor which tended to strengthen general missionary prejudice against Hinduism was the mission to the lower and exterior castes: those castes, "contact with which entails purification on the

---

[3] McCorkel (ed.), *Voices from the Younger Churches* (1939), p. 25. Cf. McGavran, *Bridges of God* (1955), p. 47: "As we look back on the last hundred years it seems both necessary and desirable for there to have been this approach. With all its limitations, it was the best strategy for the era."

[4] "Hinduism as you are aware is a gigantic system of error ..." P. Rajahgopaul, quoted in *Report of the Missionary Conference, South India and Ceylon* (1879) I, p. 105. Cf. also Bose, *The Hindoos As They Are* (1883).

[5] For high-caste Hindus baptism was in any case tantamount to excommunication.

part of high-caste Hindus".[6] In a survey of this nature it is not possible to go into the origins of this specialized missionary activity in detail. We must however mention the principal causes of this late nineteenth-century movement, since they have a distinct bearing on the problems with which we are dealing.[7]

The first is to be seen in the nineteenth-century Evangelical missionary attitude to caste (an attitude which was less universal before 1813, the Tranquebar mission being a case in point[8]). Missionaries united in condemning the caste laws—"a lie against nature, against humanity, against history"—as being contrary to the spirit of Christian brotherhood; they declared caste to be "the bane of India",[9] and demanded that caste should be utterly rejected by all converts to Christianity.[1] Many an Indian refused baptism simply because he had no desire to be disowned by society.[2]

With the lower castes and the non-Hindu aboriginals, no such problem existed. To bring such a person into the Christian Church was to better his position socially, and to place his descendants at least on a more or less equal footing with the converts of higher—though perhaps not the highest—castes.[3] There was no painful schism with Hindu society, since such a convert had no bonds to break, and in any case mass conversion was common. The outcaste had no real part in the Hindu religious scheme.

It was thus theoretically an easier matter to convert an outcaste than to convert a Brahmin.[4] (We use "convert" in the sense of "to cause formally to enter the Christian Church"; whether "conversion" in the Evangelical sense occurred in such cases as these is immaterial for our discussion.[5]) The practical occasion was largely lacking before the Mutiny; but the decades following saw an increase in avail-

[6] Hutton, *Caste in India* (1946), pp. 168, 184.
[7] Richter, *Indische Missionsgeschichte*, pp. 249 ff.
[8] *Ibid.*, p. 117. Cf. Sandegren, *Kast och kristendom i Sydindien* (1921), pp. 185 ff., Neill, *A History of Christian Missions* (1964), p. 278. Swavely (ed.), *The Lutheran Enterprise in India* (1952), pp. 14, 24, 126.
[9] *Report of the Wesleyan Methodist Missionary Society* (1858), p. 155.
[1] *Report of the Missionary Conference, South India and Ceylon* (1879), p. 421.
[2] Words spoken in the 1830's by a "respectable Hindoo" hold good throughout the period: "Others, we well as myself, are convinced of the truth of Christ's religion; but caste is like an iron chain about our necks." *Report of the London Missionary Society* (1834), p. 39.
[3] Hutton, *op. cit.*, p. 179.
[4] Beach, *Geography of Protestant Missions* (1901), p. 372 f.
[5] See however Azariah, "Living Forces behind Mass Movements", in *IRM* XVIII (1929), pp. 509 ff.

able missionary labour, and the years between 1866 and 1878 witnessed a devastating series of famines.[6] This provided the missions with their opportunity, for medical and relief work, for community rehabilitation and, finally, for the reception into the Christian Church of whole villages at a time. The mission statistics of the period show a remarkable upward trend, particularly in South India, beginning in about 1871, and continuing unabated beyond the turn of the century.[7]

We have no cause to criticize this mass influx into the Churches *per se,* though in later years it was to give rise to a number of problems. We wish merely to point out that by 1900 the greater proportion of missionary labour had been directed to the reaping of this "harvest". Christianity was tending, despite the energy of its educational efforts, to become a lower-class religion, and less and less effort was available, apart from the staffs of the missionary colleges (who were faced, as we shall see, with their own peculiar problems[8]) for work at the point of vital contact between Christianity and Hinduism—among the educated classes outside the immediate environs of the colleges and schools.[9]

But more serious, the nature of the purely religious aspects of the "mass movements" was such as to provide little incentive for the missionary to undertake this particular form of work. The religion of the majority of these castes and tribes was strictly pre-Hindu:[1] a jungle of magic, myth, taboo and propitiation, normally classified broadly at that time as "animism" or "primitive religion", but in reality extremely difficult to systematize. In the circumstances, Evangelical denunciation of "idolatry" commonly appeared to be fully justified, and the missionary's conception of the worthlessness and debilitating influence of "Hinduism"—arguing from the particular to the general—was strengthened.

---

[6] Details will be found in Dodwell (ed.), *The Cambridge History of India* VI (1932), pp. 298–301.

[7] Richter, *op. cit.,* p. 252. See also statistical table in *EB* XVIII (1911), p. 595, which shows the following rate of increase for the Christian community: 1861—52.3%; 1871—61.6%; 1881—86.1%; 1890—34.0%; 1900—52.8%; 1910—72.2%.

[8] Below, pp. 78 ff.

[9] See above, p. 24 n. 1.

[1] See Hutton, *op. cit.,* pp. 195 ff. Representative works on this aspect of the religion of the people of India include Crooke, *Religion and Folklore of Northern India* (3rd ed. 1926), Whitehead, *The Village Gods of South India* (2nd ed. 1921), Elmore, *Dravidian Gods in Modern Hinduism* (1925), and more recently Diehl, *Instrument and Purpose: Studies on Rites and Rituals in South India* (1956).

Concentration on the problems, religious and practical, of the lower castes, and on the encounter between Christianity and "animism", was in no way adequte as a preparation for the more sophisticated encounter later forced upon the Church by the rise of neo-Hinduism. Problems tended to be over-simplified or ignored altogether: the encounter between Christianity and "Hinduism" was interpreted by many as being a straightforward conflict between good and evil, between God and the devil. The missionary working among the low and "exterior" castes, compelled to treat his converts as a *tabula rasa* on which the first words were still to be written, and concentrating on replacing magic and superstition by at least some elementary form of the Christian faith,[2] could not easily keep in touch with what was happening at the university level, among the neo-Hindu intelligentsia.

The inevitable consequence was that many a missionary came to look upon his own situation as normative. Evangelical missionaries working in mass-movement areas often had little sympathy with "the higher Hinduism", or with missionary attempts to come to terms with the beliefs of the intellectuals.[3] By the end of the century, the mission to the lower castes, invaluable in itself, was tending to confirm many working missionaries in their attitude of iconoclasm, and to perpetuate still further the Evangelical attitude we have described.

The perpetuation of traditional Evangelicalism was also assisted by the conservatism of the missionary societies in the West.[4] The principles on which the societies had been formed permitted of no relaxation; impeccable orthodoxy was required of all missionary candidates. Liberal views, unless skilfully concealed, would automatically

---

[2] It has been pointed out that many have become Christians in such a situation as the result of a communal decision, and that "the elements of conscious religious conviction" in their action may be small: Firth, *An Introduction to Indian Church History* (1961), p. 196. Cf. Pickett, *Christian Mass Movements in India* (1933), *passim*.

[3] This was a potential source of conflict; see below, pp. 309 ff. But see also below, p. 55 n. 3.

[4] One important reason for this was that in virtually all cases societies were dependent for their support on public support from churchgoers, who were not in a position to keep up with developments in the scholarly world [see Glover, *Evangelical Nonconformists and Higher Criticism in the Nineteenth Century* (1954), pp. 161 f., 217, 287]. It is interesting to note that a later opponent of the "fulfilment" school claimed in 1912 that "it is such ideas as he [Farquhar] sets forth that ... are lessening self-sacrificial giving for Missions". Campbell, "The New Attitude", in *IW*, 21.5.1912, p. 408.

disqualify a man from missionary service;[5] and when expressed by an active missionary, could place that missionary in a difficult position.[6] Such occurrences were however rare. The old-established missionary societies, on both sides of the Atlantic, were, and continued to be, strongholds of Evangelical theology: suspicious of new developments in thought, and in any case too much occupied with practical matters to give much attention to theoretical discussion.

A further significant factor tending to perpetuate traditional views among missionaries was the Second Evangelical Awakening—that associated above all with the name of Dwight L. Moody.[7] It is difficult to overestimate the importance of Moody in the religious patterns of the late nineteenth century. His campaigns in Europe and America brought many recruits to the missions, and inspired many lesser imitators. Of particular importance was his work for young men; his Northfield Conferences were the source of the Student Volunteer Movement.[8] The tenets of this "new" wave of revivalism were identical with those of the original Evangelical Awakening. The Bible was still interpreted literally; a substitutionary Atonement still preached; a sharp distinction still drawn between the light of Christianity and the darkness of "the world"; the Gospel still presented to each man and woman individually, as a matter for personal decision. How much of the traditional attitude towards the non-Christian religions was strengthened by this means (in conjunction with the other factors we have mentioned) will be clear.

This is not to say that individual Evangelicals were not affected by the far-reaching changes which were taking place in theological thought towards the end of the century. Indeed it was the emergence of a new type of Protestantism (Liberal Protestantism or Liberal Evangelicalism) which enabled J. N. Farquhar to make his distinctive

---

[5] One such case, which created a stir in Congregational circles, was that of E. Evans and the London Missionary Society (1897–1900). Evans, a brilliant scholar, was on the point of being rejected on doctrinal grounds when he withdrew of his own accord. Had he not done so, Lancashire Independent College would have made this a test case on the freedom of men to hold modern theological views (material in LMS Archives).

[6] So in the case of T. E. Slater (below, pp. 98 ff.).

[7] (1837–1899). See W. R. Moody, *D. L. Moody* (1930), Smith, *An Annotated Bibliography of D. L. Moody* (1948), Brauer, *Protestantism in America* (1953), pp. 201 ff.

[8] The inaugural conference was held at Mount Hermon, Mass. in July 1886, with Moody as President; see Mott, "The Beginnings of the Student Volunteer Movement", in *The Student Volunteer Movement after Twenty-Five Years, 1886–1911* (1912), pp. 1–20, Mathews, *John R. Mott: World Citizen* (1934), pp. 41 ff.

contribution to Protestant missionary thought and practice. The history of this movement in theological thought goes back to the Enlightenment of the eighteenth century, though it did not become a force to be reckoned with until after the 1850's; and missions were even slower to make use of its distinctive premises. However, the ground had been prepared in a variety of ways for the coming of "liberalism", and we shall glance briefly at some of these ways.

Modifications in the Traditional Attitude to Hinduism

It would be incorrect to assume, on a basis of what we have said, that all Evangelical missionaries were totally devoid of sympathy for Hinduism in every shape and form. There was in fact a long tradition of sympathetic appreciation on the part of Orientalists, soldiers and civil servants of the East India Company, a tradition which was not widespread, but which individual missionaries were occasionally able to appropriate.

Sir William Jones (1746–1794) has been called "a rather rare individual" in his approach to India.[9] He had been Vinerian Professor of Law at Oxford and was appointed a judge of the Supreme Court in Calcutta in 1783.[1] Proficient in Persian and Sanskrit, he came to be impressed by Indian theology, particularly in its elevated conception of God. He warned early missionaries (E.I.C. chaplains) against the error of regarding Indian religion as necessarily the inferior of Christianity.[2] A similar attitude of respect was held by H. T. Colebrook (1765–1837)[3] and by Sir Charles Wilkins (1749–1836),[4] who published the first English translation of the *Bhagavad Gītā* in 1785. Examples might be multiplied. But we shall mention only two more names. Sir Thomas Munro (1761–1827)[5] may stand as representative of those Government officials who, while standing for the maintenance of British power in India, were sufficiently aware of the conditions of their Indian subjects to be able to appreciate the laws, literature, religious and social characteristics of India. And H. H.

---

[9] Bearce, *British Attitudes towards India,* p. 20 f. *Dict. Nat. Biogr.* XXX (1892), pp. 174–177.

[1] Chatterjee and Burn, *British Contributions to Indian Studes* (1943), p. 11 f.

[2] Bearce, *op. cit.,* p. 24.

[3] *Dict. Nat. Biogr.* XI (1887), pp. 282–286.

[4] *Dict. Nat. Biogr.* LXI (1900), pp. 259–260.

[5] *Dict. Nat. Biogr.* XXXIX (1894), pp. 309–313.

Wilson (1786–1860)[6] may be cited as representative of the pure scholar, concerned for the preservation of traditional Indian culture. Wilson and others advocated Government support for the spread of Indian literature—"the source of national imagery, the expression of national feeling, and the depository of the most approved phraseology and style"[7]—and resisted reform.[8] In 1833 Wilson became Boden Professor of Sanskrit at Oxford,[9] and in 1835 was a powerful advocate of the "Orientalist" viewpoint in the celebrated educational controversy of that year.[1]

None of these were missionaries, or particularly interested in seeing Christianity established in India. A bridge between scholarship and Protestant missions is however provided by John Muir (1810–1882).[2]

Muir was educated at the East India Company's College at Haileybury, and went to India in 1829. His most important scholarly work was his *Original Sanskrit Texts on the Origin and History of the People of India* (5 vols., 1st ed. 1858–70, 2nd ed. 1868–73). But he also did valuable work for missions; between 1839 and 1854 he published a series of pamphlets descriptive of various aspects of Christianity, written in Sanskrit verse. In this he was following a pattern set by W. A. Mill (1792–1853),[3] the first Principal of Bishop's College, Calcutta, who had published a Sanskrit version of the Gospel story in 1831. Muir's publications included *A Brief Account of Our Lord's Life and Doctrine* (1848) and *A Short Life of the Apostle Paul* (1850).[4] His position was Evangelical, but entirely respectful towards Indian culture, a position for which he argued in *An Essay on Conciliation* (1849).

Muir stressed that zeal and honesty in a disputant, particularly on religious matters, were not in themselves sufficient to bring success. Impatience and strong language in the missionary were, he claimed, likely to defeat their own object, particularly in a country like India.[5] The Apostle Paul he cited as providing a good warrant for adopting

---

[6] *Dict. Nat. Biogr.* LXII (1900), pp. 97–99.

[7] Quoted by Bearce, *op. cit.*, p. 96.

[8] Farquhar, *Modern Religious Movements*, p. 11 f.

[9] Chatterjee and Burn, *op. cit.*, p. 36. He was succeeded in this chair by Sir Monier Monier-Williams (below, pp. 49 ff.).

[1] Below, p. 69.

[2] Chatterjee and Burn, *loc. cit.*; *Dict. Nat. Biogr.* XXXIX (1894), p. 267 f.

[3] *Dict. Nat. Biogr.* XXXVII (1894), p. 400.

[4] He also published a two-part *Examination of Religions* in Sanskrit verse (1852–54).

[5] Muir, *An Essay on Conciliation*, p. 8 f.

a conciliatory attitude: this was confirmed both by the demands of justice and of prudence.[6] Missionaries must take full account of the Oriental character, social state, institutions and manners, and must be prepared to see themselves as the Indian sees them—as potential destroyers of his religion.[7]

Muir was insistent that the missionary should have intimate knowledge of Hinduism, and encouraged the missionary to admire what he could admire. "That there is much in their learning which we can honestly admire and praise, is well known to all by whom it has been studied."[8] Should an unfavourable judgment on Hinduism, or any other religion, nevertheless prove necessary, it "should be seen to proceed from a comprehensive acquaintance with all the parts, and an impartial estimate of the whole of those religions".[9] Again, this was necessary, not only for the sake of impartiality, but in order not to offend Indian religious prejudices. The demands of justice were the most weighty: Muir quoted with approval a writer in the *Benares Magazine* who had urged that we ought to acknowledge thankfully every trace of excellence in the Hindu Shastras "as we welcome every spot of verdure in the desert".[1]

Among those influenced by Muir's writings were Monier-Williams,[2] whose monograph *The Study of Sanskrit*[3] in particular shows distinct traces of Muir's ideas, and A. M. Fairbairn.[4]

It would be wrong, on this evidence, to hold that the Pietist-inspired negative attitude to Hinduism, reinforced by certain practical details in the Indian missionary situation, was the only one open to nineteenth-century Protestant missionaries. Though there can be little doubt that it was a majority view, there were important exceptions, particularly towards the turn of the century. In some of these we can see an anticipation of the attitude which developments in the study of religions were to make more common after 1900. Thus

---

[6] *Ibid.*, p. 36 f.
[7] *Ibid.*, p. 49 f., cf. below, pp. 242, 247, 251, 300.
[8] *Ibid.*, p. 54.
[9] *Ibid.*, p. 57.
[1] *Ibid.*, p. 58 f.
[2] Below, pp. 49 ff.
[3] This was Monier-Williams' inaugural lecture as Boden Professor of Sanskrit at Oxford, delivered on April 19, 1861. See especially pp. 50, 60 f. A heavily-underlined copy of Muir's *Essay*, formerly the property of Monier-Williams, is in the library of the Indian Institute, Oxford.
[4] Cf. below, p. 129 f.

individual missionaries from the time of Bishop Heber onwards,[5] while retaining their generally negative attitude to Hinduism as a religion, came to appreciate certain aspects of Indian culture. Some were prepared to spend time and energy, on the lines suggested by Muir[6] and later by Monier-Williams,[7] to make themselves familiar with at least the most important features of Hinduism. The main motive here was one of missionary strategy: conquest must of necessity be preceded by accurate knowledge of the enemy. But the bounds of strategy were sometimes transcended, as for example by the Rev. J. J. Johnson ("Pundit" Johnson) of Benares, a C.M.S. missionary who in his more than thirty-five years in India achieved a high degree of fluency in Sanskrit, both written and spoken, and was considered able to meet and confer with "Brahmin pundits" on their own terms and in their own sacred language.[8] Such attainments were however uncommon, at least among missionaries.

A further interesting group is that of the Indian converts, previously trained in Sanskrit, who were able to apply their detailed knowledge of the Hindu canonical scriptures in the service of the Christian missions. The two most prominent in this class were Nehemiah Goreh and K. M. Banerjea, both of whom were prolific writers. We shall however consider the nature of their contribution more fully in Chapter Three. Here may be noted only that the type of attitude which they represented was ephemeral: the high-caste, traditionally educated Hindu convert was to become more and more a rarity after the middle years of the century.

The trend in the direction of a sympathetic interpretation of Hinduism, vague and uncertain in the greater part of the nineteenth century, was immeasurably strengthened by the developments in the study of the religions of the world, and in the Christian theological scene, which came about after 1858. We have already pointed to

---

[5] Reginald Heber (1783–1826) became Bishop of Calcutta in 1823. Bearce writes that "his attitude was far more enlightened than those of most missionaries" and speaks of his sympathy and "broad understanding". Nevertheless he "was horrified at temple prostitution, sati and idolatry" (*British Attitudes towards India*, pp. 85–87). Ecumenically, writes Neill, Heber "was a century in advance of his time" (*A History of Christian Missions*, p. 268). See also Woodruff, *The Men who Ruled India* I, pp. 223 ff.

[6] Above, p. 36 f.

[7] Below, p. 50 f.

[8] Stock, *History of the Church Missionary Society* IV (1916), pp. 223, cf. p. 175; *Proceedings of the Church Missionary Society* 50 (1904–05), p. 202 f.; Richter, *Indische Missionsgeschichte*, p. 377.

three of these: the rise of the doctrine of evolution, the coming of historical Biblical criticism, and the launching of the "science of religion". Two further general factors might perhaps be added: increased factual knowledge of the non-Christian religions, and the general trend away from transcendentalism and towards immanentism in theological and philosophical thought. It will however suffice for our purposes if we restrict ourselves to the first of these groups; for the second, we may refer to the relevant literature.[9]

Evolution and Historical Criticism

The rise of the doctrine of evolution is generally taken to date from 1859, the year in which Charles Darwin (1809–1882) published his book *On the Origin of Species by means of Natural Selection*. In point of fact, the idea of "development", "progress" or "evolution" was very far indeed from being new. Philosophically, its roots are to be found in Antiquity. And its main scientific (in this case biological) features had already been set out by Buffon, Erasmus Darwin, Lamarck and others,[1] without however arousing very much attention. The distinctive contribution of Darwin (and A. R. Wallace, 1823–1913,[2] who had been working on almost identical lines) was to propose a theory of the way in which evolution might have happened in practice: the theory of natural selection, or "the survival of the fittest". Darwin's original biological theory was rapidly assimilated into other disciplines, thanks in no small measure to the work of Herbert Spencer (1820–1903) who claimed in a series of works that the doctrine was valid in all areas of human existence.[3] The idea of evolution struck the late nineteenth century with the force of revelation, and came to be applied to all branches of science, sociology, religion and ethics. In the words of J. H. Moulton, "A revelation of the Reign of Law invaded every field of thought".[4]

---

[9] E.g. Elliott-Binns, *Religion in the Victorian Era* (1936), idem, *English Thought 1860–1900: The Theological Aspect* (1956), Carpenter, *Church and People 1789–1889* (1933), Webb, *A Study of Religious Thought in England from 1850* (1932), Richardson, *The Bible in the Age of Science* (1961).

[1] *ERE* V (1912), pp. 615 ff., Carpenter, *Church and People* (1959 ed.) III, pp. 468 ff.

[2] See *EB* (1963) 23, p. 302 f.

[3] The most important of these were *Social Statistics* (1851), *Principles of Psychology* (1855), *Factors of Organic Evolution* (1887) and *Principles of Ethics* (1879–92).

[4] Moulton, *Religions and Religion* (1911), p. 7.

Although the idea of "development" in theology was not alto-gether an innovation,[5] it soon became evident that the evolutionary hypothesis, as stated first by Darwin and later by the more radical Spencer and T. H. Huxley (1825–1895),[6] with its implicitly naturalistic view of the origin and nature of man, could not but come into con-flict with conservative Evangelical Christianity. The Evangelical posi-tion was based on a firm belief on the inerrancy of the Bible; and Evangelicals reacted sharply against any attempt to call in question any part of that belief. It was assumed, for instance, that to deny the literal truth of the Genesis creation story, as some critics were doing, was to deny the authority of the Bible as a whole, and thus to undermine the very foundations of the Christian faith. That the controversy which began in 1860 with the celebrated exchange be-tween T. H. Huxley and Bishop Samuel Wilberforce, and intensified following the publication in 1871 of Darwin's *The Descent of Man,* still provides material for acrimony in some quarters is an indica-tion of its centrality. Discussion was equally lively on both sides of the Atlantic, though not simultaneously: the Civil War, and the prevailing left-wing Protestantism of America, were retarding factors in the debate, and the evolutionist discussion did not become wide-spread there until after 1900.[7]

In the evolutionary scheme, religion came to be viewed entirely in terms of history. Revelation tended to be ruled out *a priori,* or reinterpreted; every historical religion was treated in the same terms, without any attempt at evaluation (at least ostensibly, though the postulating of an evolutionary scale could not well take place with-out the passing of value-judgments). Scholars such as Tylor, Marrett, Frazer, Jevons, Caird and Max Müller concentrated on the analysis of legend, myth, magic, ritual and philosophy. Interest came to be centred more and more on the "origins" of religion—religion viewed as a human function, a universal fact of human experience—and on "primitive" religions.[8] In addition, growing attention was paid to the

---

[5] See A. M. Fairbairn's comments in *Christ in Modern Theology* (1893), pp. 25 ff. J. H. Newman had published his *Essay on the Development of Christian Doctrine* in 1845.

[6] See *EB* (1963) 11, p. 947 f.

[7] Sweet, *The Story of Religions in America* (6th ed. 1930), p. 492 f., Brauer, *Protestantism in America,* pp. 218 ff.

[8] This development is described and criticized by Widengren, "Evolution and the Problem of the Origin of Religion", in *Ethnos* 10 (1945), pp. 17 ff. See also James, *Comparative Religion: An Introductory and Historical Survey* (1938), pp. 3 ff.

function of religion in the development of society; in this field the main authority was Benjamin Kidd.[9] By the end of the century, although the vast amounts of material which had been amassed were far from having been fully digested, it was coming to be believed that all religions could be arranged in "stages", corresponding—for the method as such was pure analogy—to the "stages" of biological evolution.[1] We shall have more to say on this subject in connexion with Max Müller and the "science of religion".[2]

A closely related trend in the thought of the period was the new emphasis on historical method. The sense of continuity, of a cause-and-effect relationship between the past and the present, motivated a closer examination of man's past, his religious past not excepted. "Facts" were all-important. The developing science of archaeology were laying bare the monuments of vanished civilizations. Advances in linguistic studies were opening the way to first-hand examination of the literary sources in many fields. Documents and inscriptions were constantly coming to light. The evolutionary hypothesis, as well as providing a basis for the collation of existing material, had the further effect of emphasizing the importance of each "stage" in the overall pattern of development; henceforth no detail was too insignificant to be noted and incorporated into the evolutionary scheme. Scriptures, both Christian and non-Christian, came to be subjected to new techniques of historical criticism; and critical results were frequently to the detriment of traditional opinion. These two—evolution and historical criticism—were the keys which the late nineteenth century believed would unlock every door.[3]

The Christian Scriptures were by no means exempt from this process. The story of the rise of Biblical criticism, and the controversies it aroused among churchmen, is so well known as to need

---

[9] Kidd (1858–1916) has been called "a clever writer without academic training" [Webb, *op. cit.*, p. 156]. His two most influential books were *Social Evolution* (1894) and *Principles of Western Civilization* (1902). His thesis was that religion, providing a "super-rational sanction" for areas of conduct which cannot have a "rational sanction", will always have an important role in the evolution of society, and that without a religious foundation, true progress in society is impossible; cf. *Social Evolution*, pp. 20, 21 f., 100, 103, 325 ff. For this idea in Farquhar, see below, pp. 168, 255 f., 281, 311 f.

[1] Hence the use of such terms as "primitive" and "developed" and in our present study, "higher" Hinduism.

[2] Below, pp. 43 ff.

[3] For Farquhar's application of this method, see below, pp. 168 ff.

no comment here.[4] For our purposes it may however be taken as providing a further important indication of the late nineteenth-century climate of theological opinion. To subject what was regarded by the vast majority of Protestant Christians as the infallible Word of God to verbal and compositional criticism was felt to be a further blow at the foundations of the Evangelical faith, placing Christianity on a par with other religions and threatening to dispose of the idea of revelation once and for all.

But these developments could not be ignored, unless by a retreat into total obscurantism. The emergence of "liberalism" was simply an attempt to come to terms with the principle of scientific historical enquiry without abandoning more of the traditional Evangelical faith than could be helped. This involved considerable revision of the idea of revelation and of the idea of authority in religion, and was never far apart from compromise and relativism—at least as long as traditional categories were preserved.[5] Boundaries became well defined. Evolution and historical criticism, both being based on scientific historical method, were commonly accepted—or rejected—together. This was the theological crux of the age. Protestant Christianity came to be divided sharply into "liberal" and "conservative" groups, the "liberals" being those who accepted the findings of the scientific historical method, revising in the process their ideas of religious authority, the "conservatives" being those who retained the traditional Evangelical position, explaining away the work of the scientists and critics as best they might.

Within Protestant theology, the most striking results of the scholarly work of the period were a new emphasis on the figure of "the Jesus of history" and intense interest in the concept of "the kingdom of God". The Gospel material (particularly the Synoptic Gospels) was studied with renewed energy: parallel materials from Judaism, Hellenism and Gnosticism were brought to bear on the problem of Christian origins, and on the figure of the founder of Christianity. New "lives of Jesus" were published, of which the most influential were those of Strauss, Renan and Seeley.[6] This included

---

[4] See the works quoted above, p. 39 n. 9, which all treat of this subject. For the nonconformist reaction, see Glover, *Evangelical Nonconformists and Higher Criticism in the Nineteenth Century* (1954).

[5] Glover, *op. cit.*, pp. 72, 263 ff. On this subject generally, see Quick, *Liberalism, Modernism and Tradition* (1922).

[6] These were of course by no means identical in style or approach. Strauss, *Leben Jesu*, appeared in 1836 (Eng. trans. 1846); Renan, *Vie de Jésus*, in 1863;

much of the trend of the period towards immanentism.[7] Jesus was viewed "historically", in human terms, often to the detriment of anything which could be called "supernaturalism". By 1893 A. M. Fairbairn could write that Jesus "is to-day more studied and better known as He was and as He lived than at any period between now and the first age of the Church".[8] This attitude of course led to a sharp reaction. Later critics, beginning with A. Schweitzer, drew attention to the fact that the "historical Jesus" of the late nineteenth century was in many ways a construction, a projection of the spirit of the age: the century made of him an ethical and social philosopher and reformer, not a Messiah. This is substantially correct. The late nineteenth century revealed its social concern in its concentration on the idea of the "kingdom of God", which it tended to view in Utopian terms, as a divine order of human brotherhood on earth, each man owning allegiance to God as his Father and Jesus as his brother. And viewing the New Testament as a whole, the tendency was to accord absolute priority to the "teaching of Jesus", and to relegate the "work of Christ" to a subsidiary position.

This has been a very general summary of certain of the main trends of the thought of the post-1858 period. Now we pass on to a more specific area of thought: the growth of the "science of religion" or "comparative religion", a development connected especially with the name of Friedrich Max Müller (1823–1900).[9]

The Science of Religion

Max Müller was not an absolute innovator in the field of the study of non-Christian religions. We have already had occasion to note something of the work of European Orientalists in India; and in Germany, the Enlightenment had witnessed a remarkable growth of interest in Eastern religions, and a parallel tendency towards relativism in religious thought.[1] But these streams of thought were

Seeley, *Ecce Homo*, in 1865. For a late nineteenth-century Evangelical criticism, see Fairbairn, *Christ in Modern Theology*, pp. 230 ff., 278 f.

[7] Webb, *A Study of Religious Thought in England from 1850, passim.*

[8] Fairbairn, *op. cit.*, p. 3.

[9] *Dict. Nat. Biogr.*, Supplement III (1901), pp. 151–57; *EB* XVII (1911), p. 927 f.; *The Life and Letters of the Rt. Hon. Friedrich Max Müller*, edited by his wife, I–II (1902).

[1] A useful summary account of developments in the attitude to the non-Christian religions on the Continent is given by Allen, *Christianity Among the Religions* (1961).

slow to reach the British Isles. Thomas Carlyle, possibly under German influence, had delivered a striking lecture on the prophet Mohammed in 1840, and F. D. Maurice had published his much-neglected book *On the Religions of the World* in 1846, partly in order to counteract what he called Carlyle's "pantheism".[2] But these were isolated instances.

The first real impetus to the detailed sympathetic study of Hinduism in the English-speaking world was provided by Max Müller, consequent on the publication, from 1856, of his complete version of the *Rig Veda* in English. This served to give the study a new popularity, and a new foundation in literature, rather than in common observation, as had hitherto been the case.[3] The bibliographies of the last quarter of the century indicate the extent of this interest. Many specialist works on Hinduism and Hindu literature were published at that time, in England, in America and on the Continent. The works of Monier-Williams (of whom more later), Barth, Lyall, Hopkins, Garbe, Oldenburg, Hillebrandt and Geden—to name only the best known—all derive from this period.[4]

Max Müller is remembered today chiefly for the series of volumes of *Sacred Books of the East*, which he edited, and which have always been recognized as one of the foundations on which the modern study of the religions of the world rests.[5] But we must not forget the large number of essays and articles which he published over the greater part of a half-century, in which he considered, among

---

[2] This whole episode is of considerable intrinsic interest, though peripheral to our immediate purpose. See F. Maurice (ed.), *The Life of Frederick Denison Maurice* I (1884), pp. 251, 282 f., F. D. Maurice, *On the Religions of the World* (3rd ed. 1852), pp. viii–x. See also Elliott-Binns, *Religion in the Victorian Era* (1936), p. 178.

[3] This is not to disparage the work of the earlier Sanskritists, from Carey, Colebrooke and Wilkins on. The fact remains, however, that before Max Müller knowledge of Indian religions was disseminated more by travellers, soldiers and missionaries than by pure scholars.

[4] Among the relevant literature may be mentioned: Barth, *The Religions of India* (1882), Max Müller, *Lectures on the Origin of Religion* (1882), Monier-Williams, *Religious Thought and Life in India* (1885), idem, *Brahmanism and Hinduism* (1887), Hopkins, *The Religions of India* (1895), Garbe, *Philosophy of Ancient India* (1897), Oldenberg, *Aus Indien und Iran* (1899), Geden, *Studies in Eastern Religion* (1900), etc.

[5] It is less frequently recognized that they were in a sense ultimately responsible for inaugurating the new era in missionary thought which this study sets out to describe. See Macnicol, *India in the Dark Wood* (1930), p. 116. On the other hand, missionaries occasionally spoke bitterly of the work of Max Müller (and Deussen) in "arousing" Hinduism. See e.g. Dilger, *Probleme der Missionsarbeit im heutigen Indien* (1909), p. 9 f.

other things, many subjects connected with India and Hinduism, among them the Christian message to the Hindu. In December 1873, when he became the first layman to lecture in Westminster Abbey, his subject was "Missions",[6] and he was always keenly interested in missions. In fact he made a tentative missionary contribution himself, in his *naïf* attempt to persuade the Brāhma Samāj to join the Church of England.[7]

Max Müller's view of religion was immanentist and rationalist. "There is a truly human element", he wrote in 1883, "in all religions and all philosophies, and it would be strange if honest thought should not lead any one of us to the truths of Buddhism, or Platonism, or Christianity."[8] This theme he developed in great detail in his Gifford Lectures, the main object of which was to show that a belief in God, in the immortality of the soul, or in a future retribution, could be attained by the right use of reason alone, without having to turn to "what has been called a special revelation".[9] Revelation he nevertheless believed to have been given—in the spirit of God at work upon the mind of man;[1] the working of the human reason is, he claimed, the result of the direct revelation of God, whether in Christianity or Buddhism, Hinduism or Islam. "I hold that there is nowhere any belief in God except as a result of Divine revelation, the effect of a Divine Spirit working in man", he wrote.[2]

The term "the science of religion" was coined by Max Müller to describe the comparative method as applied to the study of religions.[3] For comparison there must be: not only is all "higher knowledge" acquired by comparison;[4] in the field of religion "he who knows one, knows none".[5] He drew a sharp distinction between "comparative theology" (the study of the historical forms of religion) and "theoretic theology" (philosophy of religion and

---

[6] Max Müller, "Westminster Lecture on Missions", in *Chips from a German Workshop* IV (1875), pp. 253 ff.

[7] *Life and Letters* II, pp. 390 ff.

[8] *Ibid.,* p. 148.

[9] *Ibid.,* p. 277.

[1] Cf. the words of Flemmer, descriptive of Lessing's attitude: "Gottes Wirkung ist im Inneren des Menschen lebendig. Alle Religionen sind Durchgangsstationen auf dem Weg des Menschengeschlechts zur Vollendung." *Nathan der Weise* (Goldmann ed. 1960), Einl. p. 13.

[2] *Life and Letters* II, p. 464.

[3] Above, pp. 39 ff., on evolutionary method.

[4] Max Müller, *Introduction to the Science of Religion* (*Collected Works* XIV, 1909), p. 9.

[5] *Ibid.,* p. 13.

dogmatics), believing only the first of these to be scientifically relevant.[6] In the comparative study of religion and theology, all religions must be treated as being on the same footing: it is not permissible to draw distinctions between "revealed" and "natural" religion, since that whole complex of problems belongs to "theoretic theology".[7]

Max Müller was a religious evolutionist, and believed that the "science of religion" demonstrated that the history of the world in its religious aspect was the history of a progress towards Christianity, and that non-Christian religions were to be treated as preliminary stages in the same process.[8] The non-Christian religions he considered to be part of the divine education of the human race.[9] But despite this, he would never have claimed any form of absolute supremacy for historical Christianity. He regarded Christianity as a superior stage in religious evolution, it is true, but its superiority, however desirable, was only relative. He was convinced that no religion could contain the whole truth,[1] since religion is "the light of truth as reflected in human mirrors—and however pure and spotless your mirror may be, there is none which in reflecting does not deflect the rays of light that fall on it".[2] The corollary of this belief is, of course, that as no religion can contain the *whole* truth, as Divine revelation is at work in all men, therefore all must contain *some* truth. There is no distinction in kind between one religion and another,[3] and such distinctions as we observe are artificial and man-made. Even the lowest expression of the religious instinct has its legitimacy (a thought which later occurs in Farquhar), because it is the expression of legitimate religious aspiration. "There never was a false god, nor was there ever really a false religion, unless you call a child a false man."[4]

The attitude of mind to which this gives rise—an attitude of respect and sympathy—must be practically applied in the Christian

---

[6] *Ibid.*, p. 16 f.

[7] *Ibid.*, pp. 69 ff.

[8] *Ibid.*, p. 148 f.: Christianity came "in the fulness of time, and as the fulfilment of the hopes and desires of the whole world". Cf. *Life and Letters* II, p. 464, *Chips from a German Workshop* I (1867), p. xx.

[9] *Introduction*, p. 151.

[1] This is the argument of the "Parable of the Rings" in Lessing's *Nathan der Weise*.

[2] *Life and Letters* II, p. 105.

[3] This applies to religion on all levels: Max Müller, *Last Essays* I (1901), p. 304.

[4] *Life and Letters* II, p. 135.

missionary's attitude to those to whom he is sent. The Christian must look upon the non-Christian more as a brother seeker than as a dangerous opponent in thrall to the prince of darkness.

Paradoxically enough, this does not mean that Max Müller denied the value of missionary work, though he once went so far as to say that he had "not much faith in missionaries, medical or otherwise".[5] On the contrary: he believed missionary activity to be a sign of life in any religion, classified religions into "missionary" and "non-missionary", and considered that we are fully justified in preaching Christ—the "original" Christ of the Gospels[6]—to the non-Christian.[7] In the prospectus of *The Sacred Books of the East* he appealed particularly to the missionary, for whom a knowledge of the non-Christian religions was, he thought, "as indispensable as a knowledge of the enemy's country is to a general".[8] But the attitude of superiority, whether benevolent or not, on the part of the missionary, in face of the contact between Christianity and the non-Christian religions, is utterly inappropriate. "Missionaries", he wrote, "are apt to look on all other religions as something totally distinct from their own; but this is both a sign of immaturity of thought and a misunderstanding of the true nature of religion."[9]

The missionary attitude prevalent around the middle of the nineteenth century—which we described earlier in this chapter—he found to be quite out of the question. He went so far as to call the attitude of contempt for non-Christian religious systems as a whole, blasphemous, since it ascribes to the devil what is in reality the work of God.[1] Thus the missionary must beware of indulging in indiscriminate condemnation; no one is compelled to prove all other religions to be false in order to demonstrate the truth of his own. "It is possible to put a charitable interpretation on many doctrines of ancient heathenism, and the practical missionary is constantly obliged so to do"[2]—providing always that, like Augustine, he is not

---

[5] The quotation continues: "If we get such men again in India as Rāmmohun Roy, or Keshub Chunder Sen, and if we get an Archbishop at Calcutta who knows what Christianity really is, India will be christianized in all that is essential in the twinkling of an eye." *Ibid.*, p. 310.

[6] Cf. above, p. 43.

[7] *Chips from a German Workshop* IV, p. 258 f.

[8] *Life and Letters* II, p. 9.

[9] *Chips from a German Workshop* I, p. xxi.

[1] *Life and Letters* II, p. 464.

[2] "Christ and Other Masters", in *Chips* I, p. 53. The paper in question dates from 1858.

afraid of finding traces of truth there. He must look for common ground wherever possible,[3] for the sparks of that true light which are to be found in all forms of religion.

I think it is a serious mistake if followers of different religions always dwell on the points on which they differ; it is far better to try and discover the truths on which the different religions agree. On all essential points the best religions of the world agree; there are in each inevitable fictions, and on these they differ.[4]

On the practical level, he saw the difficulties of missions as being immense, and the results as often discouraging; furthermore Max Müller was no great believer in the effectiveness of controversy in religious matters. His eirenic nature and distaste for controversy are nowhere better expressed than in his final solution: peaceful co-existence—a form of creative dialogue which calls forth the best elements in each religion, at the same time suppressing all that is felt to be of doubtful value or of uncertain truth.[5]

Max Müller evidently believed that at some date in the future there would arise a new religion, derived not from ecclesiastical Christianity as he knew it, but from all the varied repositories of truth that are to be found scattered over the face of the earth. It will be the "true religion of humanity", since humanity is the sphere of divine revelation, and it will be the essential result of the historical process, leading beyond Christianity—though in some sense still to be called Christianity. "The true religion of the future will be the fulfilment of all the religions of the past."[6]

This religion exists potentially at the heart of Christianity as the ethical and moral ideal which Jesus Christ taught, but which has been overlaid by the accretions of centuries. And it is this central ideal which is to be the final answer to the religious aspirations implanted in the mind of man by the working of God's Spirit. It is here that the true God is to be found, and it is after this ideal that all religions yearn.

Christianity must be compared

not with Judaism only, but with the religious aspirations of the whole world, with all, in fact, that Christianity came either to destroy or fulfil...

---

[3] *Ibid.*, p. xxvii: "To the true believer truth, wherever it appears, is welcome ..."

[4] *Life and Letters* II, p. 30 f.

[5] *Chips from a German Workshop* IV, p. 268 f.

[6] *Life and Letters* II, p. 135.

Every religion, even the most imperfect and degraded, has something that ought to be sacred to us, for there is in all religions a yearning after the true, though unknown, God.[7]

It will have been clear from this account that Max Müller stood apart from the traditional Evangelical missionary attitude to India and Indian religion. In Sir Monier Monier-Williams (1819–1901)[8] we have a different type of scholar: a man who combined the study of Hinduism with a firm Evangelical faith, and who did much to introduce a more sympathetic attitude to Hinduism into areas in which it was previously little known.

Monier-Williams was elected Boden Professor of Sanskrit by the University of Oxford in 1860, in succession to H. H. Wilson, and in competition with Max Müller. Monier-Williams was regarded as being much Max Müller's inferior in general attainment, but he was a capable Sanskritist, and during the period of his professorship he travelled widely in India, and published several books, mainly semi-popular accounts of Sanskrit literature and Hinduism in general.

It is perhaps not too much to claim that Monier-Williams was a typical Victorian. In the first place, he believed whole-heartedly in what later came to be called "the White Man's Burden"—particularly in its moral aspect. Several views of empire and imperialism were current in Britain at the time, and a certain amount of confusion was unavoidable in regard to its precise meaning. Some regarded it as a cloak for exploitation, while others hailed it as the religious mission of a great people elected by God. Monier-Williams belonged to the latter class.[9] He considered that this mission, this responsibility, was best fulfilled by faithful cultivation of the three causes which bulked so large in the thought of nineteenth-century Britain: education, enlightenment and christianization. "For what purpose", he asked, "has this enormous territory [India] been committed to England? Not to be the *corpus vile* of political, social or military experiments; nor for the benefit of our commerce, or the increase of our wealth—but that every man, woman and child from Cape Comorin to the Himalaya Mountains, may be elevated, en-

---

[7] *Chips from a German Workshop* I, p. xxvii.
[8] *Dict. Nat. Biogr.* Supplement III (1901), p. 186 f.; *EB* XVIII (1911), p. 722.
[9] Rudyard Kipling (1865–1936) was the greatest popularizer of this form of imperial sentiment; his poem "A Song of the English" contains the famous phrase, "Take up the White Man's Burden". See further the books quoted above, p. 29 n. 2.

lightened, Christianized."[1] Elsewhere he was able to call the British "God's trustees in India",[2] regarding the spreading of the Gospel as a British responsibility and duty.

This duty extends to the mutual study of principles of belief: for how can we enlighten, if we do not understand those to whom we are sent? And understanding must involve direct comparison, which extends to the Scriptures of the respective religions. "It may shock Christians in this Christian country of ours to think of our missionaries placing the Bible on the same platform with the Kuran and the Veda; but there is really no alternative."[3]

There is one respect in which Monier-Williams and Max Müller stand in sharp contrast. Max Müller was, it is true, a member of the Church of England, but his attitude to religion we have seen to have been broad and liberal; Monier-Williams belonged to the Evangelical wing of the Church of England, and his views were consequently more strictly defined. Unlike Max Müller, Monier-Williams insisted on the absolute supremacy of historical Christianity —and indirectly of the Western civilization with which it was so closely allied. India is to be "Christianized", and though it is possible to be fair and gentlemanly in the unavoidable process of comparison, care must be taken not to lose a sense of proportion. He thought it only right to stress, in one context, that he never aimed "at lowering in the slightest degree the commanding position occupied by our own faith", and never wrote "anything to place Christianity in an unfavourable light in relation to the other systems of the world".[4] To Monier-Williams, Christianity was "the only divine system capable of regenerating the entire human race",[5] "the only message of salvation",[6] and "the only power of God unto salvation to Jew, Greek, Hindu and Mohammedan".[7]

It follows that all other religious systems, *qua* systems, must be false.[8] Whereas Max Müller believed that the religions of the world, including historical Christianity, would in due course evolve into the ideal religion, Monier-Williams believed that eventually "the

[1] *Modern India and the Indians* (4th ed. 1887), p. 253.
[2] *The Bible and the Sacred Books of the East* (1887), p. 22.
[3] *Modern India*, p. 233.
[4] *Indian Wisdom* (1875), p. xxxviii.
[5] *Ibid.*
[6] *Ibid.*, p. 143.
[7] *Modern India*, p. 233.
[8] *Indian Wisdom*, p. xxxii.

victory of Christianity must be signal and complete" and that "Hinduism will ultimately crumble to pieces when brought more fully into contact with the truths of Christianity".[9] In the latter case, it need hardly be said, "Christianity" means "Evangelical Christianity" as a missionary force.

The fact that the non-Christian systems are inadequate for man's salvation does not however mean that no elements of truth, no flashes of true light, are to be found in them.[1] If, as Monier-Williams believed, the non-Christian religions are corruptions of some original revelation made to mankind (Rom. 1), then it must be possible to find in them some fragments of the truth contained in that revelation. But only on condition of fairness and impartiality in the seeking. We are in duty bound to make the attempt, taking the purest form of the religion in question, and not its worst corruptions, as our measuring-rod. We must try to take a just and comprehensive view, and not stop at "those corruptions, encrustations and accretions which in all religions tend to obscure, and even to conceal altogether, what there is of good and true in them".[2] We can in any case take comfort from the fact that if nothing true or sound can be shown to underly the rotten tissue of decaying religion, the truth of Christianity may be more clearly shown as a result of this process.[3] And should we succeed in finding truth, we may accept it with gratitude as being a sign of the working of the Spirit of God.[4]

There is one point on which Max Müller and Monier-Williams were for the most part in agreement: that all religions, however they are to be judged, and whatever stage of development they may have reached, are the expressions of a fundamental and deep-seated instinct in man. Although this idea was part of the common property of late nineteenth-century thought, and closely connected with the evolutionary hypothesis, it is not out of the question that Max Müller may have passed on the idea, directly or indirectly, to Monier-Williams. Be that as it may: the important thing for our purposes

---

[9] *Modern India*, p. 586. Cf. below, pp. 65 ff.

[1] *Indian Wisdom*, p. 143 f.: "Fragments of truth are to be found in all religious systems, however false."

[2] *Ibid.*, p. 3, n. 1.

[3] *Ibid.*, p. 3 f.

[4] "It must ... be admitted that the flashes of light which emerge from the mists of pantheism in the writings of Indian philosophers, must spring from the same source of light as the Gospel itself." *Ibid.*, p. 153 f.

is that it is into this context that Monier-Williams introduces *the concept of fulfilment.*[5]

By "fulfilment" Monier-Williams meant two distinct things: first, that "lower" religions are "fulfilled" by "higher" religions in the process of evolution, and that Christianity is the fulfilment of Hinduism since it exists on the highest possible evolutionary plane of development; and secondly, that Christianity is that form of religion which satisfies, or "fulfils" the religious instincts and desires in the heart of every man, of whatever religion he may be. There can be no doubt that here we have a primary source of the missionary theory of the later "fulfilment school" in India.

The passage in which this idea is expounded is of such interest and importance that we quote it *in extenso*:

And is it not proof of the Divine origin of Christianity, and its adaptation to humanity in every quarter of the globe, that some of its grandest and most essential dogmas, and, so to speak, its root-ideas, do indeed lie at the root of all religions, and explain the problems of life which sages and philosophers in all ages of the world have vainly attempted to solve? Is it not a fact that all the gropings after truth, all the religious instincts, faculties, cravings, and aspirations of the human race which struggle to express themselves in the false religions of the world, find their only true expression and fulfilment—their only complete satisfaction—in Christianity?

When I began the study of Hinduism, I imagined that certain elementary Christian conceptions—such as the Fatherhood of God, the Brotherhood of God, and the indwelling of God in the human heart—were not to be found there, but a closer examination has enabled me to detect not only these, but almost every other rudimentary idea of our holy religion. They are nearly all to be found in Hinduism, like portions of adamantine granite beneath piles of shifting sedimentary strata, and they ought to be eagerly searched for by the missionary as a basis for his own superstructure.[6]

However, Monier-Williams later rejected the "fulfilment" view altogether. A description of the attitude of mind which led him first to adopt, and later to abandon, this essentially evolutionary hypothesis, is given in *The Holy Bible and the Sacred Books of the East* (1887). This provides an interesting illustration of the tension between "liberal" and "conservative" tendencies in the religious picture of late nineteenth-century British Protestantism.

The address in which Monier-Williams made his admission was

---

[5] In the sense in which it was later taken up by Farquhar; cf. below, pp. 189 f., 200.

[6] *Modern India*, p. 234.

delivered in 1887, at the anniversary meeting of the Church Missionary Society. We are told that at its end there was a "roar of delight".[7] It is not difficult to see why. Monier-Williams had described how a desire to be fair and gentlemanly had led him to try and place the best possible interpretation on the Sacred Books of the East and Eastern religions generally. He had therefore fitted them into an *a priori* evolutionary scheme, in which Christianity appeared as "merely the climax, the complement, the fulfilment of them all".[8] But mature reflection had convinced him of the error of this superficially attractive solution, with its apparent liberality and toleration. This was "a limp, flabby, jelly-fish kind of tolerance", and "utterly incompatible with the nerve, fibre and backbone that ought to characterize a manly Christian".[9] There is no tolerance in the Bible. There is no salvation outside the name of Christ. And the Scriptures of the non-Christian religions must not be forced into an evolutionary pattern, with the Holy Bible as the consummation, "the crowning product of religious evolution". So far from being the same stuff as the Bible, these non-Christian Scriptures are all "developments in the wrong direction. They all begin with some flashes of light, and end in utter darkness."[1] Their contents say nothing to help sinful man in his quest for righteousness; they tell of no crucified, risen and ascended Saviour. Between the Christian faith and the non-Christian there is "a bridgeless chasm which no theory of evolution can ever span".[2] This chasm is to be crossed only, by the leap of faith.

In this address Monier-Williams came to terms, not only with his own past, but with the evolutionist school as a whole. Hence the enthusiasm of the Assembly. His words were interpreted as a vindication, not only of the essential truths of the Bible over against other religious scriptures, but also—and this was even more cogent— as a vindication of the fundamental missionary principle that the heathen is indeed in darkness, and cannot be saved except the light of the Gospel be brought to him.[3]

But Monier-Williams' contribution had been made. His doctrine

---

[7] Stock, *History of the Church Missionary Society* III, p. 303.
[8] *The Holy Bible and the Sacred Books of the East*, p. 11.
[9] *Ibid.*, p. 12.
[1] *Ibid.*, p. 13 f.
[2] *Ibid.*, p. 19.
[3] Cf. above, p. 25 f.

of fulfilment had been stated, plainly and forcefully, and his retraction was scarcely able to cancel out his earlier statements. We shall see in due course that J. N. Farquhar reckoned Monier-Williams among his earliest sources of information on Indian missions; and it is reasonable to suppose the "unregenerate" Monier-Williams of *Modern India and the Indians* to have wielded more influence than the rigid Evangelical of *The Holy Bible and the Sacred Books of the East,* particularly for a man in Farquhar's intellectual position.[4] We shall see, too, that the theories with which Farquhar scandalized certain Evangelical missionaries in 1912 were virtually identical with those on which Monier-Williams had turned his back in 1887.[5]

The attitude of greater sympathy for Hinduism, as it sprang from the "science of religion", was slow to make an impact on the rank and file of Protestant missionaries in India. The first to make use of the idea that Hinduism could in some sense be regarded as being "fulfilled" in Christianity were educationalists: T. E. Slater and F. W. Kellett, whose contribution we discuss in Chapter Three.[6] From thence the "succession" passed to Farquhar.

But there were others. The Rev. John Robson, a missionary of the Free Church of Scotland, published in 1876 a pamphlet on *The Science of Religion and Christian Missions,* in which he accepted, virtually without reservation, the position of Max Müller. He acknowledged the indebtedness of missions generally to Müller's work, writing that it "offers a basis on which Christianity may be studied along with other religions, alike without any assumptions in its favour, and without any prejudice to its claims".[7] And renewed scientific study of non-Christian religions was, he felt, bound to lead to a greater measure of sympathy for even the most superficially distressing of its means of expression.

When we hear of the vilest excesses of the Shakti-worshipper, or of the most senseless jabberings of the savage before his fetish, we may recognize even there the same hungering after God which prompted the highest forms of nature worship, and which the Holy Spirit may yet quicken into the worship of the same Heavenly Father that we adore.[8]

---

[4] Below, pp. 119 ff.
[5] Below, pp. 309 ff.
[6] Below, pp. 94 ff.
[7] Robson, *The Science of Religion* (1876), p. 22.
[8] *Ibid.,* p. 25.

Robson embodied this view of non-Christian religion in a monograph on *Hinduism and Christianity* which, first published in the
1870's, ran into several editions.[9]

But the impact of this "new" attitude could, and did, lead to
opposition from Evangelicals, both in Europe and India. We must
not anticipate our argument by pointing to the debate which attended some of J. N. Farquhar's published work. Here it will suffice
to point out that a precedent was established certainly as far back
as the 1880's. In India, William Miller[1] was attacked for—as some
considered—opposing current missionary methods and thereby "lowering the standards of Christianity".[2] And at the Protestant Missionary
Conference held in London in June 1888 the Rev. G. Mackenzie
Cobban[3] of the Wesleyan Methodist Missionary Society was censured
for opinions expressed in a paper on "Christianity in Relation to
Hinduism".[4] Cobban had claimed that the method of the missionary
must be discriminating and intelligent. Everything in Hinduism is
not of the devil; God and spiritual truth are not confined to the
Hebrew and Christian sacred books. The immediate reaction was
that the Acting Secretary of the Conference declared: "I can only
say that if I were prepared to concede as much as our friend does,
I should not be prepared to leave home and country to preach the
Gospel anywhere."[5]

The real conflict was however to be delayed for some years. Before the turn of the century, those missionaries who were prepared
to turn their backs on the accepted Evangelical attitude to the non-
Christian religions and strike out in the direction indicated by Max
Müller and Monier-Williams were few and far between, and often
isolated in their opinions. Nor was active missionary opinion much
influenced by the findings of the "science of religion". Not until
J. N. Farquhar began his work of interpretation after 1902 did these

---

[9] Robson, *Hinduism and Christianity* (3rd ed. 1905), p. iv.

[1] Below, pp. 82 ff.

[2] Chetty, *William Miller* (1924), p. 45.

[3] Findlay and Holdsworth, *History of the Wesleyan Methodist Missionary
Society* V (1924), pp. 231 ff. It is interesting to note that Cobban was active in
a mass-movement area, and not in higher education—an exception to the common
pattern.

[4] An abstract of the paper is given in *Report of the Centenary Conference on
the Protestant Missions of the World* (1888), II, p. 89.

[5] *Ibid.* A lively discussion followed, in which the Rev. John Hewlett of the
LMS took Cobban's part (p. 92 f.). Summing up, Cobban stressed that "Chris-
tianity stands alone; and after we have made allowances for all the truth outside
Christianity, Christianity is without a peer" (p. 98).

come to be applied to Indian missions on anything like a wide scale. But Farquhar was not breaking altogether new ground, and we must now turn our attentions to India, to see how and where a comparable adjustment in opinion had begun to take place by 1890 or so. This will involve first and foremost an examination of the concrete situation which called forth a new missionary strategy, and ultimately a new form of missionary apologetics—the situation of Protestant Christian higher education, as derived from the initiative of Alexander Duff.

CHAPTER 2

Christian Higher Education and Evangelism—
The First Phase

HAVING EXAMINED some of the more important aspects of the intellectual confrontation between Evangelical Christianity and Hinduism in the second half of the nineteenth century, we must now turn to its practical setting in Indian missions. The basic factor to be borne in mind in this and subsequent chapters is that Evangelical missions in India were committed from the 1830's on to a serious attempt to evangelize high-caste Hindus, the intellectual élite of Indian society, and that this attempt was closely bound up with the provision of higher education. Another preliminary observation is that the Hinduism of these classes of society was far different from the popular Hinduism of the villages; here the missionaries were brought into close contact with "higher" Hinduism, not indeed for the first time, but on a far wider scale than ever before, and it now became gradually easier for the individual missionary to compare Christianity as he understood it with Hinduism as practised, not by illiterate villagers, but by representatives of a cultured civilization. The result of this particular form of confrontation we shall consider in due course. In time, the "fulfilment" theory of the relationship between Christianity and Hinduism, which we have already seen to have emerged in the work of Max Müller and Monier-Williams, came to be applied in this particular situation.

But before we can estimate either the force or the nature of this theory, we must have a picture of the conditions which gave rise to it. Some of these we have discussed in Chapter 1. On the practical level, such a picture is not easily obtained from the existing literature: there is in fact no up-to-date study of the problem of Christian-Hindu confrontation in the Christian colleges, nor of the interaction of educational and evangelistic impulses in the nineteenth-century higher educational enterprise in India.[1] Nor can we hope to remedy

---

[1] There is however the extremely valuable report of the Lindsay Commission, *Report of the Commission on Christian Higher Education in India* (1931), which deals with these, and many more, problems as they appeared at a later date.

this deficiency here. It is, however, necessary for a right under-standing of the background to J. N. Farquhar's work in India that we should give a rapid outline of the higher educational enterprise —first as envisaged by Alexander Duff, secondly as taken up by the British authorities, and thirdly as modified by Duff's successors. This present chapter deals with the first two of these topics; the third is considered separately in Chapter Three.

Alexander Duff

The story of Duff's life, and of his coming to India, has often been told,[2] and we need no more than recapitulate briefly. Alexander Duff was born in Scotland on April 25, 1806. His father belonged to the Evangelical party of the Church of Scotland, and conveyed much of his conviction to his son. Duff's ultimate spiritual descent has been traced back to the English Evangelical leader Charles Simeon, who had visited the Highlands in 1796.[3] Duff himself traced his conversion to a dream in which he imagined himself to be await-ing judgment before God, and saw the dreadful consequences of unbelief.[4] These were decisive impressions. Duff was all his life an uncompromising Evangelical, and never made the slightest con-cession to any form of faith other than that in which he had been brought up. Hinduism he regarded as abhorrent.[5]

Duff's formal education took place first at Perth Grammar School, and later at the University of St. Andrews, which he entered in 1821. Two years later the great preacher and Evangelical leader Thomas Chalmers was appointed Professor of Moral Philosophy there, and it was Chalmers who was the greatest formative influence of Duff's adolescent years.[6]

---

[2] The standard biography is Smith, *The Life of Alexander Duff*; I have used the third (one-volume) edition of 1899. Also valuable are Paton, *Alexander Duff: Pioneer of Missionary Education* (1923) and Blaikie's article in *Dict. Nat. Biogr.* XVI (1888), pp. 125 ff. See also Richter, *Indische Missionsgeschichte* (2 Aufl. 1924), pp. 186 ff., Firth, *An Introduction to Indian Church History* (1961), pp. 177 ff.

[3] Smith, *op. cit.*, pp. 2 ff., Paton, *op. cit.*, p. 21. A useful account of Charles Simeon's life and work will be found in Stock, *History of the Church Missionary Society* I (1899), pp. 58 ff.

[4] Smith, *op. cit.*, p. 9.

[5] See below, p. 63 f.

[6] For a summary account of the life of Chalmers, see *Dict. Nat. Biogr.* IX (1881), pp. 449 ff. See also Sjölinder, *Presbyterian Reunion in Scotland 1907–1921* (1962), pp. 35 ff., with bibliography, p. 36 n. 8.

Chalmers appears to have accomplished something of a revolution in the spiritual atmosphere of the University during his tenure of office, on the practical as well as on the theoretical level.[7] On both levels Duff acknowledged his debt. Chalmers' main subject in St. Andrews was ethics, in which he laid great stress on the authority of conscience, a view which found considerable favour with theologians and religious teachers in Scotland.[8] Duff's biographer writes that his mind "received the impress of Chalmers' big thoughts and the form of his phraseology".[9] And on the practical side, Duff received from Chalmers the decisive impulse which turned his mind to the consideration of missionary work abroad. Soon after arriving in St. Andrews, Chalmers accepted the presidency of the St. Andrews Missionary Society (of which Duff was not yet a member). His encouragement of missions was still uncommon in the Church of Scotland, which had as yet no missionary on active service. In 1828 Chalmers left St. Andrews to become Professor of Theology in Edinburgh. This post he held till the Disruption of 1843, when, leaving the Established Church, he became principal of New College, Edinburgh, the Free Church theological college. His interest in missions never waned, and when he died in 1847 Duff, in the course of a tribute, called him "the leading missionary spirit of Christendom".[1]

The Church of Scotland was relatively late in accepting the principle of foreign missions. As far back as 1796 a proposal had been put to the General Assembly that the Church *as a body* should "contribute to the diffusion of the Gospel over the world", but the response had been negligible.[2] Not until 1824 was real progress made, when Dr. Inglis, the leader of the Moderate party of the Church, proposed the establishment of a mission to India, a mission, moreover, in which educational methods were to be the working basis.[3] Five years later Alexander Duff was appointed by the Assembly as the Church of Scotland's first overseas missionary. He

---

[7] Paton, *op. cit.,* p. 37 f.
[8] *Dict. Nat. Biogr.* IX, p. 451.
[9] Smith, *op. cit.,* p. 17.
[1] *Ibid.,* p. 24.
[2] Mathieson, *Church and Reform in Scotland* (1916), p. 77 f.
[3] The *Scotsman* reported Dr. Inglis as having said that "A barbarous people were wedded to their superstitious rites, but give them knowledge and information—open their ideas to judge in other subjects, then they first doubt and conviction follows". Quoted by Mathieson, *op. cit.,* p. 272 f.

was ordained on August 12, 1829, Chalmers himself officiating and delivering the charge. The Assembly sent Duff to the Calcutta area, with certain explicit instructions. These were however brief. Duff was recommended to avoid settling in Calcutta itself, where it was believed there would be serious drawbacks to missionary work; and he was instructed to open a school or college, "because that line of proselytising work had been neglected by the few other missionaries then in Calcutta".[4] He arrived in Calcutta in May 1830, and his reactions were immediate: he determined to ignore the first part of his commission, and to exert all his energies to fulfil the second part.

For the story of Duff's first five years in Calcutta we may refer to the standard biographies and histories of the period. The account of the starting of his first school, opened within two months of his arrival, and of the invaluable help he received from Rām Mohan Ray,[5] is a classic of missionary narrative, and we have no reason to retell it here. It is with the principles governing Duff's missionary work we are most concerned, since it was these principles that provided a foundation for the work of Christian higher education during the rest of the century. But before looking in some detail at these, it is necessary that we examine very briefly the question of education in India at the time of Duff's arrival.

Education in India before 1830

The educational situation of Bengal, and indeed of the whole of British India, before 1830, gave the Westerner the impression of being most unsatisfactory. In 1830 only a tiny minority of the population appeared to be receiving any education at all.[6] Such education as there was fell into two categories, traditional and Western, the first of which was automatically discounted by the great majority of Europeans in India. Traditional Indian education, based on the study of the Veda, also ranged over a multitude of subsidiary studies, from grammar and philosophy to demonology, divination and the

---

[4] Smith, *op. cit.*, p. 47.

[5] For details of the life of Rām Mohan Ray, see e.g. Max Müller, *Biographical Essays* (1884), pp. 1–46, Andrews, *The Renaissance in India* (1912), pp. 107 ff., Macnicol, *The Making of Modern India* (1924), pp. 171–188.

[6] Schomerus, *Indien und das Christentum* II (1932), p. 123, lays the blame for this at the feet of the British; this is hardly just.

fine arts.[7] Education was traditionally in the hands of the Brahmins, was based on the Hindu religion and was open only to members of the three "twice born" castes. And further, Hindu education was entirely voluntary, having no connexion with the state; schools and scholars were supported almost entirely by the generosity of the people.[8]

It has been argued that the "Anglicist" educationalists of the 1830's virtually ignored the existence of this Indian traditional education; but as Paton points out, the ancient Indian system of education had begun to disintegrate at the time of the Moguls and by the time of the 1835 controversy "had so far fallen into desuetude that the reformers of the day are to be excused for ignoring it".[9] And Sir Verney Lovett, writing of the same period, states bluntly that "Learning of all kinds had slunk away into the background".[1] It is a moot point whether these are in fact fair judgments. Very possibly they are not. But we do not propose to go further into the question here; the point is that such was certainly the assumption on which Duff, and later Macaulay, proceeded.

Then there was education based on Western patterns. Before 1813 little effort had been made by the East India Company to improve the educational situation in India. In 1780 Warren Hastings had set up a Mohammedan *Madrasa* in Calcutta, and in 1792 Lord Cornwallis had supported the establishment of a Sanskrit College in Benares, "for the preservation and cultivation of the laws, literature and religion of that nation [the Hindu] at this centre of their faith and common resort of all their tribes".[2] But little more had been done. The turning point came in 1813, with the renewal of the East India Company's Charter; the Act creating the new Charter laid down that such measures ought to be adopted as might lead to "the introduction into India of useful knowledge and religion and moral improvements",[3] and transferred the power to grant licenses of residence to the Board of Control from the Directors. Missionaries were not explicitly mentioned, but it was clear from the terms of the Act that the Government had them in mind.[4] In practice British

---

[7] Raichur, *Religion in Public Education in India* (s.a.), p. 14.
[8] O'Malley, *Modern India and the West* (1941), p. 139.
[9] Paton, *op. cit.*, p. 208.
[1] In *Camb. Hist. Ind.* VI (1932), p. 95.
[2] O'Malley, *op. cit.*, p. 141.
[3] *Camb. Hist. Ind.* VI, p. 102 f.
[4] *Ibid.*, p. 313.

missionary societies were for the first time given virtually unrestricted rights of access to, and activity in, the territories administered by the Company. Further, the "education clause" (Section 43) which set aside a considerable sum of money for "the revival and improvement of literature and the encouragement of the learned natives of India and for the introduction or promotion of a knowledge of the sciences among the inhabitants of the British territories in India", though slow in being implemented, set the seal of official approval on the educational enterprise.[5] The various missionary societies accepted their new-found freedom with eagerness, and the period saw a great increase in the number of missionaries at work in India. Many of these concentrated on education, at first on the elementary level, and there grew up numbers of schools, some run by missionaries, other by the Government, in which Indian children were taught in the vernacular.

The first centre of purely Western higher education in India was however started, not by the missionaries, but by the freethinker David Hare (again with the help of Rām Mohan Ray) in 1817.[6] Known first as the *Vidyalaya*, then as the Hindu College and finally as the Presidency College, this institution came into being as the result of "a semi-rationalist movement which disputed with the missionaries the control of the early stages of Western education in Bengal".[7] On the missionary side, Bishop's College was opened in Calcutta in 1820 by the Church of England, for preparation of Christians in theology and the Arts.[8] Both of these colleges however stood to one side of the main stream of development, though the Hindu College (as it then was) was to play a part, albeit a negative part, in the shaping of Duff's missionary policy.[9]

Educational progress in Calcutta was slow. There were not more than 5000 Indian children at school in the whole city of Calcutta when Duff landed, and of those not more than 500 were learning

[5] Mayhew, *The Education of India* (1926), p. 10.

[6] *Ibid.*, p. 12.

[7] *Report of the Commission on Christian Higher Education in India*, p. 63.

[8] Bishop's College was not a success; it was premature in conception, and never had a sufficient supply of Indian Christian students. Its buildings were eventually sold to the Government, and its work taken over by the Oxford Mission to Calcutta (below, pp. 88 ff.). Stock, *History of the Church Missionary Society* I, pp. 188 f., 331.

[9] Duff, *Brief Statement Relative to the General Assembly's Mission in India*, reprinted in *Missionary Addresses* (1850), pp. 26 ff.

English.[1] Outside Calcutta there were places where the situation was better—in Serampore, for instance, where the Baptists had opened their college in 1818; but Serampore was too far away to be of any practical help to the capital. Vernacular elementary education as practised by the missionaries had this further drawback, that the standard of converts produced (when it produced converts, which was not very often) was low; most, being drawn from the lower castes, were regarded by the missionaries as being unsuitable for positions of responsibility and leadership.[2] To Alexander Duff the provision of missionary higher education seemed to be a passport to the higher castes, who were impervious to Christian teaching presented in the traditional manner, and who did not attend the elementary schools.

Alexander Duff's Missionary Policy

Duff's missionary policy was strictly empirical: shaped in accordance with the demands of a situation in which the determinative factor was the position and influence of Hinduism. His object was threefold. First, if he were able to bring his school to the public notice, he would at the same time have gained some measure of access to the governing classes; secondly, in this way he would be able to spread the Christian Gospel much more widely than had hitherto been possible; and thirdly, he would, through the young men trained in his school, gain a foothold for Western culture in the leading families of the land.[3] Duff's milieu was, as Richter has expressed it, "*das Eldorado der hohen Schulen*";[4] and he had strictly only one enemy—Hinduism. His attitude to Hinduism was one of consistent and energetic opposition, as befitted a system of beliefs and practices which he could only regard as being essentially evil. Hinduism he characterized as a "huge and hideous fabric", an "old pestilent religion"; the Hindu he called

---

[1] Smith, *op. cit.*, p. 53.

[2] Paton, *op. cit.*, p. 58.

[3] The actual results of Duff's policy have been summarized, though only from the positive angle, by Azariah, *India and the Christian Movement* (1936), p. 69.

[4] Richter, *op. cit.*, p. 187.

"a poor brutish idolater".[5] The Hindu system he wished above all things to destroy; his weapon was higher education.

On Monday May 25, 1835, Duff, on his first furlough, addressed the General Assembly of the Church of Scotland, meeting in the Tron Kirk of Edinburgh. The occasion was the formal presentation of the report of the India mission, though it was in fact used by Duff as an opportunity of making an *apologia* for the methods he had used during the first five years of his work in Calcutta.[6] A general picture of the methods he advocated may be gained by studying the text of this address, for it is a striking fact that the principles he applied at the start of his missionary career remained substantially unchanged throughout his years in India.[7]

For his starting point he took the question "What has education, what has the communication of useful knowledge, to do with the missionary enterprise?" He began by picturing the efforts of a Western missionary to convince a Hindu audience of the truth of the Christian faith; the first thing a Hindu demands is proof of the missionary's authority. The missionary accordingly resorts to the methods of persuasion he has been accustomed to apply at home: the evidence of history, the argument from miracles, the argument from prophecy, and the rest. But none of these has the slightest effect on the Hindu mind; and the missionary realizes that he is faced with the insuperable difficulty of communicating with minds "that are either pre-occupied with airy subtilties, or stultified with utter neglect".[8] In other words, the missionary realizes that he must himself attempt to create the terms of reference which make a meaningful exchange of ideas possible, and the conditions on which the Hindu can appreciate the true force of the missionary's arguments.

The only possible way in which this could be done, claimed Duff, was to give the Hindu an education approximating in some way to that which the missionary himself had received: "... a sound

---

[5] Duff, *Missionary Addresses*, pp. 20, 33, 37. This view was of course that of his age (above, p. 25 f.); thus he could speak of the state of the heathen as "far too sad and awful a reality to be a fitting theme for story or song; unless it be one over which hell would rejoice, and heaven weep". *Ibid.*, p. 204.

[6] Smith, *op. cit.*, pp. 132 ff.

[7] Paton, *op. cit.*, p. 233 f.: Duff "made his great contribution to Indian policy and chose the line which was to be of such profound importance for the future of Indian education only a few weeks after he arrived in India ... The rest of his life was spent in working out the full implications of that momentous choice."

[8] *Missionary Addresses*, p. 12.

liberal education is greatly advantageous towards the establishment of the evidence and authority of the Christian revelation".[9] Greatly advantageous, but not absolutely essential, for education, while it could prepare the way for the Christian revelation, was not itself that revelation. Duff was not suggesting that education could take the place of the action of the Spirit of God on the human heart, disposing a man to receive that revelation.[1]

But Western education was desirable for a further reason. Duff was convinced that the nature of Hinduism was such, that it would be wholly unable to withstand the impact of sound Western learning. Hinduism he had seen to possess many sides and many ramifications; it was a system of religion, but it was also a social pattern and a system of traditional scholarship. It seemed to be essentially a whole, and Duff believed that to attack and undermine any one part was to attack and undermine the whole. Similarly, victory over any one part was a step in the direction of final victory over the whole of the system. Here we have the crux of the matter:

Every branch of sound general knowledge which you inculcate, becomes the destroyer of some corresponding part in the Hindu systems. And if branch after branch be communicated, one stone after another will be thrown down from the huge and hideous fabric of Hinduism; and by the time that an extensive range of instruction is completed, the *whole* will be found to have crumbled into fragments: not a shred will be left behind.[2]

But assuming it to be possible to destroy Hinduism by means of Western education, the real task of the missionary remained: that of constructing a Christian edifice on its ruins. Duff repudiated the accusation, explicit or implicit, that his system was merely destructive. His college, he claimed, was "cemented by Christian principle" throughout.[3] By this he meant that the study of the Bible

---

[9] *Ibid.*, p. 14.

[1] Duff, *Our Earliest Protestant Mission to India*, reprinted in *Missionary Addresses*, p. 278: Christianity is "*a life*—a divine life—or living energy infused by omnipotent grace into the souls of regenerated men". Education, in the form of "true literature and true science", he called "our very best auxiliaries", but insisted that they should never be allowed to "usurp the throne". *Missionary Addresses*, p. 95.

[2] *Ibid.*, p. 19 f. This was an attitude shared by many at that time. T. B. Macaulay wrote to his father Zachary Macaulay in 1836: "It is my firm belief that, if our plans of education are followed up, there will not be a single idolater among the respectable classes in Bengal thirty years hence." Trevelyan, *Life of Macaulay* (1908), p. 330.

[3] *Missionary Addresses*, p. 35.

and Christian faith and practice occupied a prominent position in all his teaching, alongside and conditioning the elements of "useful knowledge".

In this way, while we throw down, we also rebuild: while we dispossess, we replace a hundredfold: while we remove weakness, disease, deformity, we confer wealth, strength and beauty.[4]

Knowledge without religion Duff regarded as a pitfall to be avoided at all costs. This had been the result of the teaching given at the Hindu College, against which so much of Duff's initial effort had been directed.[5] He was afraid that Government policy was tending in this direction, and might succeed in producing "a nation of infidels".[6] To those who advocated Western education free from religious instruction Duff answered that, human nature being corrupt, such a process of conveying knowledge without religion would be bound to intensify, rather than relieve that state.[7] There were two errors which we wished to avoid: what he called "the bigotry of an unwise pietism", which refused to admit as theologically true what was allowed to be philosophically true (sound literature and science); and "the bigotry of infidelity", which neglected "the paramount importance of the sacred oracles, in the great work of Christianizing and civilizing a guilty world".[8]

Duff dealt with two other important topics in the course of his 1835 address: the first was the use of native agents in the work of evangelization; the second was the use of the English language in higher education. On the first count, Duff was convinced that no European could ever work in Bengal with the same degree of efficiency and effectiveness as a Bengali. This held good for a number of reasons, including language, climate and cast of mind. But the Indian evangelist must be properly qualified; and by "qualified" Duff meant "possessed of essentially European qualifica-

---

[4] *Ibid.*

[5] Above, p. 62 n. 9; Smith, *op. cit.,* p. 78 f. The prevalent atmosphere of the Hindu College has been described as "dogmatic agnosticism". Paton, *op. cit.,* p. 78.

[6] *Missionary Addresses,* p. 47.

[7] *Ibid.,* p. 149: "So, from the present constitution of the human mind, the light of secular knowledge will dispel the darkness of ignorance from the natural understanding; but will it eradicate the corruption of a depraved heart? No: its only effect may be to render that corruption more manifest."

[8] *Ibid.,* p. 95.

tions and unencumbered by European disadvantages".[9] Again the demand was for Western education.

On the central topic of the use of the English language, he began by denying most vehemently that he wanted to see English substituted for the vernaculars in each and every situation; such a demand he dismissed as unreasonable and impracticable.[1] But at the same time there were tasks for which the vernaculars were manifestly unfitted, by reason of their limited vocabulary and their lack of suitable literature. The vernaculars, claimed Duff, do not provide "an adequate medium for communicating a knowledge of the higher departments of literature, science and theology".[2] Only English is fitted for that task. But—and this is an aspect of Duff's theory which is easily overlooked—English is not for everyone. English as a medium of education Duff intended should be limited to "the thoroughly educated few": "the ordinarily educated many" must continue to be taught in the vernaculars.

Duff thus envisaged the creation of an intellectual Indian aristocracy, taught in English, thinking in English terms, capable of mediating Western education to the many. It was this aristocracy which was to be enlightened and christianized (for Duff refused to contenance the spread of Western education for its own sake, divorced from the Christian faith).[3] They would then in their turn be able to pass on what they had gained to their less privileged countrymen, making use of the vernaculars. But for the primary task of undermining the traditional Hindu religion and culture, and replacing it by Western culture and the Christian religion, English was an indispensable instrument. "The English language", concluded Duff, "... is the lever which, as the instrument of conveying the entire range of knowledge, is destined to move all Hindustan."[4]

Government Policy

Duff was not an absolute innovator in the matter of the use of the English language as a medium of education in India, though he

---

[9] *Ibid.,* p. 23.
[1] *Ibid.,* p. 42.
[2] *Ibid.*
[3] Duff called the giving of education without religion "a blind, suicidal policy". Smith, *op. cit.,* p. 266.
[4] *Missionary Addresses,* p. 44.

did cast new light on its possibilities. The process by which English came to be the "official" language of India began in the last decade of the eighteenth century.

At that time, as we have seen, the East India Company favoured a conciliating attitude to traditional Indian culture. For obvious reasons: their task was to maintain trade, and to keep the peace generally, and they regarded it as the safest policy to disturb as little as possible of the traditional Indian way of life.[5] Although little enough was done to better the situation of Britain's Indian subjects, the general trend was pro-Indian rather than pro-Western. There was as yet no consistent educational policy.

It was in this *status quo* atmosphere that a senior servant of the East India Company, Charles Grant (1746–1823) wrote a pamphlet called *Observations on the State of Society among the Asiatic Subjects of Great Britain* (1792). This was a description of social and moral conditions among the Hindus and Mohammedans of Bengal, as seen by an Evangelical layman. Its particular significance lay in Grant's plea for education, principally in English; for missionaries to teach the people new views of duty; and for the replacement of Persian (then the official language) by English in judicial proceedings. Grant ended by asserting that the English language was "the best channel for the spread of general enlightenment".[6] This document, in the hands of Wilberforce, became a powerful instrument for persuading Parliament to renew the East India Company's charter on the more generous lines we have described.

We mention this merely to show that the provision of English-language education had been considered officially desirable for some years before the opening of Duff's college. This, we must remember, was virtually a private venture, and it was as such that it gave proof of the extent to which English-language higher education might be made to serve the cause of India. Duff, though an evangelist in all he did, was not unaware that the measures he was advocating might have political repercussions.[7] In the circumstances, the Government came seriously to consider revising its traditional policy of *laissez-faire* with respect to Indian culture and learning. The revi-

---

[5] Above, p. 27 f.
[6] *Camb. Hist. Ind.* VI, p. 97 f.
[7] *Missionary Addresses*, pp. 40 ff.

sion, when it came, came suddenly, and was welcomed by Duff and his colleagues as a vindication of their ideas and methods.

The minute of the Governor-General in Council of March 7, 1835, which secured English education its official status, came as the climax of a protracted controversy between the two opposing groups commonly called Anglicist and Orientalist. The point at issue was the relative merits of the Western and classical Indian cultures as objects of study; the decision, which caused much rejoicing in the missionary camp, was that the British Government should henceforth concentrate on the promotion of European science and literature among the natives of India, and that all funds available for education should henceforth ideally be employed for the support of English-language Western education alone.[8]

The ultimate responsibility for this decision is commonly credited to Thomas Babington Macaulay (1800–1859). He was however not the prime mover. His intervention was late, and it seems likely that the Anglicists would have ultimately succeeded in their aims without his championship.[9] But to Macaulay must go the credit that the decision came when it did.

On his arrival in India, Macaulay had been appointed President of the Committee of Public Instruction. The Committee had been engaged on the problem of higher education for some time, and had become equally divided (five to five) on the subject of Western *versus* Oriental education as the basis of school curricula. Macaulay, who before coming to India had made a name as an essayist and orator, waited for the decision of the Committee before composing his celebrated minute, passed to Governor-General Sir William Bentinck (1774–1839) on February 2, 1835. Macaulay sided unreservedly with the Anglicists; furthermore, he put their case with such force as to convince Bentinck that this was the correct policy to follows. As Charles Williams has said, "It [the minute] swept the Government and the Governor-General away on its own intensity of conviction".[1]

---

[8] A useful summary of the Anglicist-Orientalist controversy will be found in Monier-Williams, *Modern India and the Indians* (4th ed. 1887), pp. 289 ff. See also Mayhew, *op. cit.*, p. 165 f., O'Malley, *op. cit.*, pp. 62 ff., Griffiths, *The British Impact on India* (1952), pp. 250 ff.

[9] Mayhew, *op. cit.*, p. 12 f.

[1] Williams, *Lord Macaulay*, reprinted in *The Image of the City*, ed. Ridler (1958), p. 11.

Macaulay knew nothing whatever about Indian culture. Nor had he any acquaintance with Indian literature (in the 1830's this was still the province of very few Europeans). But he seems not to have wanted to learn. During his short term of office in India he applied himself with remarkable diligence to a renewed study of the Greek and Latin classics,[2] at least partly as an anodyne to Indian life, which he called his "exile".[3]

The general tone of his remarks on the subject of education will be clear if we quote a few celebrated lines from the minute in question:

The question now before us is simply whether, when it is in our power to teach this language [English], we shall teach languages in which, by universal confession, there are no books on any subject which deserve to be compared with our own; whether, when we can teach European science, we shall teach systems which, by universal confession, whenever they differ from those of Europe, differ for the worse; and whether, when we can patronise sound philosophy and true history, we shall countenance, at the public expense, medical doctrines, which would disgrace an English farrier—astronomy, which would move laughter in the girls at an English boarding-school—history, abounding with kings thirty feet high, and reigns thirty thousand years long—and geography made up of seas of treacle and seas of butter.[4]

This is of course a seriously unbalanced judgment, despite its eloquence. Whatever Macaulay's prowess in other fields, he was unable to weigh the evidence in favour of Oriental studies impartially. Knowles has said that Macaulay's two great shortcomings as a historian were "his spirit of partisanship and his superficiality of judgment".[5] Both are in ample evidence here. His short term of office he himself regarded as something of an *interregnum*; he had neither the time nor the inclination to study the country and people of India. His express intention was to make the culture of the ruling class the doctrine of the ruled.[6] Government policy was at this critical juncture in the hands (and pen) of an alien;[7] a man

---

[2] For Macaulay's reading-list between Nov. 1834 and Dec. 1835, see Trevelyan, *Life of Macaulay*, p. 321.

[3] *Ibid.*, p. 307: "I have no words to tell you how I pine for England, or how intensely bitter exile has been to me ..."

[4] *Ibid.*, p. 291.

[5] Knowles, *Lord Macaulay* (1960), p. 12.

[6] Williams, *Lord Macaulay, loc. cit.*

[7] Even Max Müller was unable to make the slightest impression on Macaulay's prejudices. See *Life of Max Müller*, ed. by his wife, I (1902), p. 162.

of letters made the decision which was destined to affect the entire course of educational work in India, and the whole of the subsequent development of that nation.[8]

Macaulay's decision had the effect of introducing English-language liberal education as a major item of official policy into a country governed on autocratic principles. Had the reforms of the 1830's been restricted to the reshaping of the educational system, the results—particularly the opening of a breach with the traditional culture of India—would have been serious enough. But educational reform was associated with first efforts in the direction of granting representative government, with penal reforms and increased civil liberties, and with greater freedom of the press. The inevitable consequence was, as Bearce has pointed out, that "India had no choice but to receive a large dose of Westernization".[9] And increasing Westernization accorded ill with the principles on which India continued to be governed, even after the Mutiny of 1857–1858. It was in the conflict between the liberal mind and the autocratic system that the seeds of Indian nationalism were sown. And among the first to be affected were the students in the colleges.

From the first those young Indians who came seeking higher education in English did so from a variety of motives; but there was little outward incentive. After 1844, however, a change took place. In that year the Hardinge administration issued a resolution to the effect that henceforth candidates with a knowledge of English were to be preferred in the public service; and that even in the lowest grades "in every instance a man who can read and write be preferred to one who cannot".[1] This was regarded as being an enormous step forward, since it opened at least the lower grades of the municipal and civil services to suitably qualified Indians. The Council of Education (which had replaced the Committee of Public Instruction in 1842) instituted an agreed syllabus and graduation examinations; successful candidates were (at least in theory) entitled to employment. Of course, not all who passed were

---

[8] *Camb. Hist. Ind.* VI, p. 120: "The new policy was carried into effect in Bengal by a brilliant Whig politician who possessed no knowledge of the history of Indian thought and no understanding of the Indian mind." Other more positive aspects of Macaulay's work are stressed by Neill, *A History of Christian Missions* (1964), p. 275.

[9] Bearce, *British Attitudes towards India, 1784–1858* (1961), pp. 153 ff. Quotation from p. 155.

[1] *Camb. Hist. Ind.* VI, p. 116.

employable—a point which caused some resentment—but the precedent had been established and "Western education had been clearly declared a passport to Government service, the most coveted of all professions".[2]

This resolution was to have serious consequences for the missions, particularly in the Calcutta area. The decision of 1844 had the effect of intensifying still further the desire of the Bengali for English-language education. But a perceptible shift in motive had taken place, from the seeking of education for its own sake to the seeking of education for the sake of the rewards it might bring. "English education was now not a means to culture, but a strictly commercial proposition, with golden rewards for the proficient".[3]

Developments after 1844

English-language education thus proved popular, whatever the reasons. Duff and his colleagues found within a very short time that they had created a demand for this kind of instruction—a demand which, once recognized and encouraged by the authorities, proved increasingly difficult to satisfy.[4] It was only natural, in view of its initial success, that Duff's system should have been assiduously copied; in fact, English-language colleges were soon established, some by the Government and some by missionaries, in all the principal Indian cities. And throughout the whole of the period between 1830 and 1900 the demand continued to increase.

An important factor in this development was the Education Dispatch of 1854. This laid down, among other things, that three Universities, in Calcutta, Bombay and Madras, should be set up as examining bodies on the model of London University, that attention should be paid to vernacular education as well as education in English, and that "grants-in-aid" should be made available out of public funds not only to Government colleges and schools, but to "institutions begun and maintained by private bodies, whether Hindu, Mohammedan or Christian, indigenous or foreign".[5] This

---

[2] *Ibid.*

[3] Neill, *Builders of the Indian Church* (1934), p. 111.

[4] Macaulay wrote in 1836 that "our English schools are flourishing wonderfully. We find it difficult,—indeed, in some places impossible,—to provide instruction for all who want it." Trevelyan, *op. cit.*, p. 329.

[5] Paton, *Alexander Duff*, p. 160.

was a notable step forward, but again it gave rise to problems for the missions, since colleges in receipt of grants-in-aid were compelled to organize their teaching on the lines laid down by the authorities, and particularly to teach for the degree examinations of the three Universities. Religious teaching was not opposed in principle; but it became increasingly difficult for the mission colleges to assert their distinctively Christian character.

By 1857, taking Bengal as an example, there were four colleges—one Government and three missionary—teaching English to Bengalis in Calcutta. These three missionary colleges, the Duff College,[6] the General Assembly's Institution,[7] and the London Missionary Society's Institution at Bhowanipur,[8] were educating between them approximately a thousand young men at any given time; as the century progressed and as the educational system became better established, this number might well have been doubled. But resources were insufficient, and the initiative passed, in the course of time, to the non-missionary colleges.[9]

Not all the young men thus educated could of course be given places in the civil service, or even be found work in which their English education could be given full play. Many young men passed out of the colleges without a degree; many more were superficially Western; intellectually as often as not agnostic; to the Hindu "men without a *dharma*" and to the missionary "borderers".[1] These came to form a new class, almost a new caste: the "educated Indian" we shall be hearing so much about in the years up to 1914.

From the point of view of missions the trend of developments was disappointing and indeed alarming. In the missionary college, the examination system and growing classes forced many educational missionaries to spend up to twenty-four hours a week in the classroom, often teaching "secular" subjects apparently far removed from their missionary calling. The supply of suitable teachers became less and less adequate as the system grew: by 1910 a C.M.S. missionary

---

[6] The General Assembly's Institution of the Free Church of Scotland was founded in 1844, after the Disruption, when all the Church of Scotland's missionaries joined the Free Church.

[7] Duff's original college. The two later united, the Scottish Churches College opening on June 30, 1908.

[8] Founded in 1837; cf. below, p. 139.

[9] Below, p. 146 f.

[1] See Shay, *The Legacy of the Lokamanya* (1956), p. 38 f. for a description of the type—not however from a specifically missionary angle.

from Ceylon—where the development had been similar—was able to point to "undermanning" as the main cause of "failure" in educational missions.[2] The Scripture teaching on which Duff had laid such emphasis came to be thrust into the background. It was not abandoned, but towards the end of the century the Hindu student, under the influence of the Hindu revival and growing nationalist feeling, came to receive formal Scripture teaching with at best indifference, at worst bitter opposition. Conversions to Christianity, never plentiful, ceased almost entirely.

The early days of the educational enterprise in Bengal had seen a number of spectacular high-caste conversions in the missionary colleges.[3] It was this that Duff and his followers believed and hoped would happen when Hindus were subjected to the full force of Western education and Christian teaching together. For a time it seemed that their predictions might have been justified. But the promise of the early years could not be maintained. It is true that there continued to be a trickle of baptisms in at least some of the colleges; but it was no more than a trickle, and each individual case was welcomed all the more warmly for being a rarity. The young Hindu passed through the college, absorbing an indefinite amount of Christian "influence", often consciously turning his back on at least the outward forms of his traditional religious heritage; but seldom did he take the step of being baptized and joining the Christian community. Socially the price was too high; there came to be other reasons, as we shall see.

It is perhaps not surprising that there came to be a good deal of criticism of educational missions from those who regarded the effectiveness of a mission as measurable by the number of its converts to Christianity. Some pointed out, particularly during the last quarter of the century, that missions to the lower castes and outcastes were having striking results, in marked contrast to the missionary colleges. If the higher castes were so impervious to the forces of the Gospel, it was argued, why spend so much of the missions' money on keeping the colleges going, particularly when a good secular education was readily available elsewhere?[4]

---

[2] World Missionary Conference, 1910, *Report of Commission III*, p. 28.
[3] Smith, *op. cit.*, pp. 85 ff. Neill, *A History of Christian Missions*, p. 275.
[4] See e.g. *Report of the Centenary Conference on the Protestant Missions of the World* (1888) II, p. 247: "I do not think that this system honours God

A further cause of uneasiness in missionary circles was the employment of Hindu (less frequently Muslim) teachers in Christian colleges. In 1863 Duff's Institution had 43 non-Christian, as against 18 Christian teachers.[5] By the 1880's most colleges were unable to function without their Hindu teachers,[6] who took care of most of the "secular" teaching, leaving the missionaries to concentrate on the teaching of Scripture and the more demanding subjects. It was felt by some that "where we employ non-Christian teachers we may be filling gaps and spaces, but we are going beyond that which God has given us to do".[7] Most, however, were forced to accept their presence, *faute de mieux*.[8] This implied a tacit acceptance of certain modifications in Duff's original attitude. Duff had maintained that the Indian *Christian,* given a good education, could be of great service in spreading the Gospel to his fellow-countrymen; but it was no part of his scheme to employ Hindus to undermine the faith of their fellow-believers: the positive aspect of his theory—the subordination of all teaching to that of the Bible—ruled out the employment of any but Christians as teachers. But this is what happened, however incongruous it may seem in the light of Duff's original principles. In point of fact, however, the introduction of English-language liberal education had already begun to change the face of Hinduism; resilient as ever, it had begun to adapt itself to the new situation; and from the 1870's onward began to develop a new positive dynamic, which we shall discuss in due course. But for the present it is enough to point out that Duff's system had been modified to permit of the inclusion of Hindu teachers; and that Hinduism had been modified sufficiently to allow liberal Hindus (a new category) to teach in Christian colleges.

The decades following upon the opening of Duff's college and the adoption of English as the regular medium of all higher education in India saw the missionary movement brought into contact with the youth of the higher castes on a wide front. At the same

sufficiently, and a system which does not honour God, God will never honour ... I say if you want large results, go to the common people ..." Cf. below p. 143.

[5] Davis, *A Study of Missionary Policy and Methods in Bengal from 1793 to 1905* (Thesis, Edinburgh 1942), p. 171.

[6] *Report of the Centenary Conference,* p. 241.

[7] *Ibid.,* p. 247.

[8] Farquhar called the situation "unnatural"; see *The Higher Education of Christians in Bengal* (1896), p. 4.

time the missionary's ability to profit by the situation thus created was radically curtailed. Larger classes in which the majority of pupils were Hindus; the demands of the examination system; long hours spent in the classroom, to the detriment of personal relations with his pupils out of school hours—all these left little time for "direct" evangelism, even before the rise of Neo-Hinduism.[9] The system to which the missionary was committed was thought out in answer to the demands of a particular situation; it was intended to be used as a hammer for the destruction of Hinduism, viewed in a certain way, and envisaged the communication of a strictly Evangelical Gospel. Traditional Hinduism was indeed undermined in very many cases, but Evangelical Christianity was seldom given a chance to take its place; instead there began to grow up a new Hinduism, a Hinduism frequently modelled on the ethic and the practice of the West, though rejecting the West.

The introduction of English as the medium of higher education was intended by Duff as a means by which to communicate the full range of Western knowledge. But it was more than that. By introducing English, the educationalists of the mid-nineteenth century were introducing not only a new language, but new thought-forms, new concepts, a new way of life, and (in some cases) a new religion. Indians educated in missionary and Government schools and colleges in fact ran great risk of "denationalization", and the risk was increased if and when they were baptized and joined the Christian community.[1] It has been pointed out that under this system salvation depended "... essentially on what the West could give, and particularly the Bible: on a departure from all that Hinduism involved rather than on the adaptation and refinement of Hindu life, thought and customs".[2] And while some Indians were converted to Christianity, many more were not; large numbers had, under the influence of Western education, become dissatisfied with Hinduism without ever going so far as to accept Christianity. The nationalist movement cast many of these back into Hinduism: but in many cases a reformed Hinduism, the like of which Duff could scarcely have forseen.

One final point which may be mentioned is that the association

[9] Ibid., cf. Mylne, *Missions to Hindus* (1908), p. 142.
[1] Above, pp. 29 ff.
[2] O'Malley, *op. cit.*, p. 325.

in the Indian mind of Christianity with Western politics in India dates from the Education Dispatch of 1854, when missionaries were first given an active part to play in Government educational schemes. And the Government had since the 1830's shown itself to be in favour of the cultural theory that the planting of Western civilization in India was the only worthy object of Western education—an object symbolized by the use of the English language. It was here, as well as in the missionary work of Alexander Duff, that the seeds of suspicion were sown in the Indian mind that the ultimate object of the British in India was to destroy and replace indigenous culture with Western culture, Hinduism with Christianity. Little wonder that in later years the Indian came to look upon the missionary educationalist as a tool in the hands of the Government, bent on destroying everything distinctive in the cultural heritage of India. Even an Indian Christian (K. T. Paul) was able at the height of nationalist agitation to write of Alexander Duff and his fellow-workers as "emissaries of a foreign and denationalizing religion".[3]

---

[3] Paul, *The British Connection with India* (1927), p. 42. Cf. Andrews, *The Renaissance in India* (1912), p. 34: "We have learned since his [Duff's] day that the problem is one of assimilation, rather than substitution." Cf. also Schomerus, *Indien und das Christentum* II, p. 143 f., idem, *Kan kristendomen erövra Indien?* (translation from author's MS, 1923), p. 15.

CHAPTER 3

Christian Higher Education and Evangelism—
The Second Phase

THE SECOND and subsequent generations of missionary educationalists in India were faced with problems which differed considerably from those which Duff had had to tackle in the 1830's. Although the basic problem—how to reach the higher castes with the Christian Gospel—remained unchanged, the situation of those castes had changed, as we have suggested in Chapter Two. From being a stronghold of traditional Hinduism, the youth of the upper castes had in very many cases been profoundly affected by the coming of Western education, with consequent emancipation from traditional restraints, particularly in the field of religion. Later generations of missionary teachers thus had to try and reach "the educated classes" rather than "the highest castes". Opposition was on the increase, though its climax was not reached until the early years of the new century.

In the previous chapter we attempted to show how this situation had come about; here we shall try and show how the second generation of educationalists, from c. 1875 to 1900, attempted to solve the problems brought about, first, by the widespread copying of Duff's methods and, secondly, by the adoption of Western education as a consistent policy by the British government.

We have seen that the characteristic pattern of active evangelism in missionary education from 1830 to 1875 (the dates are of course approximate) was one of initial success, followed by gradual decline.[1] And we have looked at some of the causes which brought this about: larger and larger classes, the shortage of educational missionaries, the employment of non-Christian teachers, a rigid examination system and the imposition of a fixed syllabus of secular studies, pushing the purely Christian objectives of the colleges into the background. The number of actual conversions fell, and the colleges in India

---

[1] See above, pp. 74 ff. Cf. also Neill, *Builders of the Indian Church* (1934), p. 110.

and their supporting societies at home were forced to ask whether they might not after all be engaged on a fruitless venture.

We quoted in Chapter Two a typical criticism from one of the detractors of higher education as a missionary method: a criticism which suggested that the money being spent on missionary higher education might be spent, with more tangible results, on the evangelization of the lower castes.[2] These methods certainly appeared to be cheaper than higher education; they did not require such elaborate organization; the mass movement areas were giving proof of their effectiveness.[3] It seemed to some that the products of the missionary colleges were in fact further from Christianity than before; this too was put forward as a criticism of the educational missionaries. It was pointed out that the young Indian often had a grievously distorted picture of Christianity after his college years.[4]

But these were not the only points being made. Acute observers suggested that Evangelical missionaries could scarcely avoid becoming frustrated under the system as it was by the end of the century. For example, Bishop Mylne pointed out in 1908 that a young missionary, coming to the country for the first time in the full flush of enthusiasm, very soon found that most of his time was taken up by administration, and teaching for degrees; that direct Christian teaching formed little more than an episode in a day of secular teaching; and that the whole of his time might well be taken up with work having no apparent connexion with the Gospel. "How long", asked the Bishop, "will his early enthusiasm survive this absorption of his energies?"[5] W. E. S. Holland, a C.M.S. missionary, Warden of the Oxford and Cambridge Hostel at Allahabad, asked the same question of the Edinburgh conference in 1910.[6] This was no new problem. J. N. Farquhar, coming to Calcutta in 1891, was placed in just such a situation as this.[7]

---

[2] Above, p. 74 n. 4.

[3] This is stressed, with reference to the situation in Calcutta, by Mukerji, "Missionary Colleges", *Oxford Mission Association Paper* (*Indian Branch*) No. 14 (1889).

[4] *Ibid.*

[5] Mylne, *Missions to Hindus* (1908), p. 142.

[6] World Missionary Conference, 1910: *Report of Commission III*, p. 27: "The most serious effect of this pressure of secularisation is perhaps its reflex influence on the missionary fervour of the man himself. With little direct outlet his evangelistic fervour is apt to die away of inanition."

[7] Below, pp. 157 ff

Criticisms of this nature caused a certain amount of depression and heart-searching in the ranks of the educational missionaries themselves during this period. W. Smith of the Church of Scotland, writing to Edinburgh, suggested that unless the religious character of Christian higher education could be safeguarded, it might be better to abandon the enterprise altogether, and leave higher education to the government.[8] Although his colleagues did not agree, there was a consensus that "every precaution should be taken to prevent the religious character the Missionary Institutions should have, being subordinated to the educational requirements of the Universities".[9] The question was, how such safeguards were to be imposed.

There were actually two related problems here. On the one side there was the question of how to evangelize young Hindus attending the Christian colleges; and on the other the question of how best to look after the minority group of young Christians—converts and the sons of converts—who were being educated in the colleges side by side with young Hindus. The pastoral situation in college left a great deal to be desired. Once the young man left college, the difficulties attending both evangelization and pastoral care were immense.

One solution might be to concentrate on colleges for Christians only. By 1890 the proportion of Christians to Hindus in missionary college classes varied between 3 to 40 (in the best cases) and 3 to 100 (in the worst);[1] lessons had to be arranged with the Hindus in mind; and young Christians were often neglected, particularly when it came to Scripture teaching.[2] "In the present condition of affairs", wrote J. N. Farquhar in 1896 of the situation in the L. M. S. Bhowanipur Institution, "young Christians do not and cannot receive either the special teaching or the personal attention which are necessary, if they are to turn out fine men".[3] His solution was to propose the setting up of a new Ecumenical Institution in Bengal for the education of young Christians "of every race and creed", to be staffed by the existing societies jointly.[4] It is worth noting that a similar proposal had been put forward by Sir Charles Bernard in

[8] *Minutes of the Calcutta Missionary Conference* (Church of Scotland), 7.5.1888.
[9] *Ibid.*
[1] Farquhar, *The Higher Education of Christians in Bengal* (1896), p. 2.
[2] *Ibid.*, p. 3: "In our Missionary Institutions, since the Hindus preponderate to such an extent, the work of the classes has to be arranged to meet the needs of the Hindus."
[3] *Ibid.*, p. 7.
[4] *Ibid.*, p. 10 f.

1889; his scheme was for a Christian University of India, again to be supported by the existing societies. This he felt would ensure moral and religious teaching a secure place in the curriculum, would allay objections against devoting mission funds to educational work, and "might contribute towards the formation of a single Apostolic Church of Indian in the future".[5] Neither of these proposals came to fruition.

The most pressing problem was, however, that of evangelization. From the 1870's on there were a number of attempts made, apart from the radical solution of the proposed Christian college or university, to approach the problem of reaching the educated classes with the Gospel. It is these with which we shall be mainly concerned in the following pages.

These attempts to reach the educated Indian may be classified under three heads:

First, there were those who were willing to accept that the educational system would continue on more or less the same lines in the foreseeable future, but who modified Duff's original intentions, making the Christian college into a centre of preparation and diffusion, instead of a centre of evangelization. William Miller of Madras is the best example of this group.

Secondly, there were those who, while firm in their resolve to bring concentrated Christian influence to bear on the young educated Hindu, were aware of the risks involved in missionary higher education, and therefore avoided the setting up of schools and colleges, preferring instead to establish student hostels. This is best illustrated by the work of the Anglican communities, and in particular by the Oxford Mission to Calcutta.

And thirdly, there came to be growing awareness of the needs of those who, having passed through missionary and other Western colleges, and having absorbed a certain amount of Christian teaching without ever going so far as to accept baptism, were now beyond their sphere of direct influence. The idea of "independent evangelism" among the educated classes, former pupils of missionary and

---

[5] Sir Charles Edward Bernard was a former Chief Commissioner of Burma. The pamphlet in which he put forward his proposals bore the title "A Christian University for India", and was dated April 1889. During the nationalist period following the first world war a project of this kind was once more mooted. See Meston, *Aspects of Indian Educational Policy* (1922), p. 660.

government colleges, was to assume more and more importance as the years passed. By the turn of the century several missionary societies had set apart men for this kind of evangelism, often working in close touch with the Y.M.C.A. Here we shall examine the work of the pioneer in this field, T. E. Slater of the London Missionary Society.

William Miller: The Principle of Diffusion

William Miller (1838–1923) landed in Madras on December 9, 1862, a missionary newly appointed by the Free Church of Scotland to the staff of its educational institution, founded in 1837 by the Rev. John Anderson. Five years earlier, in 1857, the University of Madras had been founded as an examining body on the lines of London University, and it became Miller's task to direct the studies of the institution into university channels. This task was not easily accomplished, but by 1865 the first class of six students was ready for the matriculation examination; in the following year they took the intermediate examination, and in 1867 a class was opened to prepare students for the B.A. degree examination of the University. During the next ten years the college was reorganized entirely, with Miller as Principal, and in 1877 an agreement was arrived at by which the Church Missionary Society and the Wesleyan Methodist Missionary Society joined the Free Church of Scotland in the provision of a central Christian College for Southern India. The college was renamed the Madras Christian College.[6]

There followed what has been called "a period of bold and brilliant innovation and experiment",[7] inspired by Miller himself. During the years between 1877 and his retirement in 1907 he did more than merely provide Madras with a leading college; he provided the Christian colleges of India with a new and controversial *raison d'être*—not to convert, but to spread Christian thought and Christian influence throughout non-Christian India.

Further, we see in Miller's work some tentative steps in the direction of a new missionary message, embodying a new attitude to Hinduism. His lasting work was done in Madras, but the condition

---

[6] "A Hundred Years: 1837–1937. History of the Christian College", in the *Hindu*, 28.1.1937. Cf. Miller, *The Madras Christian College* (1905).
[7] The *Hindu*, 28.1.1937.

of the educated classes in Madras at this time was in many ways similar to that in Calcutta. Although we shall be very largely concerned in the main body of our investigation with the situation in Bengal after 1900, it is important at this stage to note this development in missionary thought in South India. For in a sense it is true to say that J. N. Farquhar's work in Bengal built on foundations originally laid in Madras.

We have seen that the middle years of the nineteenth century had witnessed a decline in the visible results achieved by the Christian colleges of India. And we have tried, very briefly, to indicate why this decline came about. The educational missionaries were aware that "results" were not all that had been hoped for. In 1872 the problem was discussed at the Allahabad missionary conference, where William Miller spoke on the subject of "The Place of Education as a Missionary Agency".[8]

Miller began his paper by admitting that the situation apparently left a great deal to be desired, and stated quite bluntly that "the additions made to the visible Church by means of these Institutions are fewer than they once were".[9] But he did not propose a solution; nor did he attempt to lay the blame on any of the circumstances we have described—understaffing, too large classes, and the like. Instead, returning to first principles, he asked whether the colleges had in fact been brought into existence merely as a means of increasing the *numbers* of Christians in India. His answer was that such was *not* the purpose of missions at all:

If the sole object of Christian effort be to bring the greatest number of human beings, irrespective of race, or creed, or country—simply the greatest possible number of men, into heartfelt knowledge of divine truth, then I at least should join the enemies of Indian missions and should denounce them as an immoral waste of strength.[1]

Education, he went on, is part of the overall task of the Church in India, but it must not usurp the place of preaching.[2] The Institutions must on no account be called places of preaching, or even be thought of in this way, since this "comes very near to giving educa-

---

[8] *Report of the General Missionary Conference held at Allahabad, 1872–1873*, pp. 103–116.
[9] *Ibid.*, p. 103.
[1] *Ibid.*, p. 104.
[2] *Ibid.*, p. 107.

tion as a bribe to induce the recipients to submit to exhortation".[3] The true place of education in the overall scheme of missionary strategy is, metaphorically speaking, a sowing: others will reap. The province of Christian education "is not directly to save souls, but to make the work of saving them more speedy and more certain than it would be without it".[4]

Thus he removed from the colleges the ultimate responsibility for the conversion of the higher-caste Hindus in their classes: the emphasis he placed elsewhere. In 1905 Miller published a short history of the Madras Christian College, in which he stated quite plainly that the aim of the college had never been, and would never be, to make proselytes.[5] "We do not consider that the good the College does can in any way be tested by the number of its students who are baptized", he wrote. "We put no personal pressure to induce them to take that solemn step."[6] Instead of baptism, Miller's goal was diffusion.

By diffusion he meant the spread of Christian ideas, as it were in concentric circles, from the focus of the college. Miller had rejected the limited goal of proselytism as an adequate statement of the purpose of the Christian higher educational enterprise. What he aimed at was "a change of thought and feeling, a modification of character, a formation of principles tending in a Christian direction ...".[7] And this reshaping of principles could not be limited to the individual. The college was, by its very nature and by the nature of the Hindu society in which it was placed, well able to spread Christian principles via its scholars and *alumni*. This work Miller held to be of great importance for the conversion of India. At the 1888 London missionary conference he said that:

The best thing of all would be if in any important centre the Christian college could take the foremost place. If it could thus be the leading factor

---

[3] *Ibid.*, p. 108.

[4] *Ibid.*, p. 110.

[5] This attitude was not accepted by all, though the general consensus would seem to have been that expressed by Stock, *History of the Church Missionary Society* III (1899), p. 496: "Whether or no the Madras College has aimed at conversions as definitely as some other institutions, it may be doubted whether it has not achieved results as distinct as theirs, and as clearly tokens of God's blessing."

[6] Miller, *The Madras Christian College*, p. 20 f.

[7] Idem, *Indian Missions and How to View Them* (1878), p. 30.

in the guidance of thought and feeling, the leavening of the great Society might be antedated by generations.[8]

The principle of diffusion continued to guide Miller's thought on the subject of Indian missions. Thus in a paper submitted to the 1910 Edinburgh conference (after his retirement) he stressed the same principle, that

Christian educationists have the right to hope that, few though the individuals may be whom their teaching leads to become openly members of the Church, yet the whole mass of Hindu society may in course of time become leavened with Christian thought and guided in daily life by Christian ideals.[9]

Miller held that this view implied a modification, rather than a denial, of Duff's original principles.[1] Both men were concerned to see Christian influence spread through the length and breadth of India. But while Duff assumed that Christian influence would spread *in the person of his converts* from the evangelistic focus of the college,[2] Miller felt that formal conversion was of less importance than that the force of the principles themselves should be felt.

By 1910 this view of the aim of educational missions had become fairly well established, thanks largely to the example of the Madras Christian College. But it was by no means unanimous; there were still those who, with Dr. Mackichan, held the conversion of pupils to be the primary aim.[3] This is, however, not a topic we can discuss in detail here.

The second aspect of Miller's work to which attention must be paid concerns his attitude to Hinduism. Here again he differed from Duff, on this occasion more radically. Duff, as we have seen, worked unceasingly for the absolute destruction of Hinduism, both as a religion and a social system.[4] Miller, a half-century later, refused to accept this goal; not only was it inconsistent with what he had

---

[8] *Report of the Centenary Conference on the Protestant Missions of the World* (1888) II, p. 235.

[9] World Missionary Conference, 1910: *Report of Commission III,* p. 443.

[1] *Ibid.*; cf. *Report of the Commission on Christian Higher Education in India* (1931), p. 22 f.

[2] Richter, *Indische Missionsgeschichte* (2 Aufl. 1924), p. 188.

[3] Mackichan, born in 1851, came to India in 1875 and became Principal of Wilson College, Bombay (Free Church of Scotland), in 1882. Cf. below, pp. 347 ff.

[4] Above, pp. 63 ff.

come to know of Hinduism, it was also a sure way to alienate his pupils, most of whom were Hindus. Christ, he maintained, was the friend of all that was good and true, not only in Christianity, but also in Hinduism, and the enemy of evil and error wherever found.[5] It was not true, in his view, that the Christian Church had a monopoly of divine truth.[6]

While it is no part of our purpose to enter into a full analysis of the theology behind this view, it seems, generally speaking, that it depends on Miller's conception of the universality of the human race, regardless of country and creed, under God—thus of the order of creation. This universality extends to the order of redemption. God's scheme for the redemption of the world could not, argued Miller, be limited to the commonly acknowledged contributions of the Hebrews, Greeks and Romans:

Future generations will see as clearly as we see this, that Hinduism and the Hindus are embraced within the limits of God's plan. The time will come when it will be deemed simply foolish to deny that Hindu thought, as truly as Greek philosophy, or Roman law, is a factor in the building of the historic fabric of which the foundation was laid when Abraham was called and of which the cornerstone is Christ ...[7]

Thus the Hindu ideal, being comprehended in the general revelation given to mankind everywhere, stood in the same relation to Christ as did the Israelite, Roman and Greek ideals. True, the Hindu ideal *per se* was imperfect and one-sided, but then so were all the others, apart from Christ. Concluded Miller: "India has her own contribution, and that a valuable one, for the working out of the story of the world."[8]

In 1896, William Miller was elected Moderator of the Free Church of Scotland. Before sailing to take up his duties he reminded his pupils in Madras of these principles, saying that Christianity included all that was true wherever discovered and all that was good wherever wrought out. Although Christ was the centre of human history, that did not preclude "truths" from springing up apart from the teaching of Christ. Therefore true Christians could welcome whatever elements of good Hinduism might contribute to the common store and

---

[5] Chetty, *William Miller* (1924), p. 43.
[6] *Ibid.*, p. 49 f.
[7] Miller, *The Madras Christian College*, p. 8.
[8] Chetty, *op. cit.*, p. 51.

"joyfully clasp hands" with those who brought such elements with them, regarding them as brethren who like themselves had been "perverse children of the common Father". And in his Moderator's address he attacked the established idea that the non-Christian religions (in this case Hinduism) were pure inventions of the wicked one; this he claimed to be at variance with the true spirit of Christianity.[9]

Miller also made use of the term "fulfilment" in his religious teaching, on the lines we have indicated. His biographer records that soon after coming to India he lectured on various aspects of the life and work of Christ, and that "Christ the Fulfiller" was one of the aspects dealt with.[1] But Miller's use of the term was not quite that of, for example, Monier-Williams, though it approaches that of Max Müller, as he claimed that "Christ's religion was one which sought to fulfil the aspirations in other religions and which itself sought its own fulfilment or completion by being furnished with the peculiar contributions of other religions".[2] Elsewhere he makes it clear that it is not historical Christianity which occupies a position of absolute supremacy over against Hinduism; it is Christ, who seeks "to found no sect and to upset none" who is the judge and the sole moral standard.[3] On the empirical level, there could not, he wrote, "... be complete contact between East and West without the religious ideas at work in both being frankly and lovingly laid beside each other"—not for purposes of proselytism, but for mutual enlightenment.[4]

"If the idea of Christ as the Fulfiller has become more familiar, and more agreeable, to the minds of Christians in Southern India", writes Miller's biographer, "it is largely due to the teaching and influence of Dr. Miller."[5] This may well be the case, remembering Miller's position of peculiar influence as Principal of the Madras Christian College. But his distinctive contribution is not to be sought here. It was in personal work with his students, in his energetic advocacy of Christian higher education without proselytism, and in his breadth of outlook that his lasting contribution was made.

---

[9] *Ibid.*, p. 80 f.
[1] *Ibid.*, p. 44.
[2] *Ibid.*, p. 49 f.
[3] *Ibid.*, p. 52.
[4] Miller, *The Madras Christian College*, p. 13.
[5] Chetty, *op. cit.*, p. 44.

The Madras Christian College continued to exercise the kind of influence which Miller had envisaged—a Christian influence in which religious aggression was replaced by a careful training in a Christian spirit. The College was Miller's creation, and it is in its ethos and influence that his significance lies. Though he helped create a favourable climate of opinion, the actual work of reshaping the missionary attitude to Hinduism was carried out by others.

The Oxford Mission to Calcutta: The Principle of Concentration

The Oxford Mission to Calcutta, which came into being in 1880, was one of a number of attempts made by groups within the Church of England to influence the educated classes of India by the establishment of religious communities in Indian centres.[6] The Oxford Mission was not the first in the field; nor was it the largest; but it provides a number of interesting points of contact with the work of the Evangelical missions in Bengal, and its methods are sufficiently representative to allow of our taking it as an example of this type of missionary work.

The first phase of the Oxford Movement was not characterized by its missionary enthusiasm; its first objectives were more local, and the controversies at home absorbed so much of its energy that there was never a thought of starting an independent mission. However, by the 1870's the Movement had become more stable, and its second generation of leaders were able to begin to turn their attention outward. In 1877 there was founded the Cambridge Mission to Delhi,[7] and it was suggested that Oxford might be able to start a similar graduate mission to the educated classes of the Indian universities.[8]

[6] The idea seems to have originated, as far as the Church of England was concerned, in the mind of R. M. Benson (1824–1915), the founder of the Society of St. John the Evangelist, as far back as 1859; see Woodgate, *Father Benson: Founder of the Cowley Fathers* (1953), p. 50 f. The first SSJE missionary arrived in India in 1874 (*ibid.*, p. 118 f.).

[7] There is no comprehensive published history of the CMD; see however Western, *The Early History of the Cambridge Mission to Delhi* (cyclostyled, for private circulation, 1950). Another university mission begun in the same period was the Dublin University Mission to Chhota Nagpur; see Chatterton, *The Story of Fifty Years' Mission Work in Chhota Nagpur* (1901), pp. 156 ff.

[8] *India and Oxford: Fifty Years of the Oxford Mission to Calcutta* (1933), p. 8; cf. Longridge and Hutton, *A History of the Oxford Mission to Calcutta* (1910), and Dalton, *The Story of the Oxford Mission to Calcutta* (1947).

On October 18, 1879, was passed the resolution officially founding the mission. Two clauses describe what it was hoped would be the basic genus of the new mission:

1. That the Mission shall take the form of an association of men living together in a community, though bound only by the tie of a common object.
2. That this Committee is prepared to act under the conditions suggested by the Bishop of Calcutta—namely, to keep the Mission before the public, regulate finances, and advise, but not to exercise definite control over the activities of the Mission in India.[9]

Thus the new mission was independent of the Anglican Missionary Societies from the first, and had considerable freedom to work as it thought fit. In this it differed from the Cambridge Mission to Delhi, which was associated with the S.P.G.[1]

A statement published by the mission made quite clear what were to be the objectives of the community: these were to be "to extend the Kingdom of Christ in India, especially among the more educated natives of the country: firstly, by Eucharist and prayer; secondly, by study and work among them".[2] It would have been understandable had a community of graduates attempted to emulate their Cambridge brethren and open a college of some kind;[3] but they had received forewarning of the perils of this way. Instead, recognizing that there was a very real danger that the Christian educationalist would soon find himself "bound hand and foot by the syllabus and the examiner",[4] they opened a residential hostel for university students. In this way it was hoped that they would be able to introduce Indian students to the Christian life as lived by a Christian community; and hence to "the character of Christ, not in its direct influence in civilization, but in its direct and immediate result in producing and generating Christian character".[5] Their principle was thus one of concentration in a community; their aim a demonstration of Christian presence, rather than Christian preaching.

The work of the Oxford Mission was not limited to purely passive

[9] *India and Oxford*, p. 9.
[1] Western, *op. cit.*, p. 60 f.
[2] *India and Oxford*, p. 16.
[3] The CMD took over in 1879 what had been St. Stephen's High School, and made it into St. Stephen's College; see Monk, *A History of St. Stephen's College, Delhi* (1935). It is interesting to note that the CMD also carried out evangelistic work among low-caste Chamars (tanners, cobblers and farm-workers).
[4] *India and Oxford*, p. 24.
[5] Gore, writing in *Oxford Mission to Calcutta Report for 1890*, p. 39.

evangelism, however. They organized series of lectures (Charles Gore delivered one such series in 1890),[6] published a widely-read journal, the *Epiphany*,[7] and began the circulation of tracts, many of which were devoted to apologetical subjects. Other Anglicans were suspicious of their methods and their motives, at least at first. The C.M.S., though it later acknowledged the value of O.M.C. work among educated men,[8] felt compelled in 1883 to issue a series of rival tracts to guard Indian Christian congregations from "un-Anglican statements" put forth by the new brotherhood.[9] And in 1902 J. N. Farquhar, then newly appointed to the staff of the Indian Y.M.C.A., castigated the *Epiphany* for its views, which he, as a Scottish Independent, felt to be infected by "narrow sectarianism and poisonous priestism".[1]

It is not easy to characterize the *Epiphany* briefly. Certain facts, however, emerge from an examination of numbers published around, and shortly after, the turn of the century. Its tone was often polemical.[2] Its attitude to Hinduism was almost as uncompromising as Duff's had been. A correspondent asking "Why has God created so many different religions?" was told: "He has not. The different religions have been created by men as a result of their own sin."[3] And another correspondent was told that Hinduism and Christianity differ, in that they have "a different conception of God, a different conception of sin, and a different conception of salvation".[4]

But there were occasional glimpses of a more sympathetic attitude. Thus we read: "It is necessary sometimes to point out the false ideas contained in other religions, but we think it is unwise to do so without also pointing out the truths to which they bear witness."[5] But no attempt seems to have been made to define the nature of these "truths", nor to say exactly how Hinduism "bears witness" to their occurrence. And in any case little prominence was given to views of this kind. An attempt was made, in 1907 and 1908, to

[6] Among his subjects were "Is God Partial?" and "God's Education of the Human Race". Reported in the *Epiphany*, 23.1.1890 and 30.1.1890.
[7] Richter, *Indische Missionsgeschichte*, p. 445.
[8] Stock, *History of the Church Missionary Society* III, p. 130.
[9] *Ibid.*, p. 491.
[1] Cf. below, p. 185.
[2] The *Epiphany*, 6.2.1890, p. 21 (*contra* the Brāhma Samāj) and 25.6.1910, p. 101 (idolatry).
[3] *Ibid.*, 11.6.1910, p. 96.
[4] *Ibid.*, 3.9.1910, p. 144.
[5] *Ibid.*, 13.8.1910, p. 132.

discuss the relationship of Christianity and Hinduism in a series of articles on "The Upanishads and the Christian Gospel: Some Contrasts and Fulfilments", but the anonymous writer was concerned only with the "contrasts". The "fulfilment" doctrine, in the sense in which it was popularized by Farquhar, was not mentioned.[6]

From the mid-1880's on, the Oxford Mission published a series of Occasional Papers in which various aspects of the Christian message were discussed in relation to the educated Indian thought of the time.[7] Among the writers were some Indian Christians, notably Krishna Mohun Banerjea and Nehemiah Goreh; most, however, were European members of the Brotherhood.

S. W. O'Neill,[8] writing on *Brahmoism: is it for or against Christianity?* is monitory in tone, warning his readers against "dilettantism in the prosecution of truth".[9] Christianity he equates solely with Catholicism, "and not with the opinions of any sect of separatists".[1] His thesis is that a strict attitude to truth must lead the seeker to the Church; but at the same time he allows that the Brahmos have some "light", and expresses the hope that they will not ignore it, and be drawn deeper into the error of theism.[2]

A paper on *The Catechetical School of Alexandria: its Lessons to the Missionary Clergy of India,* by C. E. Kennet, is, as its name suggests, directed less to the educated Indian than to the European missionary. Again the tone is partly polemical. Christian practice in Alexandria, writes Kennet, was to try and recover from non-Christian syncretism everything that was recoverable; not indiscriminately to condemn "the whole assemblage of heathen opinions and practices".[3] The standard of what is recoverable can only be "Divine Truth as known in the Church".[4] This attitude he recommends in all situations where there is danger of syncretism. Kennet goes on to appeal for sympathetic and informed criticism, and speaks with approval

---

[6] The attitude underlying this series of articles, in book form, was later severely criticized by Farquhar in a review in *YMI* XIX: 8 (August 1908), p. 143 f.

[7] A series of *Occasional Papers* was also published by the CMD: 34 appeared between 1879 and 1919. Their object was however informative, rather than controversial, and they were addressed to the Anglican, not the Hindu, public.

[8] The first SSJE missionary in Calcutta. See e.g. Speer, *Studies of Missionary Leadership* (1914), pp. 155 ff., Woodgate, *Father Benson,* pp. 127 ff.

[9] O'Neill, *Brahmoism*, p. vi.

[1] *Ibid.*, p. 1.

[2] *Ibid.*, p. 10.

[3] Kennet, *The Catechetical School*, p. 7.

[4] *Ibid.*

of the work of F. D. Maurice. But then he proceeds to attack what he judges to be the unwarranted liberties taken by Max Müller, T. E. Slater and others, in their treatment of the Christian Gospel in this kind of situation. Müller, he notes, admired the method of the Alexandrian Fathers, but was "destitute of the safeguard that protected them in pursuing it";[5] and Slater's views on the Divine Personality of Christ (in the book *God Revealed,* which we discuss below) he dismisses as "miserably false and misleading".[6]

A more conciliatory tone is heard in the papers by Banerjea and Goreh. Nehemiah Goreh,[7] whom Bishop Neill has called "one of the most scholarly and wise princes of the Indian Church",[8] published two pamphlets in the Oxford series on *Theism and Christianity*—a leading topic of discussion and debate in the years toward the end of the century. His attitude is sympathetic, but ultimately uncompromising.[9] He insists that theism is to be measured by Christianity, and not *vice versa,* though he allows that there is a measure of *praeparatio* in the higher forms of Hinduism. The good of Hinduism he believed to be capable of discovery only by the light of Christianity.[1] The most extensive of his many books was entitled *Hindu Philosophical System: A Rational Refutation* (1860), and shows to what extent he had broken with his Hindu past on conversion. In later years he modified his views somewhat, and was less uncompromising in his attacks on Hinduism. When his *Hindu Philosophical System* was reprinted, its name was changed to the less provocative *A Mirror of the Hindu Philosophical Systems.*[2] The semi-conciliatory tone of *Theism and Christianity* is typical of this development, which Nicol Macnicol regards as being entirely in line with the trends of the period.[3] Nehemiah Goreh was a Hindu intellectual before his conversion, and his approach to the problems of religious encounter was an intellectual approach. In him has been discerned "the imperfect mingling of a philosophic Indian per-

---

[5] *Ibid.,* p. 8.

[6] *Ibid.*

[7] See Gardner, *Life of Father Goreh* (1900); a shorter account will be found in Speer, *Studies of Missionary Leadership* (1914), pp. 135–177.

[8] Speer writes: "Nehemiah Goreh clearly discerned the uniqueness and the absoluteness of Christianity, and he neither sought nor offered any compromises", *op. cit.,* p. 168 f.

[9] Neill, *Builders of the Indian Church,* p. 128.

[1] Goreh, *Theism and Christianity* I, p. iv f. Speer, *op. cit.,* p. 161.

[2] Speer, *op. cit.,* p. 167. Cf. Macnicol, *India in the Dark Wood* (1930), p. 117.

[3] Macnicol, *loc. cit.*

sonality with the sacerdotal and sacramental type of the Christian spirit".[4] He lived in tension; his attitude to Hinduism was at best tentatively expressed, and seems to have exercised little or no influence on the subsequent course of missionary thought.

K. M. Banerjea, a Kulin Brahmin who had been one of Duff's converts[5] and who was a skilled Sanskritist, wrote on *The Relation between Christianity and Hinduism*. Banerjea goes back to the Vedas, and finds there points of contact with the Christian faith. The most important of these is discernable in the respective doctrines of sacrifice: "... the fundamental Christian doctrine in relation to the salvation of the world finds a remarkable counterpart in the Vedic principles of primitive Hinduism in relation to the destruction of sin, and the redemption of the sinner by the efficacy of Sacrifice".[6] The Vedic *Prajāpati,* the Lord of Creation, he sees as a *typos* of Christ,[7] while the Vedas "foreshadow the Epiphany of Christ".[8] And he sums up by saying that there are germs of Christian mysteries in the "heathen" Vedas,[9] and that Christianity is "a Vedic doctrine in its legitimately developed form".[1] In his peroration he draws attention to the recent publication of the Vedas "under the auspicious patronage of England's Crown" (the reference is of course to Max Müller's edition), and points the moral that, since these Scriptures have been made generally available, it is incumbent upon educated Indians to read them—as far as possible in the light of Jesus Christ.[2]

We shall not now enter into further detailed criticism of these publications, or of the methods used by the Oxford Mission. That would lead us far beyond the bounds of this introductory survey. Their methods we have seen to have had two foci: on the one hand the Oxford Mission tried to influence the educated non-Christian by bringing him into contact with the life of a Christian community; and on the other by entering into a discussion which it was hoped would develop into a creative dialogue, and by the publication of

---

[4] Speer, *op. cit.,* p. 174.

[5] Smith, *The Life of Alexander Duff* (1899), p. 86 f. Paton, *Alexander Duff* (1923), p. 84.

[6] Banerjea, *The Relation between Christianity and Hinduism,* p. 1.

[7] *Ibid.,* pp. 2, 16.

[8] *Ibid.,* p. 19.

[9] *Ibid.,* p. 20.

[1] *Ibid.,* p. 21.

[2] *Ibid.*

apologetic literature generally sympathetic in character. Neither
method bore notable fruit in conversions. A C.M.S. missionary
pointed out in 1889 that the Oxford men had succeeded in "influencing, attracting and propitiating", but not converting.[3] This
was to invite criticism. A. H. Whitehead, who relinquished the
leadership of the Oxford Mission in 1889 on his consecration to
the See of Madras, criticised the mission severely in later years for
its failure to evangelize. In Whitehead's judgment the O.M.C. had
erred profoundly in concentrating on the "philosophic aspects of
Christianity" and the method of debate and controversy, instead
of the Gospel of salvation from sin and the method of pure proclamation.[4] And Bishop Mylne has suggested that missions of this general
type could easily become, irrespective of the methods they followed,
"a hotbed of well-meaning unreality".[5]

In the most significant of the Oxford Mission's publications,
the essays by the first-generation converts Goreh and Banerjea,
we have seen that steps could be taken by academically trained
Indians toward a creative and appreciative Christian attitude to the
Hindu heritage. This might have been an approach of very great
value indeed for the future of the Indian Church—the laying of the
foundations of a genuine Indian theology of encounter. But this
was not to be. Later generations, in which consolidation might have
taken place, produced fewer and fewer such converts: Brahmins
trained in Sanskrit and philosophical Hinduism generally. Indian
Christianity came more and more to become a lower-caste religion,
and the initiative—theological and literary—was left in the hands
of missionaries, of whom T. E. Slater of the London Missionary
Society was the first.

T. E. Slater: The Principle of Fulfilment

The policy of English-language higher education in the great
cities of India—Calcutta, Madras, Bombay—had, as we have already

---

[3] Stock, *History of the Church Missionary Society* III, p. 350.
[4] Whitehead, "The New Movement in India and the Old Gospel", in *The
East and the West* IX: 33 (Jan. 1911), p. 2. It must be remembered, however, that
this criticism came *after* he had left Calcutta and after his reorientation from a
"determined Tractarian" to an equally determined ecumenical leader. Sundkler,
Church of South India (1954), p. 51.
[5] Mylne, *Missions to Hindus*, p. 108.

seen, been so far successful by the 1870's as to create a new class of Indian: the student (and ex-student) classes. Missionary and government institutions between them were educating thousands of young men annually—men whom, in many cases, English-language education had made critical of their Indian religious and cultural heritage. These young men were taught to read, write and think in English; their new terms of reference were Western; in many cases they had turned their backs on Hinduism, as a religion if not as a social system. They maintained caste for the most part, but did little more. Many were active reformers. Many had absorbed at least something of Christian principles, depending on the kind of college they had attended. But from the point of view of the missions, this was not a very satisfactory situation, even allowing for the views expressed by William Miller as to the true aims of Christian education in India. Hardly any impression had been made on the educated Hindu community as a whole. High-caste converts, always a rarity, were becoming rarer. And there was a growing band of ex-students outside the confines of the colleges—men who had come into contact with Christianity, had been in some measure influenced, but had been unwilling to take the decisive step of receiving Christian baptism. William Miller's policy of diffusion tended to aggravate the situation. Once it became clear that some colleges were no longer pressing for conversions, the question arose: Who, then, must assume responsibility for "direct" evangelistic work among the educated classes?

One solution advocated in some quarters was to appoint some well-equipped missionary to work independently among the educated classes. By the turn of the century there were a number of men set apart by the various Evangelical missions for this kind of work.[6] The pioneer in this field was Thomas Ebenezer Slater of the London Missionary Society, and it is to a brief consideration of his work that we must now turn.

In 1874 the Madras Missionary Conference sent an open letter to the Directors and Committees of all the missionary societies represented in the city. The subject was the evangelization of the educated classes of the city. The Conference pointed out that the Missionary Institutions of Madras had for many years exercised "no

---

[6] Some are mentioned by Richter, *Indische Missionsgeschichte*, p. 444 f.

inconsiderable influence" on the education of the young men of
the area, and had even brought some to renounce Hinduism and
become Christians. The letter went on:

Those who do thus decide for Christ are insignificantly few, however, compared with the vast numbers who go forth, not indeed unimpressed, but
undecided. They have become acquainted with the facts of Revelation, and
have had their minds enlightened and their moral nature quickened in
no inconsiderable degree . . . Many are in this hopeful state when they pass
from under our daily instruction; but they have no home influences of a
Christian kind, no stated assemblies for receiving light and edification, and
the temptation to forget the truths they have learned and to run into the
ways of worldliness is and will be, we fear, too strong, unless we are enabled
in some way to follow them, on an extensive scale, with the word of truth.[7]

Similarly with former pupils of government and other secular colleges, who had in many cases lost touch with their traditional beliefs
without ever being provided with an adequate replacement. The
object of the Conference in writing was to ask the societies if it
might not be possible to set apart some missionary for evangelistic
work among these young men.

There seems no hope of anything systematic being done until someone give
himself to the work entirely . . . Much of the work would plainly lie in the
way of lectures and addresses on religious subjects—in the discussion to
which these would probably give rise—in the private personal intercourse
that would slowly follow . . . But we do not pretend to be able to lay down
the course that the development of the work would follow . . . All that we
can say at present is that, beyond a doubt, the field exists, and is a very
hopeful one.[8]

T. E. Slater (1840–1912) had come to Madras in 1871 from Calcutta, where he had spent five years on the staff of the London
Missionary Society's Bhowanipur Institution. He had been engaged
on educational work, therefore, for eight years when the project
of an idependent evangelist was first mooted in Madras. He himself
wrote that during these years his own convictions and sympathies
had been gradually inclining toward the type of work indicated
in the letter, and so he offered his services.[9] The directors of the

---

[7] Slater, *Report of Work among the Educated Classes, Madras, in connection
with the London Missionary Society* (1876), p. 1 f.
[8] *Ibid.*
[9] *Ibid.*, p. 2.

L.M.S. agreed that he be given a year in which to try the suggested method of working, after which his case would be reconsidered.

Having no precedent on which to model his work, and being free to dispose of his time as he thought fit, he began along three lines: "visiting Native gentlemen in their homes, and seeing them in my own; holding meetings and classes among the student class and non-Christian teachers of our schools; and delivering public addresses".[1] Writing to the Foreign Secretary of the L.M.S. in October 1875, Slater was able to report:

I have been very much encouraged in this work—much more than I had anticipated. All here who know anything about it are now satisfied that there is a very important and hopeful field in this direction. One or two who were at first doubtful have told me that they were mistaken ...[2]

Slater's first thought was for the religious needs of the group to which he had been sent to minister. Experience had shown him that any attempt to present the Gospel to educated Hindus in the same terms as those normally used in the West would very likely prove abortive. He found in his first discussion group that the twenty-five young Brahmins who attended had benefited from Western education to the extent of being able to quote Mill, Bradlaugh, Bain, Spencer and Huxley, but that their ideas on the nature of Christianity were often distorted.[3] It was in order to remedy such deficiencies that Slater devoted his first course of public lectures to an outline of Christian doctrine.

These lectures, published in 1876 under the title *God Revealed,* dealt with such topics as the idea of revelation, the idea of God, redemption, and the life, character and teaching of Jesus. They were well received by the majority of readers and reviewers. A minority, however, disturbed by what they felt to be heterodox elements in them, complained to the L.M.S. that Slater had ceased to preach the Gospel. But before we take note of this controversy, we must say a few words about the lectures as such.

In the preface to *God Revealed,* Slater indicates what was his guiding principle:

Not to present Christianity as an antagonistic Religion among other Religions of the world, not as a voice sounding the knell of doom to non-

---

[1] *Ibid.,* p. 2 f.
[2] T. E. Slater to J. Mullens, 15.11.1875 (LMS Archives).
[3] Slater, *Report 1876,* p. ii.

7 – 644149 *Eric Sharpe*

Christian nations, but, in the firm persuasion that all are *by nature* Christians, to hold it up as that in which Hindus would find realised and satisfied the noblest and earliest ideas of their sages, and the truest sentiments and yearnings of their hearts.[4]

Further, he declined absolutely to attack Hinduism in any way, saying that

If there happen to be error, falsehood, evil, in what a man calls his religion, it may be owing to ignorance and want of light; and such a man is an object for pity and for help, and not for reproach and condemnation.[5]

This he crystallized into a significant principle:

The aspect in which I would set Christianity before you is not an aspect of antagonism but of consummation . . .[6]

It will be clear that more was involved in this statement than merely the application of a method of missionary work. Slater had, it is true, been appointed to carry out a particular kind of work among a particular class of people; but in so doing he was prepared to attempt what was at that time a novel presentation of the Christian Gospel, at least as far as Evangelical missions were concerned. This, the principle of consummation or the *principle of fulfilment,* we have seen described in the work of Max Müller and Monier Monier-Williams;[7] now we encounter it for the first (but by no means the last) time in the work of an active Evangelical missionary in India. William Miller had looked upon Hinduism as being in a position to make a definite contribution to the religious life of the world, without claiming absolute supremacy for historical Christianity: Slater, like Monier-Williams, makes of *Christianity* the fulfilment of Hinduism, and thereby points the way for the thought of a whole generation of missionary scholars.

We have said that *God Revealed* was well received by the majority. But not by everybody: there were those who found Slater's unwillingness to take up the cudgels against Hinduism distasteful; and certainly it was unusual. The generally conciliatory tone adopted by Slater in his lectures was also felt by some to show up the central Christian doctrines, and particularly the doctrine of the Atonement,

---

[4] Slater, *God Revealed* (1876), p. iii.
[5] *Ibid.*, p. 2.
[6] *Ibid.*, p. 8.
[7] Above, pp. 43 ff.

in a false light. Complaints were made (anonymously, it seems) to the Directors of the L.M.S.,[8] and Slater was called upon to give assurances that he still subscribed to the main doctrines of Evangelical Christianity, as expressed in a doctrinal statement he had made a decade earlier.[9]

In his reply, which runs to twenty-four closely-written pages, and which provides a closely-reasoned statement of his doctrinal position, Slater pointed out that though his doctrinal views had certainly developed during his time in India, they had not changed in essence. But he was not attempting to excuse himself. "I for one", he wrote, "find it impossible to remain just where I was ten years ago. Nor could I wish to do so."[1]

He supposed that the basic reason for the charges brought against him was the fact that he had tried to "set forth the *Divinity of Christ* in such a way as might best commend itself to thoughtful Hindus".[2] The attempt had led him to reject the representation of Christianity as a body of doctrine: that, he felt, had done quite enough harm already; instead he concentrated on "Divine facts and Divine life in Christianity".[3] Attempts of this nature he knew to be unusual among missionaries; there were inevitably those who looked askance upon him and his work "because I do not utter the truth exactly after their shibboleth";[4] but most recognized the centrality of the doctrines contained in the book, and approved of the effort at apologetical restatement that Slater had made.[5]

More serious was the claim that his sympathetic attitude to Hinduism was liable to do harm to the Christian Gospel. Slater in reply pointed out that the force of such arguments as these depends on the source from which they come, and observed, somewhat surprisingly, that no such complaint had been heard from Hindus.[6]

---

[8] There are in the LMS Archives a number of anonymous letters, dated March–April 1876, from Madras, and signed "True Friend of Missions". The writer makes a variety of accusations against LMS missionaries: Slater he accuses of being a "Unitarian". This may conceivably have been the source of the complaint against Slater, to which the Directors called on him to reply.

[9] Mullens to Slater, 20.10.1876 (LMS Archives).

[1] Slater to Mullens, 14.12.1876 (LMS Archives).

[2] *Ibid.*

[3] *Ibid.*

[4] *Ibid.*

[5] Slater himself quotes a number of appreciative reviews and comments in the course of his defence.

[6] "But because I have tried to do this not in a controversial and authoritative manner, but as far as I could, in a conciliatory and persuasive manner; because

Slater, like John Muir before him,[7] had felt himself compelled
to adopt a conciliatory attitude in his dealing with educated Indians;
this involved making a serious attempt to adapt his message to their
needs, or at least express it in terms they could understand and
(possibly) approve. And whenever possible, he had tried to place a
positive and constructive, rather than negative and destructive, interpretation on the ancestral faith of the Hindu. The developing
"science of religion" provided him with one of the means by which
this might be done, by suggesting that there was an evolutionary link
between even the "higher" religions, a relation of the imperfect
(Hinduism) to the complete (Christianity), fulfilling the one in the
other.

Further, the whole of the development of the period was, as
we shall discuss in detail in due course, in the direction of the
liberalizing, renewing and invigorating of Hinduism—not indeed the
traditional Hinduism Duff had known, but a new Hinduism owing
some of its *ethos* and more of its methods to the West. Neo-
Hinduism was by the late 1870's beginning to take hold of the mind
of educated India, and the old missionary attitude of disparagement
was becoming daily more dangerous to the Christian cause. This
is one of the most important factors to be borne in mind when
evaluating missionary attitudes to Hinduism—that the growth of
Neo-Hinduism and Indian nationalism, often so closely interwoven
as to be virtually indistinguishable from each other, created a climate
of opinion in which the old attitude was worthless as an apologetic
weapon. But it must also be remembered that Neo-Hinduism and
Indian nationalism were at first mainly intellectual movements; that
their most notable strongholds were the centres of higher education;
and that their most passionate supporters were the student and ex-
student classes. Alongside this intellectual movement there was, and
continued to be, the traditional "lower" Hinduism of the villages,
where, for instance, the sophistication of the Brāhma Samāj and the
political manoeuvring of the National Congress were irrelevant. Here
the traditional missionary attitude found fuel; here it was adequate,

---

I have tried to look at things from another's standpoint, and do not delight in
denying all worth to other faiths, it is supposed by some that Christianity is
compromised. But if it appear compromised to some Christians, it is not so
regarded by non-Christians, and yet succeeds in being attentively considered by
them."

[7] Above, p. 36 f.

and even necessary. But it is perhaps not surprising that it led to a cleavage of opinion among missionaries.[8]

In the 1870's few missionaries had come to recognize the signs of the times, or to sense the danger from Neo-Hinduism. This is not meant as a criticism; the problem did not become acute until thirty years later. But Slater, as his annual reports show, was in close touch with developments, and knew what they were liable to mean from the point of view of active missionary work among the educated classes. We quote once more:

If you adopt a denunciatory and authoritative tone, they [educated Hindus] simply will not listen to you, and would consign any book written in such a style immediately to the flames.[9]

Slater further points out in his letter of explanation that he had been gratified to find that his views met with the approval of Professor Monier-Williams. The two men had met at about this time and discussed the question of attitudes to Hinduism.

I was much gratified [wrote Slater] to find he [Monier-Williams] entirely sympathised with the mental attitude I have sought to take up in relation to the Hindus. He remarked that there was scarcely an idea and truth in Christianity that did not exist in some form in Hinduism, and he thought missionaries as a rule had not taken the pains to make themselves acquainted with such things, and in consequence had greatly retarded the spread of Christianity in the country.[1]

The letter as a whole was accepted by the L.M.S. as an adequate assurance of Slater's theological *bona fides*.[2]

In 1882 Slater left Madras for Bangalore, where he remained, working among educated Hindus, until his retirement in 1904. In the same year, 1882, he published his book *The Philosophy of Missions*, followed by *Keshub Chunder Sen and the Brahmo Samaj* (1884), *Studies in the Upanishads* (1897), *The Higher Hinduism in Relation to Christianity* (1901) and *Missions and Sociology* (1908).

The Philosophy of Missions was written for the British public. Its object was to justify the missionary enterprise in the face of persistent criticism at home. The book deals in turn with the nature

---

[8] Below, pp. 309 ff.
[9] Slater to Mullens, 14.12.1876 (LMS Archives).
[1] Mullens to Slater, 16.2.1877 (LMS Archives).
[2] Slater to Mullens, 14.12.1876.

and extent of modern missions, the decline of interest in missions, and what we might perhaps call the "effect" of missions. The final chapter bears the title "Missions and Religion: A Plea for the World", and is of considerable value for our study, since it takes the form of an attempt to sketch the relationship between Christianity and the non-Christian religions as a whole—a theme which Slater had touched upon in *God Revealed,* and which he was to develop in *The Higher Hinduism.*

We cannot in this context go into Slater's arguments in any great detail, but some of his conclusions may be mentioned briefly. In the first place, Slater's position is clearly evolutionist: Christianity he regards as the absolute religion, since it exists on a higher evolutionary level than any other of the living faiths of the world, which are "found wanting in those elements that the nature of man and the constitution of society require".[3] But Christianity and these "incomplete" faiths are nevertheless directly related, in a relationship of imperfection and consummation, or fulfilment. This leads to a further significant statement:

All other religions wait for their fulfilment in Christianity.[4]

The non-Christian religions have served their purpose, and have had their place in the scheme of divine providence. They have endured in measure as they have contained elements of truth, according to their fitness for the surroundings in which they have existed, and according as they have borne witness to the coming "fulfiller".[5] The coming of Christ perfected (at least potentially) these lower systems, gathered up their broken lights and completed their partial revelation. And Slater quotes 1 Cor. 13.10: "When that which is *perfect* is come, that which is *in part* shall be done away."[6]

Thus "every religion is full of presentiments of the truth";[7] "paganism waits, by a law of its own nature, for its fulfilment in Christianity".[8] And lastly:

Throughout these ancient systems there is ample evidence of that in man which *demands* a revelation, but not that in man which *gives* the revela-

---

[3] Slater, *The Philosophy of Missions* (1882), p. 111.
[4] *Ibid.,* p. 112.
[5] *Ibid.,* p. 113 f.
[6] *Ibid.,* p. 115.
[7] *Ibid.,* p. 119.
[8] *Ibid.,* p. 124 f.

tion. As religious systems they wrought no deliverance. They remain unfulfilled.[9]

Before leaving Slater, brief mention must be made of his most extensive work, *The Higher Hinduism in Relation to Christianity*.

This book was originally submitted in 1899 to the Saxon Missionary Conference at Leipzig as a prize essay,[1] and brings together in one volume the results of Slater's thinking on the subject of evangelism and missions, with particular reference to the conflict between Christianity and Hinduism for the allegiance of the educated classes of India. It carries forward into a connected system the lines suggested in *The Philosophy of Missions, Studies in the Upanishads,* and numerous occasional essays and addresses, but although it covers a wider field, bring out no new principle of interpretation. It will therefore serve to note that the theme of the book—as indeed of the whole of Slater's work from 1875 to his retirement—was the affirmation of the belief that

Christ will yet satisfy the spiritual hunger and thirst to which the great religious ideas of the East only give expression; and India ... will surely find the enlightening revelation of the Gospel to be in *complete accord* with the best sentiments of her best minds, the true realization of the visions of her seers, the real fulfilment of the longings of her sages.[2]

Such a conviction implies that the mission must have an attitude of real, and not merely assumed, sympathy toward Hinduism; and that he must acquire a detailed knowledge of the structure and beliefs of, in this case, the "higher" Hinduism, though he must also become acquainted with "its manifestations in the daily life of the masses".[3] The three pillars on which the missionary's attitude must rest are justice, courtesy and love: this is the minimum requirement, to which must ideally be added knowledge if there would be understanding.

---

[9] *Ibid.,* p. 125 f. The source of this statement is not far to seek. Cf. Maurice, *On the Religions of the World* (3rd ed. 1852), p. 55: "I ask nothing more than the Hindu system and the Hindu life as evidence that there is that in man which demands a revelation—that there is *not* that in him which makes the revelation."

[1] Richter, *Indische Missionsgeschichte,* p. 415; the prize was won by Wilhelm Dilger of the Basel Mission for his essay *Die Erlösung des Menschen nach Hinduismus und Christentum* (1902). For Farquhar's criticism of Dilger's book, see below, p. 251 f.

[2] Slater, *The Higher Hinduism* (2nd ed. 1903), p. 291.

[3] *Ibid.,* p. 1.

In Slater we find an early point of contact between the attitudes developing out of the "science of religion" and the Evangelical missionary enterprise in India. Yet his name is all but forgotten today. There are probably two reasons for this. The first is that, like all pioneers, he was ahead of his time: not far ahead, for missionary opinion was being forced into a period of rapid change, but far enough ahead to find it hard to communicate fully with his missionary generation. As a pioneer of independent work among students and the educated classes generally, he had come into direct contact with renascent Hinduism before its force had been appreciated by the majority of Evangelical missionaries in India; as a scholar he was more open to the findings of the new science of religion than any but a few of his contemporaries. But the second reason is equally cogent. Slater, unlike Farquhar in the next generation, did not have the resources of the American Y.M.C.A. behind him. His immediate chief was not John R. Mott. And though he did travel to the Chicago World's Parliament of Religions in 1893,[4] this was not the same thing as living and working in the atmosphere of the world student movement in the hectic pre-war years. It might be pointed out, with this in mind, that Slater was very much on his own, and that he was in no sense the leader or even the representative of a "school"; the question is, though, whether Slater's experimental methods did not effectively preclude him from even attempting to form a school. He was a layer of foundations: and it is commonly the fate of foundations to remain hidden.

Yet although Slater's name may be practically forgotten, there is some reason to believe that he did exercise some influence on Farquhar in later years. It is impossible to state with any degree of certainty just how extensive was the use which Farquhar was able to make of Slater's studies; but that he did so use them is obvious.[5] It would also be inaccurate to claim that Slater was working during these years in *complete* isolation. The real extent of his influence on his contemporaries is uncertain, the data being for the most

---

[4] He delivered two papers there: "Concessions to Native Ideas, having Reference to Hinduism" [Barrows (ed.), *World's Parliament of Religions* I (1893), pp. 456 ff.], was designed to demonstrate some of the "links by which a Christian advocate may connect the religion of the Incarnation with the higher phases of religious life and thought in India". His second paper, "The Present Religious Outlook in India" [*ibid.* II, pp. 1172 ff.], is a characterization of the religious state of India in the 1890's.

[5] Cf. below, p. 208 n. 8.

part missing, but there was at least one other missionary writer in the Madras area, working under similar conditions, whose approach was esentially similar to that of Slater.

Frederick William Kellett (1862–1904), a missionary of the Wesleyan Methodist Missionary Society, then on the staff of the Madras Christian College,[6] and later an independent student evangelist in Triplicane, published in 1896 a 23-page pamphlet entitled *Christ the Fulfilment of Hinduism*,[7] in which the influence of Slater (and probably of Miller also) is clearly to be seen.

Kellett's paper is of course not to be compared with Slater's *Higher Hinduism*: it is in fact no more than a tentative sketch, a suggested line of thought, the implications of which are left to others to work out. Kellett's basis is however that of the evolutionist school generally: that history provides the record of God's progressive revelation of himself to man, that all the historical religions have their place in this pattern, and therefore that no historical religion is without its "fragment of truth".[8] In the case of Hinduism these fragments have not found their "completeness"; but in Christ they find that missing completeness—in other words, they are "fulfilled". Kellett felt that it would not be difficult, given time, to show

how Christ as the Teacher has fulfilled Hinduism, how He has carried forward the teaching of this sect and that sect in the doctrines of each into one harmonious whole; how the scattered lights on man's future life He has gathered within the light His Resurrection shed upon it; how His practical teaching on conduct corrects, sums up and develops all that Indian sages had written or taught on the duties of life; how there is no department of sacred lore but He has illuminated it and made it rich and full.[9]

It is interesting to note that Kellett was not content to limit his study to the ethical problems summed up in the *teachings* of Jesus. The Person and Work of Christ he regarded as the real heart of the matter, and even here he claimed that Hinduism foreshadowed both or, in Paul's phrase, might prove a "schoolmaster" to lead the Hindu to Christ. For instance, Vedic ideas on sacrifice are seen to have a meaning in the light of the sacrifice of Christ (an idea touched upon

---

[6] For a brief account of Kellett's missionary career, see Findlay and Holdsworth, *History of the Wesleyan Methodist Missionary Society* V (1924), pp. 236 ff.

[7] No. 10 in a CLS series of *Papers for Thoughtful Hindus*.

[8] *Christ the Fulfiller of Hinduism*, p. 4.

[9] *Ibid.*, p. 5.

by K. M. Banerjea); the Vedantic theory of knowledge is a *typos* of the knowledge of God revealed in the Son and in the work of the Holy Spirit; the questions of the omni-penetration of God and the reality of sin—so hardly reconciled in Hinduism—find their answer in Christ.[1] An unusual piece of typology is that Kellett suggests that Yama, the Vedic god of the dead, is

a type of Jesus, who having overcome Death brought life and immortality to light . . .[2]

And he concludes:

Such, as it seems to me, are some of the elements in the *praeparatio evangelica* of India. I do not pretend that all these taken together—and still less any one singly—*demonstrate* the truth of Christian doctrine. But anyone who considers them carefully and who has regarded the Hinduism to which I have referred as deserving respect and support will find less difficulty in accepting Christianity.[3]

It would be unwise to place too much emphasis on Kellett's essay. It is short, and its points are not fully developed. Yet it is enough to place Kellett alongside Robson,[4] Miller and Slater—pioneers of a more sympathetic approach to Hinduism. That Farquhar's views were in basic agreement with Kellett's will be seen in due course,[5] while the continued acceptability of Kellett's essay is shown by the fact that it was still in print in 1923.

Both Slater and Kellett had turned to what was in some ways a new form of apologetic in the context of missions to the educated classes. A third missionary whose period of service overlapped those of Slater and Kellett, and whose influence on students was profound, was the Dane Lars Peter Larsen (1862–1940),[6] who arrived in Madras in 1889, and whose student work began under Y.M.C.A. auspices in 1899. In July 1910 Larsen became Principal of the newly-founded Union Theological College in Bangalore. Though he thus belongs to the same period as Farquhar, it is appropriate to introduce him here, since it was in the Madras area that his early work was done.

---

[1] *Ibid.*, pp. 7 f., 11.
[2] *Ibid.*, p. 22.
[3] *Ibid.*
[4] Cf. above, p. 54 f.
[5] Below, p. 201.
[6] The standard biography is Bindslev, *L. P. Larsen: hans Liv og Gerning* (1945). An English edition has recently been published in India.

The question of Larsen's attitude to Hinduism is one which is deserving of fuller treatment than can be given it in this study. As a Lutheran—albeit a Lutheran whose orthodoxy was called in question by some[7]—his background was in many ways different from that of Slater and Kellett, Miller and Robson. That he was never an evolutionist seems clear; thus at no time did he claim that the whole of Hinduism could be "fulfilled" in Christianity. Yet his personal attitude was one of sympathy, and he held that there were many assonances between Hindu and Christian beliefs.[8] He was a scholar and a linguist, and a close student of Hinduism, and particularly of Hindu spirituality. His contribution was however made, as we have indicated, after the turn of the century, his most important book in this field, *Hindu-Aandsliv og Kristendommen* (Hindu Spirituality and Christianity), appearing in 1907. We shall therefore return to Larsen in a later context, pausing only to emphasize once more that his formative years as a missionary were spent in the Madras of Miller, Slater and Kellett.

Summing up, the period from c. 1875 to the end of the century was one of expansion and consolidation in Christian higher education in India, but it was also a period of trial and experiment. On the practical level, the strategy of Duff and his immediate successors gave way to a greater variety of approach, in which evangelism was more and more divorced from the classroom. Theologically, the initiative taken by Max Müller and Monier-Williams in England began to make some impression on the better-informed among the educational missionaries, particularly among those who had come into contact with the early stages of the Hindu revival. Factual knowledge of the Hindu scriptures was increasing, thanks largely to the publications in the *Sacred Books of the East* series. And at the same time it was becoming more usual to look upon Christianity itself as one of the religions of the world, related to Hinduism within the evolutionary pattern. Less emphasis was being placed

---

[7] Bindslev, *op. cit.*, p. 72, has this statement by Larsen: "Jag er ganske paa det rene med, at jeg i mange Stykker tænker meget forskelligt fra gode luthersk-troende Mennesker derhjemme om Kristendom og Kristenliv. — I mine Tanker om Daab og Nadver er jag saa bestemt hverken luthersk eller dansk-luthersk." This statement dates from 1897. Cf. however *ibid.*, pp. 95 ff.

[8] See e.g. Larsen's review of Dilger's *Die Erlösung des Menschen*, in *MCCM* II: 12 (June 1903), p. 639.

by missionaries of this type on the *sui generis* character of the Christian revelation, and more on its superiority within the category "religion".

But it must be stressed that there were still comparatively few active missionaries prepared to abandon or modify the traditional Evangelical methods and assumptions, however cautiously. The 1875–1900 period was preparatory: foundations were being laid on which the next generation were to build. The nature of this edifice was conditioned, as Slater's had been, by both practical and theoretical factors, and it is to an examination of these we must now turn, exemplified in the early missionary career of J. N. Farquhar.

CHAPTER 4

J. N. Farquhar's Religious and Intellectual Background, 1861–1890

IN OUR study so far we have described something of the climate of opinion on the frontier between nineteenth-century Evangelical missions and Hinduism. We have examined the attitudes of representative Evangelical missionaries, and seen how these were affected by the practical demands made on them in the Indian situation, and by developments in Western theological, philosophical and scientific thought; we have also looked at the Christian higher educational enterprise in India in its beginnings and later development, with a view to tracing its root ideas and peculiar problems. We have seen the way in which an originally evangelistic undertaking was forced by the pressure of circumstances into new paths, and some of the attempts which were made to meet basic missionary requirements in a period of growing secularization in the colleges, and growing opposition on the part of renascent Hinduism.

This was the situation in which J. N. Farquhar was placed on his arrival in India at the beginning of 1891. But before we proceed to consider his first encounter with "educated India" it is necessary that we should have some picture of his background and missionary qualifications. It would however be well to state at the outset that a detailed picture of his development is out of the question, due to the scarcity of source materials. We have little documentary evidence covering the first thirty years in Farquhar's life. But we do know a certain amount about his background, and there is some information given in his missionary candidature papers and elsewhere about his religious and intellectual development. The overall picture which emerges is clear, and in some measure distinctive. First, however, some salient facts.

Born in Aberdeen, Scotland, on April 6, 1861, John Nicol Farquhar was brought up a member of the Evangelical Union, a small branch of Scottish Independant Protestantism, having affinities with Congregationalism; after serving his apprenticeship as a draper, he entered Aberdeen Grammar School in 1882, Aberdeen University in 1883, and Christ Church, Oxford, as Exhibitioner in 1885. He took his B.A. in 1889 and was accepted by the London Missionary Society in 1890, sailing for India in December of that year.[1]

It will be clear from this summary that we have to take account of two distinct phases in Farquhar's religious and intellectual development before 1890. Twenty-five of his first twenty-nine years were spent in Aberdeen, and these years were obviously formative; while for four years he studied in the University of Oxford, at a time which coincided with the emergence of nonconformity as an active ingredient in the intellectual and religious life of the University. We shall examine the main features of each of these in turn, after which we pass on to consider some details of Farquhar's missionary candidature.

Aberdeen: The Evangelical Union

Farquhar was, as we have said, a member of the Evangelical Union during his Aberdeen years. On his own evidence, he was trained by his parents in the principles of Evangelical Christianity, and was in due course received into full membership of the Evangelical Union (the date is unknown); but he never became a very active member. This is not to say that he was altogether passive, but the nature of his religious development was such as to keep him, as he himself put it, rather in "the place of the hearer than of the speaker" during his student days.[2]

Nevertheless, there is every reason to believe that the distinctive atmosphere of the Evangelical Union, made up of evangelistic fervour, theological and intellectual seriousness, and a comparative disregard of ecclesiastical controversies, played a notable part in his development, establishing certain habits of mind which were in course of time to find their application in the context of Indian missions.

The distinctiveness of the Evangelical Union cannot however be understood fully without first knowing something of the history of

---

[1] For further details of Farquhar's family background and early life, see Sharpe, *J. N. Farquhar* (1963), pp. 2–5.
[2] L. M. S. Candidature papers: J. N. Farquhar (1890).

that denomination. Such information is not readily accessible today.[3] The Evangelical Union ceased to exist as a separate denomination before the turn of the century, and there is no modern study of its history and principles. For that reason we must first of all discuss the background and origins of the Evangelical Union; only when this has been done shall we be in a position to estimate the nature of its contribution to the religious picture of late nineteenth-century Scotland, and the extent of its influence on a layman such as Farquhar.

There were two great topics of controversy in mid-nineteenth-century Scottish Christianity, one ecclesiastical, the other doctrinal. Both came to a head in May 1843, though independently, in two separate and distinct Churches: the ecclesiastical question was thrashed out in the Established Church; the doctrinal question on this occasion in the United Secession Church.[4] The Disruption of the Church of Scotland over the question of patronage is a subject which does not concern us here. Of more immediate interest is the formation, some few days earlier, of an independent evangelistic society, the Evangelical Union. The main point at issue here was doctrinal, centring on the question of the extent of the Atonement. This was far from being an isolated instance of this kind of doctrinal conflict; rather is it to be seen as the climax of a trend which had been felt for some years throughout the Scottish Churches. The Church of Scotland's classical "case" was that of the Rev. J. Macleod Campbell, who was tried for heresy and deposed in 1831 for preaching the universality of the Atonement—a doctrine which conflicted with the teaching of the Subordinate Standards (the Westminister

---

[3] Most of the available literature dates from the late 19th century, and generally suffers from parochialism. See Ferguson, *A History of the Evangelical Union from its Origin to the Present Time* (1876), *The Worthies of the Evangelical Union* (1883), *Evangelical Union Jubilee Conference Memorial Volume* (1893), and Adamson, *The Life of the Rev. James Morison, D.D.* (1898). There is also an unpublished Ph.D. thesis by C. E. Kirsch, *The Theology of James Morison* (Edinburgh University, 1939), in which the E.U. is given full consideration. See also Selbie, *The Life of Andrew Martin Fairbairn* (1914) and idem, *Congregationalism* (1927), *passim*.

[4] This is not to say that the doctrinal and ecclesiastical developments were altogether independent of each other. There were common factors conditioning both. See e.g. Mathieson, *Church and Reform in Scotland* (1916), *passim*, and Sjölinder, *Presbyterian Reunion in Scotland 1907–1921* (1962), pp. 49 ff. For a graph illustrating the position of the Scottish denominations relative to one another, see Sjölinder, *op. cit.*, p. 379.

Confession and the Shorter Catechism), that the death of Jesus Christ was a propitiation for the sins of the elect only.[5] An almost identical situation obtained in the United Secession Church, which acknowledged the same Subordinate Standards. There the controversy centred on the figure of James Morison, and the ultimate result was, as we have indicated, the founding of the Evangelical Union, whose motto was from the first "salvation without distinction or exception".

James Morison (1816–1893),[6] a minister of the United Secession Church, became convinced of the inadequacy of the "official" doctrine of the Atonement in a semi-missionary situation, amid the atmosphere of revival. This is recorded as having taken place while he was still a theological student.[7] It is also recorded that he had been reading *Lectures on Revivals,* by the American revivalist preacher Charles G. Finney.[8] As early as 1840, when the time came for Morison's ordination, it was suspected that he was unorthodox on the question of the Atonement, and his ordination was almost refused.[9] His ministry in the United Secession Church did not last long: in the following year, 1841, he was tried and expelled from his pulpit, as Macleod Campbell had been.[1] But the temper of opinion in the churches was not altogether unfavourable to his cause; again like Campbell, he was able to continue preaching as an independent.

In 1843 Morison was joined by three other ministers, his father Robert Morison, A. C. Rutherford and John Guthrie, all of whom had been similarly treated by their Presbyteries. A meeting was convened at Clerk's Lane Church, Kilmarnock, on May 16–18, 1843, at which the Evangelical Union was formally constituted.[2]

A further point of doctrine remained in dispute: what was known as the "double reference theory of the Atonement". This was the main weakness of the Evangelical Union at its inception: a doctrine

---

[5] See McNeill, *The History and Character of Calvinism* (1954), pp. 396 ff.

[6] Adamson's life, despite its faults, is still the only biography available.

[7] Adamson, *Life of Morison,* pp. 55 ff.

[8] Ferguson, *History of the Evangelical Union,* p. 7.

[9] Adamson, *op. cit.,* pp. 90 ff. For Morison's definition of the Atonement, see *ibid.,* p. 106 f.: "It is an expedient introduced into the divine moral government, consisting of the obedience unto death of Jesus Christ, which has completely removed all the obstacles standing between man and salvation, except obstacles within him." Cf. Kirsch, *op. cit.,* pp. 145 ff.

[1] For accounts of Morison's trial and defence, see Adamson, *op. cit.,* pp. 124 ff., Ferguson, *op. cit.,* pp. 51 ff.

[2] Ferguson, *op. cit.,* pp. 261 ff., Adamson, *op. cit.,* pp. 238 ff.

which stated that although Christ had in theory died for all men, the Holy Spirit calls only some men to repentance and faith.[3] Morison, who held this view at the time of his trial and dismissal, expressed it as follows: First, that God saw that all men would be "hell-deserving sinners"; secondly, that he resolved to provide an atonement sufficient for all; but thirdly, he also saw that men would not be willing to receive salvation on these terms; therefore, fourthly, "... he resolved to bestow on some, such influences of his spirit as would infallibly *dispose* them to accept what all others are able and welcome to take".[4] This was, as Morison himself soon realized, to postulate a contradiction within the Godhead, and he was later able to assert the universal work of the Holy Spirit as one of the "three universals" on which the theology of the Evangelical Union rested.

The Evangelical Union was a voluntary association of Christians who had come together "for the purpose of countenancing, counselling; and otherwise aiding one another; and also, for the purpose of training up spiritual and devoted young men, to carry on and to carry forward the work and 'pleasure of the Lord' ".[5] There are three things to be said here.

First, that the Union was a form of "gathered church", an *ecclesiola* in which like-minded Christians were able to meet according to the Pietist principle of mutual edification and growth in holiness.[6] Secondly, that its intellectual standards were from the first as high as those of its parent body. Morison was deeply concerned with the provision of ministerial training; his own intellectual acquirements were considerable, and he saw the careful education of the ministry as being an elementary requirement. He opened a theological college in Kilmarnock (later removed to Glasgow), the courses at which were so arranged as to enable students to attend

---

[3] This theory was derived ultimately from a book by Edward Fisher called *The Marrow of Modern Divinity* (1645). Condemned by the General Assembly in 1720, it nevertheless continued to exercise some influence, and reached the Secession Churches by way of Thomas Boston and Ebenezer Erskine. See McNeill, *op. cit.*, pp. 326, 356.

[4] Morison, *The Question "What must I do to be saved?" Answered*, quoted by Ferguson, *op. cit.*, p. 22.

[5] *Evangelical Union; Its Origins, and a Statement of its Principles* (1845), p. 12.

[6] The wish was early expressed that E.U. churches should be distinguished by "the striking peculiarity of eminent holiness", *Evangelical Union Report for 1845*, p. 10.

university lectures parallel with their theological studies.[7] Hebrew and Greek were taught. A further point is, that the Union published a quarterly theological journal, the *Evangelical Repository*. And thirdly, that the object of the Union was revivalist and missionary; it was in no sense static—clearly a reflection of Morison's own positive experience in the Kilsyth revival. The work was to be "carried on"; but it was also to be "carried forward".

Perhaps not surprisingly, the Union had no Subordinate Standards, looking only to the Bible as the source of faith. It did however have a "statement of principles", though these were not binding upon members. The first of these principles bears out what we have said about the Union's evangelistic aims:

The objects of our Union are, mutual countenance, counsel, and co-operation in supporting and spreading the glorious, simple, soul-saving and heart-sanctifying 'gospel of the grace of God'.[8]

The faith of the Evangelical Union was finally crystallized into the "three universals", which may be briefly summarized as the universal love of God, the universal purpose of Christ in his atoning death, and the universal grace of the Holy Spirit.[9] It was thus clearly Trinitarian, as well as being considerably less forensic than the prevailing Calvinism of early nineteenth-century Scotland. Breadth of outlook was also characteristic of the Union's ecclesiastical position. In practice the Union was hardly concerned with the ecclesiastical conflicts of its own day; in fact it was claimed that "an entire Synod of godly Presbyterians" or "a body of pious Episcopalians" would be welcome, should they so desire, to join with the Union in its work of evangelism.[1] In theory at least, such questions as those of church government were subordinated to the need for "winning souls".[2]

---

[7] This "meant a real saving of time, and was carried out at the express desire of the theological professors", Selbie, *Life of Fairbairn*, p. 9.

[8] *Evangelical Union* (1845), p. 5. Other "principles" were that the nature of the Union was strictly voluntary, and that the Union accepted the Bible as "the Book of God". The principle of the universal Atonement was likewise stated forcefully: God, it was maintained, has made propitiation for "every sin of every sinner in the world", *ibid.*, p. 8.

[9] *Evangelical Union Memorial Volume* (1893), p. 30. For a fuller statement, see Selbie, *Life of Fairbairn*, p. 18.

[1] A. C. Rutherford, in 1845 *Report*, p. 24 f. Elsewhere the E.U. principle of co-operation was stated to be "friendship and brotherly love" with like-minded Christians: Ferguson, *op. cit.*, p. 379.

[2] *Memorial Volume*, p. 31.

There seems little doubt that the Evangelical Union conceived of its task as being primarily to arouse the people of Scotland, little or no mention being made in the histories of the work of foreign missions, though it is hardly likely that the subject could have been ignored altogether.[3]

The question of the position and influence of the Evangelical Union relative to other Scottish Churches is not one which we can consider in any great detail here. Some points may however be mentioned briefly.

A number of factors were at work in late nineteenth-century Scotland, as a result of which there came to be widespread acceptance of the principals for which the Evangelical Union stood. Some of these factors were strictly non-theological, having to do with the political and economic situation of the time; others had to do with later waves of revivalism, notably the campaigns of Moody and Sankey. Among theological factors may be mentioned the Scottish "Broad Church" movement, centring on Macleod Campbell and Erskine of Linlathen; Scottish Congregationalism, whose leading theological mind had been Ralph Wardlaw (1779–1853);[4] and similar influences from across the border, from F. D. Maurice and F. W. Robertson. Ritschlianism came in time to exercise an undoubted attraction, particularly on the many Scottish students who spent periods of study on the Continent. And finally, the personal influence of James Morison and his denomination must not be overlooked.[5] All these contributed in varying degrees to a decline in strict Calvinism, at least in its doctrines of Election and Atonement. A. M. Fairbairn wrote in 1861:

Let theological special pleaders say what they choose, it is a simple and indisputable matter of fact that the people will not tolerate Calvinism in its ultra or original form. The very mention of limited atonement or eternal election is dreaded . . .[6]

---

[3] Before 1890 the Union had only one missionary in active service: Alexander L. Allan, whose field was Nagercoil, S. India.

[4] See Hyslop, *Ralph Wardlaw, 1779–1853* (unpublished Ph.D. thesis, Edinburgh 1947), especially pp. 202 ff.

[5] For a fuller account of these and other factors, see Kirsch, *The Theology of James Morison*, pp. 254–256. McNeill writes, *op. cit.*, p. 398: "His [Morison's] *Nature of the Atonement* (1890) presented his case so effectively that the doctrine of a limited atonement virtually ceased to be advocated by Scottish theologians." This is an exaggeration. The doctrine in question had to all intents and purposes been abandoned long before 1890.

[6] Selbie, *Life of Fairbairn*, p. 46.

On the literary level, the most influential book seems to have been Macleod Campbell's *The Nature of the Atonement* (first published in 1856), about which D. S. Cairns wrote that

this strange, obscure, but profoundly spiritual book has probably had a deeper and more widespread influence on later thinking in Scotland on its great theme than any other book in the language.[7]

The main result of these influences was to discredit the idea of limited atonement—a change incorporated into the official doctrinal statements of at least the United Presbyterian Church.[8] In 1876 A. M. Fairbairn, then an Evangelical Union minister in Aberdeen (a circumstance to which we shall return) wrote that "Had theological thought been as liberal thirty years ago as it is to-day, our denomination had never been".[9]

In this same year, 1876, the proposal was first mooted that the Evangelical Union and the Congregational Union of Scotland should join forces.[1] An official statement to the same effect was delayed for some years, but finally appeared in 1892.[2] Union was consummated in 1896, the Evangelical Union then having enjoyed independent existence for fifty-three years only.

J. N. Farquhar's parents, George and Christian Farquhar, belonged to John Street Evangelical Union Church in Aberdeen, and it was as a member of that fellowship that their son was brought up. Of the details of his Christian upbringing we know very little, save that it was not restricted to his church: "I grew up", he was able to write in later years, "with all the words of the New Testament ringing in my ears."[3] We know, too, that he was in due course received into full membership of the Evangelical Union; and further, that he took an active, though limited, part in the life of his own church, and that of the other Evangelical Union church in Aberdeen, St. Paul Street. In 1890 the minister of John Street Church, the Rev. Alexander Stewart, wrote that Farquhar had always been ready to

---

[7] Cairns, *Life and Times of Alexander Robertson MacEwen* (1925), p. 81.

[8] In the Declaratory Act of 1879.

[9] Selbie, *op. cit.*, p. 75. The term "liberal" in this context has nothing to do with later "Liberal Protestantism"; it refers to "liberal" as against "conservative" Scottish Calvinism, particularly in its interpretation of the Atonement.

[1] Ferguson, *op. cit.*, p. vi f.

[2] *Memorial Volume*, p. 78 f. The actual initiative was taken by the Congregational Union.

[3] L.M.S. Candidature papers (1890).

assist in church work, "and specially by addressing the Sabbath Morning Bible-class"; he further testified that in his opinion Farquhar was at this time "a Christian in the real and truly evangelical sense".[4] A similar testimony was borne by the Rev. Alex. Brown, minister of St. Paul Street Church, who had heard him read "papers on Biblical and experimental themes", and who spoke highly of his Christian character.[5] This is the sum total of our information concerning Farquhar's Christian position in these early years. There are however a number of further points which can be deduced from his general background.

First, Farquhar appears in no sense to have been in conflict with his Evangelical Union background as such. He had, as we shall see, his period of doubt and conflict, but this was due more to the impact of the scientific world-view than to the specific teachings of his denomination.[6] His ecclesiastical position was clear; problems of church government concerned him not at all, and like A. M. Fairbairn he found the transition from the atmosphere of the Evangelical Union to that of Oxford nonconformity natural.

Secondly, we have drawn attention to the expressly revivalist and evangelistic atmosphere of the Union. This, too, Farquhar found congenial, once his period of doubt and uncertainty was resolved.[7] The influence of Finney and of Sankey and Moody was considerable, and had as its natural corollary the aim of "winning souls". It will be clear from what we have said in an earlier chapter about the origins of the nineteenth-century missionary movement that a man brought up in this kind of atmosphere would have no difficulty in finding his place in the Protestant Evangelical missionary enterprise of the period.[8] It may also be worth noting that the American Y.M.C.A., with which Farquhar was later to serve, was revivalist in tone, while the ethos of the Student Volunteer Movement was essentially that of Dwight Moody.[9]

---

[4] A. Stewart to R. Wardlaw Thompson, 20.10.1890 (LMS Archives).

[5] Alex. Brown to Thompson, 23.10.1890 (LMS Archives).

[6] See below, p. 119 f. It is worth noting that Farquhar remained a Congregationalist until 1923, when he joined the Church of England. Even then his change of allegiance was not theologically motivated: cf. Sharpe, *J. N. Farquhar*, p. 84 f.

[7] See below, p. 131.

[8] See above, pp. 25 ff.

[9] See below, pp. 175 ff., on the theological background of the American Y.M.C.A. and its work in India.

Thirdly, although the main concerns of the Evangelical Union were with "heart-religion", and with evangelism, intellectual standards we have seen to be high.[1] The theological college and the *Evangelical Repository* we have mentioned. A further factor, the importance of which will be clearer as we proceed, was the presence of Fairbairn as an Evangelical Union minister in Aberdeen (St. Paul Street), from 1872 to 1877. It is in the person of Fairbairn that we see the point of contact between the evangelicalism of the Union and developments in British and Continental theology, and particularly the "science of religion". This we shall consider separately in due course.[2]

Fourthly and lastly, the Evangelical Union was prepared to enter into wide co-operation on an "evangelical alliance" basis of common faithfulness to the Bible and the call to evangelize. A person acquainted with such a conviction would obviously have little difficulty in finding his place in the late nineteenth-century missionary enterprise, since virtually all the missionary societies were prepared for some degree of fellowship and co-operation on the same basis, and the interdenominational groups exercised widespread influence.

As we have said, there is little more than this to be deduced from Farquhar's Aberdeen background, at least as far as his religious development is concerned. There is however one final point which calls for comment: that although his minister had in 1890 no hesitation in calling him a Christian "in the real and truly evangelical sense",[3] he did not regard himself as having undergone a classical "conversion experience". We may quote the relevant passage from his missionary candidature form:

I was carefully trained in the truths of the Gospel by loving Christian parents; I thus grew up with all the words of the New Testament ringing in my ears, but I was not a follower of Christ. Rather more than five years ago I formed a very close friendship, which led me to think and feel and fear anew; good companionship in Oxford helped to deepen these thoughts and feelings: I looked into the face of Christ, and accepted him. But I cannot tell the moment, nor the day, nor the month of my conversion; only the beginning of that close friendship is the turning point of my life.[4]

---

[1] W. Robertson Nicoll wrote in 1912 that "The ministers of the Evangelical Union were, as a rule, men of popular gifts and on some subjects well ahead of their time ..." The *British Weekly*, 15.2.1912.

[2] See below, pp. 126 ff.

[3] A. Stewart to R. W. Thompson, 20.10.1890 (LMS Archives).

[4] L.M.S. Candidature papers.

The close friendship referred to was with Euphemia Watson, the daughter of his former employer, whom he married in 1891. Under her influence, and that of Mr. William Brebner, a teacher at the Aberdeen Mechanics' Institute,[5] Farquhar determined to leave the drapery business at the first opportunity, to educate himself and become a teacher. This he did on his twenty-first birthday. He returned to school, among boys some seven years his junior. In fifteen months' time (1883) he had won a bursary to Aberdeen University, and two years' further study brought him, in 1885, as Exhibitioner to Christ Church, Oxford—an academic record which speaks for itself. This he looked upon as a call from God, but although teaching continued to be the primary objective for which he strove, he did not consider the possibility of teaching on the mission field until he came to Oxford.

Oxford: Undergraduate Years

We quoted above a statement made by Farquhar in 1890 which suggested that his religious development was by no means unbroken and untroubled, and that the final resolution of his religious difficulties came only during his studies at Oxford. We may compare this further statement, made twenty years later, that

Under the influence of modern ideas, I lost my childish belief in Christianity while still young, and it was only to faith in the deeper things that I fought my way during undergraduate days.[6]

Such crises of faith were far from uncommon at this period. The 'seventies and 'eighties of the last century were a time of transition in theological and religious thought: from "old" to "modern" ideas, from an uncritical to a critical view of the Bible, from the literal acceptance of an established authority to the historical weighing of evidence. In the process, many traditional assumptions had to be revised, notably the idea that ultimate religious authority rested nowhere but in the word of Scripture. Other concepts followed, for if the Bible were proved to be historically unreliable in even one particular, then Christians brought up on the dogma of verbal in-

---

[5] In Farquhar's papers there is a reference to "Mr. William Brebner, a man thoroughly well known in educational circles here, and who has been a priceless friend to me for ten years". Cf. Sharpe, *J. N. Farquhar*, p. 5.

[6] Edinburgh Conference 1910: Manuscript Answers to Commission I Questionnaire (MRL New York).

fallibility were unable to see why other particulars should not also be called in question. The divinity of Christ; the birth narratives; the historicity of the Resurrection; the Ascension—these and many other ideas, from being unquestioned assumptions, became disputed territory. Many Evangelical Christians, unable to ignore the findings of the higher critics, the discoveries of the natural scientists and the "comparative religion" school, were forced radically to revise the whole of their traditional view of the foundations on which their faith rested.[7] Such was evidently the crisis through which Farquhar passed.

But at the same time Evangelical nonconformists were rapidly coming to assimilate the general atmosphere of criticism, if not the entire body of its conclusions, finding little in the "new" teachings which was not capable of ultimate reconciliation with the tenets of Evangelical doctrine. This process has been well described by W. B. Glover in his book *Evangelical Nonconformists and Higher Criticism in the Nineteenth Century*,[8] and we need do no more than summarize his findings.

Before 1880, most British nonconformists tended to react negatively to biblical criticism, and orthodox biblical scholars still found it possible

to consider higher criticism as the temporary form taken by infidelity in Germany and confidently to predict the scholarly victory of tradition.[9]

Between 1880 and 1887, however, a large proportion of the foremost scholars, though they did not in every case adopt a critical approach to the Bible, at least learned to tolerate such an approach on the part of others.[1] The scholars' findings penetrated to the rank and file Christian only very gradually, however, and this process was complicated by a number of bitter controversies. One which must have come to Farquhar's notice was the celebrated case of Professor Robertson Smith, dismissed his chair in Aberdeen by the Free Church of Scotland in 1881.[2] Another was the "Down Grade" controversy among the Baptists, which was begun by C. H. Spurgeon

---

[7] We have discussed certain aspects of this development above, pp. 39 ff.

[8] First published in 1954. Another valuable survey which covers the same ground, though from a different angle, is J. W. Grant's *Free Churchmanship in England 1870–1940* (s.a.).

[9] Glover, *op. cit.*, p. 36.

[1] *Ibid.*, p. 110.

[2] *Ibid.*, pp. 118 ff.

in 1887, and which dragged on for a number of years.[3] The Congregationalists, however, escaped the full force of the "higher criticism" dispute, due in no small measure to the influence of A. M. Fairbairn, who after 1877 "threw his growing influence behind a critical approach to the Bible".[4] Though Glover is often unnecessarily harsh in his judgment on Fairbairn, he allows that

... nobody could affirm evangelical truth with more dignity nor hold in greater scorn those unwilling to submit the Bible to the test of historical and critical study.[5]

When it is remembered that Fairbairn was originally a minister of the Evangelical Union, that he had had a pastoral charge in Aberdeen, and that after 1886 he became the most outstanding representative of nonconformity in Oxford, it will be clear that in coming to Oxford, Farquhar was coming into the sphere of influence of one with whom he had a number of natural affinities, and who might be expected to play some part in resolving his religious crisis in a particular way. The evidence for this we shall discuss later.

The religious scene in Oxford at the time of Farquhar's arrival reflected the concerns and tensions of the age. Many of these were peripheral to the nonconformist, whose position was still somewhat underprivileged. The Universities' Test Act had been repealed as recently as in 1871, and there were as yet only about a hundred nonconformists in what was still a fortress of the Establishment. But negotiations were in progress for the building of the first nonconformist theological college, Mansfield College being finally opened in 1889. The influence of Benjamin Jowett (1817–1893), Master of Balliol, and the liberal Anglicanism he represented, was at its height.[6] The Oxford movement was now in its second generation, and well able to exercise a powerful influence among students: Pusey House, under the principalship of Charles Gore, had been founded in the

---

[3] *Ibid.*, pp. 164 ff.
[4] *Ibid.*, p. 111.
[5] *Ibid.*, p. 140. As an example of Glover's criticism may be quoted his statement on the same page, that Fairbairn "was pompous and verbose, and none of his work proved of lasting worth". On p. 154 he goes even further, calling Fairbairn "a pompous windbag".
[6] Fairbairn, *Catholicism: Roman and Anglican* (1903), pp. 406 ff., 437 ff.; Webb, *Religious Thought in England from 1850* (1933), pp. 93 ff.

previous year, 1884, and the Oxford Mission to Calcutta was in its sixth year.[7]

Oxford theological opinion in 1885 might thus be very roughly divided as follows: there was the unemphatic college Anglicanism of the majority, modified by the high-churchmanship of the "Anglo-Catholics" on the one side and the broad-church liberalism of Jowett on the other; in addition the Evangelical party of the Church of England had its outstanding representatives: one such was Monier-Williams, Boden Professor of Sanskrit, though the actual leaders of the Evangelicals in Oxford were Christopher and Chavasse.[8] The nonconformists were few, and took little part in the active life of the university as yet. These groups were of course liable to subdivision; there were, and there continued to be, many shades of Christian and non-Christian opinion in University circles. The fires of controversy occasionally flared up, as for example in 1885, when Fairbairn and J. H. Newman debated—at complete cross purposes—the Catholic interpretation of Christianity.[9] Further, the presence in Oxford of the controversial figure of Max Müller was a constant reminder that the traditional Evangelical interpretation of the nature of Christianity and of the non-Christian religions had been, and was being, called in question. But at the same time, the Boden Chair of Sanskrit was, as we have said, occupied by Monier-Williams, who, while he was prepared to allow that there were "truths" in the non-Christian religions, was nevertheless a staunch Evangelical in all matters pertaining to the Christian faith. The conservative Evangelical mind found Max Müller suspect theologically, whatever may have been his contribution to scholarship;[1] Monier-Williams, on the other hand, was much more of a *persona grata* in these same circles;[2] some tension there undoubtedly was. But theological controversy seems not to have interested Farquhar: we must remember that he was not a theological student, that his view of the Christian life was

---

[7] Above, pp. 88 ff.

[8] Selbie, *Fifty Years at Oxford* (1936), p. 7.

[9] Selbie writes: "The fact is, the two men were working on different planes and using language each in a way that was hardly intelligible to the other ... Though their interchange of views created some stir at the time and has a certain historical interest, it remains an example of the futility of such controversy." *Life of Fairbairn*, p. 207.

[1] See e.g. *CMI* XVIII N.S. (1893), in which a commentator claimed that Müller "uproots the foundations of the Christian religion that he may erect another structure which is the shrine of nobody's faith but his own" (p. 502).

[2] Above, pp. 52 ff.

still taking shape, that he came from a milieu in which the characteristic emphases were practical, rather than speculative, and—most important—that he had a good deal of leeway still to make up in his studies.[3] A contemporary of his bears witness to the intensity of his studies and the long hours he spent at his books.[4] In due course he took his First in Classical Moderations, in 1887, and his First in Literal Humanities (B.A. degree), in 1889, at the age of twenty-eight.

It was during his years at Oxford that Farquhar reached his decision to undertake some form of Christian service abroad. Again, we have little information as to the precise way in which this came about; we do however know that contact with other Christians, as he put it, "purified my desire as to profession, and made me feel that I ought to help in the spread of the Gospel, if possible".[5]

This impulse can hardly have been derived from books. His missionary reading at the time of his candidature in 1890 was modest—surprisingly so. He admitted to having read biographies of Moffatt and Livingstone, Carey and Wilson (of Bombay), but this was nothing unusual in an Evangelical Christian. Apart from these he had no distinctively missionary publications on his reading list, but he had read a number of works by H. M. Stanley, Monier-Williams and Hunter, from which he claimed to have derived most of his knowledge of modern missions.[6] Principal Fairbairn wrote in his letter of recommendation that it was addresses delivered in Oxford by missionaries of the London Missionary Society which first turned Farquhar's thoughts specifically in the direction of work abroad.[7] Unfortunately we do not know who these missionaries may have been; nor do we know anything of the subjects on which they spoke. The Oxford University Nonconformists' Union has left no records;[8] Mansfield College did not publish a magazine before 1895.

---

[3] Cf. Sharpe, *J. N. Farquhar*, p. 11.
[4] Obituary in the *Manchester Guardian*, 25.7.1929.
[5] J. N. Farquhar to R. W. Thompson, 24.10.1890 (LMS Archives).
[6] Candidature papers.
[7] Farquhar was "very much influenced by the addresses of missionaries from your Society, which were the first influences which turned his thoughts to educational work in the foreign field". Fairbairn to Thompson, 27.10.1890 (LMS).
[8] The four principles of the Nonconformists' Union were (i) to remove nonconformist students' feeling of isolation, (ii) to investigate the principles of Nonconformity, (iii) to study the Bible, in English and Greek, and (iv) to represent Nonconformity to the Establishment. See Selbie, in *Mansfield College* (1890), p. 31. The Union was dissolved in 1886. The Oxford Inter-Collegiate Christian

But that he was in fact influenced in this way is backed up by Farquhar's own testimony, first, that his experience in Oxford had made him aware of a call to help in the spread of the Gospel, and secondly, that personal contacts in Oxford—together with the fact that he had friends working abroad (including a cousin on the Congo)—were a means of bringing him to the decision to undertake educational work on the foreign field.[9] It seems that in making this decision Farquhar was thinking of missions (in this case Indian missions) in largely traditional terms. This is in no way remarkable. What is noteworthy is that, as we shall see later, he was prepared to undertake language studies in order to fit himself for the work of evangelization, even though he was proposing to enter a field in which much of his work would be in English. And further, that having read Monier-Williams, whose inaugural lecture (delivered in 1861) had been on the study of Sanskrit in its bearing on missionary work, and whose *Indian Wisdom* (1875) had placed a favourable interpretation on much of Hinduism, he must have had at least some insight into the positive aspects of the religion of the Indian people before this date. But his candidature papers show that he was nevertheless preparing to assist in the work of "leading a people to change its religion". Contact with the Hindus themselves, though it affected his presentation of Christianity, did nothing to alter either of these basic principles.

In due course, then, Farquhar offered himself as a candidate for missionary work with the London Missionary Society. His candidature papers provide the first real evidence of his theological opinions which we possess. But before we pass on to discuss some of the details of his candidature, it may not be out of place to ask what were the main influences which can have helped mould his thought at the time of his departure for India.

Any answer to this question must remain partly conjectural. In no case does Farquhar provide clear indications of the course taken by his own religious and intellectual development. Further, we have his own evidence that his theological ideas were still at the formative

---

Union had been founded in 1879 [Tatlow, *The Story of the Student Christian Movement of Great Britain and Ireland* (1933), p. 6], but there is no direct evidence of its having played any positive role in Farquhar's development.

[9] Candidature papers.

stage. He had read no theology—a lack which he was to regret all his life.[1] The only exception was that he does seem to have taken some interest in New Testament exegesis, possibly in the Nonconformists' Union Greek Testament class.[2] His time at Oxford was fully occupied with his regular studies (mainly Classics). So while his religious convictions were firm, he had still not come to the stage at which it was possible for him to express them in terms of theological propositions. In 1910 he wrote retrospectively of his theological position at this time:

I held no elaborate creed when I began my work, but was still in the process of forming my own body of beliefs. I saw clearly in a general way the superiority of Christian theology to every other system, and I held to Christ, the Son of God crucified for us, but I had no defined theological ideas... Similarly I had no clear perception of the nature of the Church, nor had I reached firm standing-ground with regard to Baptism.[3]

In the circumstances it is difficult to claim categorically that he was influenced by any specific writers or thinkers during his years at Christ Church. There are however two names which must be mentioned in this connexion: two scholars whose distinctive ideas are to be found in some form in his later work. In neither case can we claim that the writer in question exercised a formative influence on Farquhar's life and thought at this stage.[4] It seems rather to be the case that he built on the work of these and later writers as circumstances warranted. Nowhere does he acknowledge any direct indebtedness to either.

We have discussed the work of the two scholars in question at some length in Chapter One: they are Sir Monier Monier-Williams, Boden Professor of Sanskrit,[5] and Friedrich Max Müller,[6] both of

---

[1] Farquhar "often regretted that he had no adequate theological preparation", A. J. Appasamy, "Dr. J. N. Farquhar", in *YMI* XLI: 9 (September 1929), p. 685.

[2] "My studies in theology have been almost altogether confined to New Testament exegesis; I have, as yet, rather attempted to understand the spirit of the various writers of the New Testament than to formulate precise doctrines from their writings." Candidature papers.

[3] Edinburgh Conference 1910: Manuscript Answers to Commission I Questionnaire (MRL New York).

[4] Farquhar was not in the habit of providing his books with an extensive critical apparatus, and in any case his first published works did not appear until 1900–1901; it is not safe to draw from these any hard and fast conclusions regarding his reading of a decade earlier.

[5] Above, pp. 49 ff.

[6] Above, pp. 43 ff.

whom held posts in the University of Oxford at the time of Farquhar's undergraduate period. In the case of Max Müller influence
cannot be shown to have extended beyond sympathetic appreciation
of certain aspects of his work; of other aspects Farquhar was openly
critical.[7] Monier-Williams, as we have seen, had made use of the
concept of "fulfilment" in his statement of the relations between
Christianity and Hinduism.[8] We shall find Farquhar making extensive use of this idea in his books—indeed it was one of the pillars
on which his missionary thought rested—but while he may have
derived it from his reading of Monier-Williams, he may equally well
have taken it from the missionary scholars T. E. Slater and F. W.
Kellett.[9] Direct influence can neither be proved nor disproved. There
is however the further significant factor that Monier-Williams, unlike Max Müller, held an altogether uncompromising insistence on
the supremacy and sole final validity of Christianity among the
religions.[1] This view is in ample evidence in Farquhar's later books.[2]

A third scholar with whom Farquhar was in personal contact at
Oxford was Andrew Martin Fairbairn (1838–1912),[3] who we have
already mentioned in passing on a number of occasions. Here there
is more conclusive evidence, as well as a greater intrinsic likelihood,
of direct influence. This we must examine in a little more detail.

Fairbairn was an ordained minister of the Evangelical Union,
and had served in churches in Bathgate and Aberdeen before coming Principal of Airedale College, Bradford. In 1886 he came to
Oxford as Principal of the newly-founded Mansfield College. Be-

---

[7] "Müller calls himself a historical student, but the excessive strain he puts
upon *words* in all his studies in religion and mythology decisively separates his
work from the labours of the historians. His acceptance of the *Rigveda* as evidence
for the character of *primitive* religion is also quite sufficient by itself to set him
in a school of his own. Further he contaminates his work by the introduction
of a most curious philosophic theory of the rise of religion from the perception
of the infinite. Yet we owe a very great debt of gratitude to Max Müller, for his
pioneering work in the science of religion, for the large quantities of materials
he has gathered, for his edition of the *Rigveda* and above all things for *The
Sacred Books of the East.*" Farquhar, "The Science of Religion as an Aid to
Apologetics", in *HF* XII N.S. (Oct. 1901), p. 372.

[8] See above, pp. 51 ff., with references to Monier-Williams' works.

[9] Above, pp. 94 ff. (Slater) and p. 105 f. (Kellett).

[1] Above, p. 50.

[2] Below, pp. 205, 256, 308.

[3] The standard biography is Selbie, *The Life of Andrew Martin Fairbairn*
(1914). There is an unpublished modern study by A. W. Loos, *The Theology of
A. M. Fairnbairn* (Ph.D. thesis, Edinburgh, 1939). See also works quoted by
Glover, *op. cit.*, p. 140.

tween 1865 and 1866 he had studied in Berlin, and had been influenced by the *Vermittlung* school of dogmatic theology, and in particular by Dorner, though he had also attended the lectures of the orthodox Hengstenberg.[4] This period in Germany, coming as it did at a time of spiritual crisis, was of decisive importance for the whole cast of Fairbairn's mind: so much so, that it has been suggested that he was never able to break free from the patterns of thought it imposed upon him.[5]

The question of the precise extent of Fairbairn's influence on Farquhar is one which it is very difficult to decide with any great certainty. There are however a number of indications which taken together seem to show that Fairbairn did in fact exercise a not inconsiderable influence on his younger countryman. Two we have already mentioned: briefly, that both were from the Evangelical Union, and that Fairbairn had spent five years as a minister in Aberdeen while Farquhar was still an apprentice draper. That Farquhar had at least heard Fairbairn preach in Aberdeen, and may well have attended his lectures, is a safe assumption. But there is a more tangible piece of evidence in the form of a letter of recommendation written by Fairbairn on the occasion of Farquhar's missionary candidature in 1890. Such a letter could not have been written without a fair degree of personal acquaintance on Fairbairn's part, as its contents indicate. Part reads:

He [Farquhar] is a man of fine parts and spirit. He is a scholar, took a first class in Literal Humanities and was throughout his entire course up here a simple-minded active Christian worker. His first application to me was to be allowed to attend Communion at George Street and when Mansfield was founded he was one of our most constant friends ... You may be sure that if he offers himself it is because he has been impelled to do so by conviction and the highest motives and you may be no less certain that whatever he undertakes to do, he will do with the most rigid conscientiousness. I would support this application therefore in the strongest possible way ...[6]

And personal acquaintince of this order in the university milieu makes intellectual influence, not indeed certain, but highly likely.

There are three aspects of Fairbairn's thought which are of

---

[4] Selbie, *op. cit.*, pp. 38 f., 253; *idem, Congregationalism*, p. 173.
[5] *Idem, Congregationalism, loc. cit.*
[6] Fairbairn to Thompson, 27.10.1890 (LMS Archives).

especial interest in this connexion, since all recur in some measure in Farquhar's later work. One we have already mentioned: the problem of biblical criticism and Evangelical theology. The others are Christology and Comparative Religion. These we shall consider very briefly.

Fairbairn was not primarily a biblical critic. His main field of interest and competence was the history of doctrine, in which he had read widely, and on which he wrote at great length.[7] It is true that he specialized to some extent in New Testament theology, but he was never in any sense creative in the biblical field. Indeed, it has been pointed out that in Old Testament criticism he remained at the pre-Wellhausen stage, while in theology generally he made no attempt to understand Ritschl—a remarkable omission in a theologian of his period and standing. What is generally regarded as his best work, *Christ in Modern Theology,* though it first appeared in 1893, has nothing to say on Ritschl. Fairbairn was nevertheless well aware of the importance of biblical criticism for the study of theology. We have quoted Glover on the subject.[8] Here we may add the judgment of Fairbairn's biographer, that "though he never kept pace with the advance of criticism in his own time, he was fully alive to its importance, and was quite prepared to accept and use in theological teaching such results of it as were available".[9] But at the same time he was firmly opposed to any diminution of Evangelical theology merely on critical grounds, and it may well be that this was an important stabilizing influence on Farquhar in his own crisis of faith.

Secondly, Fairbairn's distinctive emphasis was Christological, that is, he laid stress on the doctrine of the Person of Christ, and on its determinative function in Christian theology. In this, Fairbairn was making use of the new emphasis on the historical side of New Testament studies which by 1885 had begun to supersede the Tübingen school, and which he had come to know during his time in Germany.[1] He considered that the progress of historical research

---

[7] Fairbairn's most important works are *Christ in Modern Theology* (1893), *Religion in History and Modern Life* (1895), *Catholicism: Roman and Anglican* (1899), *The Philosophy of the Christian Religion* (1902) and *Studies in Religion and Theology* (1910).

[8] Above, p. 121 n. 5.

[9] Selbie, *Life of Fairbairn*, p. 225.

[1] For a detailed account, see Loos, *op. cit.,* p. 27 f.; cf. Selbie, *op. cit.,* p. 225 f.

into the life of Christ had brought the Church of the late nineteenth century more nearly face-to-face with Christ—the Jesus of history—than at any time since the Apostolic age.[2] This meant that all societies, conventions and systems must be compared with "His mind and ideal": "As He is the source and authority of all the Churches, no Church can refuse to be measured and judged by Him. No development can be legitimate that is alien to His spirit and purpose."[3] Further, in Fairbairn's case, as so often during this period, emphasis on historical method and acceptance of evolution as a working theory went together. As Loos has pointed out, at a time when many theologians considered that the theory of evolution jeopardized theism, "Fairbairn accepted it as a highly significant comprehensive hypothesis which would be of value in gaining a better understanding of the universe".[4]

The third point at which it is likely that Fairbairn exercised some influence on Farquhar is in respect of the study of the "science of religion" or "comparative religion". It is tempting, in view of Far-quhar's later development, to assume more than a mere cursory contact here. But that would be to go beyond the evidence; again, we have no more than a certain degree of probability. Fairbairn's interest in non-Christian religions is known to date back at least to the early 1870's.[5] At that time he was studying Indian, Chinese and Semitic religions, partly under the stimulus of his friendship with the Sanskritist Dr. John Muir.[6] Through Muir, Fairbairn came into contact with Max Müller, and had his first published essay, on "The Genesis and Development of the Idea of God", accepted by the *Contemporary Review* (this was in 1871).[7] During Fairbairn's ministry in Aberdeen, comparative religion is said to have been his main scholarly interest; he corresponded with Muir, Max Müller, Tiele, Chantepie de la Saussaye and others, and lectured on the

---

[2] "Our age ... knows Him as no other age has done as He lived and as He lives in history." Fairbairn, *Christ in Modern Theology*, p. 20.

[3] *Ibid.*, p. 296.

[4] *Op. cit.*, p. 62 f. On evolution generally, cf. above, pp. 39 ff. It is also interesting to note that Henry Drummond's *Natural Law in the Spiritual World* had been published in 1883; there is however no direct evidence that Farquhar had been influenced by Drummond at this date.

[5] Selbie, *Life of Fairbairn*, p. 35.

[6] On John Muir and his advocacy of the method of conciliation in Indian missions, see above, p. 36 f.

[7] Selbie, *op. cit.*, p. 50 f.

subject, in Edinburgh as well as in Aberdeen.[8] Between 1878 and 1882 he was Muir lecturer in the science of religion in Edinburgh, and in 1892 he delivered a series of Gifford Lectures on the religions of the world in Aberdeen. It was expected that he would publish his material, but other interests supervened, and it appears that some of his material had in any case become out of date, requiring a degree of re-working for which he had not the time.[9] He also held occasional courses in comparative religion at Mansfield College. After his death, a contemporary wrote that

Dr. Fairbairn was a pioneer among Christian theologians in the importance he attached to be comparative study of religions.[1]

These are suggestive emphases, but must not be over-stressed. As far as Farquhar was concerned, any or all of these may have influenced Farquhar's intellectual development and at the same time have helped to resolve his perplexities in the field of personal religion. But all three were in some measure the common property of the age, as we have already pointed out.[2] In the case of the "science of religion", the Oxford of the 1880's was also the Oxford of Max Müller and Monier-Williams, whose position in nineteenth-century thought we have discussed.[3] So much is however clear, that Farquhar was a member of the circle around Fairbairn in these years, and that he was thereby in a position to derive from him religious and intellectual impulses. In his acceptance of biblical criticism as a working method, in the stress he laid on the Person and the teachings of Christ as the foundation of Christian theology, and above all in his study of one of the great non-Christian religions we have the essence of Farquhar's later position as a missionary leader. The seeds of any or all of these attitudes and concerns may well have been sown in Oxford, under Fairbairn.

Missionary Candidature

Farquhar's missionary career began when, on the completion of his studies in Oxford, he offered himself to the London Missionary

---

[8] *Ibid.*, pp. 66 f., 76 f.
[9] *Ibid.*, pp. 120 f., 306 f.
[1] Dr. A. E. Garvie, quoted by Selbie, *op. cit.*, p. 238.
[2] See above, pp. 41 ff.
[3] Above, pp. 43 ff.

Society as a candidate for educational work abroad. We have already seen that he left the world of trade in order to educate himself and become a teacher, and we have the testimony of the Principal of Mansfield that the first influence which turned him towards the idea of work overseas came from the London Missionary Society.[4] And it was as an unordained educational missionary that he offered his services. He remained a layman all his life.[5] But at the same time he had a lively appreciation of the missionary's responsibilities in the field of evangelization, recognized that he was about to join in the attempt to persuade a people to "change its religion", and stated that he intended

> to work in all things with the single aim of promoting the knowledge and sway of Christ in India, yet chiefly through the special branch of work which the Master has given me, the teaching of young men.[6]

The answers which he returned to the London Missionary Society's candidature questions are in no way outstanding; they are brief, and from the evangelical point of view perfectly orthodox, making use of the conventional evangelical vocabulary of religious experience. They are not the work of a man who had learned to think either philosophically or theologically on matters of religion, and accord well with Fairbairn's estimate of him as "throughout his entire course ... a simple-minded active Christian worker".[7] His categories are those of the Evangelical Union, particularly in his stressing of the universality of the Atonement [see (ii) below]. He traces his call at least partly to the commandment of Jesus in Matt. 28.19—the evangelical missionary commandment *par excellence*. At this stage, and in this connexion, he naturally uses the current missionary terminology, which he retained for a short period in India,[8]

---

[4] Above, p. 123 n. 7.

[5] Sharpe, *J. N. Farquhar*, pp. 16, 102. Farquhar's daughter has informed the present writer that this was a point of strong conviction on her father's part, since he believed his sphere of usefulness to be wider as a layman than it could be in the ordained ministry.

[6] Farquhar to R. W. Thompson, 24.10.1890 (LMS Archives).

[7] Above, p. 127 n. 6.

[8] In later years he was to look back with mixed feelings on his early attitude to India and Hinduism. In 1913 he wrote: "The writer here wishes to make public confession that during the first years of his life in India unguarded expressions fell from him in teaching, in public addresses, and in literature, of which he is now heartily ashamed." *The Crown of Hinduism* (1913), p. 57.

but later abandoned altogether, when he writes about "the thrice-noble work of spreading the Gospel of Christ among the heathen".[9]

His own Christian experience he sums up in these words:

I have accepted Jesus Christ as my redeemer from sin, and I believe his promises. He has forgiven my many transgressions; and he is daily giving me grace and strength to win the victory over sin, and to live a holy life.[1]

One of the questions on the candidature form asks, "What are your views of the principal and distinguishing doctrines of the Gospel?" It may be of interest at this stage to quote his answers *in extenso*:

(i) *Truth:* The Son of God became man and lived among men, full of all grace and speaking heavenly truths. He died a sacrifice for the sins of men, and rose from the dead, that we might know about the life to come.
(ii) *Salvation:* All those who throw themselves by faith on Christ receive forgiveness of sins and are freed from the power of sin. The Spirit is given them, so that they receive of the fulness of the Grace of Christ; and 're-flecting, as mirrors, his glory, are transformed into his image from glory to glory'.
(iii) *Work:* Christ's life, death and resurrection must be proclaimed among all men; and every Christian is bound, as he has received salvation, to be a herald of salvation to others.[2]

We shall not comment further on these short statements, beyond pointing out that this is the background against which Farquhar's first contacts with Hinduism are to be seen and judged. They are of little or no permanent significance, since we shall see in due course that Farquhar's missionary thinking was conditioned very largely by the needs of an empirical situation; nevertheless they are of interest in this context, as they show the point reached by Far-quhar in 1890 in his religious thinking. At the same time, it must be pointed out that reasons of space (on the candidature form) and diplomacy precluded speculative thought—not that this is likely to have been a temptation in Farquhar's case.

From the practical point of view, Farquhar recognized that his coming task would not be without its difficulties. Asked what he believed to be the general qualifications for the work of a Christian missionary, he specified "intellectual gifts and attainments" as neces-

---

[9] Candidature papers.
[1] *Ibid.*
[2] *Ibid.*

sary for "the work of leading a people to change its religion"; further, he stressed the need for "practical business qualities", patience and tenacity.[3] As a capable linguist, he understood that an early knowledge of Indian languages would be of great value in understanding the people among whom he was to work. He had in fact made a private start on this side of his missionary activity before leaving England, since at that time there was nothing resembling pre-service training for the purely educational missionary.

I shall want to learn them [the languages] as quickly as possible [he wrote] in order to use them in evangelistic work, if I am capable for it, and also to come more closely into touch with the life and civilization of India. I have indeed begun Bengali and Hindustani already.[4]

The Directors of the London Missionary Society accepted Farquhar's offer. He was appointed to the teaching staff of the Society's Institution at Bhowanipur (Bhowanipore), Calcutta, and sailed in the S.S. *Ravenna* for India a few days before Christmas, 1890.[5] He arrived in Calcutta early in February 1891, and took up his teaching duties immediately.

---

[3] At the same time it should be pointed out that he wrote first that "... above and beyond everything else a man must have the Spirit and Grace of Christ in rich measure, if he is to be an ambassador for Christ". *Ibid.*

[4] Farquhar to Thompson, 3.11.1890 (LMS Archives).

[5] Farquhar to Thompson, 29.12.1890, 14.1.1891, 5.5.1891 (LMS Archives).

PART TWO

J. N. Farquhar in India

CHAPTER 5

A Christian College and the Hindu Renaissance, 1891–1902

CALCUTTA in 1891, when Farquhar arrived, was still the capital of India, as well as being her largest city, with a population of 700,000, and growing rapidly. During the previous seventy years the population had expanded from c. 230,500 (though the figures for earlier periods are most unreliable)[1] to its 1891 figure; the rate at which the city was expanding can be gauged from the fact that in 1961 the figure stood at 2,926,498.[2] Calcutta was the natural centre for the internal trade of N.-E. India, by road, rail and river, but its growth was due rather to its external, than to its internal trade. From 1860 onwards Calcutta and its neighbours were largely affected by an expansion of foreign trade, a general increase of prices, and a rise in the standard of living. Large industrial works were started, conducted by machinery and offering employment to numbers of labourers who came to the villages and returned to their lands at certain seasons. Thus, to take only one example, in 1881 there were nineteen jute mills with 39,000 operatives; by 1911 there were fifty-eight jute mills and 200,000 operatives.[3] The opening of the Suez Canal in 1869 had brought changes in the pattern of Asiatic trade: the administration was shortly to be removed to New Delhi. But the character of the city did not change—industrial, fast-expanding, the centre of a wide hinterland and a clearing-house for the whole of Bengal.

But even more important, Calcutta was also the intellectual centre of Bengal and North-East India. This is not the place to give a

---

[1] Art. "Calcutta", in Balfour (ed.), *Cyclopaedia of India* (1899), p. 547 f.

[2] For a summary of the situation and history of Calcutta, with select bibliography, see *EB* 4 (1963), pp. 605 ff. The 1961 figure is for the city proper. The total population of the metropolitan area, including suburbs, now stands at over 6,500,000.

[3] For a more detailed account, see *Camb. Hist. Ind.* VI (1932), pp. 251 ff., Tyson, *The Bengal Chamber of Commerce and Industry* (1953), pp. 55, 64.

review of the developments which had brought this about.[4] Suffice it to say that by 1890 English-language higher education had been established in a dozen large colleges—many of which owed their existence to the Christian missions and their working patterns to Alexander Duff[5]—apart from many smaller institutions and secondary schools. The University of Calcutta had been established in 1857 as an examining body on the model of London University.[6] The student population had by 1890 reached over 3000, which meant that every political, religious and social development was at once reflected in the ranks of the students;[7] Calcutta could on this account be reckoned as the barometer by which the climate of Indian opinion as a whole could be estimated. Further, the Bengali people had always shown a particular receptivity to, and appetite for, English education, with the result that the ideals of Calcutta very soon spread to the *bhadralok* (middle classes) of the rest of Bengal. This increased intellectual awareness brought with it an increased political susceptibility, as the events of 1905–10 were to show.

Missionary Higher Education in Calcutta

Education and missionary work had long run parallel courses in Bengal. As we have seen, the years from 1813 onward had seen an unprecedented expansion of missionary activity all over India, as a result of the terms on which the East India Company's charter had been renewed in that year.[8] Parliament had declared that such measures ought to be adopted as might lead to "the introduction into India of useful knowledge and religious and moral improvements",[9] and had transferred the power to grant licenses to missionaries from the E.I.C. Directors to the Board of Control, which in practice meant virtual freedom to exercise missionary work, at least for British missionaries. And the "education clause" which set aside a con-

---

[4] See however above, pp. 58 ff.

[5] Above, pp. 63 ff.

[6] *Camb. Hist. Ind.* VI, p. 118 f.

[7] The significance of this for the missions is increased by the fact that by 1900 the "native" colleges were educating more young men than all the government and missionary colleges put together. In 1900, out of a total of 8000 students in Bengal as a whole, the missionary colleges accounted for no more than 1120. J. N. Farquhar to R. W. Thompson, 6.3.1902 (LMS Archives).

[8] Firth, *An Introduction to Indian Church History* (1961), pp. 153 ff.

[9] *Camb. Hist. Ind.* VI, p. 102 f.

siderable sum of money for "the revival and improvement of literature and the encouragement of the learned natives of India and for
the introduction or promotion of a knowledge of the sciences among
the inhabitants of the British territories in India" set the seal of
governmental approval on the educational enterprise.[1] The way in
which the various missionary societies each accepted this new-found
freedom lies outside the scope of this work, but we must nevertheless
make some brief remarks about the work of the London Missionary
Society in Calcutta.[2]

The L.M.S. had entered Calcutta in 1816.[3] Their first representatives concentrated on education, opening three elementary
schools within the first few months.[4] Five years later, in 1821, was
opened the first Congregational Church in Calcutta. The L.M.S.,
following the general trend of the period, entered the field of higher
education in 1837, when the Bhowanipur Institution came into
being. The language controversy having been decided in favour of
the Anglicists, the teaching was to be in English; the College itself
was modelled on Duff's famous Institution,[5] and a start was made
with 22 pupils, of whom 16 were the sons of Christians and 6 were
Hindus. By 1851 the total of pupils had risen to something in the
region of 800 (if the Bhowanipur College's two branches are reckoned
in the overall total) and between 1851 and 1854 it was found necessary to rebuild the college.[6] A further fact of importance is that at
no time was the teaching at the Bhowanipur college entrusted to
non-Christians; in this L.M.S. policy differed from that of many
Christian institutes of higher education.[7]

The sheer numbers of students flocking into Calcutta's educational
centres had by 1890 become a distinct missionary problem.[8] In the
first place, it was fast becoming evident that purely educational missionary work was no longer having the desired effect on young India;
the expected rapid infiltration of the upper classes had not ma-
terialized. And secondly, the Hindu element of Indian society had
begun, for reasons which we shall enumerate elsewhere, to develop

[1] Ibid.
[2] Richter, Indische Missionsgeschichte (2 Aufl. 1924), p. 166 f.
[3] Lovett, History of the London Missionary Society II (1899), pp. 46 ff.
[4] 39th Report of the London Missionary Society (1833), p. 32.
[5] Cf. above, pp. 63 ff.
[6] 60th Report of the London Missionary Society (1854), p. 19.
[7] Above, p. 75.
[8] See e.g. Lovett, op. cit., p. 191 f.

a positive dynamic. The very students who ought in theory to have
been most deeply influenced by Christianity had begun to hold
themselves more and more aloof from organized Christianity, despite
their professed admiration for Jesus. The result of all this was a
practical problem of the first magnitude. The Calcutta Decennial
Review of 1890 included this statement by a member of the Bhowanipur staff, the Rev. F. F. Longman:

There is a great work to be done in Calcutta among the students who
come here from all parts of Bengal to attend the different colleges. Most
of them reside in the neighbourhood of the larger colleges... They are of
course a most important class, as they must necessarily exercise considerable
influence for good or evil in time to come upon the thoughts and opinions
of their fellow countrymen. Here in Calcutta, at all events, the time of one
missionary might well be devoted to evangelistic work among them.[9]

It is interesting, and important, to take account of this slight
indication—for it is no more than an indication—of dissatisfaction
with missionary policy in Calcutta as it was understood in the period
immediately prior to Farquhar's arrival in India. It will be at once
evident that this is a striking parallel to the situation in Madras,
fifteen years before.[1] Longman, like Slater in Madras, was concerned lest the purely evangelistic side of missionary work in Calcutta
should unwittingly be neglected by a continued emphasis on the
indirect evangelism of Christian education. Duff's own original experiment had been enormously successful in terms of the propagation of Duff's educational principles, and at least partly successful—
during the first generation—from the missionary point of view.[2] For
example, there can be no doubt that it was this type of higher
education which turned so many Indians to a study of the life and
teaching of Jesus. But several factors combined to make it less successful with the passing of years.[3] First, Duff's experiment was by
1890 no longer an experiment, but an established fact; the element

---

[9] *Ibid.*, p. 192.

[1] Above, pp. 95 ff.

[2] For instance, there were a number of outstanding Brahmin converts, among
them K. M. Banerjea; see Smith, *The Life of Alexander Duff* (1899), p. 86 f.
Neill, *A History of Christian Missions* (1964), p. 481.

[3] A deputation appointed by the Free Church of Scotland in 1889 had noted
that the education which was the best *praeparatio evangelica* for the Hinduism
of 1830 may have borne little relation to the Hinduism of 1889; the Lindsay
Commission added that it "may be even less what is wanted for the Hinduism
of 1930". *Report of the Commission on Christian Higher Education in India*
(1931), p. 25 f.

of novelty had gone, and an educational routine had been worked out, with a consequent concentration on education as an end in itself. Secondly, Government and native educational schemes, though slow in starting, made great progress from 1879 onward: it goes without saying that these did not provide for the teaching of Christianity and often actively opposed it; non-Christian—with which must be included anti-Christian—education was thus a feasible alternative to higher education in a missionary college. In other words, higher education and the spreading of the Gospel were no longer necessarily synonomous; developments had arisen which Duff could not possibly have foreseen, and certain otherwise faithful educationalists were beginning to feel the problem rather acutely.[4]

A. I. Mayhew sums up in these words:

The early advocates of Christian advance through Christian secondary schools and colleges did not foresee the development of a system of education in which Christian institutions would be merged... What they had in mind was a system dominated by the Christian point of view... They hoped also as a result of rapid conversion that the staffs and pupils of all Christian institutions would be predominantly Christian, and that the Christian influence on the non-Christian minority would be correspondingly great.[5]

But this was not the case—at least not in Bhowanipur—and certain of the more acute observers were beginning, in the years before the turn of the century, to recognize the signs of the times.[6] We shall see that in Farquhar's own case it was the discrepancy between the needs of the situation and the conservative attitude of the mission which was a large contributory factor in his final withdrawal from this kind of educational work.

Teaching at Bhowanipur

Farquhar's period of work with the L.M.S. is best seen in retrospect, from the point of view of his resignation. It would scarcely

---

[4] Farquhar to J. R. Gaunt, 12.3.1902 (LMS Archives): "Is that not a prodigious revolution that has taken place since 1857? The beginning of the change was visible before 1879, but only the beginning. Practically the whole of this extraordinary change has taken place during the past 23 years. Is it not absolutely clear that another engine is necessary besides the colleges, if we are to seriously influence the educated classes of Bengal?"

[5] O'Malley (ed.), *Modern India and the West* (1941), p. 329.

[6] Nor were these all missionaries; for a contemporary Indian judgment, see Mukerji, "Missionary Colleges", *Oxford Mission Association Paper (Indian Branch)* No. 14 (1889), p. 5 f.

be an exaggeration to say that despite his early enthusiasm, he was really a misfit in a college of the Bhowanipur type. But the circumstances surrounding his resignation provide a remarkable survey of the period in question—the last decade of the nineteenth century—as seen by an acute observer. From the point of view of the study of Hinduism, and of Farquhar's own contribution to the study of Christian-Hindu relationships, the period is preparatory. Farquhar is constantly being compelled to play the part of the observer, saying little and writing little. But such a period of observation was indispensable; in it we see the establishment of those conditions which led Farquhar to undertake the study of Hinduism, and to attempt to arrive at a workable theory of the relationship between Christianity and Hinduism. He was aware of the need for such a theory almost from his first moments in India; the pattern of aggressive Hinduism was beginning to take shape, and the doors were being shut, one by one, in the face of the Christian missionary. We see reflected in his work something of the emergence of the new India, particularly in student circles; in Farquhar himself we see a young educationalist growing more and more disillusioned with the progress of a work which he feels to be getting more and more out of touch with the needs of the age. During this period, too, we see the growing conviction of his own inability to do anything to help the situation as long as he remained in a routine teaching post.

Farquhar was eager to avoid misunderstanding of the reasons which led to his resignation, which seemed to some of his colleagues as a piece of wilful folly, carried out in a fit of bad temper; he thus wrote at length explaining his own position.[7] It is clear that he hoped by this means, not only to justify his own actions, but also to influence the L.M.S. authorities into taking steps to reorganize and improve their own work in Calcutta. We have no reason to give a full account of all the reasons which led to his resignation, as a number of them have no direct bearing on the problems with which we are most closely concerned; we shall thus attempt only to summarize the situation on a basis of Farquhar's own later explanations.

When Farquhar arrived in Calcutta in 1891, he was at once thrown into college work. He lived with one of his senior colleagues,

---

[7] Two such letters are in existence: 6.3.1902 to the Foreign Secretary of the LMS, and 12.3.1902 to J. R. Gaunt (LMS Archives).

the Rev. A. P. Begg, an experienced, though conservative educationalist, and was thus given every opportunity to allow a sense of the importance of educational work to enter his mind. And as he was prepared to be influenced, it did so.[8] His first letter to the Secretary of the L.M.S., written on February 23, 1891, contains these words:

My little experience and few scraps of observation since I came here confirm my belief that the educational work done here is of extreme value and importance. That these young Hindus should be taught by earnest Christians rather than by careless Christians or by Hindus is of immense importance, even if we do not consider the actual Scripture work and direct Gospel teaching. And the magnificent set of educated native Christians dependent upon our mission here is an evident proof of the power of Christian educational work.[9]

He later bore repeated witness to his conviction that the higher education carried out by the Protestant missions in Bengal was "the greatest piece of mission work done in Bengal between 1830 and 1900".[1] But at the same time he saw that the rapid evolution of events in Calcutta was in the process of creating an altogether new situation. In Duff's day, the intellectual movement of the day was centred upon the colleges; by 1890 the centre of gravity had shifted to the ex-students who were by that time active participants in the work of Government, in commerce, in law and in education. The actual process of education had been "clipped into shape" and was becoming a matter of routine. Farquhar soon recognized that it was becoming impossible to influence the mind of Bengal by means of work in the colleges, and that the evangelistic opportunity in these same colleges was dwindling steadily in comparison with the 1840's and 1850's.

It is significant that possibly the strongest of Farquhar's "first impressions" was just that of the difficulty of carrying out, in the process of college education, a programme of "direct" evangelism.

---

[8] "I do not allow any thoughts of mine to influence me in my work as yet: I am doing my best to work loyally along with, and under the direction of, Mr. Ashton and Mr. Begg ..." Farquhar to Thompson, 23.2.1891 (LMS Archives).

[9] *Ibid.*

[1] See e.g. Farquhar to Gaunt, 12.3.1902 and Farquhar, *The Higher Education of Christians in Bengal* (1896), p. 7. Goodall, *A History of the London Missionary Society 1895–1945* (1954), p. 36, is mistaken in supposing that Farquhar was referring in this connexion to the LMS work at Bhowanipur only. His terms of reference were much wider.

The educational work of the college had become an end in itself[2]—a state of affairs which evidently caused Farquhar some surprise and not a little disquiet. It was not merely that the young men he had to teach were indifferent to Christianity; by 1890, as a result of the work of the Ārya Samāj, Rāmakṛishṇa and the Theosophists, "there was a general uprising of the educated Hindu spirit in defence of Hinduism".[3] Active criticism of all things Christian was becoming more common.

Nothing impresses me so deeply [he wrote] as the extreme difficulty of leading the class of men we have to deal with, educated Bengalis, to become Christians; they are ... proud of their own hoary cult and filled full of arguments drawn from the purer and nobler parts of its teaching... And the fear which is felt by Hindus concerning the advance of Christianity has led them to form almost a sacred dread of allowing any shred of Christian teaching to find a place in their heart.[4]

The Hindu Revival

The origins and development of the national movement in India have formed the subject-matter of a good many books, particularly since India's independence.[5] But as far as I am aware there has been no definitive study of the interaction of religion and politics during the nationalist period in India's history. Nor can we pretend to remedy the deficiency here. Some observations may however be useful at this stage.

The letter quoted above was written in 1891, by which time the Ārya Samāj and the Theosophical Society had been in existence for sixteen years;[6] nine years earlier, in 1882, a student, Narenda Nath Datta—later more widely known as Swāmī Vivekānanda—had been taken to visit the Hindu religious leader Rāmakṛishṇa. Vivekānanda, who dated his "conversion" from this meeting, was to become a most potent force in religious nationalism.[7] In the same year, 1882, Dayānanda Sarasvatī had founded the *Gaurakshinī Sabhā* (Cow-protecting Association),[8] a movement which grew to great pro-

---

[2] This was of course no new problem. See above, pp. 78 ff.
[3] Farquhar, *Modern Religious Movements in India* (1914), p. 316.
[4] Farquhar to Thompson, 23.2.1891 (LMS Archives).
[5] See e.g. works by Dasgupta, Griffiths, Masani, Panikkar and Raguvanshi (bibl.).
[6] Farquhar, *Modern Religious Movements*, pp. 101 ff., 208 ff.
[7] *Ibid.*, p. 200 f.
[8] *Ibid.*, p. 111.

portions in the Hindu world. These are perhaps the most significant dates in the early history of the Hindu renaissance, preceding by some years the effective beginning of the national movement as a political force.

Most observers are agreed that the immediate cause of the revival within Hinduism was the impact of the West, in one form or another. It is probably true to say that in no other field was there a more profound antithesis between East and West than in the realm of religion. We have described in some detail how the Western missionary came to India, bent on persuading India (or at least individual Indians) to apostasize from Hinduism and embrace one or another form of Christianity, Evangelical or Catholic. There was a deliberate *Auseinandersetzung* in which Christianity was contrasted, in outline and in detail, with Hinduism. And since the Christian missions and Government combined to revitalize the Indian mind by means of education it is not surprising that there was a reaction. Valentine Chirol wrote in 1910 that the Hindu revival of the latter part of the nineteenth century was largely stimulated and to some extent prompted by Europeans and Americans. This stimulus came from two sources. On the one hand, the studies of Western Orientalists had convinced many Indians that their ancient religion contained treasures such as they had never before realized. Max Müller in particular played an important part in this new realization. And on the other, the writings of anti-Christian apologists, of whom Bradlaugh exercised the widest influence, served to provide Hinduism with a basis on which the Christian missions might be attacked.[9] The Hindu Tract Society of Madras, whose object was the dissemination of anti-Christian polemical books and pamphlets, was started in 1887.[1]

The alliance between religious nationalism—the Hindu revival—and political nationalism came later. It is true that the founder of the Ārya Samāj taught, implicitly if not explicitly, that "a return to the pure teachings of the Vedas would gradually fit the people of India for self-rule and that independence would ultimately come to them".[2] But his immediate objectives, as Farquhar has shown,

---

[9] Chirol, *Indian Unrest* (1910), p. 28.

[1] *Ibid.*

[2] Griswold, in the *Indian Evangelical Review* (Jan. 1892), quoted by Farquhar, *Modern Religious Movements*, p. 112.

were religious rather than political, and in any case the main influence of the Ārya Samāj was limited to the Punjab and the
United Provinces.[3]

It is a well known fact that political nationalism in India dates
from 1885, the year of the foundation of the Indian National
Congress. We have no reason to discuss the early years of Congress
in detail here, beyond remarking that the methods they employed
were fully constitutional, and that Congress politicians were at first
eager to avoid all suspicion of disloyalty to the British Crown. It has
been said that the first years of Congress were marked by the lack
of a fully constructive ideal.[4] Resolutions were passed, but little was
done. However, it is not with purely political nationalism we are
concerned here; we shall see in due course that intensifying *religious*
nationalism led in time to a split in Congress, but not before the
"Curzon" period had strained East-West relations in Bengal almost
to breaking-point.[5]

In 1891, then, we find a situation in which the students of
Bhowanipur were being subjected to increasing anti-Christian propaganda, from the Ārya Samāj, from the Theosophical Society and
from the disciples of Rāmakrishṇa, to name only the three most
potent sources. From the first came the rallying-cry "Back to the
Veda"; from the second an express statement of the superiority of
Indian over Western religion; from the third the postulate that all
religions are ultimately equal, and that although Christianity may
be a good religion, there can be no conceivable need for a Hindu
to transfer his allegiance from the faith of his ancestors. At the same
time the Christian educational situation, as we have described it in
Chapters Two and Three, was making it difficult for the educational
missionary to combat these views. The national movement, both
religious and political, was gathering momentum.

Hindu schools and colleges, often set up in answer to the efforts
of the missionaries, were beginning to train large numbers of men
highly receptive to nationalist teaching. These young Hindus were
beginning to form a large circle entirely outside the influence of
the educational missionary. Beyond them were the ex-students (an
even larger group)—those who were setting the new intellectual stan-

---

[3] Farquhar, *op. cit.*, p. 127.
[4] Tagore, *Nationalism* (1918), p. 112.
[5] This will be discussed more fully in Ch. 7, below, pp. 209 ff.

dards of India: these were even further away from the missionary educationalist. There seemed little hope, as the situation then stood, of improvement; as Farquhar himself expressed it, "the overworked professor could only look out of his classroom in pain, and see the main current of the times sweeping past him".[6]

In the circumstances, it is interesting to note that, although individual missionary bodies had been known to appoint commissions to inquire into the state of higher education on the mission field —the Free Church of Scotland commission of 1889–1890 being a case in point—no full-scale examination was carried out until 1929–1930,[7] and when the Principal of the Presidency College, Calcutta, published his short study, *Education and Statesmanship in India, 1797–1910,* he was in favour of retaining the whole educational system essentially unaltered, despite its admitted imperfections.[8]

The Mansfield Settlement

The L.M.S. staff in Calcutta was not entirely unaware of the critical aspects of the situation; it is however significant that they sought to solve the problem by turning to England, and to the newly-founded Mansfield College, rather than attempting to deal with the problem on the spot. The way in which they set about the problem is reflected in this extract from the minutes of the Calcutta District Committee of the L.M.S., dated December 29, 1892:

The Committee have observed with much interest, and with deep thankfulness to God, the active part now being taken in Foreign Missionary work by University men and Colleges; and they earnestly request the Mansfield College, Oxford, to send out men under the auspices of the L.M.S. to locate themselves in a Mansfield mission here in Calcutta, where there are unusual facilities and opportunities for reaching all classes of people, *and the educated classes in particular,* with a view to bringing them to a saving knowledge of the Gospel of our Lord Jesus Christ.[9]

---

[6] Farquhar to Thompson, 6.3.1902. Farquhar was by no means the only missionary to have this experience. Bishop H. Whitehead had come to doubt the value of Christian higher education for similar reasons [Sundkler, *Church of South India* (1954), p. 52], and the 1889–90 report of the Free Church of Scotland stated: "Professors in our mission colleges have to work much harder and in a far more exhausting way than before. The educational missionary is a hard-working man—overworked in our opinion ..." *Christian Higher Education in India,* p. 25.

[7] See *Christian Higher Education in India,* pp. 1 ff.

[8] See pp. 136 ff.

[9] LMS Archives.

The hope that the small L.M.S. staff at Bhowanipur might be reinforced from Mansfield, thus enabling direct evangelistic work to be undertaken on the level of the educated Indian, bulked large in the minds of the Bhowanipur missionaries during these years. Farquhar himself wrote in 1893, "I earnestly hope and pray that the Mansfield Settlement, in spite of the difficulties that at present surround it, may soon be a realized fact ... I have every hope that great help will come to Calcutta from Mansfield."[1] There can be no reasonable doubt that, had it been possible to arrange for the settlement in Calcutta of a body of university graduates, committed to an attempt to reach the educated classes with the Christian Gospel, considerable results might have been achieved. The practical difficulties, however, proved insurmountable.

The prototype Mansfield Settlement[2] had been started in Canning Town, a district of London's East End, in September 1890, largely on the initiative of A. M. Fairbairn; it was directly inspired by the Christian Socialism of the period, and was a direct outcome of the settlement movement begun by Samuel Barnett and Arnold Toynbee (Toynbee Hall was opened in 1884).[3] The proposed Calcutta Settlement was, however, not of this type; its main aim was not the amelioration of poverty and the carrying out of a policy of neighbourliness *vis-à-vis* the poor. It was aimed instead at the educated classes, and its primary object seems to have been much more missionary in character than was the case with the Canning Town settlement. It is not unlikely that Farquhar, being the only member of the Bhowanipur staff to have come to India subsequent to the establishment of the London settlement, had some hand in the attempt to bring Mansfield students to Calcutta.

But nothing came of the attempt. The L.M.S. was chronically short of money,[4] and would not undertake to support more men in Calcutta, even had men been available. The project was reluctantly shelved—though it enjoyed a new lease of life in 1898, in connexion

---

[1] Farquhar to Thompson, 18.10.1893 (LMS Archives).

[2] Selbie, *The Life of Andrew Martin Fairbairn* (1914), pp. 297 ff.

[3] See art. "Social Settlements", in *EB* 20 (1963), pp. 905 ff., with bibliography.

[4] Nevertheless, in 1891 the Society had entered upon a policy of expansion, aimed at adding 100 additional missionaries to its staff before 1895; this was a venture of faith, but it was not supported, and led in 1894 to a complete suspension of all new appointments. See Mathews, *Dr. Ralph Wardlaw Thompson* (1917), pp. 83 ff.

with A. M. Fairbairn's visit to India[5]—and was never realized. This was a blow to the whole of the Bhowanipur staff, but most particularly to Farquhar, who had believed that it afforded a practicable way of coming to terms with the sophisticated exponents of resurgent Hinduism who were to be found everywhere in college and university circles.

Reinforcements

By the end of 1893, after the disappointment over the Mansfield Settlement, Farquhar had begun to press for an addition to the Bhowanipur staff: preferably one who could be fully responsible for evangelism among students and educated men generally.

One name that suggested itself was Alex. Booth, who had been a fellow-apprentice with Farquhar in Aberdeen, and whom Farquhar regarded as likely to prove a useful acquisition to the College. Although sympathetic consideration was given Booth's case by the L.M.S. Directors, no appointment could be made, probably again because of lack of funds.[6] But Farquhar did not wish the project to be forgotten. In October 1893 he wrote

If the Directors are unwilling to increase the Educational staff here, might they not consent to a new Educational Missionary being sent out, on condition that one already here be set free for direct Evangelization? I am receiving almost daily further proofs of the great work waiting to be done here among the students and educated men.[7]

Farquhar's letter of May 2, 1894, combines enthusiasm—over the enormous opportunities awaiting the right man—with despondency—over the impoverished financial situation that made it impossible to do anything about it. "I am still impressed", he wrote, "with the need there is for a vigorous evangelist to work among the educated young men. The tide is rising steadily, I believe. Almost every day we have indications of the deep hold Christ has taken of numbers of young men around us. They want to be looked out, to be helped, taught, guided and encouraged." Then he continues in a much more sombre vein. "But in the present straitened condition of our finances

---

[5] Selbie, *Life of Fairbairn*, pp. 347 ff. It was proposed during Fairbairn's visit that the entire work of the Bhowanipur college should be handed over to the projected settlement; see *Minutes of the United Half-Yearly Meeting of the Calcutta D.C., at Bhowanipur*, 6–9.12.1898, § 4 (LMS Archives).

[6] Farquhar to Thompson, 22.8.1893, 18.10.1893 (LMS Archives).

[7] Farquhar to Thompson, 18.10.1893.

I can scarcely hope that the Directors will so be able to strengthen this depleted mission as to make it possible for a man to be set aside for this particular work."[8]

In point of fact, we learn from Farquhar's own letter of resignation that he had by this time been seized by the conviction that he ought, if at all possible, to enter this independent evangelistic work.[9] This implies that he felt himself, in some sense at least, qualified to meet aggressive Hinduism on its own ground, although his serious study of Hinduism did not begin until after 1902. The same letter which we have quoted above (May 2, 1894) contains hints to this effect, assuring Wardlaw Thompson, the L.M.S. Secretary, that although he is still convinced of the value of educational work, he feels that its focus has become somewhat misplaced, the means having been confused with the end. "I came out here for work in the Institution; and I am still in full sympathy with Educational work. But the work of leading these young men to Christ is the natural crown of our education; and I should count myself happy were I counted worthy to do it. If however a man with a higher spiritual endowment than myself can be found, I shall gladly continue to teach English in the classrooms, and do my utmost to prepare men for him."

It goes without saying that such an attitude—however moderately expressed—was hardly likely to commend itself to this colleagues, particularly the older educationalists, to whom Bhowanipur and its work were all in all. His difficulties with his colleagues A. P. Begg and J. P. Ashton dated from this time, and did little to help the strained situation brought about by his own inward frustration. They regarded him as "a prig and an upstart" (the words are Farquhar's) for wanting—as they saw it—to abandon the work of teaching so soon after having embarked upon the career. Their lack of understanding is perhaps symptomatic of the routine of missionary higher education, which was failing to consolidate the ground it had won, and tending to throw away opportunities, not recognizing them for what they were.

---

[8] Farquhar to Thompson, 2.5.1894.
[9] Farquhar to Thompson, 6.3.1902: "By this date [1893–4] the conviction that I ought myself to get into this free work had taken possession of my mind. I forget when I first mentioned this conviction to you; but I fancy I did not do so until later."

The Y.M.C.A.—the Third Alternative

In July 1894, the Secretary of the L.M.S. received this letter, which we quote in its entirety:

After thought and prayer I feel led to write to you about Mr. J. N. Farquhar, of Bhowanipur, Calcutta. For eight months I have watched him. Two things are clear to me. First, the students of your college love him and like to have personal talks with him about salvation. Secondly, he is much drawn to the students and loves to do personal work among them.

It does seem to me a great pity that through pressure of work he cannot devote his whole time and strength to inquirers. Were he free to devote himself entirely to these men, I believe great results would quickly follow. With possibly one or two exceptions he is the best man I know in Bengal for such work ...

Pardon the liberty taken by me in asking if your committee cannot set him free for evangelistic work among students. *He is just the man for the work.*[1]

The writer of this letter, Robert Parmalee Wilder[2] was one of the founders of the Student Volunteer Movement (originally known as "The Princeton Foreign Missionary Society"). Born in India of American missionary parents, he had been in Calcutta, working under the joint auspices of the S.V.M. and the Y.M.C.A., since the beginning of July 1893.[3] He had thus had ample opportunity to meet and discuss with Farquhar the present trends in student evangelism and missions. This kind of personal work which Wilder was advocating for Farquhar was that in which he himself had considerable experience.[4] His opinion of Farquhar was not hastily formed, and he must obviously have been aware of the urgency of the situation before taking the step of writing as he did.[5]

The letter appears to have had little effect on Farquhar's position, but it brings into the picture for the first time the *Young Men's Christian Association*, which was to play such a vital role in future

---

[1] LMS Archives.

[2] See Wilder Braisted, *In This Generation: The Story of Robert P. Wilder* (1941), particularly p. 16 f., and Eddy, *Pathfinders of the World Missionary Crusade* (1945), pp. 40 ff.

[3] His original appointment by the Presbyterian Board of Foreign Missions was to work among students in India "on an undenominational basis", Braisted, *op. cit.*, p. 52.

[4] *Ibid.*, p. 70 f.

[5] "Wilder ... wrote to you (I should think it was in 1894), and advised you strongly to set me free for student work. He did so absolutely without my knowledge." Farquhar to Thompson, 6.3.1902 (LMS Archives).

developments in Christian-Hindu relations. This is not the place
to give a detailed account of the history of the Y.M.C.A. in Calcutta,[6]
or the principles on which it functioned, but we must nevertheless
mention certain important facts. (a) The Calcutta Y.M.C.A. had
been founded in 1857, the year of the Mutiny. (b) Its period of
real influence dates from 1893, with the coming of J. Campbell
White as General Secretary. (c) The modern Calcutta Y.M.C.A. was
American in origin, and was comitted to a far more definite evangelistic and missionary programme than that normally associated
with the European Y.M.C.A. movement. This latter factor cannot
be stressed sufficiently, in the light of subsequent developments. The
point is, that Farquhar was able to see in this specialized form of
missionary activity the very agency he had been seeking for evangelistic work among young men. It mattered little, in Farquhar's
opinion, that it stood to one side of the main stream of church life,
and was affiliated to none of the organized missionary societies.[7]

Here was Farquhar's third—and decisive—alternative. The Mansfield Settlement had failed to materialize; the L.M.S. Directors were
unable to sanction the appointment of any extra missionaries; in
December 1895, on Farquhar's own initiative, the Y.M.C.A. Bhowanipur Branch was opened.

Work: The foundation of the work of the branch will be religious. Weekly
meetings for Christians and for Hindus and other forms of religious effort
are being organized and will be commenced with the New Year (1896).
Membership: Any young man of good character, without distinction of race
or creed, may become an Associate Member ... Any young man who is a
member of a Christian Church may become an Active Member. The pro-
moters of the Association, believing that all stable progress must rest on
religion, are desirous of attracting as many of the members as possible to
the religious meetings, but, beyond a friendly invitation, no pressure will
be brought to bear on them.[8]

The opening of the Y.M.C.A. College Branch had preceded the
opening of the Bhowanipur Branch by some months, and had begun
to give direct evidence of one way in which advantage might be
taken of the opportunities which existed among the educated men

---

[6] See however Nish, *Young Men's Christian Association of Calcutta 1857–1957*
(1957); also Farquhar, *Old Stalwarts of Bow Bazaar* (1904), idem, "Calcutta—
Then and Now", in *FM* XIII: 5 (Sept.–Oct. 1906), pp. 17 ff.

[7] For a more detailed discussion of YMCA principles and practice in Calcutta,
see below, pp. 175 ff.

[8] Brochure on YMCA Bhowanipur Branch, in LMS Archives.

of Calcutta. It was not then surprising to find that Farquhar himself was largely responsible for the organization of the Bhowanipur Branch[9]—or that his work came to the attention of such men as Campbell White and Robert P. Wilder. He was—not for the first time—enthusiastic about the possibilities offered by the new Association, but a little more cautious in his estimate of the practical situation. In June 1896 he wrote that "although it [the Bhowanipur Branch] has been successful in point of numbers and in some other things, we have not been able to use it as a basis for aggressive evangelistic work. We hoped to get hold of the Hindus of the district by this means ... but in consequence of pressure of work ..." It is thus the old story, of resources insufficient to meet the needs of the situation. The fact however remains, that "it forms a magnificent basis for evangelistic work, and is proof to us of the almost limitless scope there is for personal work among young men here".[1]

Early Religious Nationalism: Śivaji, Swadeshi, Vivekānanda

The following years in Calcutta saw little change in the situation of missionary education as it affected Farquhar; the mid-1890's however witnessed a number of significant developments in the Hindu world—developments which were to have a profound effect on the religious conflict of the years after the turn of the century. Three in particular must be noted here: the Śivaji festival of 1895; the first swadeshi exhibition of 1896 and the return of Swāmī Vivekānanda to India in 1897.

The first Śivaji festival was organized by Bal Gangadhar Tilak (1856–1920), a Chitpavan Brahmin Vedic scholar, educationalist and journalist.[2] Tilak had received an English education, but has been called "far less deracinated" than many of his contemporaries, thanks to his Sanskrit studies.[3] This was not the first time Tilak had

---

[9] "All the work of organizing and starting this Association was done by me during our brief Christmas vacation ..." Farquhar to Thompson, 1.6.1896 (LMS Archives).

[1] Ibid.

[2] Tilak is discussed in all the standard works on Indian nationalism, though from widely differing standpoints, according to the political sympathies of the authors concerned. The facts will be found in Shay, The Legacy of the Lokamanya: The Political Philosophy of Bal Gangadhar Tilak (1956). Cf. Kraemer, World Cultures and World Religions (1960), pp. 137 ff.

[3] Shay, op. cit., p. 53.

advocated radical measures in politics: his journalism was already notably left-wing. But the Śivaji festival enabled him to establish a firm connexion between politics and religion, as well as providing Hindu political extremism with a figurehead of heroic stature.

Śivaji, a Marāṭha chieftain of the late seventeenth century, had made his tribes into a nation capable of resisting the Mohammedan invasions,[4] and had been personally responsible for the treacherous assasination of the Mohammedan general Afzul Khan. Whence Tilak derived the idea of this modern festival is immaterial.[5] The point is that Tilak emerged by this action as a "new Śivaji", prepared even to condone violence for the sake of his country. At the 1895 festival at Raighar a Brahmin professor is reported as having said, "Had Śivaji committed five of thirty crimes more terrible, I would have been equally ready to prostrate myself ... before the image of our lord Śivaji."[6] Events were to prove that Tilak himself commanded hardly less reverence. Although he expressly forbade the use of violence, at least later, his followers were not always conscious of the distinction.[7] So while Tilak came to be looked upon by young Indian nationalists as something of a Messiah, and "the one possible leader for a revolutionary party",[8] the British authorities regarded him as "one of the most dangerous pioneers of disaffection".[9] Even a moderate observer like Farquhar could write in 1915 that the Śivaji celebrations "contain the poison of anarchy".[1] Shortly afterwards, Tilak was imprisoned for sedition, and the full extent of the movement he had been instrumental in starting was not seen until after 1905. But the seeds of violence in the name of religion had been sown.

The first *swadeshi* exhibition was held in Calcutta in 1896. Again, this was little more than the seed from which the later *swadeshi* movement was to grow. The main features were however clear even

---

[4] Farquhar, *Modern Religious Movements*, p. 359.

[5] See however Chirol, *Indian Unrest*, p. 45.

[6] Quoted by Chirol, *op. cit.*, p. 46; cf. Lovett, *A History of the Indian Nationalist Movement* (1920), p. 50 f.

[7] "It is not preached nor is it to be expected that the methods adopted by Śivaji should be adopted by the present generation ... It is the *spirit* which actuated Śivaji in his doings that is held forth as the proper ideal ..." *Speeches of Bal Gangadhar Tilak* (1918), p. 48 f.

[8] Mukherjee and Mukherjee, *Sri Aurobindo's Political Thought, 1893–1908* (1958), pp. 35, 37.

[9] Chirol, *op. cit.*, p. 40.

[1] Farquhar, *Modern Religious Movements*, p. 359.

at that early date. The left-wing press had during the 1890's concentrated very largely on economic questions. India, it was argued, was being drained of her resources, plundered and oppressed by aliens.[2] The early *swadeshi* movement was an attempt to encourage home industries, and the early exhibition was on a small scale. Not until 1905 was the movement as such coupled with the idea of economic boycott of foreign goods.[3]

The third significant event in the Hindu world during the mid-1890's was connected with the name of Swāmī Vivekānanda. We have seen that the meeting of N. N. Datta (Swāmī Vivekānanda) with Rāmakrishṇa in 1882 was of decisive importance for the religious development of the younger man. When Rāmakrishṇa died in 1886, Vivekānanda became a *sannyāsī* and spent some years in retirement, from which he emerged in 1892. In the following year, 1893, he represented Hinduism at the World's Parliament of Religions in Chicago,[4] where he made a profound impression. He had preached the Vedantist gospel of universal religious toleration. "I am proud", he had said, "to belong to a religion which has taught the world both tolerance and universal acceptance. We believe not only in universal toleration, but we accept all religions to be true. I am proud to tell you that I belong to a religion into whose sacred language, the Sanskrit, the word 'exclusion' is untranslateable."[5]

For four years the Swāmī travelled in the West, preaching and teaching; everywhere he was well received. In January 1897 he returned to India, where large audiences of Hindus acclaimed him as their first "missionary", and as the Saviour of their ancient faith. Many believed that he had succeeded in winning many adherents

---

[2] Lovett, *op. cit.*, p. 52 f.

[3] Cf. below, p. 218 f.

[4] The question of the precise significance of this remarkable and enigmatic demonstration for Protestant missions as a whole is one which we have not ventured to discuss in this study. The motives of the participants seem to have been as diverse as their backgrounds; some came in the spirit of the organizers and preached universal toleration; others carried out thinly-disguised propaganda. Evangelicals criticized it bitterly: a writer in the CMS *Intelligencer* called it "this menagerie of religions ... the most profane and the most unpardonable outrage upon Christianity that the world has known" [*CMI* XLV (1894), pp. 161–175]. Among its supporters were however Max Müller and William Miller; among its speakers T. E. Slater; and among its visitors John R. Mott. However, as far as Indian missions are concerned, there can be no doubt that it was Vivekānanda's appearance which was to have the most lasting effect.

[5] For a complete text of Vivekānanda's address, see Barrows (ed.), *The World's Parliament of Religions* II (1893), pp. 968 ff.

in America and Europe for Hinduism.[6] The real significance of his home-coming is well expressed by a modern Hindu writer, D. S. Śarma:

It is impossible to read without emotion the accounts of the reception that was given to Swami Vivekānanda when he returned to India in triumph after four years of glorious work for the Motherland and her ancient religion ... The event was great not only because a fitting reception was given by India's millions to a samnyasin, who was after their own heart and who had made them all feel an inch taller, but also because the stir created by his triumphal tour made the present Hindu Renaissance self-conscious and adolescent.[7]

Last Years in Bhowanipur

After this excursus we return to Farquhar's affairs. During the summer of 1896, J. Campbell White spent some time in England, and met Wardlaw Thompson. Farquhar was particularly eager that this meeting should take place, because he felt that it would strengthen his case for the reinforcement of the Bhowanipur staff. "My object in asking you to have this interview", he wrote to Thompson, "is to strengthen in your mind the impression I believe we have already made as to the need for setting apart some one to work among the young men here. Mr. White will tell you of the opportunities such work affords ... Bhowanipur is probably more ripe for such work than any other quarter of Calcutta."[8] The interview did little good. Thompson was prejudiced against the Y.M.C.A. from the start,[9] and although White pressed Farquhar's case, it appears—for no record of the interview survives—that no headway was made. Farquhar's letters continue to hold out hope,[1]

---

[6] Farquhar, *Modern Religious Movements*, p. 202.

[7] Śarma, *Studies in the Renaissance of Hinduism in the Nineteenth and Twentieth Centuries* (1944), p. 281.

[8] Farquhar to Thompson, 1.6.1896 (LMS Archives).

[9] This is clear from certain phrases in a later letter of Thompson's written on the occasion of Farquhar's resignation. "Certainly the opportunity provided by the proposal of the YMCA seems a most tempting one. I confess, however, that there are aspects of the proposed new arrangement which make me look at it very doubtfully. I should not have felt so much hesitation if the offer had come to you from some well-established Society with a continuity of policy and of power to carry it out ... I feel ... that you are embarking upon a hazardous course in the interests of your own permanent opportunities of service ..." The root of the matter is revealed a little later, as Thompson writes, "I should not like myself to be dependent upon some of those who are influential in YMCA circles in this country." Thompson to Farquhar, 7.2.1902 (LMS Archives).

[1] Farquhar to Thompson, 16.12.1896, 13.1.1897 (LMS Archives).

but by the end of 1897 there was no material alteration in the situation. His own personal sense of frustration was however increasing.

Then in January 1898, Farquhar was compelled by bad health to return temporarily to England on a combined sick-leave/furlough.[2] Before leaving India he went before the Calcutta District Committee of the L.M.S. and explained his position to them, saying that he was convinced he ought to get out of college work and begin evangelistic and literary work "outside". He also informed them of his intention to lay his case before the Directors of the L.M.S. when he arrived in London. This he did in the summer of 1899, but though the Directors were not unfavourably disposed towards Farquhar's scheme as such, they were not prepared to take any positive steps: the whole matter was referred back to Calcutta.[3]

There followed what Farquhar himself described as his "time of trial". He was on the point of resignation from sheer frustration; he shrank from the "joyless, hopeless work of college".[4] Nevertheless, a sense of duty kept him at his work, and he determined to wait until some suitable opportunity should present itself.

When he returned to Calcutta, a token effort was made to find some method of keeping Farquhar on the Bhowanipur staff. At the first committee meeting held after his return, Ashton proposed that Farquhar should receive a certain amount of freedom, this to be made possible by the transfer of some of his work to other members of the staff. Farquhar would not accept this proposal, first, because he knew that it would never work: the staff at Bhowanipur was so small that any innovation was quite out of the question. Secondly, he was not prepared to accept freedom at expense of his colleagues, each of whom had quite enough work of his own, without taking on an extra burden. Thirdly, it is tolerably clear from Farquhar's own evidence that Ashton made this proposal because he imagined that Farquhar had come back from England in a bad temper, after

---

[2] The diagnosis was "utter nervous prostration with acute neuralgia of the spine". Farquhar to Thompson, 28.11.1897 (LMS Archives).

[3] *Minutes of LMS Eastern Committee (India Department)*, 12.6.1899, § 6 (b). It was recommended "*That* the Directors regarded favourably the proposal of Mr. J. N. Farquhar that on his return to Calcutta he should be set free from educational work in order to engage in evangelistic effort among English-speaking students, but that they leave the D.C. free to make such rearrangement of work as they may deem best in providing for this promising branch of work." (LMS Archives).

[4] Farquhar to Thompson, 6.3.1902 (LMS Archives).

his unsympathetic reception by the L.M.S. Directors: in short, it
was a placatory gesture, and on these terms Farquhar was unable
to accept it.[5]

The next two years were a time of waiting, and for Farquhar
"almost a time of anxious suspense", as he saw so much happening
outside college and felt himself so impotent to do anything about it.
It must be remembered, too, that in 1901 he was forty years old,
and apprehensive lest increasing age should bring with it diminished
elasticity of mind and consequently a diminished ability to adapt
himself to the change which he was convinced would come sooner
or later. It seems to be the case that during his stay in England,
Farquhar was promised that, as soon as circumstances should permit,
he was to be released from educational work. Whether there was
ever any real likelihood of this happening is a moot point. A letter
written on August 30, 1900, contains this rather plaintive remark:
"Things go on much as they have done for several years: there is
little to chronicle. I am still looking forward to release from educational work, and fully believe that sooner or later my enfranchise-
ment will come."[6]

But although the years 1900–1902 were outwardly static, a new
conviction had been growing upon him. We have seen that from
his very first years in India he had been aware of the *opportunity*
afforded by the educational system as it then stood. His own personal
destiny—whether or not he ought personally to attempt to do anything to remedy the situation—came next. The new conviction, which
crystallized the first two, was that the situation was assuming more
and more *urgency*. It is this latter aspect which compelled his final
decision. We quote his own words:

There are not only great opportunities for the work outside: the time is
now come when it must be taken up, unless we are to lose the flood-tide.
The work of college itself will get poorer and poorer, until there is this
free spiritual work created outside and around it. And it is really a matter
of grave urgency. The uneducated masses are still happy in their idolatry:
the educated classes have had their old religion destroyed for them, and are
wandering around in doubt, in fear, and in anger, anxious to build up
again their beautiful edifice, but daily finding the work more hopeless.[7]

---

[5] *Ibid.*

[6] This letter was written shortly after his return from Britain; Farquhar to
Thompson, 30.8.1900 (LMS Archives).

[7] 6.3.1902.

This was in fact the situation which drove him from the active work of the L.M.S., and the attitude of mind which inspired his resignation. He never opposed college work as such, never proposed that the college should be weakened as a matter of policy—though this was one inevitable outcome of his action—and declined absolutely to accept a partial freedom, which would have been unsatisfactory in every way. He maintained consistently that the "new work" should be set up by the side of the old, and that it ought not to be started unless an additional missionary could be appointed. The majority of his colleagues—with the exception of Begg and Ashton—agreed with his analysis of the situation, and were prepared to support his attempt at a solution.[8]

Resignation from the L.M.S.

The turning-point in Farquhar's career came, quite unexpectedly, in January 1902, in connexion with a visit to Calcutta of John R. Mott.[9]

J. R. Mott has been epigrammatically described as "a statesman among missionaries and a missionary among statesmen".[1] His major gifts were in the fields of organization and administration; his work in America, and above all his role in the foundation, seven years before, of the World's Student Christian Federation,[2] had begun to give evidence of his world vision, his energy and his ability as an organizer. His first two world tours, in 1896–97 and 1901–02, were undertaken on W.S.C.F. business. The first was a tour of establishment, the second a tour of encouragement. Mott also had great gifts as an orator and evangelist, and much of his success as a leader of world student opinion can be traced to his power to grip and hold mass meetings of students, and his skill in presenting a Gospel of personal commitment in simple, direct and forceful language.

---

[8] Some drew different conclusions, maintaining that Bhowanipur ought to be made into a college for Christians only; Farquhar felt, on the other hand, that such an exclusively Christian college could only be run satisfactorily on an interdenominational basis. See *The Higher Education of Christians in Bengal*, p. 8.

[9] Regrettably, there is as yet no definitive biography of Mott. Mathews, *John R. Mott: World Citizen* (1934) contains much valuable material, but lacks perspective. See also Fisher, *John R. Mott: Architect of Co-operation and Unity* (1952), and Neill, *Men of Unity* (1960), pp. 13 ff.

[1] Quoted by Fisher, *op. cit.*, p. 164.

[2] Rouse, *The World's Student Christian Federation* (1948), *passim*.

Alongside his "public" abilities as an organizer and evangelist must be mentioned Mott's outstanding capacity for recruiting helpers. The list of prominent men and women whose first introduction to ecumenical work can be traced back to John R. Mott is impressive.[3] Whenever he came into contact with someone whom he felt could be of value to one of his many international enterprises, his first impulse was to set that person to work, irrespective of his or her earlier commitments. Such was his tenacity and force of personality that he seldom experienced difficulty in gaining his ends.

We have seen that by 1902 Farquhar had been in touch with the Y.M.C.A. in Calcutta for at least seven years, and that his work at Bhowanipur had come to the notice of Wilder and Campbell White.[4] It seems that it was on the recommendation of these and other Y.M.C.A. leaders that Mott approached Farquhar in January 1902 with the offer of a post as a Secretary in the College Department of the Calcutta Y.M.C.A., in which he would be free to concentrate on evangelistic work among students. In Farquhar's own words:

Here was an offer of the very work I was waiting for, perfect freedom to do it along my own lines, and the best field, not only in Calcutta, but actually the greatest in all Asia, to do the work in.[5]

Mott was in Calcutta for only a short time; Farquhar had to decide quickly. On January 15 he wrote to London:

I write to resign my appointment as a Missionary of the Society. I have accepted an offer made to me a few days ago by Mr. John R. Mott, to take up work in the College Department of the Calcutta Y.M.C.A. ... I am very sorry to leave the L.M.S. I had hoped to continue to work under the old Society. But this offer—complete freedom to do the work which I have asked for, in vain, in the L.M.S., for so many years—seems to me to be a door opened for me by my Master.[6]

---

[3] Fisher, *op. cit.*, pp. 79 ff., Mathews, *op. cit.*, pp. 332 ff. Mott himself wrote: "Recruiting is the most important single thing that I have to do. I have given the greater part of my life to discovering, enlisting and selecting men, opening up avenues of opportunity for them, helping to train them, raising money to support them ..." Quoted by Mathews, p. 332.

[4] Above, p. 152. It is perhaps not altogether without significance that Campbell White was Mott's brother-in-law.

[5] Farquhar to Thompson, 6.3.1902 (LMS Archives).

[6] Farquhar to Thompson, 15.1.1902. See also *Minutes of LMS Eastern Committee (India Department)*, 10.2.1902, § 4—the meeting at which his resignation was accepted (LMS Archives).

Farquhar's resignation caused near-consternation, both in Calcutta and London. Missionaries wrote, deploring his "loss";[7] Thompson tried to persuade him to change his mind;[8] letters passed back and forth, discussing the educational situation, and asking whether Farquhar might not have been right after all.[9] But little was achieved. Farquhar's plans were not put into practice in Bhowanipur, nor was it possible at this stage to effect a reversal of his decision. "To draw back now", he wrote, "would be to make the grand refusal, to run away from the opportunity of my life."[1]

As far as his new post was concerned, he anticipated having no educational work to do. He recognized that there must be a considerable amount of organizing and secretarial work to be overtaken, but reflected that, as there were already four secretaries in the College Department, he was not likely to be greatly troubled by that side of the situation. Although events were to prove that his earlier expectations were no altogether justified, the original intention was that he should devote his entire time to (1) evangelistic work, Bible classes and personal interviews, (2) literature.

Concerning the Y.M.C.A. itself, doubts had been expressed as to whether the non-denominationalism of the Association, and its avowed liberalism[2] might not seriously compromise Farquhar's own intellectual integrity. Farquhar's answer to this objection is indicative, not only of the standing of the Y.M.C.A. itself, but also of the Y.M.C.A. in relation to the ordinary missionary. To quote Farquhar's own words, "The type of man I have met here in Y.M.C.A. work is far above the average missionary: Campbell White, Wilder, Wilbert White, Mott, Anderson of Bombay, McConoughy, are all giants."[3]

These words were not unnecessary. There was at this time, and there continued to be, as we shall see later,[4] a good deal of bad feeling against the Y.M.C.A. in Calcutta, and in fact in many parts

---

[7] W. R. Le Quesne to G. Cousins, 16.1.1902 and 27.2.1902; J. H. Brown to Thompson, 4.2.1902 (LMS Archives).

[8] Thompson to Farquhar, 7.2.1902 and 14.2.1902 (LMS Archives).

[9] *Calcutta D.C. Minute* 22.1.1902; A. P. Begg to Thompson, 23.1.1902, 6.2.1902; Thompson to Begg, 14.3.1902; Le Quesne to Cousins, 6.3.1902 (LMS Archives).

[1] Farquhar to Thompson, 6.3.1902 (LMS Archives).

[2] Organizational, not theological liberalism is meant. The YMCA at this time was still firmly Evangelical; see below, pp. 175 ff.

[3] Farquhar to Thompson, 6.3.1902 (LMS Archives).

[4] Below, p. 242 n. 10.

of the world. Wardlaw Thompson, for example, when he heard of Farquhar's resignation, confessed that, had the offer come from "some well-established Society with a continuity of policy and the power to carry it out", he would have been far less apprehensive. But the Y.M.C.A. was suspect. It lacked history and tradition: there was no telling what its position might be in a few years' time. As for its leaders, although Campbell White was above suspicion, Thompson would not care "to be dependent upon some of those who are influential in Y.M.C.A. circles in this country". Worst of all, the Calcutta Y.M.C.A. was of American origin.[5]

Farquhar recognized that this prejudice existed, and that there was perhaps some ground for it. The Y.M.C.A. was intended to be an auxiliary to the churches, and yet its activities were often far more congenial than those offered in the churches themselves; its outlook was wider; the result was that it sometimes absorbed young men who would otherwise have been of great value to the individual churches. But on the other hand, the Y.M.C.A. in America had taken hold of university undergraduates in a way which it had never been able to do in Europe. As a mission from students to students, on an Evangelical basis, it had considerable appeal; and it was this side of its activity which was represented in India. We shall, however, return to this topic.

There is very little which is obscure about the workings of Farquhar's mind in the course of events which we have related. He most certainly did not leave the L.M.S. in a fit of disappointment, angry because a private scheme of his was not carried out. Nor had the undeniable personal tensions between Farquhar and certain of his senior colleagues very much to contribute to the final result. The crux of the matter lay in the policy followed by the L.M.S.[6]

---

[5] Cf. above, p. 152 n. 6.

[6] The lines of this policy were determined very largely by financial considerations. The "forward movement" (above, p. 148 n. 4) had placed great strain on the Society's finances. Farquhar's resignation caused a serious debate to take place on this matter of policy. Thompson wrote to Begg: "The subject is so vital and such changes [as those which Farquhar had proposed] would be so radical, that we cannot afford to do things hastily. Unfortunately the opinion expressed in the Minute you forwarded to the Board, while very valuable, seems to force us to the conclusion that we have come to a parting of the roads ..." 17.10.1902 (LMS Archives). Things went on for a time as before, but in 1909, the college ceased to teach to degree standards, and became an Intermediate Arts college. It was closed altogether in 1918.

in face of a changing and developing situation in which nationalism, both political and religious, was the chief factor.

This is to me by far the greatest matter in the mission field of Bengal at this time. It is a most serious question of policy, nay, a tremendous fact, that we must lay hold of and deal with, on pain of being flung aside as useless in the fierce religious struggle we are now engaged in.[7]

Early Literary Work

We have seen that the terms on which Farquhar was offered a position as a Y.M.C.A. Secretary intended that he should divide his time largely between "direct" evangelistic work and literature. We have so far been concerned mainly with the first of these categories, and have said nothing about Farquhar's literary work during these years at Bhowanipur, since the main significance of the period lies in evangelism rather than literature. But Farquhar's early written work, though modest in extent, must not be overlooked. It furnishes us with a number of valuable indications of the way in which his mind was working at this time. From the years before 1900 we have only one paper, that on *The Higher Education of Christians in Bengal* (1896); but in 1900 Farquhar published his first book, *The Crossbearer*, a school commentary on St. Matthew's Gospel; and three separate essays survive, dated 1901: *Christ and the Gospels*, *Criticism and Christianity* and *The Science of Religion as an Aid to Apologetics*. In addition there is the text of a paper on *Great Religious Books*, prepared to be read before the Calcutta Tract and Book Society but never delivered; it is undated, but appears to be from the years around the turn of the century, and so we include it here.

Christian Higher Education

In *The Higher Education of Christians in Bengal*[8] Farquhar discussed the possibility of establishing an interdenominational Christian Institution of higher education in Bengal. The college education of Indian Christians, as distinct from that of Hindus, Farquhar regarded as being highly unsatisfactory, for a number of reasons. In

---

[7] Farquhar to Gaunt, 12.3.1902 (LMS Archives).

[8] A paper originally read before the Calcutta Missionary Conference in February 1896, and published, with revisions, in the *Indian Evangelical Review* for April 1896. We use pagination of the offprint.

the first place, the small proportion of Christians in college classes had led to the teaching—and Scripture teaching in particular—being given mainly with Hindus in mind. "The consequence is that the young Christian receives little or no help in religion or in morality from his regular college course."[9] And the situation which had come about during the mid-nineteenth century, in which Hindus were appointed to the teaching staffs of missionary colleges, and set to teach Christians, Farquhar characterized as "unnatural".[1] These defects in the system might be remedied by personal attention from missionaries, but missionary professors, teaching long hours, normally had no leisure to devote to their students. Higher "college" education had moreover failed to keep pace with primary and secondary education: Christian bodies frequently had no colleges to which they might send boys from their secondary schools; and where individual missionary bodies ran schools *and* colleges "for Christians only", the colleges were normally too small to be effective.

Such was the problem. Farquhar's proposal was

That there should be established in Calcutta an Interdenominational Institution, consisting of a High School and College, for Christians only, and that each one of the missions now at work in Bengal should provide one missionary to teach in the Institution.[2]

Whether or not the project belonged to the sphere of practical politics is strictly immaterial. Its significance for our purpose is, first of all, that it provides further evidence of the breadth of Farquhar's sympathies and his readiness for co-operation. He even went so far as to suggest that the proposed College might serve as an interdenominational centre for preliminary theological training, at which teaching might be given in such "neutral" subjects as Hebrew, Greek, Exegesis, Apologetics, Homilitics and Indian Religion, Philosophy and Literature—other, more controversial subjects being left in the hands of the denominational bodies.[3] And then secondly, we see that Farquhar is at this date still suspicious of Indian "speculation" in the Church. The Indian mind, he claimed, was very speculative, and the development of the Indian Church was bound to bring with it an increase in theological speculation.

---

[9] *Higher Education*, p. 3.
[1] How this situation arose is described above, p. 75.
[2] *Higher Education*, p. 8.
[3] *Ibid.*, p. 12 f.

This he felt to be dangerous. But the proposed College "would ...
be able to correct the evils of these theorisings, without hampering
freedom".[4] This is in striking contrast to the views expressed some
years later by another L.M.S. missionary, who looked forward to
the coming of "heresy" as an infallible sign of life in the Indian
Church. "A real live heresy asserting itself in the midst of our Indian
Christian orthodoxy, would be an incalculable blessing in the
stimulus it would give to indigenous thinking."[5] In 1896 Farquhar
was firmly on the side of orthodoxy.[6]

The Crossbearer

The essentials of Farquhar's theological position are to some
extent to be found in the pages of *The Crossbearer,* a commentary on some three-quarters of the English text of St. Matthew's
Gospel. In this book, completed whilst on furlough in 1899 and
published in the following year, Farquhar showed that despite his
lack of formal theological training he had managed to keep well
abreast of progress in exegetical studies. We shall however discuss
this point more fully below, particularly since in a commentary
of this kind the author had no call to discuss the "machinery" of
criticism; his object in writing was to meet the need of his Scripture
class for an up-to-date, reliable and straightforward introduction to
Matthew: in this he appears to have succeeded.

Commenting on the basic doctrines of Evangelical Christianity,
Farquhar expresses himself almost entirely in traditional terms. Thus
on the subject of the Death and Resurrection of Christ, he asserts
that "on the cross He [Christ] bore the sin of the world",[7] though
he declines to commit himself to any express theory as to *how* this
took place. But the Death of Christ "purchases" forgiveness[8]—a forgiveness conditional upon the individual's willingness to forgive
others.[9] The Resurrection is set forth as a plain statement of fact.
"If there had been no Resurrection, there would have been no
Christian Church ... Jesus rose from the dead, and the Christian
Church is the fruit of the Resurrection." Further, the Resurrection

---

[4] *Ibid.,* p. 14.
[5] Lucas, *Our Task in India* (1914), p. 159 f.
[6] Cf. below, p. 352 n. 6.
[7] *The Crossbearer* (1900), p. 116.
[8] *Ibid.,* p. 119.
[9] *Ibid.,* pp. 77, 99.

is "the divine seal set upon the work of Jesus as a whole ... the token that His death as a sacrifice for the sins of men has been accepted."[1]

The Christian Church is "a new Community, the Community of the Messiah, which would take the place of the old religious Community of Israel".[2] But there is no express statement of the relation between the visible and invisible Churches, nor of the relation of the Church to the Kingdom of God—a concept which Farquhar discusses separately. In the preaching of John the Baptist the Kingdom is already revealed as "sternly moral";[3] in Jesus it becomes "completely moral and spiritual".[4] It is thus related only indirectly to earthly order, since it produces character, not organization: its "citizens" are characterized by humility, purity, unworldliness, love and trust.[5] Not only does it come from heaven (as a spiritual manifestation), but returns to—"culminates in"—heaven.[6]

There is however a close connexion in the missionary situation between the Kingdom and the Church. For where the Kingdom is received, the Church must be entered. "To refuse baptism is to refuse to enter the Church, and to refuse to enter the Church is to break the religion of Jesus in two."[7] The nature of baptism is nowhere discussed, save as a confession of faith indispensable to the missionary Church.

One final point which is worth noting here is that Farquhar's commentary on Matt. 5.17 ("I have not come to destroy, but to fulfil") makes no mention of the fulfilment of any religion other than Judaism.[8] Hinduism is not discussed at all in this connexion—a significant fact in view of the later development of Farquahr's thought on the subject of Christian-Hindu relations.

---

[1] *Ibid.*, p. 120.
[2] *Ibid.*, p. 95.
[3] *Ibid.*, p. 62.
[4] *Ibid.*, p. 66 f.
[5] *Ibid.*, p. 99 f.
[6] *Ibid.*, p. 120.
[7] *Ibid.*, p. 121.
[8] Farquhar paraphrases the passage thus: "Do not imagine that I have come to destroy the authority of the Law or the Prophets: not destruction, but *completion* is My work. For I warn you most solemly that no single part of the Law can pass away, until all God's purposes therein have been fulfilled." And he comments: "a) Jesus came to fill up *the sketch of religion* given in the Law and the Prophets. b) The followers of Jesus must not rub out any of the lines of the sketch, since it forms the outline of *the completed picture.*" *Ibid.*, p. 71 (the italics are Farquhar's own).

The Crossbearer is not a treatise in systematic theology, and it is idle to treat it as though it were. The most we can gain from it is a very general indication of some of the ways in which Farquhar's thought moved, and of the basic conservatism of his theology. Ten years later he was to revise this commentary altogether, and republish it as *The College St. Matthew*. We shall compare the two versions in due course.[9]

Criticism and the Gospel

In 1901 Farquhar published three short articles, *Christ and the Gospels, Criticism and Christianity* and *The Science of Religion as an Aid to Apologetics*. The first two are in the form of open letters "to the thinking men of Calcutta"; the third appeared in the October, 1901, number of the *Harvest Field*. The three together are important as showing Farquhar's attitude to the theological thought of his time, and as a statement of the position at which he had arrived prior to leaving the L.M.S. It is not too much to say that the intellectual position expressed in these pamphlets was one which Farquhar never really relinquished. On the one hand they demonstrate the comparative breadth of his reading, and his acceptance of the fundamentals of the critical thought of his day; on the other they reveal his continued insistence on the Evangelical tenet of personal commitment to Jesus Christ. It was in this sense he was later able to call himself a "liberal evangelical" or "progressive conservative". He was "liberal" in his attitude to the problems of the Gospel and modern thought, his unreserved application of modern scientific method to religious matters,[1] and his emphasis on "the historical Jesus"; "evangelical" in the unchanged foundation of his Christian faith as a Gospel of personal, individual redemption.

Both elements are evident in the pamphlet *Christ and the Gospels*. This was written in answer to a type of anti-Christian propaganda common in late nineteenth-century India—a type which attempted to prove, often with the help of far-fetched arguments, that Jesus never lived, and that the Gospels were utterly fraudulent. Farquhar appeals to history; he marshals all the available evidence, from Jewish and Roman as well as Christian sources, to prove the historicity of Jesus. Similarly he quotes from his reading of Harnack,

---

[9] Cf. below, pp. 259 ff.
[1] Cf. Quick, *Liberalism, Modernism and Tradition* (1922), p. 1.

Zahn, Hastings, Moffatt, Hatch, Kennedy, Deissmann and other scholars to demonstrate that the Gospel accounts are in fact generally considered as essentially reliable. But he is no fundamentalist: the literal inspiration of the Scriptures he rejects summarily:

To us an inspired book is not one written by the finger of God, and miraculously handed to men, but a book written by a man under the ordinary conditions of history, only with the Holy Spirit working in his heart. An inspired book, we hold, cannot be known to be inspired by any outward authoritative declaration . . .[2]

His acceptance of the "liberal" position is complete, as he appeals for "the application of sound methods of criticism to Christian literature" and as he urges his readers to turn to the "real Jesus" (i.e. the historical Jesus): "Will you not study the Gospels, and try to understand the secret of this extraordinary influence?"[3]

This position is developed in *Criticism and Christianity*, which is an account of the impact of modern thought on the Christian faith. Here Farquhar presents the case for evolution as a working hypothesis, and the historical method as a basis of investigation. As far as history is concerned, "The history of a thing is its best, indeed its only real explanation. It is this that gives history its value to the modern mind." And evolution he calls "the Master Idea, which, more or less unconsciously, inspires historical students to-day".[4] Historical criticism, writes Farquhar, must be applied to everything which has its roots in the past. Christianity cannot be exempted. That is in fact what has happened in recent years. Rationalists and sceptics thought that history would undermine Christianity, but despite the vigour of the assault, Christianity has emerged unscathed.[5] The position of Christ in history has been confirmed, not weakened.

Discussing the conditions of human progress, Farquhar reveals for the first time a measure of reliance on Benjamin Kidd, whose *Social Evolution* had appeared in 1894.[6] However, he takes Kidd's argument a step further. Kidd had stressed morals based on "super-rational sanctions" as a *sine qua non* of progress; Farquhar writes:

---

[2] *Christ and the Gospels* (1901), p. 25.
[3] *Ibid.*, p. 27.
[4] *Criticism and Christianity* (1901), p. 2.
[5] *Ibid.*, p. 3.
[6] Above, p. 40 f.

The decisive factors in human progress are moral; and the moral influence of Christ to-day is infinitely greater than that of any other leader.[7]

Further, he quotes Kidd in support of the historicity of the Resurrection and the miracles of Jesus. Kidd had emphasized the non-rational, supernatural character of religion. "Is not supernaturalism the very life-breath of religion?" asks Farquhar.[8]

Nor is it surprising, in view of what we have seen of Farquhar's Oxford career, that his main authority for the statement that thanks to modern historical research Christ was better known in 1901 than at any time since the Apostolic age, is A. M. Fairbairn.[9]

In these two pamphlets the point at issue was the nature of the Christian faith. In *The Science of Religion as an Aid to Apologetics* Farquhar makes the first of many appeals to the missionary to take a scientific interest in the religious conflict around him, a conflict of which he is at least in part the cause. Farquhar begins by taking up the question of apologetics, which he regarded as a self-evident need. "If the first duty of a Christian is to hold up Christ to the world", he writes, "surely the second is to remove difficulties and to stimulate the intellect by a reasoned apologetic."[1] There will always—so he reasoned—be difficulties to be removed and intellects to be stimulated. The only question is what form this inevitable apologetic is to take. Two possibilities—the appeal to authority and the appeal to history—he dismisses, the first as being inconsistent with the age, the second as being irrelevant to the Indian mind. What then remains?

His answer is highly suggestive, not only in this context, but for the whole of his later development as a leader of missionary thought.

---

[7] *Criticism and Christianity*, p. 4.

[8] *Ibid.*, p. 7; cf. Kidd, *Social Evolution* (1894), pp. 107–113.

[9] Fairbairn, *The Place of Christ in Modern Theology* (1893), pp. 3, 19. Cf. above, pp. 127 ff. A slightly later article covering practically the same ground as *Criticism and Christianity*, and entitled "The Church and Biblical Criticism", was published in the liberal Indian journal *East and West* I: 12 (Oct. 1902), pp. 1313–1321. On this occasion Farquhar made a powerful plea for higher criticism, pointing out that most of the leading British "higher critics" were orthodox and practising Christians (p. 1316). In an interesting aside he notes that the Ritschlian school "is hardly recognized as orthodox in Britain" (ibid.)—a judgment which may be paralleled with Fairbairn's refusal to concern himself with Ritschlianism (above, p. 128).

[1] "The Science of Religion as an Aid to Apologetics", in *HF* XII N.S. (Oct. 1901), p. 369. On the term "apologetics", see above, p. 16 f., and below, p. 255 f.

We want a criticism [he wrote] that will set Christianity clearly and distinctly in its relations with other faiths.[2]

The significance of this statement cannot be stressed too highly,
since it poses the problem to which Farquhar was to devote the
remainder of his missionary career to finding an answer. In fact
The Crown of Hinduism is his own answer, twelve years later, to
this very question.

It goes without saying that Farquhar here allows no approach
but the *historical* approach. The idea of "the Science of Religion"
had been current since Max Müller coined the term in 1867; but it
had not yet reached the missions in its full significance. In Farquhar's
view it nevertheless held out "boundless possibilities", since it
provided a factual basis on which the student of Christianity and
other faiths might work. In this article there follows a short account
of the rise of the science, which we need not consider in detail; it
ends with an appeal to missionaries to devote themselves to a study
of religions, the better to be able to fulfil their calling. This was a
theme to which Farquhar was to return again and again, notably in
Missionary Study of Hinduism.[3]

The final paper in this group, *Great Religious Books,* is a brief
consideration of the role of high-class literature in the religious
context—again a topic which was to occupy much of Farquhar's
time and energy in later years. The argument need not however
detain us, save in one particular. Farquhar is discussing the effect
of "great" literature (and particularly "great" religious literature)
on its readers, and suggests that even one book of this kind would
be of inestimable value in the evangelization of India. But such
books are not easily come by. The demands are high. A book, in
order to qualify as "great" must be well written, since a book that
is to persuade must first of all attract. Its author must have considerable imaginative and spiritual gifts. But most important, it
must be suited to its readers, both in point of form and matter. Here
we must quote *in extenso*:

... we shall never write a book that will capture the Hindu mind, until
we not only understand Hindu thought, but so sympathize with it in its
various manifestations as to thoroughly appreciate whatever of good and
true it has brought to Hindu life. Scorn never yet led men to truth; only

---

[2] *Ibid.*
[3] Below, pp. 206 ff.

humility and self-distrust and a passion for knowledge can do that. Let us beware of despising Hindu thought. Doubtless it is mostly error; but God did not leave Himself without a witness in India.[4]

Summing up, we have seen in this chapter, besides the practical situation in which Farquhar was introduced to the Indian religious conflict, and his choice of the Y.M.C.A. as a field of practical missionary work, the emergence of certain firm theological and missiological convictions. These were to gain in depth and intensity with the years, as our later account will show. His mature Evangelical Christian faith proved to have been undisturbed by modern critical research; indeed, before leaving the service of the L.M.S. he had come to accept the conditions of the scientific method without question, and also the essential validity of the evolutionist position. He had come to demand historical investigation as the only reliable pathway to truth and understanding. He had come to realize the need for a comprehensive theory setting forth the relationship of Christianity to Hinduism, though he had as yet had no chance to do any serious work on this problem. And most important, he had come to the fundamental realization that sympathy must replace iconoclasm in literature, for without sympathy the truth must be distorted and listeners will invariably be alienated.

We shall see in our next chapter, which deals with Farquhar's first period as a Y.M.C.A. Secretary, how each of these basic requirements came to be met in his own literary work, and later in the work of those fellow-missionaries to whom he communicated something of his enthusiasm.

---

[4] It is this last sentence which marks the offprint from which this quotation is taken as pre-1902. In the circumstances, since its source has not been traced, no page references can be given.

CHAPTER 6

The Y.M.C.A. and the Hindu Renaissance, 1902–1905

In this chapter we shall examine some aspects of J. N. Farquhar's first years as a Y.M.C.A. Secretary in Calcutta. In the previous chapter we saw how he was brought into contact with the Association movement, and how he came to adopt its methods as an attempt to resolve the practical difficulties in which he was placed as an educationalist and evangelist in a missionary college run on traditional lines. But the Bhowanipur Branch of the Y.M.C.A. was a spare-time venture, and had had to be organized and run alongside Farquhar's regular work in the classroom. It had given an interesting indication of the role which a movement of this independent type might be expected to play, given favourable circumstances, in the Evangelical missionary enterprise; but it was strictly limited in scope. From 1902 onward, Farquhar was engaged in full-time Y.M.C.A. work. John R. Mott's invitation had given him the opportunity of examining and testing the effectiveness of the movement in a wider context, among the students of Calcutta as a whole.

Our first task will be to examine the position occupied by the Association in the Protestant missionary situation of Calcutta.[1] We shall look briefly at its basic theological presuppositions, and review the methods used by the Association in its attempt to reach the students of Calcutta. We must examine the developing use of literature in Y.M.C.A. work, and observe the independent role which Farquhar came to fill as a writer during these years. This will involve an examination, first, of his work as editor of the monthly journal the *Inquirer,* and secondly, of the three books written as a result of his study of the *Bhagavad Gītā.* But before we turn to these written works, we must attempt to gain a picture of Y.M.C.A. work in Calcutta at the time of Farquhar's accession.

---

[1] This is dictated by the fact that Calcutta was Farquhar's main sphere of work during these years. It should not be taken to imply that YMCA work in other cities—Madras for example—is uninteresting or unimportant.

The Calcutta Y.M.C.A.

We have earlier had occasion to mention the early history of the Y.M.C.A. movement in Calcutta, and there is no need to repeat what we said there,[2] beyond stressing once more the work of J. Campbell White. The College Branch building, completed in 1897,[3] was opened as a result of White's efforts, which a contemporary writer described as "unique, unconventional, specific and to the point".[4] The Branch became, by the turn of the century, a centre of varied activities, which we shall discuss in more detail shortly. During the year 1900–1901 there were 768 meetings of all kinds held, with a total attendance of 32,000. Frequent Bible classes were organized, both for Christians and non-Christians; thus 214 non-Christian Bible classes attracted 845 participants, and 107 Christian Bible classes 1201 participants.[5] On the national level—for the Indian Y.M.C.A. also had its headquarters in Calcutta[6]—the years between 1899 and 1902 saw a sharp increase, both in numbers of affiliated organizations and in membership.[7] The Association as a whole gave Farquhar the impression of being a lively and forward-looking organization. "I have watched the work here for years from the outside (he wrote) and have had some idea of its scope and depth, but my experience these four months has led me to see that the opportunity here is much greater than I ever dreamed it was."[8] The site of White's College Branch building he called "simply magnificent", and he confessed himself impressed by the work done by White in laying the foundations of the Calcutta Association work.[9] In fact he went so far as to claim that the College Y.M.C.A. occupied a

---

[2] Above, p. 152.

[3] Latourette, *World Service* (1957), p. 111.

[4] An anonymous writer quoted from the *Congregationalist* in *FM* VIII: 2 (April 1901), p. 11.

[5] *Ibid.*, p. 8.

[6] For a list of officers and account of working methods, see Wilder, "The Indian National Association of Young Men's Christian Associations", in *FM* IX: 3 (July 1902), pp. 15 ff.

[7] During the past two years the general Associations have increased from 104, with a membership of 4275, to 110, with a membership of 4504, a gain of 229, and the Student Associations have increased from twenty-seven in 1899, with a membership of 990, to forty-one in 1901, with a membership of 2052, an increase in two years of 1062." *Ibid.*, p. 17.

[8] YMCA Secretaries' Reports: J. N. Farquhar 1902, p. 62 (YMCA Hist. Lib.). Hereinafter *Report 1902*.

[9] *Ibid.*

strategic position in the Calcutta of 1902 similar to that of Alexander Duff's original institution in the Calcutta of 1830.[1] Indeed the basic strategy involved was similar—evangelism directed at the upper classes, reinforced in practice by experience with similar methods among students in the West, and particularly in America.

Farquhar's satisfaction with his new post was fully reciprocated by his new colleagues, the American Secretaries of the Calcutta Y.M.C.A. Previously they had known him by reputation, both as a scholar and evangelist: now they welcomed him as a colleague, and looked upon his transfer as an indication of the esteem in which Calcutta missionaries as a whole held Y.M.C.A. work in the city. "It is very cheering to us", wrote General Secretary J. Campbell White, "that one of the strongest and most successful missionaries in this part of India, Professor J. N. Farquhar, M.A., has just resigned from his Society in order to become one of the Secretaries of the Student Branch. He is a tower of strength, both intellectual and spiritual."[2] And Guy W. Sarvis, another American Secretary on the Calcutta staff, reported to the International Committee in New York that Farquhar's coming had filled a manifest need. He called Farquhar "invaluable" in work among students, and wrote: "He has been long connected with mission work and brings to the Association the benefit of that experience ..."[3] Farquhar in his turn was personally appreciative of his new colleagues. Writing to the Foreign Secretary of the L.M.S. in London, Wardlaw Thompson, he stated as his conviction that the type of man he had met in Y.M.C.A. work was "far above the average missionary".[4] He was, it seems, referring to intellectual attainment (most of the American Secretaries having been drawn, via the Student Volunteer Movement, from American colleges and universities), but there may also have been overtones of personal and spiritual attainment involved. This is however a question which we do not propose to discuss here. The only slight observation we might make is that Farquhar's last years with the L.M.S. were not made easier by certain personal tensions, and he may have looked upon the Y.M.C.A. men as being above such things.

---

[1] *Ibid.*, p. 65.
[2] Circular letter, dated 27.2.1902 (YMCA Hist. Lib.).
[3] YMCA Secretaries' Reports: Guy W. Sarvis 1902 (YMCA Hist. Lib.).
[4] J. N. Farquhar to R. W. Thompson, 6.3.1902 (LMS Archives).

Be that as it may, Farquhar regarded his release from college work as providential. Freed from a situation he had come to look upon as intolerable, and placed in a congenial environment, he was prepared for constructive work. The question at once arose: What pattern should that work take? Was Farquhar's freedom to be absolute, or circumscribed by the Y.M.C.A. methods then in general use, and by the terms of his appointment?[5] We shall examine these basic methods in turn, but first something must be said about the theological basis of the movement within which Farquhar had come to work.

Theological Basis of the Indian Y.M.C.A.

This is not the occasion to give a detailed critical account of theological developments in the world Y.M.C.A. movement down to the turn of the century.[6] There are, however, one or two points which must be borne in mind in our dealings with the Indian Y.M.C.A. during the pre-1914 period.

The doctrinal foundations of the Y.M.C.A. were essentially Evangelical.[7] The "Paris Basis" adopted in 1855 attempted to define the purpose of the new Association around two foci, discipleship and evangelism. It was this basis which was accepted, virtually without question, by the European Y.M.C.A. movement during the period we are discussing. The "Paris Basis" was as follows:

The Young Men's Christian Associations seek to unite those young men who, regarding Jesus Christ as their Saviour according to the Holy Scriptures, desire to be His disciples in their faith and in their life, and to associate their efforts for the extension of His kingdom amongst young men.[8]

It will be noticed that although due emphasis was laid on the priority of the Holy Scriptures, nothing was actually said about their interpretation. Further, although a clause stressed the "desire" of members for discipleship, no attempt was made to express in words

---

[5] He was to concentrate on (i) seeing inquirers, and (ii) literary work. See above, p. 161.

[6] Hopkins, *History of the Y.M.C.A. in North America* (1951), pp. 361 ff.; Shedd (ed.), *History of the World's Alliance of Young Men's Christian Associations* (1955), *passim*, under *Paris Basis*.

[7] In the sense in which we have defined the term in Ch. 1, above, pp. 25 ff.

[8] Hopkins, *op. cit.*, p. 78.

the mode of that discipleship. Nor were intending members required to subscribe to any declaration of belief, either on the nature of the Divinity of Christ, or on the Atonement.

The Paris Basis was felt by many American Protestants to be too vague. It left too many questions unanswered in a period when close definition was held to be of importance, due to the intense rivalries which existed between Protestant Churches on the American continent.[9] At the Detroit Convention of 1868 it was therefore determined to limit at least the control of the Association by some further definition. A resolution was put forward, laying down that henceforth only those who fulfilled certain conditions could vote, or be eligible for office, in the Association. The resolution limited control to "those who profess to love and publicly avow their faith in Jesus, the Redeemer, as divine, and who testify their faith by becoming and remaining members of Churches held to be Evangelical . . .".[1]

This gave rise to a further question: What constitutes an Evangelical Church? Once more the need was for further definition. At the Portland Convention of the following year, 1869, a closer definition was formulated, and it was this statement, in conjunction with that of 1868, which served throughout our period, and incidentally did much to determine the patterns of work followed by the Indian Y.M.C.A. in the crisis years. It will be of value to have the "Portland Basis" in mind when the American Y.M.C.A. is being discussed. The following words were added:

And we hold those Churches to be Evangelical which, maintaining the Holy Scriptures to be the only infallible rule of faith and practice, do believe in the Lord Jesus Christ (the only begotten of the Father, King of Kings, and Lord of Lords, in whom dwelleth the fulness of the Godhead bodily, and who was made sin for us, though knowing no sin, bearing our sins in His body on the tree), as the only name under heaven given among men whereby we must be saved from everlasting punishment.[2]

It must be emphasized once more that the Indian Y.M.C.A. was organized, from the 1880's on, from America; its Secretaries were appointed by the International Committee in New York; its theological basis was strictly and explicitly Evangelical. The movement

---

[9] *Ibid.,* p. 368.
[1] *Ibid.,* p. 364.
[2] *Ibid.,* p. 366.

to which Farquhar was now attached was, at least in theory, committed to the Holy Scriptures as its infallible rule of faith and practice, and to a substitutionary doctrine of the Atonement. In this it was of course at one with practically the whole of the nineteenth-century Protestant missionary movement; where it differed was in its ability to accept and make use of advances in Biblical scholarship and criticism generally, and the rapidity with which it assimilated certain aspects of the emerging "liberalism" which we have discussed in Chapter One.[3] It will be clear that Farquhar's position was already rather more advanced than was compatible with a literal acceptance of this doctrinal basis.[4]

Relations between the Y.M.C.A. and the equally Evangelical Student Volunteer Movement were of course intimate. Many leaders held prominent posts in both movements. John R. Mott is the most obvious example; Robert P. Wilder was another,[5] being both a founder-member of the S.V.M. and a prominent member of the staff of the Indian Y.M.C.A. at this time.[6] In fact the Indian Y.M.C.A. *was* the Indian Student Movement, affiliated to the World's Student Christian Federation, throughout the pre-war years. Student Movement reports supplied to the W.S.C.F. conferences of 1905 (Zeist), 1907 (Tokyo) and 1909 (Oxford) come from the Indian Y.M.C.A.

Bearing this in mind, it is only natural to find the Indian Y.M.C.A. adopting the S.V.M. and W.S.C.F. watchword ("The evangelization of the world in this generation") as its own watchword. The decision was made at the Sixth National Convention of December 1901, the same convention which determined to press practical evangelistic work more energetically than formerly as the basis of the work of the Association.[7]

It was this famous watchword, rather than the Portland basis, which served as the "ideological" foundation for the work of the

---

[3] Above, pp. 39 ff.
[4] Above, pp. 167 ff.
[5] For Wilder's attempt to have Farquhar set apart for student work, see above, p. 151.
[6] Wilder Braisted, *In This Generation* (1941), *passim*.
[7] Wilder, "The Indian National Union of Young Men's Christian Associations", in *FM* IX: 3 (July 1902), p. 17 f. A further interesting point was that the Convention resolved to take steps "to secure and train an increased number of Indian secretaries". At this time the only Indian on the national staff was V. S. Azariah; see Hodge, *Bishop Azariah of Dornakal* (1946), p. 15.

Y.M.C.A. in India during our period. The conflicts which had brought the Portland Basis into existence had little or no practical significance in the Indian situation. The pressing need was for expansion. Hence a generation of evangelists accepted a Watchword which committed them to precisely this programme, and at the same time aligned them with the Student Christian Movements of the world, and particularly with the energetic Student Volunteer Movement. Whether the theological presuppositions of the old declaration were assumed to underly the Watchword is a moot point. The theological climate of opinion was changing rapidly, and the Y.M.C.A. was becoming more "liberal". But not until after the first world war was the Declaration replaced.[8] The emphasis of the period in India was practical, rather than theoretical, and the Y.M.C.A. secretaries concentrated rather on the preaching of the Evangelical doctrine of personal commitment than on the theological basis of that doctrine. Definition was for the time being laid aside in the interests of action.

Evangelization in Practice

The coming of Farquhar to the staff of the Calcutta Y.M.C.A. prompted Campbell White to call for a discussion on the whole of the student work in Calcutta, the object being to define a policy which might serve as a guide for future work.[9] The point at issue was *method*. The question uppermost in many minds was raised by the new patterns Association work was taking in America.[1] Should the Indian Y.M.C.A. regard itself as a permanent evangelistic agency —in other words, as a missionary society working among young men— or as an "association of men" only? The Calcutta staff seem to have been unanimously in favour of the former alternative, though it was agreed that more emphasis might with advantage be placed on internal work.[2] At this time, to take only one example, Bible classes

---

[8] Hopkins, *op cit.*, pp. 519 ff. Cf. Tatlow, *The Story of the Student Christian Movement of Great Britain and Ireland* (1933), pp. 624 ff.

[9] "We are planning to have the best part of several days next week given to a thorough discussion of our whole student work here in Calcutta. It seems an opportune time now when Farquhar has joined the force ... to carefully review the work and if possible get a clearly defined policy with reference to it." J. Campbell White to J. R. Mott, 19.6.1902 (YMCA Hist. Lib.).

[1] Hopkins, *op. cit.*, p. 452 ff.

[2] YMCA Secretaries' Reports: Guy W. Sarvis 1902 (YMCA Hist. Lib.).

for Hindus outnumbered those for Christians by as much as five to one.[3] It was agreed that this was quite in order, according as it did both with the basic aims of the Association in India, and with the needs of the religious situation of the time. "There can be little question", wrote one of the Calcutta Secretaries, "of the need of just such a body as the Y.M.C.A. *in evangelistic work* under the present religious conditions."[4]

Y.M.C.A. evangelistic work at this time may be classified under four heads: preaching, Bible classes, private interviews and literature. These we shall now discuss in turn.

1. *Preaching*

The public preaching of the Gospel occupied a position of importance in the Calcutta Y.M.C.A., as indeed in all Protestant missions of the period. The Y.M.C.A. Secretary was expected to be an evangelist, and not merely an organizer. Each Secretary of the College St. Y.M.C.A. preached on an average two or three times a week, either in the open air or indoors, often to difficult audiences.[5] Occasionally special series of meetings were organized—evangelistic "campaigns" aimed directly at a particular class. John R. Mott's student meetings of 1902 provide a case in point.

Mott's meetings were held in the Overtoun Hall of the Calcutta Y.M.C.A., but had been planned by a joint sub-committee of the Calcutta Missionary Conference and the Student Branch of the Y.M.C.A. The Chairman was an Indian, Mr. Kali Charan Banurji,[6] and a choir of Indian Christian students led the singing. Mott's emphasis was on personal commitment. Beginning with "The Attitude of Educated Young Men towards Christianity", he went on to speak of "Purity, Social and Personal", and concluded with an address on "The Battle-Ground of Young Men", after which a large number of men signed cards expressing a desire "to follow Jesus Christ as personal Saviour up to their present light".[7]

[3] Thus between January 1 and March 31, 1900, there were 59 daily Bible Classes for non-Christian students, with an aggregate attendance of 570, and only eleven Bible Classes for Christians, with an aggregate attendance of 209. See table given by White, "Seven Years in Calcutta", in *FM* VII: 3 (Sept. 1900), p. 5.

[4] YMCA Secretaries' Reports: Guy W. Sarvis 1902 (YMCA Hist. Lib.).

[5] *Ibid.*

[6] Registrar of Calcutta University, and at that time Chairman of the YMCA Student Branch.

[7] Barber, "Mr. Mott's Visit to Calcutta", in *FM* IX: 2 (April 1902), pp. 27 ff.

These meetings were typical on at least two levels. First, typical of Y.M.C.A. methods. The object of this type of missionary work was to bring the individual to a sense of sin and knowledge of salvation. The "big meeting" method continued to be used throughout the period for this purpose. But secondly, they were typical in the difficulties they raised.

It was recognized that the hardest task remained to be done after the "campaign".[8] But the real measure of the task was not immediately apparent. Farquhar, writing to Mott, called his campaign "a wonderful piece of work", but was puzzled to account for the lack of result. There seemed to have been "much genuine conviction" in the minds of many of the young men present, but it had led to no apparent conversions.[9] But at the same time Farquhar had been long enough in India to be aware of the differences in attitude between the Indian and the European or American in religious matters: the educated Indian he knew to be able "to go a very long way indeed in expressing a personal interest in religious teaching without having the slightest idea of really adopting and following the teaching".[1] This criticism of those who came to hear Mott he also applied to those who regularly listened to outdoor addresses given by Y.M.C.A. Secretaries.

Discussing Y.M.C.A. evangelistic methods in his 1902 report, Farquhar placed preaching in the open air and in the hall first, as "our first line of attack on the non-Christian educated community around us".[2] He regarded indoor work as "useful", but the open-air work as being of greater significance. College Square, which was near the Y.M.C.A. building, was a regular meeting-place for educated Indians, and there the Y.M.C.A. Secretaries had their preaching stand. Most listeners (and there were commonly between a hundred and two hundred Hindus in their "congregation") were attentive, but Farquhar was not over-optimistic. Again the problem lay in the attitude of the Indian listener than in the method used by the preacher; for

the educated Indian believes that he will get moral and spiritual good from listening to religious addresses no matter of what religion the speaker may be, and many regard such listening as actually meritorious.[3]

---

[8] *Ibid.*, p. 29.
[9] J. N. Farquhar to J. R. Mott, 16.11.1902 (YMCA Hist. Lib.).
[1] *Ibid.*
[2] *Report 1902*, p. 62.
[3] *Ibid.*

As long as the missionaries could be sure of a receptive audience, this method was at least potentially valuable. But increasing political tension came to have an adverse effect on open-air preaching.[4]

It is noteworthy that Farquhar laid down two conditions for success in preaching to the non-Christian. The first was central Christian proclamation.[5] Controversy Farquhar regarded as dangerous and sub-Christian—a view he continued to hold throughout his time in India.[6] The second condition was understanding—of the Indian, his habits of mind and the conditions of his life and thought. "The better we get to understand our constituency and the more carefully we prepare our addresses for this open-air work", he wrote, "the deeper and more lasting will the effects be."[7]

The twofold demand for centrality and sympathy extended to the second of the Y.M.C.A.'s main evangelistic methods, the method of Bible study.

2. Bible Classes

It is hardly necessary to motivate the priority of Bible teaching in an Evangelical mission such as the Y.M.C.A. of this period. The Bible had its given place as the supreme rule of faith and conduct, and it was an accepted part of mission strategy to place the Scriptures in the hands of non-Christians as soon as possible—whether in vernacular translation or in English. Since the 1830's Scripture teaching had been an essential part of the curriculum of every missionary institute of higher education. Farquhar himself had taken an active part in such teaching, and had kept abreast of developments in Biblical criticism as far as circumstances allowed. In 1900 he had published his elementary commentary on St. Matthew's Gospel, and in 1901 a pamphlet on *Criticism and Christianity,* in which problems of Gospel criticism were discussed in relation to the historical person of Christ. Both were written from the teacher's standpoint.[8]

We have seen how Bible teaching in Bhowanipur had been

---

[4] See below, Ch. 7, *passim.*

[5] "Whenever some great truth from the Gospel of Christ or some deep lesson from his death is being pressed home one can see that members of the audience are deeply moved." *Report 1902,* p. 62.

[6] This is perhaps most clearly expressed in his paper on *The Study of Hinduism;* see below, p. 206 f.

[7] *Report 1902, loc. cit.*

[8] Above, pp. 167 ff.

hampered, by the pressure of secular teaching and by Hindu unwillingness to listen: the situation in the Y.M.C.A. was rather different. Instead of the Scripture lesson being directed to an entire
class of youths, irrespective of their wishes, the Bible classes were
conducted in smaller groups, on an entirely voluntary basis. There
were Bible classes for Christians, and for non-Christians, conducted
for the most part separately. Farquhar felt that the fact of fifteen
to twenty Hindus coming to study St. John's Gospel was a most
encouraging experience.[9] Most of those attending were young clerks,
but there were also a number of students and middle-aged men who
attended regularly. On their motives, Farquhar was not prepared to
commit himself too deeply.[1]

Farquhar had no personal doubt as to the value of the work
done in such classes. Writing in 1904, he pointed out that in order
to draw a man from Hinduism to Christianity, a long course of
training was necessary. The first stage must always be the reading
of the Bible, followed by direct personal contact with "an earnest
Christian".[2] Much of the groundwork was however done in these
Y.M.C.A. non-Christian Bible classes.

In the Bible classes, as in preaching, the same basic requirements
obtained: centrality and sympathy. Farquhar observed that in his
experience the greatest attention and interest was aroused by "the
faithful exposition of the great truths of Christianity".[3] And he
believed that the classes might exercise much influence, provided the
missionaries were prepared to study the men and prepare their
work with a view to their particular needs.[4]

The Bible class method of evangelization could not be regarded
as an end in itself. We have seen that Farquhar recommended
personal contact as the next stage. Elsewhere, writing on basic
method, he stressed the value of private interviews, as the stage at
which the missionary could come to close quarters with the young

---

[9] *Report 1902*, p. 63.
[1] "So far as one can judge the majority attend from true religious motives
but a proportion of the men come merely from intellectual interest in the
religious questions discussed, while a few come from mere curiosity or to benefit
by the English they hear." *Report 1902, loc. cit.*
[2] J. N. Farquhar to J. L. Macpherson, 12.12.1902 (YMCA Hist. Lib.).
[3] *Report 1902*, p. 63.
[4] *Ibid.*

men they were attempting to influence, and could form some estimate of the value of the work that was being done.[5]

3. *Private Interviews*

Farquhar enjoyed something of a reputation among Calcutta missionaries in the field of personal evangelism.[6] He himself regarded the personal interview as of inestimable value in missionary work, and tended to set this method on a considerably higher level than classroom work. Although he recognized that it could be a "severe test" to the young Hindu, his own personal view was that it enabled the missionary to see much more clearly where a man stood in relation to the Christian faith than the collective methods of classroom and platform.[7] Sympathy of course was a *sine qua non*; further, the Evangelical missionary must go as soon as possible to the Bible and its "living verities" in order to bring the inquirer into direct contact with the Christian message in its most concentrated form.

It will be clear that the value of this method depended almost entirely on the pastoral qualifications of the missionary concerned, and on the degree of personal trust between the Hindu and the missionary. The crisis years saw a progressive diminution in the practical value of the private interview, the Hindu often being suspicious of the motives of the Western missionary.

4. *Literature*

The fourth basic method used by the Calcutta Y.M.C.A. was the method of literature; it was to assume more and more importance as Hindu opposition intensified.

In 1902 the literature published by the Y.M.C.A. (as indeed by Evangelical missions as a whole) was extremely limited in its range and quality.[8] It was a generally recognized fact that Christian li-

---

[5] *Ibid.*

[6] See above, p. 151.

[7] "I need not say how exceedingly valuable this personal work is. In the quiet of one's own room, with only one soul to deal with, it is often possible to lead that soul on in a short time much further than many hours of teaching in a class would do." *Report 1902*, p. 63.

[8] See *Report of the Conference of the World's Student Christian Federation held at Eisenach, Germany, July 13-17, 1898* (1898), p. 98 f., and *Report of the Conference of the World's Student Christian Federation held at Zeist, Holland, May 3-7, 1905* (1905), p. 170 f. It will be seen from these how little literary work was being done at this time by the Indian YMCA.

terature *might* exercise wide influence; but little had been done to publish books and pamphlets suitable for the educated classes. There were the Tract Societies of Calcutta and Madras; and we have described some of the publications of the Oxford Mission to Calcutta.[9] But Farquhar was not satisfied that they were meeting the needs of the situation. At this time the Y.M.C.A. had only their monthly paper the *Young Men of India,* with its supplement the *Inquirer,* which was devoted largely to the answering of questions on religious subjects, and was issued free to anyone in India, Burma or Ceylon who wished to receive a copy.

One of the conditions of Farquhar's appointment to the Y.M.C.A. staff was that he should devote himself to literature, and one of his first tasks was therefore to take over the editorship of the *Inquirer.* It seems to have been this work which gave him most cause for satisfaction in his early Y.M.C.A. years. It is important that we should recognize why this was so. Farquhar himself stated plainly his reasons for pinning so much faith to literature as a method of missionary outreach, in his 1902 report. The Y.M.C.A. in Calcutta had been accustomed to concentrate on the non-Christian population in the immediate vicinity of its buildings—in short, to those men who could be reached by the three methods we have described. But Farquhar was dissatisfied with the situation as it stood, and wondered how it might be possible to widen the influence of the Association so as to touch the educated community of Calcutta, and the rest of Bengal.[1] This community he divided up into two groups: those whom he called "prepared souls"—men who had been educated in mission colleges, or who had at least some acquaintance with the Bible, or who had been introduced to the figure of Christ by the preaching of the Brāhma Samāj[2]—and the rest of the educated classes, who had not been "prepared" in any way.

---

[9] Above, pp. 90 ff.

[1] *Report 1902,* p. 65.

[2] Rām Mohan Ray (1772–1833), the founder of the Samāj, had a deep reverence for the person and teachings of Christ, and this was perpetuated by his successors, Keshab Chandra Sen and P. C. Mazoomdar. Farquhar points out that they "regarded Jesus as the eternal Son, but they lived the life of theists, following now one master, now another". *Modern Religious Movements in India* (1915), p. 68. Nevertheless the Samāj was well acquainted with the Bible (or parts of it) and Christian teaching. Cf. Datta, "Causes of the Expansion or Retrogression of Religions in India", in *IRM* III: 12 (Oct. 1914), p. 649: "To the Christian the Brahmo Samaj is the best expression of the spiritual instincts of modern India..." For a contemporary Brahmo statement, see Gupta, "The Christ-Ideal in the Brahmo Samaj", in *East and West* I: 13 (Nov. 1902), pp. 1434–1444.

The Y.M.C.A. Farquhar believed to be "the strategic centre whence these men must be effectively influenced".[3] He felt that the Association held a distinct advantage here over the mission colleges, thanks largely to the freedom and elasticity of its methods.[4] And he placed the provision of suitable literature first among these methods.

In 1902 there was very little being done to meet this need. The educated Indian, often with a deep interest in religious matters, was an avid reader: but the missions lacked the resources to meet his need. The *Epiphany*, a paper published by the Oxford Mission, we have discussed elsewhere.[5] It had a circulation of about 20,000 weekly, but neither its layout nor its theological and ecclesiastical position were acceptable to a man of Farquhar's background.[6] Then there was the extensive work of Dr. John Murdoch,[7] published for the most part by the Tract Society in Madras. Murdoch was a journalist by temperament, and belonged to an older theological generation.[8] His books, attacking Hinduism from every angle, Farquhar allowed might have some value in helping to destroy faith in Hinduism, but were in no sense constructive in their criticism.[9] In Farquhar's eyes this was clearly inadequate. His ideal was constructive criticism which, like that of T. E. Slater, took account of the most recent developments in the study of the New Testament and the non-Christian religions.[1]

---

[3] *Report 1902, loc. cit.*

[4] *Ibid.* Here he was thinking primarily of its freedom from the old-established (and hence conservative) societies, and from the demands of educational routine.

[5] Above, p. 90 f.

[6] "It might be a force of very great value indeed, but it depends largely for its popularity upon this, that three-fourths of its space is filled with correspondence, the bulk of which, while interesting to half-educated Hindus and Mohammedans, is practically of no value for the extension of the Kingdom. It has this second defect, that being published by the brethren of the Oxford Mission, it is often tainted by the narrow sectarianism and poisonous priestism of the High Church party of the Anglican Church." *Report 1902*, p. 65.

[7] Morris, *The Life of John Murdoch* (1906). Richter, *Indische Missionsgeschichte* (2 Aufl. 1924), p. 407 f.

[8] Appasamy, "Dr. J. N. Farquhar", in *YMI* XLI: 9 (Sept. 1929), p. 689. Cf. Richter, *op. cit.*, p. 408: "Für sie [CLS] hat er über alle brennenden Tagesfragen, über alle Phasen des wechselnden indischen religiösen Lebens Flugblätter und Schriften verfasst, welche vielfach zündend und klärend gewirkt haben."

[9] Murdoch's books Farquhar judged as being "exceedingly valuable as helping to destroy faith in Hinduism and to clear away prejudice against Christianity, but hardly go much further". *Report 1902*, p. 65. It is interesting, in view of this, to see what Farquhar has to say about Murdoch's edition of the *Mahābhārata* in the bibliography of his *Primer of Hinduism*: "A useful outline of the vast poem. The criticism is crude." *Primer* (2nd ed. 1914), p. 207.

[1] He does not however mention Slater at this stage.

Farquhar felt that, if the contents of the *Inquirer* could be adapted to the needs of its readers, it might wield very great influence indeed. "There is simply no limit", he wrote, "to the power such a little paper may exercise in this land ...".[2] But first it must be made interesting, and filled with "strong Christian teaching in effective form".[3]

The *Inquirer* provided Farquhar with his first opportunity of undertaking sustained literary work. We shall therefore examine some of the ways in which he sought to use the journal as a medium of evangelism. We shall see that the first clear application of the "fulfilment" concept from Farquhar's pen was made in the pages of the *Inquirer*; we shall note some of his ways of meeting objections to Christianity; and we shall see something of his personal attitude to the Christian claim to be the final and absolute religion.

The Development of Christian Literature—The Inquirer

Farquhar took over the editorship of the *Inquirer* in August 1902, and remained in office until January 1906. We shall however concern ourselves mainly with the issues up to the end of 1903, after which time the interest shifts to other publications on the subject of the relationship of Christianity to Hinduism. At the end of 1903 Farquhar was able to report that his paper had "a steadily growing circulation", but that he was not enough of a journalist to be able to make a popular paper.[4] His period as its editor is therefore best regarded as a further stage—largely experimental—in his literary apprenticeship, and while it gives us a number of interesting insights into the development of his thought, it was not an unqualified success.

The issues up to the end of 1902 are characterized by a consistent effort to assert the exclusiveness of Christianity, and the altogether uncompromising character of its claims to be the only true religion.[5]

One correspondent asked why Christians were so intolerant as to condemn every religion but their own. Farquhar wrote in answer

---

[2] *Report 1902*, p. 64.
[3] *Ibid.*
[4] YMCA Secretaries' Reports: J. N. Farquhar 1903, p. 108. Hereinafter *Report 1903*.
[5] It ought perhaps to be pointed out that practically the whole of the paper was written by the Editor.

that truth is necessarily intolerant of falsehood, and that Christians believe that Christianity alone contains the full truth, and that every other religion contains "very serious errors".[6] Religion, he pointed out, is not merely "a means of searching God"; the value of a religion depends upon the amount of truth and the amount of error contained in its conception of God.[7] The implication is that the Hindu conception of God, being non-moral, must be false.[8] This condemnation of other systems is not merely a matter of theory, but is carried out in practice: that is why a man, when he becomes a Christian, has to accept baptism, thereby giving up his old religion.[9] Elsewhere he stressed that it was the absolute duty of every Hindu who might become convinced of the truth of the teaching of Jesus, "first to renounce Hinduism utterly and secondly to join the Christian Church".[1] This was clearly a shaft directed at the Brāhma Samāj.

But this aspect of exclusiveness was only one facet of Farquhar's interpretation of Christianity—a facet which came to be stressed less and less. Like Slater before him, he came to recognize the risks inherent in continued stress on Christian exclusiveness. Thus he was able to assert that the man who follows all the light he has, even though he may not have heard of the Gospel, will be saved.[2] This is a decisive step away from the Evangelical doctrine of the non-salvability of the heathen, though that particular doctrine was by this time regarded by many as totally obsolete.[3] But Farquhar was still only feeling his way towards a distinctive position. The core of his later doctrine of "fulfilment" was likewise in process of formation during these early Y.M.C.A. years. This is clearly seen

---

[6] The *Inquirer* IV: 1 (Sept. 1902), p. 6.

[7] *Ibid.*

[8] This point continued to be stressed by Farquhar. Thus: "Hinduism remains from first to last crippled, because the idea of God was never moralized." *A Primer of Hinduism* (2nd ed. 1914), p. 49. "The fundamental weakness of the Indian moral theory is that it stands apart from God." *The Crown of Hinduism* (1913), p. 152.

[9] Christianity, wrote Farquhar, condemns all other religions as imperfect or untrue, "and this condemnation of other systems is not merely a matter of theory, but is carried out in practice: when a man becomes a Christian, he has to give up the racial organization in which he grew up". The *Inquirer* IV: 2 (Oct. 1902), p. 4.

[1] *Ibid.* IV: 6 (Feb. 1903), p. 8; IV: 7 (March 1903), p. 6.

[2] *Ibid.* IV: 5 (Jan. 1903), p. 6; cf. IV: 9 (May 1903), p. 7.

[3] Above, p. 25 f.

in a series of articles written in 1903 under the title "Is Christianity the Only True Religion?"

The first requirement of a "true" religion, in Farquhar's view, is that it must be universal, i.e. capable of being adopted by men of every class, language, race and latitude.[4] Hinduism fails at this point, for a number of reasons, mostly connected with its traditions. Neo-Hinduism, though in the process of breaking away from many of its traditional attitudes, is otherwise deficient in having no real historical foundation.[5] Further, Christianity is prepared to honour the genuine religious insights of the non-Christian world—an important element in its claim to universality.[6] This is the first indication in this context of an idea which we have noted as playing a large part in the thought of the period—the idea of "partial truth" in non-Christian religion. Already well established in the West, it had hitherto found few missionary advocates, since it accorded ill with the traditional Evangelical view of the absolute and final validity of the Christian revelation. It had been expressed in various ways, by Max Müller and Monier-Williams in England, by the Chicago Parliament of Religions in America, and by Miller, Slater and Kellett in India, and there can be little doubt that it was no novel idea to Farquhar. Here he was beginning to make use of what was to be the foundation of his missionary thought, and in a later article developed it more fully.

But first he turned to the practical aspect of the Indian situation. The Indian religious scene is complex, and yet it is possible to distinguish between the various faiths. Pantheism and polytheism he condemns; "Mohammedanism, Unitarianism and Brahmoism" he judges far less severely. The Brāhma Samāj is even commended for its good qualities. It has in it "something noble ... something substantial ... something that touches the very foundations of things".[7]

---

[4] *Ibid.* IV: 10 (June 1903), p. 5. Further: "The very idea of the absolute religion carries with it the concept of the unity and homogeneity of the human race, and implies that the truth is applicable, suitable and necessary for all men." *Loc. cit.*

[5] "Our chief criticism of Neo-Hinduism is that it simply cannot stand, because it has no historical foundation." *Loc. cit.* This was the chief of Farquhar's criticisms of the religion of the *Bhagavad Gītā*, see below, pp. 198 ff.

[6] "We Christians frankly recognize the real greatness of the ancient philosophical systems of Hinduism; we rejoice in the large amount of lofty ethical teaching to be found in the best Hindu literature; and we also recognize that in popular Hinduism many of the leading principles of true religion find expression ..." *Ibid.* IV: 11 (July 1903), p. 3.

[7] *Ibid.* IV: 12 (August 1903), p. 4.

By this Farquhar meant that it was closely related to "the religion of Israel", and is therefore closely related to Christianity in its ethical monotheism.[8] And perhaps most important, it was able to make an appeal to Indians as a "native growth", in contrast to the foreign missionaries, who come bringing a foreign faith.[9] It is perhaps no wonder that nineteenth-century missionaries looked upon the Brāhma Samāj as their most powerful rival. But the Samāj made no progress whatever during the last decade of the nineteenth century. "Has not history", concludes Farquhar, "already written the epitaph of Brahmoism?"[1]

The fourth article in Farquhar's series brings to a conclusion the idea which we have already touched upon, that God has not left himself without a witness in the non-Christian world, and in so doing introduces, for the first time in Farquhar's written work, the concept of "fulfilment".

Christianity is the only truly universal religion, recognizant of truth wherever it may be found, appreciative of the best in even its closest rival; but this is not enough: "modern" religion must also be "truly spiritual" and must "stimulate the moral life to the uttermost".[2] Christianity is the only religion which satisfies all these conditions, and at the same time completes those glimpses of ethical and spiritual truth which are to be found in other religions. Farquhar's conclusion must be quoted *in extenso*. Here begins the unbroken line of thought which stretches forward to the publication of *The Crown of Hinduism,* ten years later.

Now Christianity is the only faith in all the world which is purely spiritual and essentially ethical on the one hand, and on the other offers us historical facts of the largest significance and the mightiest emotional power, which fully satisfy the demand of the human heart for sacrifice and an object of worship more imaginable and comprehensible than the God of the Vedanta. The life of the Son of God on earth satisfies at once the instinct that has produced the avatars of Hinduism and the idols of all the earth; for the story of his life in the Gospels appeals to the feelings and imagination more completely than any mythical incarnation or any idol of stone or wood. And his death on the Cross gives us a sacrifice which satisfies the

---

[8] *Ibid.*

[9] The recognition of this attitude, which was becoming increasingly common among Indians, must be seen as an important element in Farquhar's later efforts to free the Christian (in this case Evangelical) mission from the charge of "denationalization". Cf. below, pp. 242, 247, 251, 300.

[1] The *Inquirer* IV: 12 (August 1903), p. 4.

[2] *Ibid.* V: 1 (Sept. 1903), p. 6.

human desire to make atonement for sin, and thereby explains in a satisfactory manner all the animal and human sacrifices that have ever taken
place on this earth of ours.

Thus the belief, that Jesus Christ, the Son of God, died for our sins on
Calvary, produces a religion which satisfies the modern mind, and which
also proves to be the fulfilment and goal of all the religions of the world,
the crudest as well as the loftiest.[3]

This is essentially an evolutionist position, and represents in a
highly compressed form (remembering the nature of the *Inquirer*
as a semi-popular pamphlet) views which Farquhar was to hold
throughout his active missionary career. Whence he derived them
we do not know; one conceivable "direct" derivation is from T. E.
Slater, whose book *The Higher Hinduism in Relation to Christianity* had appeared two years before, in 1901.[4] But the idea was not
new, and can have come from any one of a number of sources. The
essential thing is to recognize its ethos, and its connexion with the
developments in Western thought we have sketched in Chapter
One.[5] Farquhar was of course to develop the idea of fulfilment
considerably, and apply it in far more detail to the Hindu-Christian
dialogue, but it is already here in essence. Farquhar has interpreted
the religions of man as demonstrating the existence of a religious
need, or instinct—which is only to be satisfied in Christianity. That
he had also begun to look upon the religions as occupying relative
positions on the evolutionary scale can scarcely be doubted, remembering his earlier pamphlet on *The Science of Religion as an
Aid to Apologetics*.[6] However, at this early stage he made little
mention of that aspect of the fulfilment hypothesis. But the evolutionist basis of the doctrine must be recognized, along with the
historical emphasis on the person of Jesus which was its complement
in the thought of the period, since it is this double focus which
provides the basis for the understanding of Farquhar's missionary
theories.

In the *Inquirer* Farquhar dealt with religious questions on a
basis of "religious" arguments. But it was seldom possible to isolate
religion in this way in the India of that period. There had already

---

[3] *Ibid.*
[4] Above, pp. 96 ff.
[5] Above, pp. 43 ff.
[6] Above, p. 169 f.

grown up a certain connexion between religion and politics, religion and national feeling, in the mind of the Indian, and this connexion was destined to become more and more clearly marked with the passing of the years. It is therefore necessary that we now turn our attention to the development of Indian nationalism in the years after 1902, to see in what way the ground came to be prepared for this important alliance.

The Growth of Nationalism after 1902

Indian nationalism has been well termed "the child of the British raj".[7] Based from the first on the liberal principles of individual dignity and "all-round development",[8] as introduced by the reformers of the mid-nineteenth century, its original idea was one of constitutional reform, based on the belief that good government is no substitute for self-government. The early years of the Indian National Congress, founded in 1885, were remarkable for the docile attitude of the nationalist leaders in council; but beneath the surface there was growing discontent with the passive attitude which refused even to countenance any measures more radical than the filing of petitions. We have noted the growth of anti-Western feeling, particularly in the left-wing press, and the emphasis which came to be placed on economic factors in the national situation.[9] We have seen, too, something of the early religious impact of nationalism on the Bengali student, revealed in a renewed appreciation of Hinduism, particularly as a result of Swāmī Vivekānanda's "mission" to the West.[1]

The years from 1902 to 1905 are in a sense to be seen as the prelude to the storm. The intensification of nationalist feeling which preceded the anti-British outburst of 1905 was steady, and for the most part contained within constitutional limits. Economic agitation continued, assisted in no small measure by three books, each of which drew attention to the far from satisfactory state of the Indian economy. Dadabhai Naoroji, who had long been an

---

[7] Coupland, *The Indian Problem, 1833–1935* (1942), p. 23.

[8] Shukla, *A History of the Indian Liberal Party* (1960), p. 93. On this subject generally, see *Camb. Hist. Ind.* VI (1932), pp. 538 ff., Griffiths, *The British Impact on India* (1952), *passim*, McCully, *English Education and the Origins of Indian Nationalism* (1940), pp. 240 ff., Lovett, *A History of the Indian Nationalist Movement* (1920), pp. 31 ff.

[9] Above, p. 154 f.

[1] Above, p. 155 f.

influential figure in the Congress, published his *Poverty and un-British Rule in India* in 1901; in the same year appeared a book by a British civil servant, William Digby, entitled *"Prosperous" British India: A Revelation from Official Records*; and in 1902 was published *The Economic History of British India,* by Romesh Dutt. All pointed to the breakdown of the Indian village community as the root of all economic evil in the country.[2]

But while the village communities declined, the cities grew. In Calcutta, to name only one example, the number of jute and cotton mills doubled between 1891 and 1911.[3] At the same time, efforts were being made to restore some measure of economic independence to India. The first *swadeshi* exhibition had been held in 1896, paving the way for the economic measures of 1905 and the following years.[4] And schemes had been set on foot for subsidies and technical education, though they were slow in being implemented.

"Religious nationalism" was also on the increase. We shall have occasion to discuss the phenomenon of Neo-Krishnaism in some detail below, but first we must see in what way the student community was affected by the increasing pressure of pro-Indian (and often anti-Western) thought.

A picture of the life of the Indian student shortly after the turn of the century is drawn by Valentine Chirol,[5] who draws largely on an address given by Garfield Williams.[6] Neither can be called an impartial observer: the facts seem nevertheless to be clear. Overcrowding; the lack of communal life; moral laxity—these are just some of the factors mentioned by Williams as conditioning the life of the average Indian student in Calcutta. One important result of these conditions was incontestably the creation of a group among which political agitation could easily spring up: "political disease", as Williams calls it.[7] This is a missionary's interpretation of the

---

[2] Panikkar, *Asia and Western Dominance* (1954), p. 149.

[3] In 1891 there were 126 cotton mills in Calcutta, employing 112,000 men: by 1911 the figure had risen to 232 mills employing 236,000 men; in 1891 the jute mills of Calcutta employed 61,000 men: in 1911 they employed 192,000 men. Figures from Raguvanshi, *Indian Nationalist Movement and Thought* (2nd ed. 1959), pp. 77 ff.

[4] Above, p. 154 f.; below, pp. 216 ff.

[5] Chirol, *Indian Unrest* (1910), pp. 216 ff.

[6] A missionary of the Church Missionary Society.

[7] Chirol, *op. cit.*, p. 219.

situation in 1909; but there can be no doubt that political feeling was beginning to run high—for instance among the members of the student community served by the Y.M.C.A.—as early as 1902–1903.

Thus in 1903 Farquhar was able to write that the most noteworthy phenomenon in the life of India at that time was "the rapid growth of *the national movement*" (Farquhar's italics).[8] He commented that the movement was making more progress than ever, and extending its influence rapidly. Anti-Western feeling was also on the increase, and with it a desire to justify everything Indian, whatever its nature.[9] Farquhar's main interest in the nationalist movement was directed towards its religious aspect. He comments briefly on certain of its social and educational results, but only as a prelude to his main concern as a missionary: "... we are most interested in the movement as it affects the *religion* of the people; and there can be no doubt that the religious aspect of the national spirit is of very great importance".[1]

We shall see in due course that Farquhar had serious reservations with regard to many aspects of nationalism, and particularly its religious affiliations.[2] Nevertheless it was vital to understand the movement, since he felt it to be the most effective obstacle raised in men's minds to the progress of Christianity since the introduction of Western civilization into India. And in order effectively to combat its influence, high-class Christian literature would be called for.[3]

The first attempt on Farquhar's part to achieve a thorough understanding of a particular branch of Neo-Hinduism, and at the same time to state the Christian position with regard to that branch, took place in connexion with the Neo-Krishnaism of Bengal. Beginning

---

[8] *Report 1903*, p. 102.

[9] "Nowadays ... feeling has gone so far that there is a strong disposition on all hands to condemn everything Western and praise everything Indian. Apologists are not wanting for polytheism, idolatry, and the grossest of ancient customs; that they are Indian is quite sufficient reason for belauding them as super-excellent." *Ibid.*

[1] *Ibid.*

[2] This is perhaps most clearly seen in his attitude to the *Kalighat* meeting of the *swadeshi* movement, which we discuss below, p. 221.

[3] "Clearly if we are to combat this great movement we must understand Hinduism and understand all the thoughts and motives of the leaders of this reactionary movement, and we must use the most effective literary methods if we are to produce results of any great value." *Report 1902*, p. 66. "We want men who know Sanskrit, and understand Hinduism, who know something about the history of religions generally, and who are really trustworthy scientific students of the New Testament ..." *Report 1903*, p. 109.

with a close study of the *Bhagavad Gītā*, it resulted in the publication of three closely-related books, *Gita and Gospel, The Age and Origin of the Gita* and *Permanent Lessons of the Gita,* the origin and characteristic ideas of which we must now examine in some detail.

Kṛishṇa and the Bhagavad Gītā

The complex of religious, social and political factors which went to make up the Hindu Renaissance is, as we have tried to indicate, by its nature extremely difficult to systematize. There are however certain fixed points by the help of which some degree of orientation is possible, certain emphases which may fairly be said to be characteristic of the movement as a whole. These are not very numerous. But in the case of Kṛishṇa and the *Bhagavad Gītā* we can isolate a double theme which was of considerable significance to the revival as a whole. Neo-Krishnaism had its roots in Bengal; the students of Bengal were deeply affected by the movement; and for Farquhar, working among these Bengal students, the *Bhagavad Gītā* was a necessary field of study.

The origin of Neo-Krishnaism in Bengal was of comparatively late date. Before about 1880, Vaishnavism had only a limited following among the high-caste Hindus of Bengal, the high-caste Bengali being by tradition a Śaiva or a Sakta rather than a Vaishnava. But the first years of the Hindu Renaissance (reckoning from 1875[4]) saw a new emphasis on the religion of *bhakti* (loving devotion), on the figure of Kṛishṇa as the ideal object of devotion and on the *Bhagavad Gītā* as the record of the avatar (incarnation) of Kṛishṇa.

Although the growth of Neo-Krishnaism was due in no small measure to the influence of Rāmakṛishṇa Paramahaṁsa, Keshab Chandra Sen and other reformers—an influence which we cannot discuss in detail here—there was a second contributory factor. Not only were the ancient Vaishnava books brought out and read with new interest; the last two decades of the nineteenth century saw the publication of a stream of new *Vaishṇava* literature, in Bengali and in English, the work of a small number of authors who, in

---

[4] The year in which both the Ārya Samāj and the Theosophical Society were founded; cf. Farquhar, *Modern Religious Movements,* p. 109 f.

Farquhar's words, "threw themselves into painting the character of Krishna with extraordinary enthusiasm".[5]

Foremost among these authors was Bunkim (or Bankim) Chandra Chatterji, whose *Krishnacharitra* Farquhar accounted the most influential of the twenty-six notable works he listed as having been published on the subject between 1884 and 1903.[6] *Krishnacharitra* was a book of essays in Bengali prose on the character of Krishna; other books published during the period included lives of Krishna, theological treatises and—most typically—numerous editions, with or without commentary, with or without translation, of the *Bhagavad Gītā*. Neo-Krishnaism, closely connected as it was with the national movement, like the national movement spread from Bengal to other Indian centres.

Neo-Krishnaism was observed with growing interest and concern by a number of Protestant missionaries, and several attempts were made to combat its growing influence. J. P. Jones' book *India's Problem: Krishna or Christ?* (1903) is basically Evangelical, and reaffirms the absolute demands of the Christian Gospel in the Indian situation. A. G. Hogg's *Karma and Redemption* (1904–1905) takes up the basic philosophical and theological problems raised by the confrontation of Christianity and Neo-Krishnaism.[7] L. P. Larsen was another who devoted much attention to the problem in these years.[8] Farquhar's approach, as we shall see, was historical.

The influence of Neo-Krishnaism continued to increase throughout our period. By 1912 C. F. Andrews was able to record that the *Bhagavad Gītā* had been elevated within living memory into "a common and well-read scripture for the whole of educated India".[9]

During the first decade of the twentieth century, then, the students of India were coming to read the *Bhagavad Gītā* and to regard Krishna with a new reverence.[1] The Krishna of the *Gītā*, unlike the Krishna of the *Bhāgavata Purāṇa*, held an intellectual, and not merely an emotional, appeal.[2] "Active" and "gracious", he was com-

---

[5] Farquhar, *Gita and Gospel* (1903), p. 94.
[6] *Ibid.*, pp. 94 ff.
[7] We discuss some of these elsewhere; below, pp. 284 ff.
[8] Bindslev, *L. P. Larsen, hans Liv og Gerning* (1945), p. 147.
[9] Andrews, *The Renaissance in India* (1912), p. 146; cf. *ibid.*, p. 103.
[1] Cf. *Report 1903*, p. 104.
[2] Cf. Lucas, *The Empire of Christ* (1907), p. 100: "Among the common people it is the Krishna of the Puranas who holds sway over the heart; amongst the more thoughtful classes it is the Krishna of the Bhagavad Gita who embodies the highest thought and the most profound wisdom."

mended as the goal and refuge of the man of knowledge and devotion. And if, as Mrs. Besant was claiming, it was possible to discern
in Kṛishṇa "half-heard melody" and "elusive fleeting grace, scarce
seen but sensed", it was equally possible to see in him "human
greatness as politician, as statesman, as a guide of nations".[3] Judgments such as these, coming when they did, were in no small measure
responsible for increasing to appeal of Kṛishṇa to a politically-
minded young India.

Farquhar's experience as a missionary educationalist had shown
him that those representatives of young Indian with whom he was
likely to be in the closest contact as a Y.M.C.A. Secretary—the students of Bengal—were being subjected to increasing pressure from
Neo-Krishnaism. The pressure being brought to bear on them by
the Christian missions was also considerable. The battle seemed to
be between Christianity and Neo-Hinduism. The student was offered
Christ; he was offered Kṛishṇa. In Calcutta he could join the
Y.M.C.A.; or he could join its Hindu equivalent, *The Dawn Society*.[4]
His devotions might be based upon *The Imitation of Christ*; or upon
The Imitation of Sree Krishna.[5] If the pressure of Hinduism called
upon him to abandon the Gospels, it provided him with a cheap
copy of the *Bhagavad Gītā*.

Compromise was not encouraged in these years. The eclectic and
eirenic Brāhma Samāj was feeling the force of the new climate of
opinion, and was losing ground rapidly. The teaching of Rāmakṛishṇa, that all religions are essentially one and that all paths lead
in the end to the one goal,[6] was becoming overlaid by nationalist
intolerance. The nationalists ostensibly held all religions to be good
and all divine; but Hinduism was at least as good as Christianity

---

[3] Quoted by Sarma, *Studies in the Renaissance of Hinduism* (1944), p. 202 f.
See also Jhaveri, "Krishna: the Hindu Ideal", in *East and West* I: 6 (April 1902),
pp. 657–662, and I: 7 (May 1902), pp. 746–752. The aim of these articles was
to show Krishna as "a man—not an ordinary but an ideal man" (I: 6, p. 657)—an
interpretation which invites comparison with certain aspects of the Christian
thought of the time.

[4] "We have near by us here a society which is a distinct imitation of the
Y.M.C.A., only purely Hindu; it is called *The Dawn Society*, and is a close copy
of our methods even down to its advertisements." *Report 1903*, p. 103.

[5] Published in 1901 by the Secretary of *The Dawn Society*, S. C. Mukhopadhaya:
a daily textbook, containing extracts in English from the *Gītā*, the *Mahābhārata*
and the *Bhāgavata Purāṇa*. Cf. Farquhar, *Modern Religious Movements*, p. 440.

[6] "A truly religious man should think that other religions also are paths
leading to the truth." "Every man should follow his own religion." Max Müller,
Ramakrishna, pp. 153, 177, quoted by Farquhar, *op. cit.*, p. 198.

as a religion, while as a native Indian growth it was immeasurably superior.[7] There could thus be no possible motive for a Hindu to become a Christian. And more: the fact of Christianity being Western was quite enough to ensure its rejection in the eyes of most nationalists. And the fact of Neo-Krishnaism and the *Bhagavad Gītā* being Indian went a long way to ensure their acceptance. It was for this reason that leaders of Hindu society and orthodox Hindu parents exhorted their sons to study the *Gītā* reverently and carefully, if they would be good Hindus, and, by implication, good Indians.

It is possible that for many, the priorities were reversed, and that it was more important to be a good Indian than a good Hindu. In reality, of course, "Indian" and "Hindu" were well on their way to becoming synonyms within the phenomenon called Indian nationalism, and the *religion* of the *Gītā* was but one element among many in that complex phenomenon. So, for instance, the more militant agitators are said to have shown a remarkable catholicity in their reading habits. They laid down that certain text-books were to be read by all who regarded it as their *religious* duty to expel the European from India. The first of these was the *Bhagavad Gītā*; the others included the lives of Mazzini and Garibaldi, Russian methods of revolutionary violence, military manuals and books on explosives![8] From about 1890 onward inflammatory propaganda, directed against the British, became more and more widespread, and was often linked with ideas derived from the *Gītā*.

Thus when in 1895 Bal Gangadhar Tilak first introduced the cult of Śivaji,[9] he turned to the *Gītā* to find sanction for Śivaji's assassination of the Mohammedan general Afzul Khan. "Did Śivaji", he wrote, "commit a sin in killing Afzul Khan? The Divine Kṛishṇa teaching in the *Gītā* tells us we may kill even our teachers and our kinsmen, and no blame attaches if we are not actuated by selfish desires. Śivaji did nothing from a desire to fill his own belly."[1] From this Tilak drew the conclusion that similar action was entirely permissible against the British, exhorting his countrymen to "rise above the Penal Code into the rarefied atmosphere of the sacred *Bhagavad*

[7] *Report 1903*, p. 104.
[8] *Camb. Hist. Ind.* VI (1932), p. 552.
[9] Above, p. 153 f.
[1] Quoted by Chirol, *Indian Unrest*, p. 46 f.

Gītā".[2] His words fell upon good ground. The murderer of Sir William Curzon Wylie, assassinated in July 1909,[3] stated before his execution that he believed a wrong done to his country to be an insult to the gods. "Her cause is the cause of Śri Rām; her service is the service of Śri Kṛishṇa."[4]

This is however to anticipate developments. In 1903 the agitations had not yet reached their height: Bengal had not yet been partitioned.[5] But the *Gītā* was beginning to be put to non-religious use, and it would be well to keep that fact in mind. Farquhar was impressed by the *Gītā* as a work of religious genius; so was A. G. Hogg; so were other missionaries, whatever the public attitude they were forced to adopt. But if we fail to take account of this political undercurrent in Neo-Krishnaism, we run the risk of oversimplification and of underestimating the pull of the *Gītā* on the younger Indian generation. The use of the *Bhagavad Gītā* in nationalism was, in Farquhar's words, "one result of that potent spirit whereby India has become conscious of her unity, and her sons have been roused to a vigorous defence of all that they have inherited from the past".[6]

Literature on the Bhagavad Gītā

Farquhar's own approach to the *Bhagavad Gītā* was along the lines of historical inquiry. This approach he regarded as furnishing the only key for its true understanding as a religious document.[7] He bore repeated witness to its literary and religious merits, speaking in various contexts of its "great literary power", "deep religious feeling", and "genuine moral aspiration"; he called the *Gītā* "the noblest expression of (modern) Hinduism" and "the loveliest flower in the garden of Sanskrit literature". But judgments such as these may be passed irrespective of the historical standing of the work concerned. And it was the historical approach to the *Gītā* which revealed, in Farquhar's view, its essential weakness as the source—or potential source—of a nation's faith.

---

[2] *Ibid.*

[3] *Camb. Hist. Ind.* VI, p. 554.

[4] O'Malley, *Modern India and the West* (1941), p. 750.

[5] See below, pp. 216 ff., on the partition of Bengal.

[6] *Gita and Gospel*, p. 98. We use pagination of first edition (1903); later editions differ considerably. Farquhar published this book originally under the pseudonym of Neil Alexander.

[7] For Farquhar's emphasis on historical method, see above, pp. 167 ff.

We have seen that the great religious question of the period was Kṛishṇa or Christ—which was to have the mastery? The historicity of Jesus could not be called in question: he had lived, and died, in a certain place at a certain time. What of Kṛishṇa? Were it possible historically to demonstrate that Kṛishṇa had spoken the words of the *Gītā* on the battlefield of Kurukshetra, then the struggle might take on a different character in the eyes of the educated classes. And conversely, to prove that the *Gītā* could not possibly have been spoken there might do much to undermine faith in Kṛishṇa. Such was Farquhar's argument.

The first problem taken up by Farquhar in *Gita and Gospel* and *Age and Origin* (and to some extent in *Permanent Lessons* as well) is thus the problem of dating. He begins by placing the *Gītā* in the history of Sanskrit literature; this does not involve setting a definite date; although he inclines towards a date around, or just after, the beginning of the Christian era, he is clearly more concerned with the relative position of the *Gītā* in the religious literature of India.[8] This position is late: the *Gītā* is contemporaneous with the *Dharmaśāstras* and earlier Atharvan Upanishads (a position confirmed by internal and external evidence).[9] The conclusion is simple: it cannot have been uttered by Kṛishṇa at the battle of Kurukshetra, which took place practically a thousand years earlier. There is no mention of Kṛishṇa as an incarnation of the Supreme until this late period. Farquhar concludes that the story "that Kṛishṇa uttered the Song on the battlefield, is a pious imagination".[1]

But the *Gītā* is nevertheless an extremely effective piece of imaginative writing, which has succeded in welding together ancient Brahmanical thought and law on the one hand, and the popular cults on the other.[2] Literary skill, however, is no substitute for historical accuracy, and the fact remains that Kṛishṇa is a mythical figure, skilfully drawn but the product of a human mind.

What then is the missionary to make of the *Gītā*? First, he must

---

[8] *Gita and Gospel*, p. 10 f.; *Age and Origin*, p. 13.
[9] *Age and Origin*, p. 14.
[1] *Gita and Gospel*, p. 15.
[2] "The author ... formed the idea of combining the loftiest philosophy of his country with the worship of Krishna. He would intertwine the speculative thought that satisfied the intellect with the fervid devotion which even the uncultured felt for a god who was believed to have walked the earth. Philosophy would thus come nearer religion, while religion would be placed on far surer intellectual ground." *Gita and Gospel*, p. 16; cf. *Age and Origin*, p. 22 f.

approach it with reverence, not as the record of a new revelation, but as the summing-up of centuries of earlier religious development.[3] In it we see "the Hindu people ... reaching out after God". This is the crux of the matter for the missionary. The creation of the Kṛishṇa myth proves that the Hindu people felt the need of a personal Saviour; the missionary answers that the needs thus revealed can never be met—fulfilled—by a myth. Only in the historical figure of Jesus Christ can this need be satisfied.

On the one hand ... we have the imaginative portrait of Krishna, surrounded by millions of adoring worshippers—touching spectacle! On the other stands the historical Jesus of Nazareth, Son of Man and Son of God... Rightly read, the *Gītā* is a clear-tongued prophecy of Christ, and the hearts that bow down to the idea of Kṛishṇa are really seeking the incarnate Son of God.[4]

In *Permanent Lessons* Farquhar goes even further in the enunciation of this principle, claiming that "Jesus is the reality of which the *Gītā* gives an imaginative picture", and that "The author of the *Gītā* would have been a Christian, had he known Jesus".[5]

Leaving aside the somewhat extravagant final statement, we have here the basic pattern—or one of the basic patterns—of the "fulfilment" doctrine. And since it was this which was to exercise most influence in future years (more so, for example, than the idea of the evolutionary classification of Hinduism as a less developed religion than Christianity) it is necessary that we should define it with some care. It can be divided into three stages.

1. The phenomena of Hinduism reveal the existence of a religious need.

2. That need cannot be satisfied by those same Hindu phenomena.

3. Jesus Christ is able to satisfy—to fulfil—that need.

It might be objected (though the point was not made then)[6] that the onus of proof in this case rests upon the missionary. How can he be sure that "religious needs" are not satisfied by Hindu phenomena? On what is his judgment based? Is it not so that it is the Christian view which determines his estimate of Hinduism? What

---

[3] "It is the concentrated essence of Hinduism. It is the expression of all the highest hopes, aspirations and ideals of the best Indians that have ever lived ... It is the revelation of the Indian people." *Age and Origin,* p. 23.

[4] *Gita and Gospel,* p. 59.

[5] *Permanent Lessons,* p. 31.

[6] This was later Hogg's criticism, however.

is to happen when the Hindu claims to have found what he was seeking *within* Hinduism? But these questions were not asked by Farquhar. A. G. Hogg was to object to this aspect of the "fulfilment" doctrine on just such grounds as these.[7] F. W. Kellett, whom we have seen to have been an earlier exponent of this theory,[8] commented with approval on *Gita and Gospel,* recognizing in it the same ideas which he had expounded practically a decade earlier.[9]

The relation of the "myth" of Kṛishṇa to the figure of Christ was not the only topic discussed by Farquhar in *Gita and Gospel.* For instance, he also discusses the term "fulfilment" in its Biblical application, to the relationship between Judaism and Christianity.

The subject of the teaching of Jesus, writes Farquhar, was the Kingdom of God.[1] Special preparation had been made among the people of Israel, who had come to know God, not only as righteousness, but also as love, mercy and redemption. But Jesus the Messiah had come; a new era had begun, an era of love and mercy—the Kingdom of God. It was this for which the history of Israel had been preparing.

On the ground cleared in Israel, and on the basis of the revelation already made to them, God would now reveal Himself to all men. The destiny of Israel—'I will give thee for a light to the Gentiles'—would now be fulfilled.[2]

In Christ the history of Israel is thus brought to completion—fulfilled. The true nature of God is shown finally and decisively as resting on his Fatherhood. In the process the figure of the "Suffering Servant" is fulfilled too.[3]

Elsewhere Farquhar discusses the relation of the Old Testament law to the authority of Christ, writing that "Christ taught us that he came to *fulfil* the Old Testament, to take the imperfect teaching therein given and complete it".[4] And again that Jesus came to fulfil the ancient religion of the Jews, by taking their national moral law and making it into a universal standard of conduct, and by taking and universalizing their existing religious conceptions.[5]

---

[7] See below, p. 289 f.
[8] See above, p. 105 f.
[9] Review of *Gita and Gospel* in *MCCM* III: 6 (Dec. 1906), p. 307.
[1] *Gita and Gospel,* p. 53.
[2] *Ibid.,* p. 54.
[3] *Ibid.,* pp. 26–35.
[4] The *Inquirer* V: 2 (Oct. 1903), p. 6.
[5] *Ibid.* V: 4 (Dec. 1903), p. 12.

It will be clear that the actuating principle in this interpretation is the idea of "progressive revelation", and that that has been ultimately derived from the evolutionary hypothesis. Religion is subject to the same laws of progress, development and "evolution" as the physical universe, a development called forth by the basic religious instinct present in each man individually, and in races and nations collectively. Thus Farquhar is able to write of the "fulfilment" of an existing system of laws and ethics (in respect of Judaism) and the "fulfilment" of basic religious needs (in respect of Hinduism); hence, too, he can claim that the "ideals" of Israel, Greece, Rome and India "are reconciled in a loftier unity".[6] Among the difficulties aroused by this view is the question of the exegesis of Matt. 5.17.[7] But Farquhar himself saw no such difficulty, though his writings as a whole constantly refer back to that text.

The publication of these works on the *Gītā* gave Farquhar a great deal of satisfaction, and opened the door to useful future contacts.[8] In 1904 he was able to write that his literary work had brought him into touch with many "fresh minds" and widened his influence.[9] Now he turned his attention to a study of the Upanishads, under the guidance of Pundit Siradhan Vidyarnava, a minister (*Āchārya*) of the *Ādi Brāhma Samāj*.[1] At the same time he was responsible for the formation of a Theological Circle, a discussion group aimed at bringing together Christians, Brahmos and Hindus for the discussion of tropics of common interest; the response from Indians was however disappointing,[2] and little more was heard of its activities.

There remain two works from this period which we must consider. The first, *The Future of Christianity in India,* is, as its title implies, a review of the Christian prospect in an Inda stirred by nationalism. The second, *Missionary Study of Hinduism,* is of particular im-

---

[6] *Gita and Gospel,* p. 65.

[7] The crux here is whether the text as it stands refers only to the fulfilment of the Jewish Law, or whether it may legitimately be extended to refer to other non-Christian religions. Cf. the interpretations advanced by Farquhar in *The Crossbearer* (above, p. 165 f.), and later in *The College St. Matthew* (below, p. 260 f.).

[8] So e.g. his meeting with the Dewan of Mysore, of which an account is given below, p. 241.

[9] YMCA Secretaries' Reports: J. N. Farquhar 1904, p. 153 (YMCA Hist. Lib.). Hereinafter *Report 1904.*

[1] *Report 1904,* p. 152.

[2] *Report 1904,* p. 156.

portance for our analysis, since it lays down the programme which Farquhar wished to see applied in face of the changing Indian situation.

The Future of Christianity in India

A striking characteristic of Farquhar's reports during his first period of service with the Y.M.C.A. is the way in which "difficulties" and "encouragements" frequently go hand in hand. Thus in 1903, and again in 1904, we find him referring to Neo-Hinduism as "the greatest of all obstacles to our work";[3] nevertheless he regarded the Neo-Hindu movement as a source of encouragement. For while the Hindu was coming to reject the Christian message, as preached by the Western missionary, as being too intimately connected with the West, he was still imitating missionary *methods* extensively. This Farquhar interpreted as demonstrating "most distinctly and most deeply the influence of Christ".[4]

Then there was the parallel which was beginning to be drawn between the siuation in India and the revival of paganism in Europe in the second, third and fourth centuries A.D.[5] The point was that Christianity, or, as some preferred to call it, "the religion of Jesus",[6] had already won a resounding "victory" over paganism, and that in a situation in many ways reminiscent of that subsisting in twentieth-century India. Added to this was the belief—which was certainly in part justified—that the new movement within Hinduism was the direct result of Christian influence, and would eventually revert in some way to its true source. Or, as Farquhar put it, "When

[3] *Report 1903*, p. 102; cf. *Report 1904*, p. 158.
[4] *Report 1903*, p. 102. Cf. p. 103: "One sees the influence of Christianity everywhere. *Monotheism* has taken altogether a new place in the minds of Hindus; *Righteousness* is now beginning to be seen to be the most important element of religion; *Practical Results* are demanded from faith; and men are beginning to see that true religion must be universal." The imitation of Christian missionary practice has already been touched upon (above, p. 196 n. 4); here may be added that a Vedic Salvation Army was later started in Lahore by Lala Lajpat Rai. Farquhar, *Modern Religious Movements*, p. 127.
[5] Andrews, "A Missionary's Experience", in *Ind. Interp.* IV: 3 (Oct. 1909), p. 103; *idem, The Renaissance in India*, pp. 36 ff.; Ewing, "Christianity in India and in the Roman Empire—An Analogy", in *MCCM* IV: 5 (Nov. 1904), pp. 225 ff.
[6] Ewing, *op. cit.*, p. 235: "Friend and foe alike can scarcely fail to observe that all that Hinduism, ancient and modern, has to put forward has already gone down before the religion of Jesus ..."

the Hindu reaction passes the flood, we may be sure there will be large accessions to the Christian Church".[7]

The pamphlet *The Future of Christianity in India* was written in this spirit of (as it turned out, ill-founded) optimism. Its immediate cause was the religious statistics provided in the Census of India for 1901, which showed an increase of 30.8% in the Christian community over the last ten years as compared with an increase of only 2.5% in the population as a whole over the same period. Farquhar was not prepared to attach undue importance to these figures, however encouraging in themselves. They nevertheless provided him with a starting-point for an outline of "the historical characteristics of Christianity *as an aggressive religion*".[8]

Farquhar began by quoting figures to show that the increase in the number of Christians in India in the period 1871–1901 was not an isolated phenomenon, but part of a world-wide movement. How is this to be explained? His answer takes the form of a brief review of the early history of Christianity. Greek, Roman and Egyptian religion are passed in review, largely in order to make the point that Hinduism is to be classified together with these, as "national polytheisms".[9] Farquhar's main authority here is Benjamin Kidd.[1] But Christianity has already overcome earlier examples of this class of religion, and there is every reason to believe that Christianity will emerge victorious from the present conflict:

Let Hindus ... realize that Christianity met and conquered in the early centuries an enemy quite as great as Hinduism, an enemy, too, which in many respects closely resembled Hinduism.[2]

This conclusion Farquhar proceeds to elaborate under eight headings—eight characteristics which in his judgment were common to the two situations. We may enumerate them briefly:

1. Fierce opposition on the part of the old faith.
2. Extreme contempt for the Christian Church.

---

[7] *Report 1903*, p. 104. Others were less optimistic. Five years later Nicol Macnicol recognized that there were signs of new life in India, but that it had not yet come to fruition, and commented: "Whether that fruition will be a new Hinduism or a further phase in the unwearied life of Christianity remains to be seen." Review of Percy Gardner's *The Growth of Christianity*, in *Ind. Interp.* II: 4 (Jan. 1908), p. 196.

[8] *The Future of Christianity in India*, p. 6.

[9] *Ibid.*, p. 9 f.

[1] *Ibid.*, p. 10. Cf. above, p. 41 n. 9.

[2] *Ibid.*, p. 11. This idea was taken up by A. H. Ewing; cf. above, p. 203 n. 5.

3. Steady increase of the Church's membership.
4. Many converts from the lower classes.
5. Steady diffusion of Christian ideas.
6. A great tendency to praise Christ.
7. A revival of the old faith.
8. Philosophical reorganization of the old faith (a parallel between Neo-Platonism and Theosophy).

A remarkable final paragraph gives striking confirmation of the depth to which Farquhar's thinking at this time was conditioned by the evolutionary hypothesis. In it is introduced an impartial judge—"some impartial biologist"—who is asked to comment on the evidence for the future of Christianity in India, and who delivers the scientific judgment that

Christianity has proved itself an organization of such unparalleled vitality and of such invincible aggressiveness in the past, and in circumstances so exceedingly similar to those we now see around us in India, that, *from the point of view of biology,* I am inclined to think that the younger faith is likely to gradually weaken Hinduism and finally supplant it.[3]

The Future of Christianity in India is characterized by its insistence on Christianity as an aggressive religion, and by the conviction that Christianity's ultimate victory is assured. Its analogical argument appears naïve and unconvincing, it is true, but that it was in line with much "liberal" thought of the period cannot well be denied. But this was only one side of the picture. Victory in a religious conflict could not be achieved in a vacuum; great demands still would be made of the individual missionary *vis-à-vis* renascent Hinduism. Although aggression is an inevitable aspect of Christianity, it must be sympathetic aggression—paradoxical though that may sound. Aggression is characteristic of Christianity as a religious organism, but must be tempered with sympathy in the individual, when faced with the actual phenomena of Hinduism. The attitude proper to the missionary apologist Farquhar discusses in a paper, *Missionary Study of Hinduism,* which we shall now examine.

---

[3] *Ibid.,* p. 24.

Missionary Study of Hinduism

Farquhar's important paper on *Missionary Study of Hinduism* was first read to the Calcutta Missionary Conference in May 1905; it was then published in the *Harvest Field*,[4] and later as a pamphlet.[5] It is divided into two sections, aimed at answering two questions: Why ought a missionary to study Hinduism? and How ought he to set about it?

The first point Farquhar makes is that the success of a preacher or teacher cannot but be relative to his knowledge and understanding of the people he wishes to influence. Religion is "the deepest of all the influences that go to make up their mental and moral constitution"; therefore knowledge of Hinduism paves the way to a thorough knowledge of the Indian people.[6] Some Christians are inclined to suspect this kind of enterprise, on the grounds that the study of Hinduism may usurp the study of the Bible. But this, says Farquhar, is easily guarded against. Granted that the missionary ought to study Hinduism, yet "in ninety-nine hundredths of his work he ought to keep his knowledge strictly in the background".[7] The missionary's task is to preach, not to dispute: "a discussion of Hinduism, whatever else it may do, will never save a human soul".[8] Study is therefore to be undertaken for the sake of the missionary's own attitude, and his understanding of the people, and not as a basis on which the Christian message is to be interpreted. Used carefully, such a study is of immeasurable value. When the missionary has mastered some aspect of his subject, he may be able to *lecture* on it: but he is not called to preach it.[9]

An important statement of principle may be quoted:

All our study of Hinduism and everything we write and say on the subject should be sympathetic. I believe incalculable harm has been done to the Christian cause in India in times past through unsympathetic denunciation of Hinduism. Even if the severe condemnations passed on certain aspects of the religion be quite justifiable, it is bad policy to introduce these things

---

[4] *HF* XVI: 5 (May 1905), pp. 166–178.

[5] We use the pagination of the offprint. Part has also recently been reprinted as an appendix to the present writer's *J. N. Farquhar: A Memoir*, pp. 123–128.

[6] *Missionary Study of Hinduism*, p. 3.

[7] *Ibid.*

[8] *Ibid.*

[9] What Farquhar was advocating was primarily a change of *attitude*, and this must be kept in mind.

into our addresses and tracts; for the invariable result is that our audience is alienated. There can be no doubt that a great part of the bad feeling which so many Hindus harbour against Missionaries is a direct result of such denunciation.[1]

The key word here is perhaps "policy". Sympathy and diplomacy were closely allied in Farquhar's mind, as in Slater's before him.[2] And not without reason, for many educated Indians had long been wary of the authoritarian approach, and the coming of the nationalist spirit had only served to intensify that feeling. Yet this was not the whole story: the missionary must also be prepared to attend to the claims of justice. He cannot, claims Farquhar, be just and accurate in his estimation of another religion unless he is sympathetic.

An unsympathetic student of the Gospels invariably misinterprets them; and the same is true of an unsympathetic student of the Upanishads, the *Mahābhārata,* or the Purānas. The attitude of the great scholars of the West to Hindu literature ought to be the ideal of every Missionary.[3]

Farquhar hastened to add that this was not tantamount to saying that the missionary ought to praise everything they praise, and condemn everything they condemn; but he must be prepared to be patient, and try to see every text with the eyes of those to whom it was first addressed: every rite with the eyes of those who first practised it. It is this which constitutes the sympathetic attitude necessary for fruitful study of Hinduism.

The remainder of the paper is concerned with technical matters: *How* to study. We have no cause to enter into a detailed discussion of this part of Farquhar's paper; we mention only his insistence on *historical method*—the only safe pathway through "the vast jungle of tropical growths which Hinduism is"—and his equal insistence on the use of the latest scholarly literature on the subject.[4]

Farquhar brought his paper to a close with an appeal—one of many[5]—for more concentrated work by missionaries on Sanskrit, and on the subject of Christian-Hindu relations generally.[6] And he

---

[1] *Missionary Study of Hinduism,* p. 5.
[2] See above, p. 101.
[3] *Missionary Study of Hinduism,* p. 6.
[4] *Ibid.,* pp. 6 ff.
[5] See above, p. 170, and below, pp. 257, 267, 305 ff.
[6] This, too, he was to repeat frequently; see e.g. his address at the 1909 Oxford WSCF conference (below, pp. 255 ff.), and cf. D. S. Cairns' article "The Need for Apologists", in the *Student World* IV (April 1911), pp. 49 ff.

pointed out that the task of taking the literature of Hinduism as a whole, as well as Hindu rites and practices, and showing its true relationship to Christianity "has scarcely been touched yet".[7] A significant footnote suggests that Kellett's *Christ the Fulfilment of Hinduism* and Slater's *Higher Hinduism* are "on the right lines".[8]

This paper largely speaks for itself, and leaves us in no doubt as to the direction in which Farquhar's mind was turning at the end of his first period of service with the Y.M.C.A. We have seen that he had taken the theory of "fulfilment" and applied it to one particular branch of modern Hinduism, viz. Neo-Krishnaism. But he clearly believed the theory to be valid throughout the field of religion, and applicable as a missionary doctrine to the whole of Hinduism "the whole literature of Hinduism, with all its rites, ceremonies and sacrifices". Nothing less would serve, in his opinion, to clarify the position of the Church in India.

This may be described as the theoretical foundation of Farquhar's work. But it is important that we should take adequate account of the practical circumstances which made it more and more imperative that some theory of relationship should be stated, and the reasons which led Farquhar to concentrate on Christian literature as the vehicle of such a statement. Some years were to elapse before the full implications of the new attitude were clearly seen. Those years witnessed a notable deterioration in East–West relations in India as a whole, but particularly in that part of India in which Farquhar was working. The immediate causes of that deterioration are of an extent and importance which preclude their being incorporated into a summary account. We shall accordingly devote Chapter Seven to a review of the various events which combined to render Protestant missions more dependent than previously upon literature as a method of evangelism, and to Farquhar's interpretation of the crisis situation of 1905 and the following year.

---

[7] *Missionary Study of Hinduism*, p. 14.

[8] We have discussed the contribution of Slater and Kellett above, pp. 94 ff. A copy of *Missionary Study of Hinduism*, annotated by Farquhar himself, has a third name added here; unfortunately, while the words "and Dr. K. M. Banerjea's" are fully legible, the title of the book in question has been removed in the process of binding.

CHAPTER 7

A Year of Crisis, 1905–1906

WE HAVE seen that the political temperature of Bengal had been rising steadily for some years when J. N. Farquhar joined the staff of the Calcutta Y.M.C.A. in 1902. The three following years did nothing to moderate the discontent and agitation of the capital city and the province of which it formed the centre. We saw how missionary work had come to be hampered very seriously indeed by the growing popularity and militancy of Neo-Hinduism; and how Farquhar had begun to concentrate on the method of literary evangelism, believing this to be the most promising method to use in the complex situation brought about by the coming of nationalism. The events of 1905 had the effect of creating a crisis of East–West relations in Bengal such as had not been seen since the Mutiny. A new form of nationalism emerged: a nationalism prepared to abandon constitutional principles whenever and wherever necessary, for the furtherance of its ends. Relations between Indian and European came in very many cases to be tainted with suspicion verging on hatred. Standard missionary methods were seriously disturbed—at least temporarily—and the importance of Christian literature to the missions increased still further.

The actual cause of the crisis cannot be summed up briefly, and in a work of this kind it is out of the question to attempt to do so. Something must however be said about its immediate causes, which were three in number.[1] First, the victory of Japan over Russia caused a wave of optimism to sweep through India: if Japan could thus effectively oppose a Western power, it was argued, why should not India do likewise? Secondly, the methods employed by the then Viceroy, Lord Curzon, aroused great indignation, particularly among students. The Viceroy's Convocation Speech, delivered before the University of Calcutta in February 1905, was a particular source

---

[1] Kraemer, *World Cultures and World Religions* (1960), p. 137, mentions only two: the Russo-Japanese War and the partition of Bengal, overlooking altogether the role of Curzon in irritating Indian opinion.

of dissatisfaction, and made many enemies. Thirdly and lastly, the Partition of Bengal, coming after several decades of growing discontent, led to the most serious consequences, both for the Government and the missionaries at work in North-East India.

The Russo-Japanese War

The Russo-Japanese War began in 1904 as a result of Tsarist Russia's refusal to evacuate Manchuria (occupied in 1900) and ended with the Treaty of Portsmouth in 1905; Russia, having been defeated on sea and land, surrendered the strategic centre of Port Arthur to the Japanese and finally agreed to all Japan's territorial and diplomatic claims.[2] The actual details of the struggle are of no real significance in this context; the impression made by Japan's victory was however of great importance for the situation in India, and indeed the whole of Asia.[3]

Japan's rapid assimilation of Western culture, and her economic progress, had aroused attention in both East and West even before the war.[4] By 1905 it was no exaggeration to claim, as a Japanese leader claimed, that "the eyes of the world are focussed upon the Orient".[5] But the impact of Japan's victory was perhaps most strongly felt in India, where the war was regarded as symbolizing the struggle between East and West.[6] The victory of Japan was welcomed, particularly in nationalist circles, as a sign that European domination in the East was fast approaching its end. Japan's success was felt to be the result of two factors, national unity and individual capacity for self-sacrifice, and what had proved possible

---

[2] There is an extremely useful short account in *EB* 19 (1963), pp. 759–765, with bibliography.

[3] Some would go even further. So e.g. Lloyd, *The Church of England in the Twentieth Century* I (1946), p. 204: "The balance of power between the nations was changed, the calculations of economists and financiers had to be redrawn, and the whole world situation was permanently altered."

[4] Beach, *Geography and Atlas of Protestant Missions* (1901), pp. 204 ff.

[5] K. Ibuka, speaking at the 1905 Zeist conference of the WSCF: see *Report of the Conference of the World's Student Christian Federation, held at Zeist, Holland* (1905), p. 113.

[6] "As between Korea and Japan, the Queen of the East stands up for civilisation; as against Russia, she stands up for political rectitude; as against the aggressive West, she represents the worm that will turn. She has deserved our best wishes, and in her victory we shall recognise the triumph of all that we hold sacred in the political morality of nations." Editorial in *East and West* III: 29 (March 1904), p. 314.

for Japan now seemed to be within the grasp of India.[7] Indian leaders were loud in their praise of Japan[8]—echoed by John R. Mott, who spoke at the Zeist W.S.C.F. conference of "the brilliant Japanese nation".[9]

The 1905 Indian National Congress noted the profound "moral impression" made by Japan's successful struggle.[1] And Jawaharlal Nehru later described the outcome of the war as "a great pick-me-up for Asia".[2] The impression was greatest on the nationalists, who saw in Japan's example evidence that an Asiatic nation could beat a powerful European nation at its own game of war, and that Europe *qua* Europe had no essential element of material or moral supremacy. (The rightness or otherwise of Tsarist Russia's right to be regarded as typical of Europe need not concern us.) India's efforts to achieve nationhood and independence were no longer isolated. Japan had shown the way. Now for the first time it became possible to speak of what O'Malley has called "a pan-Asiatic spirit", and what Meredith Townsend called "a comity of Asia".[3] The underlying feeling was that Asia had now demonstrated her potential superiority to the West,[4] and that nothing could now stand in the way of the ultimate control of Asia by Asiatics themselves. What Japan had done, India could—and would—do. A further moral drawn by Indian nationalists was that although Western methods might well have their place in war, politics, education and commerce, there was no such need in the realm of culture or of religion.[5]

But although Japan's victory lifted the morale of the Indian nationalists, it is unlikely that it would have led to any serious repercussions, had it not coincided with a period of intense dis-

---

[7] O'Malley, *Modern India and the West* (1941), p. 95.

[8] Ghose, "Japanese Polity", in *East and West* IV: 46 (August 1905), p. 875.

[9] *Zeist Report,* p. 23. Cf. World Missionary Conference 1910, *Report of Commission I,* p. 32: "For a long time Japan has furnished the most inspiring and powerful example [to Asia] of free and triumphant nationality."

[1] Lovett, *A History of the Indian National Movement* (1920), p. 61.

[2] Moraes, *Jawaharlal Nehru* (1957), p. 27.

[3] O'Malley, *op. cit.,* p. 741, Raguvanshi, *Indian Nationalist Movement and Thought* (2nd ed. 1959), p. 83, Farquhar, *Modern Religious Movements in India* (1915), p. 28, Panikkar, *A Survey of Indian History* (3rd ed. 1960), p. 221.

[4] "The victory of Japan over Russia ... was represented as the turning of the tide of conquest in favour of Asia against Europe." Ker, "Subversive Movements", in *Political India 1832–1932,* ed. Cumming (1932), p. 228.

[5] *Ibid.,* cf. O'Malley, *op. cit.,* pp. 95 ff., Paul, *The British Connection with India* (1927), p. 109.

satisfaction with the British Government—dissatisfaction centring on the convenient figure of the Viceroy of India, Lord Curzon.

Lord Curzon

It is not easy to sum up the Viceroyalty of Lord Curzon in a few words. This is at least partly due to the difficulty of finding literature on the period, and on the man, which is written from the point of view of objective history. The Indian nationalist press was unanimous in condemning Curzon as no true friend of India—as an oppressor and a foreigner. Panikkar calls him "the apostle of imperialism".[6] And Lord Ronaldshay, Curzon's "official" biographer, is cautious with regard to much in Curzon's life. The result is inevitably a somewhat distorted picture. Perhaps the most telling comment on Curzon's character was that made by Clemenceau: "*orgueil immense—justifié*".[7] Pride, ability, and yet a surprising lack of tact and discernment seem to have characterized his term of office—or rather two terms of office, for he served from 1899 to early in 1904, and again from late in 1904 to 1905, when his Indian career came to an abrupt end as the result of a semi-personal quarrel with Lord Kitchener.

"Lord Curzon's Viceroyalty", writes the Earl of Ronaldshay, "left India a little breathless."[8] It was a period of intensive administrative reform, similar in some ways to the liberal period from 1835 to 1854. "Efficiency of administration, is, in my view", wrote Curzon himself, "a synonym for the contentment of the governed."[9] This is perhaps the key to the understanding of the Curzon period in India. But to regard efficient administration as the be-all and end-all of Indian government was a view, which, however suitable it may have been in the 1830's, largely failed in its object amid the tensions of the earlier twentieth century. Taking Bengal as a measure of the Indian situation as a whole, it is abundantly clear that the Bengali was far from being contented; and the administrative reforms proposed by Curzon tended only to increase his discontent.[1]

---

[6] Panikkar, *Asia and Western Dominance* (1954), p. 150, cf. p. 163.

[7] Quoted by Mersey, *The Viceroys and Governors General of India 1757–1947* (1949), p. 118.

[8] Ronaldshay, *The Life of Lord Curzon* II (1928), p. 413.

[9] *Ibid.*, p. 328.

[1] Thus, to take only one example, there was a widespread feeling that Curzon's legislation was aimed to benefit only the English-speaking fraction of the people

Sir Verney Lovett has pointed out that Curzon was led by this means seriously to underestimate the force of Indian opposition to his reforms.[2] This weakness was to some extent recognized by Curzon himself. On one occasion he confessed in public that he failed to understand what was in the mind of "young India". It goes without saying that this admission was hardly calculated to increase the confidence of "young India"—i.e. the student body—either in the person of the Viceroy, or in the measures which he sought to implement.[3]

The nationalist press criticized Curzon bitterly and often. Criticism was directed against five separate measures introduced by the Viceroy between 1899 and 1905: the Official Secrets Bill, the Delhi Durbar, the Indian Universities' Act of 1904, an episode which was characterized as "remarks against the Indian character", and lastly, the Partition of Bengal.[4] Details of all these will be found in the political histories of the period, and we shall accordingly concentrate on points four and five in the Indian indictment, since these have the greatest relevance for the missionary situation in Bengal at this time.

The occasion of Lord Curzon's "remarks" was the Annual Convocation of Calcutta University on February 11, 1905. It is probably true to say that Curzon had no intention of including in his speech anything of a deliberately derogatory nature; he nevertheless showed what appears in retrospect as a remarkable lack of tact in taking for his subject a discussion of personal qualities, foremost among them truthfulness. He did not, as his opponents afterwards claimed,

---

of India; see Rowji, "A Petition on behalf of the Rural Poor of India to H. E. Lord Curzon", in *East and West* I: 3 (Jan. 1902), pp. 265–278. Yet Curzon himself claimed in 1905 that the Indian peasant "has been in the background of every policy for which I have been responsible, of every surplus of which I have assisted in the disposition". Philips (ed.), *Select Documents on the History of India and Pakistan* IV (1962), p. 659.

[2] Lovett, *op. cit.*, p. 59.

[3] His actual words were, "I do not pretend to know what lies in the mind of young India, or even of that small section of it which I am now addressing". *Lord Curzon in India* (1906), p. 489. This was undoubtedly true, but tactless in the extreme. As Woodruff has well said, "He was too self-centred to see how his words or actions would hurt other people ...". *The Men who Ruled India* II (1954), p. 194.

[4] These "acts of blazing indiscretion" are enumerated by Raguvanshi, *op. cit.*, p. 79 f.

say that Indians were habitually untruthful; but he did say that truth had occupied a high place in the moral code of the West before being similarly honoured in the East. And he went on to suggest that "craftiness and diplomatic wile" had always been part of the Eastern pattern of business, and advanced as proof the "common innuendo" that "Oriental diplomacy" must mean a process which is "rather tortuous and hypersubtle".[5]

The Viceroy then proceeded to enumerate some of the commonest forms of "untruth" in India: exaggeration, invention and imputation. "I know no country", he said, "where mares'-nests are more prolific than here. Some ridiculous concoction is publicly believed until it is officially denied ..."[6] As well as this attack on rumour, he warned his hearers against the abuse of authority, pointing out that an atmosphere of constant strife could not possibly benefit the growth of the national spirit. Students he recommended to try and form an independent judgment on all matters of personal and national importance. This was a shaft directed against the popular press, undue reliance on which he called "not thought, but very often an abnegation of thought".[7] Furthermore, students must learn moderation in their dealings with authority, since nothing could be more offensive than arrogance or license in youth.[8] They must also learn to avoid "the absurd and puerile tyranny of words".[9] This was of course said in criticism of the numerous conferences and political meetings then being held all over India, but which were particularly rife in Bengal. The Viceroy recommended in no uncertain terms more action and less empty talk:

I sometimes think that if fewer resolutions were passed and a little more resolution was shown—resolution to grapple with the facts of life, to toil and labour for your country instead of merely shouting for it—the progress of India would be more rapid.[1]

And in his peroration Lord Curzon delivered a judgment on the future of India which did a great deal to confirm in the minds of his hearers the unfavourable impression conveyed by the speech

---

[5] *Lord Curzon in India*, p. 491.
[6] *Ibid.*, p. 492.
[7] *Ibid.*, p. 494.
[8] *Ibid.*, p. 495.
[9] *Ibid.*
[1] *Ibid.*, p. 495 f.

as a whole, striking as it did against the self-esteem of the whole national movement:

I do not think that it can yet be said that there is any Indian nation, though in the distant future some approach to it may be evolved.[2]

The Indian reaction was immediate and scandalized. The general impression was that the Viceroy had gone out of his way to insult the people (and particularly the young people) of India, by accusing them of being untruthful, and by pouring scorn on their nationalist aspirations. The liberal journal *East and West* observed that in the case of Lord Curzon, valour had triumphed over discretion. Statesmen do not as a rule "present their knuckles to machines charged with electricity. Lord Curzon is bold and has drawn off a spark. It may or may not have hurt his nerves, but the lesson is plain: the machine is charged."[3] Curzon's "nerves" seem in fact not to have been affected. His biographer records that no one was more surprised than Curzon himself at the storm of denunciation to which his speech gave rise.[4] Indian self-esteem had however been wounded, not merely on the personal level, but, as Lord Tweedsmuir has pointed out, because Curzon's speech "seemed to postpone the realization of Britain's solemn pledge [to grant self-government] to the Greek Kalends".[5] At all events, Curzon's speech made many enemies; an Indian historian has passed judgment that "never was a deeper affront afforded to the people of India by the representative of the Sovereign".[6]

Curzon did not intend to insult the Indian people: so much is tolerably certain. But it is an undeniable fact that India interpreted his didactic tones in that light. And as Curzon was the highest representative of the Crown, his speech was taken as reflecting the views of the Government, and of the ruling nation as a whole. It is not then surprising that the reaction was felt by most Europeans (and Americans) in Bengal at that time. The missionary body was no exception.

---

[2] *Ibid.*, p. 499.
[3] *East and West* IV: 42 (April 1905), p. 457.
[4] Ronaldshay, *op. cit.*, II, p. 364.
[5] Buchan (Lord Tweedsmuir), *Lord Minto: A Memoir* (1924), p. 230.
[6] Raguvanshi, *op. cit.*, p. 79. For a more moderate view, see Masani, *Britain in India* (1960), p. 79.

The Partition of Bengal

J. N. Farquhar's report for 1905 contained these words:

Lord Curzon's speeches and policy have excited and irritated the people of Bengal to an extraordinary degree. I have never before seen one quarter of the wild agitation and anger that are now apparent in this city and province ... Lord Curzon is the real cause of the trouble and is very seriously to be blamed both for his words and his actions ... Nothing, however, has excited Bengal at all comparably with Lord Curzon's scheme for the partition of the country ...[7]

The partition of Bengal into two independent provinces was made for what the Government obviously believed to be the best of reasons. The Eastern Provinces had long been suffering from administrative starvation: the area lacked adequate police supervision, adequate troops, adequate schools and adequate employment.[8] It seemed only reasonable, therefore, to create an independent province in which these needs could be met. But the outcry when this was done was enormous: first and foremost because the new Province of East Bengal would have a Mohammedan majority; but also because Curzon's measure, coming on top of the Universities' Act (which Indians interpreted as an attempt to curtail the influence of the educated classes) and the Convocation speech, was felt by the Bengali to be the crowning insult to his motherland.

The twentieth Indian National Congress of 1904 had viewed with alarm the proposed partition, and had passed a resolution to the effect

That this Congress records its emphatic protest against the proposals of the Government of India, for the Partition of Bengal in any manner whatsoever ...

The reasons for this protest were recorded as being that the division of the "Bengali Nation" into two separate units would seriously interfere with its "social, intellectual and material progress".[9] The official report of the twenty-first Congress—the first after partition—

---

[7] YMCA Secretaries' Reports: J. N. Farquhar, 1905, p. 163 (YMCA Hist. Lib.). Hereinafter *Report 1905*.

[8] *Camb. Hist. Ind.* VI (1932), p. 252.

[9] Resolution XIV of the 20th (Bombay) Congress, quoted by Besant, *How India Wrought for Freedom* (1915), p. 412; cf. Philips (ed.), *Select Documents* IV, p. 155.

stated that never "since the dark days of Lord Lytton's Viceroyalty had India been so distracted, discontented, despondent",[1] while the Congress itself passed a resolution—the first of many—condemning the partition.[2]

But the protests of Congress went unheeded; and meanwhile the popular reaction had begun, assisted no doubt by the voices and publications of the extremer nationalists, who recognized in the partition the opportunity they wanted to stir up anti-British feeling. Riots broke out. Between 1905 and 1909 the courts of law had to deal with no less than 557 disturbances in East Bengal alone arising from the partition, and this figure takes no account of the innumerable riots which went unprosecuted.[3]

Lord Curzon himself seems to have been quite indifferent to the storm of public opinion aroused by his legislation. Before the partition became law he claimed to have found no valid argument, "nothing but rhetoric and declamation", in the articles and letters he had read on the subject.[4] And the outcry, when it came, he believed to be based only on sentiment. He was concerned only with administrative efficiency, and met passion with cold logic. This of course did nothing to improve the situation.

Outside Bengal, lone voices were raised in support of Curzon's measure. Thus the Maharaja Dhiraj of Burdwan poured scorn on the student demonstrations of 1905, asking, "Could anything be more ridiculous than this schoolboy demonstration?"[5] But in Bengal, condemnation appears to have been universal. The nationalists led the outcry, treating the partition as the supreme example of what an irresponsible alien government could do to spite the wishes of the people and endanger the good of the country. Many believed that the real reason for partitioning Bengal was to divide the politically and educationally most advanced province of India, thereby weakening the pressure its leaders were able to bring upon the Government.[6]

---

[1] *Ibid.*, p. 415.

[2] *Ibid.*, p. 436. Similar resolutions were passed at each succeeding Congress from 1906 to 1910. Cf. Dasgupta, *The Indian National Congress* I–II (1946), *passim*.

[3] *Camb. Hist. Ind.* VI, pp. 252 ff.

[4] Ronaldshay, *op. cit.*, II, p. 322.

[5] *East and West* IV: 48 (Oct. 1905), p. 1017.

[6] Shay, *The Legacy of the Lokamanya* (1956), p. 89. This attitude has persisted in some quarters; cf. Raguvanshi, *op. cit.*, p. 86: "It [the partition] was manifestly a Machiavellian measure. It was intended to break the solidarity of the Bengalee race and encourage rift between the two communities." Cf. however Panikkar,

G. K. Gokhale, a radical, though not one of the most extreme of the Indian nationalist leaders, expressed the reaction, and the hopes, of many educated Bengalis when he claimed that

The tremendous upheaval of popular feeling which has taken place in Bengal in consequence of the Partition, will constitute a landmark in the history of our National progress ... Bengal's heroic stand against the oppression of a harsh and uncontrolled bureaucracy has astonished and gratified all India ...[7]

As to the riots, he was sanguine. Such "little excesses" he regarded as inevitable; "they must not be allowed to disconcert us too much".[8] Other, more militant, nationalist leaders seem in fact to have seized upon the partition as an ideal opportunity for agitation, irrespective of the merits and demerits of the situation. B. G. Tilak, speaking in Calcutta in June of the following year, 1906, urged his listeners to "make a permanent cause of grievance ... Partition grievance will be the edifice for the regeneration of India."[9] It may thus have been that in pressing the partition Curzon was unwittingly playing into the hands of the nationalists.

One important result of the partition was the renewed impetus it gave to the *swadeshi* movement (the movement for the furtherance of home industries). The movement as such was not altogether new,[1] but its progress had so far been unspectacular. On August 7, 1905, however, Bengali leaders, meeting in Calcutta Town Hall, declared a general boycott of British goods as a practical protest against the approaching partition.[2] A *swadeshi* vow was inaugurated at the temple of Kali:[3] Indians in sympathy with the national movement refused to buy British goods, Hindu priests even declining to of-

---

A Survey of Indian History, p. 221: The partition of Bengal "was fully justified by the events that followed"—i.e. the development of the Indian nationalist movement.

[7] Besant, *op. cit.*, p. 419.

[8] *Ibid.*, p. 419.

[9] Tilak, *Speeches* (1918), p. 46.

[1] See above, p. 154 f.

[2] Rai, *Young India* (1927 ed.), p. 177. For a moderate account from the Indian angle of the aims of the movement, see Baijnath, "The Swadeshi Movement", in *East and West* IV: 48 (Oct. 1905), pp. 1035–1045. G. K. Gokhale felt it necessary to distinguish between a negative aspect (boycott) and a positive (*swadeshi*); Philips (ed.), *Select Documents* IV, p. 156 f.

[3] "Invoking God Almighty to be our witness, and standing in the presence of after generations, we take this solemn vow that, as far as practicable, we shall use home made articles and abstain from the use of foreign articles." Quoted by Raguvanshi, *op. cit.*, p. 87 f.

ficiate at ceremonies where foreign stuff was intended as an oblation to the gods![4] Although the actual boycott was restricted to Bengal, the idea of *swadeshi* spread rapidly throughout India, and continued to influence the thinking of Indian nationalists, even after the partition had been revoked and the "Curzon period" was no more than a memory.[5]

The events of 1905, viewed as a whole, affected not only the political, but also the religious scene in Bengal, and presented very serious problems to the Protestant missionary force of Bengal. We shall now see how J. N. Farquhar and his co-workers in the Y.M.C.A. reacted to the new situation thus forced upon them.

Missionary Work in Calcutta, 1905–1906

We have seen what were the main methods of missionary work practised by the Calcutta Y.M.C.A. immediately prior to the crisis.[6] These were four in number: preaching, in the hall and in the open air; Bible classes; private interviews; and literature. It will be clear that the first three of these methods relied on a measure of co-operation from the Hindu: unless he were willing either to listen to the missionary, or to meet him personally, there could be no question of communication. Hitherto there had been little difficulty on these grounds; the attitude of the Hindu had often been one of friendly interest; he had usually been prepared to listen to what the missionary had to say, even if he were not prepared to submit to baptism.[7] The crisis of 1905 had the effect of alienating, at least for the time being, the average Bengali (not least the Bengali student) from Western influence, including that of the missionary. It also placed the Bengali Christians in a difficult position.[8] It had

---

[4] *Ibid.*, p. 87.

[5] The obvious example here is M. K. Gandhi.

[6] Above, pp. 179 ff.

[7] On the Hindus' motives for listening to the missionaries, see above, p. 180 n. 3.

[8] *Report 1905*, p. 163 f.: "The strained relationships which the best informed amongst missionaries know very well to exist between missionaries and Indian Christians have shown themselves in our College Branch work very seriously during the last few years. There has been a decided indisposition on the part of young Bengali Christians to attend meetings in the building or to assist in work. With Mr. Sircar's coming a very great change for the better seemed to be imminent. For a month or two young Christians came about the building quite freely and even helped with the meetings; but the excitements I have described above have laid hold of Christian Bengalis quite as seriously as Hindus;

become virtually axiomatic that the West was engaged in a policy of exploitation and repression *vis-à-vis* Indian national aspirations, and the mere fact of the missionary being a European (or an American, for close distinctions were not drawn) was enough to destroy a good deal of whatever confidence may have existed before the start of the crisis.

The first standard method to feel the force of the new situation was open-air preaching. On one occasion, reported Farquhar, it was almost impossible for the missionaries in College Square to gain a hearing, and even a stranger (who happened to be an American) was hooted and pelted with mud. Some days later the Bengali mob took the furniture which the missionaries used on their preaching stand and threw it in the water tank. Farquhar himself went to try and rescue it, and was followed down the street by an angry crowd, throwing stones and mud; Farquhar was struck and injured by a piece of brick.[9] It is not without significance that on this latter occasion the immediate cause of the riot was an ill-judged attack on Hinduism by a Bengali Christian speaker.[1] For Farquhar, this was a painful illustration of the consequences of trying to press the traditional missionary attitude of denunciation in a tense situation. Hinduism was part of the nationalist movement, and to attack Hinduism was to attack India; in the new situation the Indian retaliated without hesitation.

But preaching was not the only method to suffer. Farquhar pointed out in the course of his 1905 report that the agitation over partition, as well as putting a temporary stop to preaching in College Square, had greatly decreased the attendance at Y.M.C.A. Bible classes and indoor meetings generally. Interviews also became less common. And he commented that "men are too excited over politics to give time to religion".[2]

However, one of the existing basic methods seemed not to have been affected by the crisis. That was the fourth, the method of Christian literature. Although in public a man might easily be

and the result is that we are not a bit better off than we were before ... We trust and pray that the new scheme for a National Missionary Society will do a great deal to better the state of affairs."

[9] *Report 1905*, p. 164. He was not unduly perturbed by this, however. He wrote, "The true Apostolic succession is usually acquainted with blood and prison and persecution". Farquhar to J. L. Macpherson, 27.3.1905 (YMCA Hist. Lib.).

[1] Farquhar to Macpherson, 27.3.1905.

[2] *Report 1905*, p. 163.

converted into a member of an anti-Christian mob, at home he was still generally willing to read the publications of the Christian missionaries. This continued to hold good during the entire period up to the outbreak of the first world war, and is one of the main reasons for the growing emphasis which was to be placed on Christian literature in India by Farquhar, and by others with him.

A special problem for missionaries in Bengal was posed by the *swadeshi* movement, and particularly by its religious affiliations. This movement provides a particularly good illustration of the interaction of politics, economics and religion. Politically, it was an expression of intense nationalism, coupled with anti-Western feeling; economically, it was an attempt to place Indian home industries on a firmer footing; while a religious sanction was provided by the *swadeshi* vow, taken before Kali, the mother-goodess, representing the motherland, India.[3] The occasion of the vow was a mass meeting organized by nationalist leaders at the temple of Kali, *Kalighat,* in 1905. Farquhar, though not unsympathetic towards certain of the aims of the movement,[4] was deeply disturbed by this particular manifestation, and wrote:

That educated Bengal must go to Kalighat for its religion, where Kali the blood-thirsty stands with her tongue hanging out of her mouth and a necklace of skulls about her neck, is surely an appalling thought. It becomes every day more clear that educated Indians must choose between Christ and gross idolatry.[5]

This episode, and the strong terms in which Farquhar's aversion was expressed, are worth bearing in mind when estimating his attitude to Hinduism as a whole.

Farquhar's sympathy with the *swadeshi* movement as representing a genuine Indian aspiration was not however affected unduly by *Kalighat* episode. In fact he was disposed rather to attempt a reorientation of the movement than to abandon it altogether. In the measures taken by Farquhar and the Calcutta Y.M.C.A. to meet this particular problem we see an interesting example of the way in which the Association was able to adapt its attitude and its methods to meet the needs of a rapidly developing situation.

---

[3] Below, pp. 248 ff.
[4] Below, p. 222.
[5] *Report 1905*, p. 162.

Farquhar left India on furlough at the end of March 1906.[6] Immediately prior to his departure there was held in the Calcutta Y.M.C.A. a *swadeshi* exhibition—an event of particular importance in the history of the Protestant missions of the period. In it we see a Christian movement adopting a position of sympathy towards Indian national aspirations, at least partly in order not to jeopardize its own position as an instrument of the Gospel.

No mention of this exhibition is to be found in Farquhar's own reports and letters. But we find in the report of one of his colleagues on the Y.M.C.A. staff, the Dane F. W. Steinthal, that Farquhar had in an open letter to a Calcutta public meeting expressed his sympathy with the *swadeshi* movement.[7] This letter seems to have been regarded as laying down a policy to be followed by the Y.M.C.A. At all events, there was organized an exhibition of Indian-made goods, planned and carried out by Y.M.C.A. members under the direction of a Bengali secretary, B. C. Sircar. The exhibition was favourably received by public and press, and, as Steinthal pointed out in another context, "has helped to create a more sympathetic appreciation of our work".[8] A further interesting feature of the exhibition was a visit of two leading Japanese Christians, sent at the request of the Indian National Council as delegates from the Japanese Y.M.C.A. It is not surprising, in view of the intense interest shown at that time by Indians in Japanese affairs, to learn that their visit "created quite a sensation".[9] The basic purpose of the exhibition, and of the Japanese visit, was clearly expressed by Steinthal as follows:

This our policy, to be in full sympathy with the national movement without committing ourselves in any way towards its extravagances, has so far been successful and must be continued in order to gain the ears and confidence of the student community ...[1]

The key-word in this important statement is "policy". We have no way of knowing to what extent the individual Western members of the Y.M.C.A. staff were in fact in full sympathy with *swadeshi*:

[6] YMCA Secretaries' Reports, J. N. Farquhar, 1906, p. 211 (YMCA Hist. Lib.). Hereinafter *Report 1906*.

[7] YMCA Secretaries' Reports: F. W. Steinthal, 1906, p. 222 (YMCA Hist. Lib.).

[8] Steinthal, "National Character in Making", in *FM* XIII: 4 (July–August 1906), p. 23.

[9] *Ibid.*

[1] YMCA Secretaries' Reports: F. W. Steinthal, 1906, p. 223.

Farquhar, as we have already seen, was critical of its religious basis, and we may assume that most shared his views. But it was imperative in a time of tension and mutual distrust that the Y.M.C.A. should not fall under the same condemnation as the British authorities. The confidence of the student population of Calcutta must be retained, and it was thus imperative that a stand should be made on the side of nationalism—in so far as such a stand could be taken without compromising essential Christian principles—as a matter of policy.

We do not wish to lay too much emphasis on this aspect of the situation in 1905–1906: merely to point out its existence. But it must be recognized that the thought of "policy" and "strategy" was seldom wholly absent from missionary work at this time. It may have been partly unconscious; partly a result of the inherent activism of the Evangelical missionary enterprise. Yet it was as a matter of policy—to demonstrate that Christianity was no enemy of Indian nationalist aspirations—that the *swadeshi* exhibition was arranged; and the same idea is to be discerned at the back of a great deal of Farquhar's later written work. In reality, of course, policy was one aspect of apologetics, as understood at the time: and conversely, apologetics could never be wholly freed from an element of policy.[2] The Y.M.C.A. *swadeshi* exhibition might be characterized as an essay in practical apologetics. Its lessons were however to reflect on the literary apologetics practised by Farquhar and supported by the Y.M.C.A. in later years. But the time was not yet ripe for Farquhar's full contribution.

The National Missionary Society

The 1905 crisis, with its upsurge of national feeling, did not pass by the Indian Christian community. Ever since the days of Duff the Indian Christian had tended to find himself in an ambiguous position, drawn one way by traditional loyalties, and another by his religious affiliations. Open conflict seldom occurred, but there had long been tension, which nationalist agitation served to intensify. The "great wave of national aspiration"[3] which swept

---

[2] On the term "apologetics", see above, p. 16 f. and below, pp. 231 ff.

[3] The phrase is taken from Chaturvedi and Sykes, *Charles Freer Andrews* (1949), p. 42.

over educated India in 1905 had as one of its results the formation in Serampore, on December 25, 1905, of the Indian National Missionary Society (*Bharat Christya Sevak Samaj*)—a notable step towards indigenization in the Indian Church.[4]

The N.M.S. was not the first attempt to organize a "missionary society" for Indians. As far back as 1839 the American Madura Mission had had local "native evangelistic societies"[5] and a general society for the whole Mission since 1853.[6] But these had been supervised by Western missionaries. The immediate forerunner of the N.M.S. was the Indian Missionary Society of Tinnevelly, founded in 1903, with Dornakal as its "field" and V. S. Azariah (later Bishop of Dornakal) as its leader.[7] Impulses from these earlier experiments, together with a desire to create a form of organization genuinely *swadeshi* in character, bound to no Western body, and run by Indians, took concrete form in 1905. Its ethos was essentially that of the Y.M.C.A., though directed more towards the villages than the educated classes. An important role in its organization was played by G. Sherwood Eddy, an American Y.M.C.A. Secretary at that time working in Madras.[8]

Describing the formation of the N.M.S.,[9] Eddy stated its aims as follows:

Founding no new denomination, but preserving the strongest loyalty to the churches; soliciting no funds outside of India, but laying the burden of India's evangelization upon her own sons, we believe the Society is organized on a sound and safe basis.[1]

The governing council was to consist of some sixty Indian Christians; the executive committee was based on the Y.M.C.A. building

---

[4] For the history of the movement, see Ebright, *The National Missionary Society of India 1905–1942* (1944); this is however poorly written. There is also an earlier symposium, printed in India, *The First Ten Years of the N.M.S. 1905–1916* (s.a.).

[5] Chandler, *Seventy-Five Years in the Madura Mission* (s.a.), p. 134.

[6] *Ibid.*, p. 265.

[7] Firth, *An Introduction to Indian Church History* (1961), p. 247.

[8] For a brief appreciation of the work of G. S. Eddy, see Sharpe, "G. Sherwood Eddy 1872–1963", in *SMT* 51: 3 (1963), pp. 173 ff. Another prominent leader of the NMS was Prof. S. Satthiandan of the Madras Christian College. V. S. Azariah was however able to claim at the Tokyo WSCF conference of 1907 that "It was the students, the student leaders and the young men of the country that ... organized this society". *Report of the Conference of the World's Student Christian Federation, held at Tokyo, Japan* (1907), p. 125.

[9] Art. "The Evangelization of India by Indians", in *FM* XIII: 3 (May–June 1906), pp. 16 ff.

[1] *Ibid.*, p. 16.

in Madras; and an advisory board of experienced missionaries was set up. The first President was Sir Harnam Singh; the first Secretary V. S. Azariah.[2] It was thus intended to be run by Indians, for Indians; and implicitly to stand as far as possible outside the sphere of Westernization represented by the existing missions.

Farquhar hailed the foundation of the new Society as a "momentous" event. For three reasons: first, because it demonstrated the influence of the Y.M.C.A. on the Indian Church; secondly, because he felt it to be proof of the real unity underlying the denominational divisions of Christianity in India; and thirdly, because it was "the first general movement tending towards the evangelization of India by her own sons".[3] As one of the signs of the times, he found it highly encouraging evidence of a new spirit of evangelism, in which Indians would be able to make their rightful contribution, as well as being evidence of an active ecumenical intention.[4] In fact he was slightly carried away by his own enthusiasm, writing that a Society of this type would "take the Indians themselves by storm, and ... lead to such an outburst of missionary enthusiasm as we have never yet seen".[5]

The National Missionary Society was never quite the force Farquhar hoped it would be. By 1934 it had 160 workers,[6] mainly in the Punjab villages. But after 1914 the emphasis in India began to move from "missions" to the Church, and the N.M.S. was placed in a difficult position.[7] However, the idea of the Christian *ashram* was first mooted at a N.M.S. conference (in 1912),[8] and the important Chakkarai-Chenchiah theological group were at first associated with the N.M.S.[9]—both of much significance for the future of the Indian Church.

---

[2] Hodge, *Bishop Azariah of Dornakal* (1946), p. 16, Graham, *Azariah of Dornakal* (1946), pp. 26 ff.

[3] *Report 1906*, p. 212. Others, too, were enthusiastic: G. Hibbert Ware of the Cambridge Mission to Delhi (SPG) wrote that "The inaguration of this scheme promises a new era in the evangelization of India". *The East and the West* IV (1906), p. 214. Similar sentiments were expressed by W. E. S. Holland of Allahabad: see *Proceedings of the Church Missionary Society* 51 (1905–1906), p. 135.

[4] The founding of the Union Theological College at Bangalore, first mooted at this time, was another source of encouragement. Farquhar had been advocating this kind of move for more than a decade. See above, pp. 163 ff.

[5] Art. "A National Missionary Society for India", in *HF* XVII: 2 (Feb. 1906), p. 60.

[6] Azariah, *India and the Christian Movement* (1936), p. 94 f.

[7] Firth, *op. cit.*, p. 248 f.

[8] Chaturvedi and Sykes, *op. cit.*, p. 73 f.

[9] Sundkler, *Church of South India* (1954), p. 86.

That a movement of this kind should have emerged from out of the midst of such a crisis as that we have described, was symptomatic of the general movement away from what had come to be regarded as Westernization. The National Missionary Society was essentially *swadeshi,* and was a challenge to the missions: Could they be satisfied with anything less? For Farquhar, and others with him, the implications were clear: the process of Indianization in the Church, once begun, could not and must not be halted; but could the Indian Church of the future be provided, surrounded as it was by renascent Hinduism, with an adequate intellectual foundation?[1]

Summing up, we have seen in this chapter how the political crisis of 1905 rendered standard missionary methods less effective than formerly. This was no transitory phase. The influence of the Neo-Hindu movements was increasing: opposition to the West and to Christianity as a "denationalizing" religion was to survive, even after the political climate had become temporarily more stable.[2] It is therefore of the utmost significance for the future development of Farquhar's work to note that along with an emphasis on policy, and the growth of the national spirit in Christian circles, there came to be a new emphasis on the potentialities of literature. Farquhar was absent from the Indian scene during the greater part of 1906 and part of 1907. Yet his first report after his return emphasizes precisely this point—the opportunity open through literature, even when other doors appear to have been closed.[3] The

---

[1] A closely related subject, which we cannot go into here, is that of the position of Indian leaders in the missionary organizations, and that of the first steps towards the establishment of the Indian Church. We may note that the first Principal of a missionary college was appointed in 1907, when S. K. Rudra became Principal of St. Stephen's College Delhi [A most interesting collection of material relative to this appointment is preserved in the CMD Archives, London, in a folder entitled "Correspondence re Appointment of Prof. Rudra as Principal, 1907]. The first Indian bishop, V. S. Azariah, was consecrated in 1912.

[2] Below, p. 300.

[3] YMCA Secretaries' Reports: J. N. Farquhar, 1907, p. 286 f. (YMCA Hist. Lib.): "Every experienced man all over India agrees that there is no way of reaching the average educated Hindu or Mohammedan throughout the country comparable with literature. There are thousands of men, especially those who have come under the influence of the Hindu revival or the Theosophical movement, who would scorn to enter a Christian building or listen to a Christian preacher in a public square. Yet these same men are perfectly willing to read Christian literature, if it is presented with a special view to their class ... The educated classes are steadily increasing in numbers, education and influence; a large proportion of them are resolutely opposed to mission work: yet they are quite open to literature."

provision of such literature was henceforth to be Farquhar's greatest concern. But when he returned to India in 1907 it was in an administrative capacity, and five more years were to elapse before he was given the opportunity of meeting what he had come to regard as a personal challenge. The developments of those years we shall consider in our next chapter.

CHAPTER 8

Student Evangelization and Religious Nationalism
1907—1911

UP TO 1906, as a teacher in a missionary college and a Secretary on the staff of the Y.M.C.A. College Branch, Farquhar's main task had been the interpretation of the Christian message to the Bengali student. The period which we are to consider in this chapter has a number of distinctive features which were not present in these earlier phases. Farquhar spent the years between 1907 and 1911 as National Student Secretary of the Indian Y.M.C.A. (though for a period he served as National General Secretary). This involved incessant travelling, speaking and organizing. During these years he was brought into contact with the leaders of the World's Student Christian Federation on an increasing scale, and some of the problems on which he had been engaged since coming to India began to be debated in the wider context of the student movements of the world.

It is thus symptomatic of the period that it began and ended at W.S.C.F. conferences. His first action as Student Secretary was to represent the Indian Y.M.C.A. at the Tokyo W.S.C.F. conference of 1907; while his release from the immediate responsibility for student work in India was negotiated at the 1911 Constantinople conference of the W.S.C.F. His own development as a missionary leader owes a great deal to the contacts he established as Student Secretary, and to the subjects discussed in the debate of the period. This was a period, too, of greater co-ordination in student work the world over. Not least thanks to the travels of John R. Mott and to the conferences which he organized, the problems of the student movements of China, Japan, Russia, India and the West came to be seen as part of an overall pattern; and if Farquhar was able to derive information and encouragement from the progress of the movement in other parts of the world, the movement looked to

Farquhar as an interpreter of the Indian situation—a role he filled in Tokyo and at the 1909 Oxford conference.

This does not mean that Farquhar was less concerned with the details of the Indian problem. On the contrary; the complicated relations between Christianity and Hinduism, and their struggle for the allegiance of the students of India, assumed new importance in view of the wider perspective in which Christian student work came to be seen. Furthermore, the main features of the Indian situation had already become peculiarly distinctive—more so than in other Far Eastern lands—and in no other country was the problem at that time quite so clear-cut. India thus became something of a test case, and the work done by Farquhar and other student leaders in India helped to clarify the position for their colleagues in other countries.

We have said that the period began with the Tokyo W.S.C.F. conference of 1907, and it is here we must start our account of Farquhar's work as Student Secretary.

Tokyo 1907

The only one of Farquhar's private diaries which has been preserved[1] covers the period of the 1907 Tokyo conference and a subsequent journey through China, Hong Kong, Burma and Singapore. Unfortunately there is little in it but a bare account of his travels, names of his companions and notes of the addresses he heard. It is however useful in supplementing our information on a number of points. We learn from this diary that he left Aberdeen on February 19, 1907, and travelled to Japan via America and the Hawaiian Islands, landing in Yokohama on March 26. The conference began on April 3.

The Tokyo conference was notable principally as the first international conference of this kind to meet in the Far East and the first world Christian conference to be called in a non-Christian country.[2] It had three main foci. The first of these was information: a comprehensive series of addresses was given on the contemporary situation of Christianity in the countries of the

---

[1] Farquhar collection.
[2] Tatlow, *The Story of the Student Christian Movement of Great Britain and Ireland* (1933), p. 275 f., Rouse, *The World's Student Christian Federation* (1948), pp. 124 ff.

modern world—Germany, Great Britain, France, America, Africa, India and Japan. Farquhar was responsible for the address on "India and Christianity"[3] which we shall consider shortly. Secondly, attention was paid to the three main objects of the World's Student Christian Federation—evangelization, the building up of converts and their utilization in further missionary work. And thirdly, an attempt was made to combine the conference with evangelistic campaigns in Tokyo and the surrounding districts. Farquhar himself, as we learn from his diary, took part as a speaker in such meetings.[4] Commentators are agreed that although there were a number of conversions as a result of these services, the main effect of the conference as a whole was to dispel anti-Christian prejudice, rather than to swell the ranks of committed Christians.[5]

Farquhar, as we have indicated, addressed the conference on the subject of "India and Christianity". His object was to provide information, and his paper accordingly was concentrated and possibly over-systematized. It need hardly be said that he approached the problem entirely from the side of Evangelical missions, particularly as these missions were affected by the "movement towards Western thought among the educated classes".[6] Farquhar interpreted this movement as evidence that the defensive armour of Hinduism had been finally and decisively pierced, since in his view all the ruling ideas of this movement were diametrically opposed to the spirit of Hinduism, and since all the new ideas at work in India society and religion were "definitely Christian".[7] The causes of this new movement he saw as being four in number: Western education, Christian teaching, Christian philanthropy and Government action.[8] And the situation of the Protestant Churches he described as hopeful in the extreme, being characterized by growth, progress, and—most important of all—"the rise of missionary zeal".[9] He concluded on an optimistic note, saying

[3] *Report of the Conference of the World's Student Christian Federation held at Tokyo, Japan* (1907), pp. 37 ff.

[4] No details are however given, except that on April 4 he spoke together with V. S. Azariah, and that after the conference he travelled for a while with G. S. Eddy.

[5] Rouse, *op. cit.*, p. 125, Honda, "Some Results of the Federation Conference in Japan", in the *Student World* I (1908), p. 4.

[6] *Tokyo Report,* p. 39 f.

[7] *Ibid.*, p. 41.

[8] *Ibid.*, p. 41 f.

[9] The reference was to the National Missionary Society—"a new, glorious enterprise", *ibid.*, p. 44. Cf. above, pp. 223 ff.

The hand of God is visibly stretched out over India; His quickening Spirit is working both within and without the Church of Christ; the tide is rising slowly, but irresistibly: let us be faithful; Christ will conquer.[1]

Farquhar was also one of those who contributed "impressions of the conference" to the official report. His main personal impression was that it proved Christianity to be "a world-wide religion of great vitality and strength",[2] and he also noted that the conference had evidently had at least some effect on the non-Christian religions of Japan—a judgment in which he was borne out by Japanese Christian leaders.[3] Unity was another aspect of the conference which impressed him; yet—and here we return to the theme of optimism which was so prominent a feature of the missionary conferences of the period—"the thought which controlled the conference, the shore to which the tide of spiritual power continuously swept, was the evangelization of the world".[4]

Unity there undoubtedly was; yet a potential source of controversy was to be seen in the introduction of "Apologetics" into the conference. While a detailed consideration of this theme would lead us far beyond the bounds of this present work, a brief review of the coming of this new attitude into international student Christian work will be helpful for our understanding of Farquhar's role in the Indian debate. This is to be seen as the penetration into a previously conservative Evangelical sphere of certain of the ideas we have discussed in Chapter One of this study.

Apologetics or Evangelism?

The World's Student Christian Federation was born at a time when the spirit of evangelism—in the sense of the direct presentation of the claims of Christ on the allegiance of the individual—was at its zenith, on both sides of the Atlantic. In fact the first "line of activity" laid down by the Federation in 1895 was "To lead students to become disciples of Jesus Christ as only Saviour and God".[5] This was fully in accordance with the principles of the

---

[1] *Ibid.*, p. 45.
[2] *Ibid.*, p. 193.
[3] "The direct spiritual results of the Conference were not very striking, but the indirect results were vast." Honda, *loc. cit.*
[4] *Tokyo Report*, p. 195.
[5] Rouse, *op. cit.*, p. 62.

Student Volunteer Movement, the Y.M.C.A. and the British College Christian Union—to name only the three most prominent parent bodies.[6]

The question of apologetics—in this case the attempt to remove hindrances to the acceptance of the Christian faith by means of a reasoned intellectual discussion of problems and difficulties—was first raised in the British student movement, where the climate of opinion differed somewhat from that of America.[7] It was closely linked with the question of the doctrinal basis of the movement. Though the evangelical basis was at first accepted in Britain, as it had been in America,[8] British student opinion was far from unanimous.[9] The student movement there was coming more and more into contact with newly-won Christians and doubters; theology in Britain was in an unsettled state, and many questioned the wisdom of having any basis at all. For such people the most that could be accepted was a statement of attitude, rather than of belief.[1] But the conservative element was still strong enough to ensure the retention of the old basis, and at the same time to reject the suggestion that more time ought to be spent on discussing intellectual problems—in other words, on apologetics.[2]

The turning point, as far as Britain was concerned, came in the autumn of 1905, on the initiative of Tissington Tatlow,[3] when a series of apologetical meetings held in London were received with such interest as to convince the S.C.M. committee of their value to students.[4] On the international level, John R. Mott himself, speaking at the W.S.C.F. conference at Zeist, Holland, in May 1905, had advocated the apologetical approach as a necessary preliminary

---

[6] For SVM principles, see Brown in *The S.V.M. after Twenty-Five Years* (1911), p. 33; for YMCA, see above, pp. 175 ff.; for BCCU, see Tatlow, *op. cit.*, p. 65 f.

[7] Tatlow, *op. cit.*, p. 199 f. Cf. above, p. 40.

[8] Thanks partly to the influence of Mott: see Tatlow, *loc. cit.* The basis of 1901 was formulated thus: "I desire in joining this union to declare my faith in Jesus Christ as my Saviour, my Lord and my God." *Ibid.*, p. 208.

[9] A parallel stage in the American debate was not reached until after the first world war, though when it came the rejection of the Evangelical position was even more decisive. See Hopkins, *History of the Y.M.C.A. in North America* (1951), pp. 519 ff.

[1] Tatlow, *op. cit.*, pp. 380 ff., 472, 474.

[2] *Ibid.*, p. 259. This attitude came to govern the British SCM after 1908, *ibid.*, p. 311.

[3] Then General Secretary of the BCCU.

[4] *Ibid.*, p. 260: "The meetings were crammed and the Bible readings parallel to them deserted; this convinced the committee that the new element must be added to the programme at the summer conference."

to evangelism in some cases. This he felt would help meet philosophical and scientific difficulties among students.[5] The idea was
echoed by Tatlow, who considered that such an approach would
attract, not only men weak in the faith, but "men who may have
been harbouring a suspicion that the union (i.e. the W.S.C.F. and
S.V.M.) is ready to make an appeal on behalf of Christ to men's
hearts, but ignored Christ's appeal to their intellects".[6] No apologetical addresses were delivered at Zeist; the principle had however reached an international student forum.[7]

At the Tokyo conference both streams were represented. Alongside the traditional evangelical approach there had appeared the
intellectual, or apologetical approach. A section of the conference
report is devoted to "Doctrinal, Apologetical and General Addresses". Apologetical lectures were given by such distinguished speakers
as Professor Alex. Macalister, Professor of Anatomy in Cambridge,
who spoke on "The Scientific attitude towards Christianity",[8] and
Sir Alexander Simpson of Edinburgh, who spoke on "The Science
of Knowing God".[9] The innovation—for innovation it was—was not
welcomed by all. G. Sherwood Eddy was oppenly suspicious of the
appeal to the intellect. "Let us", he said, ". . . avoid the apologetical
method and seek rather the personal appeal to the heart and the
conscience."[1] In his view the method as such postponed rather than
hastened the acceptance of the Gospel; if we concentrate on the
message of Christ crucified, the Saviour from sin, he claimed, conversions will result, without the need for apologetics.[2] This was
however to mistake the function of apologetics. What Mott and
Tatlow had envisaged was not that the intellectual approach should
replace the direct appeal to the heart and conscience, but that it
should *pave the way* for such an appeal. Mott, despite his advocacy
of apologetics two years earlier, was firm in his conviction that the

---

[5] Mott, "A Decennial Review", in *Zeist Report* (1905), p. 26.
[6] Tatlow, "How to Enlarge the Range of the Influence of our Union", *ibid.*,
p. 38 f.
[7] The contrast between the later and earlier approaches stands out even more
clearly by comparison with the report of the Eisenach conference of 1898, where
the emphasis was purely evangelistic.
[8] *Tokyo Report*, pp. 73–87.
[9] *Ibid.*, pp. 87–90.
[1] *Ibid.*, p. 112.
[2] *Ibid.*

distinguishing characteristic of the World's Student Christian Federation was "the spirit of evangelism".[3]

The acceptance of the apologetical position by the W.S.C.F., though reserved, was one element which helped create a favourable atmosphere on the international level for the work which Farquhar was attempting to do on the local Indian level. Since coming to the Y.M.C.A. he had been concerned with the question of Christian-Hindu relations: not, it is true, as matter for preaching,[4] but as apologetics, as the intellectual foundation on which evangelical preaching might be based. In this we have seen that he was moved very largely by the practical considerations of gaining a hearing among Hindus. A short article published in the *Student World* in the following year, 1908, further emphasized this need.[5] Although only the presentation of Christianity "has any positive value", and the most potent addresses appeal to the conscience, rather than to the intellect, "in these days it is hard to get the average Hindu to listen to such themes", wrote Farquhar.[6] Denunciation is of no value whatever; Christ must be set forth as "the great Consummator of the faith of Asia"; the preacher's message must be "Through Hinduism to Christ".[7] But at the same time Farquhar was, as we have seen,[8] aware of the practical limitations of preaching. Literature he considered to be of more value, since many Hindus were prepared to read Christian literature where they were unwilling to listen to a Christian preacher. We have already noted something of the form Farquhar wished such literature to take.[9] A further decisive impulse came from John R. Mott.

Alongside the 1907 W.S.C.F. conference in Tokyo John R. Mott took the opportunity to arrange a small private conference of national Y.M.C.A. secretaries, in order to discuss the situation of the Y.M.C.A. in the larger context of the world student movement, and to outline the large-scale policy which was to be followed in future.

---

[3] *Ibid.*, p. 108. It is not too much to say that "evangelism" and "evangelization" were Mott's characteristic emphases throughout his active life. See the introduction to his symposium *Evangelism for the World Today* (1938), p. 7 f.

[4] Farquhar, *Missionary Study of Hinduism* (1905), p. 4.

[5] Idem, "The Most Fruitful Apologetic Methods among Hindu Students", in the *Student World* I (April 1908), pp. 60–62.

[6] *Ibid.* A practical illustration of the problems facing the preacher is given above, p. 220.

[7] *Ibid.*

[8] Above, pp. 184 f., 220 f.

[9] Cf. literature on the *Bhagavad Gītā*, discussed above, pp. 198 ff.

This subsidiary conference was held in Yokohama, March 29–31, 1907 (before the main conference), in the presence of secretaries from America, Japan, China and India.[1]

The minutes of this conference have been lost, but it seems that matters of some importance were discussed, including a programme of "mission-study" involving the production of high-class literature. In February 1908 Farquhar wrote to E. C. Carter

As you know, we have been earnestly carrying out the programme sketched for us by Mott in Japan. Azariah's book on India[2] is in the press, and will be out by the first of April; ... and my own work on Hinduism[3] will follow ...[4]

"Mission-study", as advocated by Mott, fell into six categories. First came (i) the study of mission fields; then in turn (ii) the study of non-Christian races, (iii) the study of the great non-Christian religions "including a comparison of these with one another and with Christianity and an examination of the best methods of presenting Christianity to the people of these faiths"; (iv) the history of overseas missions and (v) home missions; and finally (vi) the study of the Biblical basis of missions.[5] Of these, category (iii) was of particular importance for Farquhar's work.

The launching of this scheme does not necessarily mean that Mott explicitly advocated at this stage the production of large-scale works on the relationship of Christianity to the non-Christian religions, but that he provided a further impetus for the starting of such work in India seems clear.[6] Mott's policy provided high-level confirmation of the views which Farquhar had held for a number of years.

One necessary presupposition for the writing of this kind of li-

---

[1] Others present were: G. M. Fisher and V. Helm of Japan, F. S. Brockman and D. W. Lyon of China, E. C. Carter and G. S. Eddy of India, E. T. Colton, C. D. Hurrey and J. R. Mott from America. The record of this conference carries the following note: "The minutes of this important conference have never been found. The above notes were sent by Mr. Barber from the Mott archives in Florida." (YMCA Hist. Lib., New York.) Farquhar's private diary states only: "Friday March 29th: Went down to Yokohama ... Very fine conference lasting until Sunday afternoon."

[2] Azariah, *India and Missions* (1908).

[3] Farquhar, *A Primer of Hinduism* (1911).

[4] J. N. Farquhar to E. C. Carter, 2.2.1908 (YMCA Hist. Lib.).

[5] Murray, *The Organization of Mission Study among Students* (1908); cf. Farquhar, *The Crown of Hinduism* (1913), p. 16.

[6] On the subject of Mott's attitude to the non-Christian religions, see Mathews, *John R. Mott: World Citizen* (1934), pp. 264 ff. Much remains to be done in this field.

terature in India was the availability of scholars sharing Farquhar's attitude of sympathy towards Hinduism. Ten years earlier the project would have been altogether remote from the sphere of practical politics; now it was at least feasible. The question of the intellectual, apologetical approach had been raised, and had received at least a partly affirmative answer; the question now was who was to provide the literature it called for.

Changing Attitudes

The exact stages by which Evangelical missionaries in India came to be convinced of the need for a sympathetic approach to Hinduism are not easily determined. For obvious reasons: the field was enormous and diverse; so much depended upon the background and education of the individuals concerned; the lines of demarcation between those favouring the "old" and "new" attitudes often cut across denominational boundaries; and these were in any case indistinct. But an examination of representative literature from this period shows that more and more missionaries were coming to regard sympathy, "points of contact" and—in some cases—"fulfilment" as standard items of their equipment. This process dates back, as we have seen, to the 1880's; but only now, in the years between 1905 and 1910, did it come to be applied on anything like a wide scale, and even then with notable dissentients. We may take a number of illustrative examples.

During these years the "old" and "new" attitudes are often found to be existing side-by-side, among missionaries from the same society—one distinguishing factor being apparently the kind of Hinduism the missionary in question was called upon to face. Thus in 1905 two articles were contributed to the Baptist *Missionary Herald* by a village missionary, T. R. Edwards, under the title "Face to Face with Hinduism".[7] There is little to distinguish these from the "heathen darkness" articles of the previous century: little but contempt is shown for the Hindus' "cunningly-devised priest-craft". Yet in the following year, 1906, an educational missionary, G. Howells (later Principal at Serampore) began in the same journal a series of "Short Papers on Non-Christian Religions" in which it was stressed that the missionary is compelled by loyalty to the truth in

[7] *MH* VIII N.S. (1905), pp. 488–91, 533–36.

Christ to recognize truth wherever it may be found. "Our aim", wrote Howells, "should be not to destroy, but to preserve everything that is consistent with the essentials of the Christian faith."[8] A similar opinion was expressed in 1907 by another Baptist missionary, E. E. Hayward.[9]

The same juxtaposition of "old" and "new" may be observed among missionaries of the Church Missionary Society. In this case the process of modification had begun earlier: two articles in the 1896 *Intelligencer* take almost contradictory positions with regard to Hinduism.[1] Occasionally, in later years, the claims of both attitudes could be felt by the same missionary. As when W. E. S. Holland, who had been working among students at Allahabad since 1900,[2] saw for the first time the excesses of popular Hinduism (at the *Kumbh Mela* of 1906) and confessed: "The shock to me was to realize that this existed alongside of one of the sublimest, profoundest and most spiritual philosophies in the world."[3] On the "official" level, the C.M.S. was reticent as to the extent of sympathy that was justified. Reviewers in the *Intelligencer* spoke equally highly of Slater's *Higher Hinduism* and Dilger's *Erlösung*—two books with vastly different approaches to Hinduism.[4] And as late as 1912 an anonymous writer could state that Hinduism is "on the whole not an evolution from darkness to light, but a degradation in ever-increasing degrees of darkness".[5]

But in India, a growing number of missionaries were willing to follow the example of N. C. Mukerji, a Presbyterian from Allahabad, who wrote in 1908:

---

[8] *MH* IX N.S. (1906), p. 16. Howells was later to contribute an interesting paper to the Edinburgh conference (Comm. IV), in which he developed the argument that a Christian preacher must look for, and use, the "large elements of truth" in the Hindu scriptures, and concluded: "The new Christian apologetic for India must be on such lines, or it will fail altogether of its purpose." *Edinburgh MS.*

[9] "Impressions of India", in *MH* X N.S. (1907), pp. 83–85.

[1] Articles by W. St. Clair Tisdall (positive) and J. P. Haythornthwaite (negative) in *CMI* XXI N.S. (1896), pp. 569–76 and 578–90.

[2] Sen, *Memoir of the Revd. Canon W. E. S. Holland* (1951).

[3] "Never till now have I seen what Hinduism meant. This is a side of things one may never see while working among educated men ... Yet this is Hinduism, natural, naked, hideous." *Proceedings of the CMS* 51 (1905–06), p. 155 f. But in 1910 he wrote that the missionary's attitude must be "generous and delighted in the recognition of the good wherever found". *Edinburgh MS.*

[4] *CMI* XXVIII N.S. (1903), p. 12 (review of Slater); *CMR* XXXIV N.S. (1909), pp. 37 ff. (review of Dilger).

[5] *Proceedings of the CMS* 57 (1911–12), p. 90.

But let us, above all, preach Christ as He who came not to destroy, but to fulfil. Let us make it quite clear that in becoming a Christian a Hindu does not give up what is best in his religion, but gets it back in a fuller and richer form.[6]

The periodical in which Mukerji was writing, the *Indian Interpreter,* is worth a special mention. Started in 1906 by two Scottish missionaries in Poona, Nicol Macnicol and A. Robertson of the U.F.C.S., its initial statement of policy—which was that of Macnicol— made it quite clear on which side of the "attitude" question it stood:

The attitude of the paper will be one of sympathy with all that is worthy in the religions of India and the aspirations of the Indian people, as pointing to and finding their fulfilment in the Christian faith.[7]

Another journal which exercised a not inconsiderable influence of the same kind in South India was the *Madras Christian College Magazine,* to which A. G. Hogg (then Professor of Philosophy in the College) was a frequent contributor. The tone of the magazine may be judged from this editorial comment, again from 1908:

"I came not to destroy but to fulfil", is not a word to be limited in its application to Judaism. All that there is of truth and inspiration in other religions must find its fulfilment in Jesus Christ.[8]

Of Hogg's own attitude we do not propose to speak at length here; his contribution was distinctive, since he was convinced of the need for an altogether new approach to the problem of Christian theology in India, and could not rest content with a mere theory of "relationship" between Christianity and Hinduism. We shall return to this topic later.[9]

Two other individual missionaries whose growing influence in these years was altogether on the side of the sympathetic approach, but who were not primarily theorists, may be mentioned here: C. F. Andrews of the Cambridge Mission to Delhi and L. P. Larsen of the Danish Missionary Society (then working under Y.M.C.A. auspices in Madras). In neither case can we however speak of the same kind of influence as that later exercised by Farquhar on the problem of confrontation. Andrews was to leave missionary work

---

[6] *Indian Interpreter* IV: 1 (April 1908), p. 34.
[7] From Macnicol's prospectus, quoted in *HF* XVII: 3 (March 1906), p. 119.
[8] Editorial notes, in *MCCM* VII: 12 (June 1908), p. 646.
[9] Below, pp. 284 ff.

altogether in 1914; Larsen's lasting contribution was in the field of theological education and Bible translation. In Andrews' case, though standing in a tradition of sympathetic appreciation of Hinduism,[1] the years from 1905 to 1910 were taken up by an attempt to show that the Western missionary could be altogether sympathetic to all things Indian, and not merely to the "quests" or "truths" of Hinduism.[2] Larsen's attitude was conditioned by a theological background which the British and American missionaries did not possess. Though he had earlier spoken of Christ coming to India to "fulfil",[3] he was later to concentrate more on the defective, than on the preparatory, aspects of Hinduism. Metaphysics, he felt, could never be a substitute for moral stringency; the missionary's appeal must be to the conscience, not to the imagination and emotions.[4] Lecturing in Uppsala in 1906, he stressed that there must be no compromise in Christianity in India; there is indeed a *praeparatio,* but it is to be found rather in Western (British, not German) culture than in Hinduism as such.[5] And in his most notable book, *Hindu-Aandsliv og Kristendommen* (1907), he allowed there to be "points of contact" (*Tilknytningspunkter*) between Christianity and Hinduism, but stated that these were of little practical value to the missionary.[6] For Larsen the whole problem was one of sin and guilt, and the only solution the Cross of Christ. To this there were no short cuts, and on the subject of "relationships" and "attitudes" he was not prepared to theorize further.[7]

A still more uncompromising position tended to be taken up by Continental missionaries in India, of whom Wilhelm Dilger of the Basel Mission may serve as an example. For Dilger, the issue was plain: the Gospel of Redemption through the Cross and Resurrection of Christ was *sui generis,* and might not be modified in any

---

[1] A tradition beginning with Westcott and persisting throughout the early history of the CMD. See e.g. Lefroy, *Christ the Goal of India* (CMD Occasional Paper 15, 1889). Lefroy later became Bishop of Lahore.

[2] Shown with great clarity in the question of the appointment in 1907 of S. K. Rudra as Principal of St. Stephen's College, Delhi. See correspondence in CMD Archives referred to above, p. 226 n. 1.

[3] Review in *MCCM* II: 12 (June 1903), p. 639.

[4] Larsen, "The Interest of Mystical Christianity to Missionaries", in *HF* XVI: 1 (Jan. 1905), p. 36 f., and XVI: 2 (Feb. 1905), p. 54.

[5] Larsen, "Kristendom och folkkaraktären i Indien", in *Nutida Missionsuppgifter* (1906), pp. 101 ff., 112.

[6] *Hindu-Aandsliv*, p. 219 f.

[7] Larsen did not contribute to Commission IV at Edinburgh.

way, least of all by missionaries lacking an adequate theology.[8] However, at this stage missionaries from the Continental churches and societies were scarcely in a position to influence the course of the missionary debate in India, though the position was in time to be changed.

Here we have seen that during these years there were a number of conflicting views on the question of the attitude to be taken up in principle towards Hinduism. The attitude of sympathy, which depended on the recognition of elements of truth and goodness in Hinduism, and which might in some cases rest on the foundation of evolutionary theory, was gaining support, mainly among British missionaries. It had indeed received episcopal sanction, in the book *Mankind and the Church* (1907), written entirely by bishops of the Church of England.[9] Articles were continually appearing, stressing the need for sympathy; but others were stressing equally vehemently the danger of compromise. However, it seemed that Farquhar's plans for scholarly, sympathetic literature might well bear fruit, since there was now a body of missionary opinion sufficiently well-defined to be enlisted in this cause. In December 1907 a conference was called in Calcutta on "Christian Work for Educated Indians", at which a literature committee was appointed. Nothing seems to have come of the conference as such, but the names of the committee may be placed on record: the first name is that of Farquhar; and the others, C. F. Andrews, V. S. Azariah, D. J. Fleming, W. E. S. Holland, R. A. Hume, L. P. Larsen, N. Macnicol and N. C. Mukerji. This was in effect the nucleus of what came to be called the "fulfilment school".

After Tokyo

As Student Secretary, Farquhar was compelled to be constantly on the move, visiting, organizing, preaching and lecturing. His route to India after the Tokyo conference took him to Hong Kong, Canton, Burma and Singapore, and from the beginning of August

---

[8] Dilger, *Probleme der Missionsarbeit im heutigen Indien* (1909), p. 11. Cf. idem, *Krischna oder Kristus: eine religionsgeschichtliche Parallele* (1904); see also above, p. 103, and below, p. 251 f.
[9] Dewick, *The Christian Attitude to Other Religions* (1953), p. 48 f.

1907 he was on tour in South India and Ceylon,[1] arriving back in Calcutta in December.

A letter written a few days after his arrival[2] stresses three important points: first, that he was convinced that his own work ought to be mainly in the field of Christian literature; secondly, that he had found an encouraging interest in Y.M.C.A. work in East Asia and the South of India; and thirdly, that a meeting in Bangalore had given him great personal satisfaction. We shall deal with these points in reverse order.

1. In Bangalore Farquhar had called on the Dewan (Prime Minister) of Mysore. His reception was most cordial. He found that the Dewan had read all that he had written, and was particularly interested in his books on the *Bhagavad Gītā*.[3] Furthermore the Dewan not only agreed to preside at Farquhar's first lecture, but also held a reception for him, at which he was able to speak for twenty minutes on "the genius and methods of the Y.M.C.A.".[4] This Farquhar called "a gathering of extraordinary importance", since never before had he had such an opportunity of expounding Y.M.C.A. methods to influential non-Christians.[5] The reception also provided an index of the influence his literary work had already exercised, and might be expected to exercise in future. The Dewan said in the course of his address of welcome,

The critical spirit in which you have traced the origin and age of the *Gita,* and the appreciation you have evinced of the teachings of that great book, show how well equipped you are for the new field of activity on which you have entered ... You belong to the new type of Christian missionary who have made a critical study of the life and customs of the Indian people, and can readily enter into their feelings and aspirations ... We Indians cannot be too grateful to you and other Europeans possessing true insight into Indian character and sympathy with Indian aspirations, for your interpreting our religion and our thought to your fellow-countrymen, thereby bringing a better understanding between the two races.[6]

It is significant that this mark of appreciation came as a direct result of books which advocated Christianity and yet at the same

---

[1] Farquhar's diary for this period provides little more than a record of places visited, names and dates.

[2] J. N. Farquhar to J. R. Mott, 5.12.1907 (YMCA Hist. Lib.).

[3] Above, pp. 198 ff.

[4] Farquhar to Mott, 5.12.1907.

[5] *FM* XV: 2 (March–April 1908), p. 19.

[6] Copy of an address given to J. N. Farquhar at a reception given in his honour by the Prime Minister of the Mysore State (YMCA Hist. Lib.).

time took a sympathetic view of the Hindu phenomena criticized—in this case the doctrines of the *Bhagavad Gītā*.

2. The second point stressed by Farquhar at the end of his 1907 tour was the suitability of the Y.M.C.A. in the religious situation of the day. In the first place, he felt that the Association provided an excellent focus for Indian Christians of all denominations.[7] But this was not all. He felt, too, that it was "the only organization ... able to bring Europeans and Indians effectively together in real social intercourse";[8] and as an instrument of evangelization "the Association is the one form of work able to bring a powerful Christian influence to bear on the educated classes of India".[9] This influence Farquhar wished to see widened by means of literature. At the same time there was a certain amount of bad feeling against the Y.M.C.A. in India, for a variety of reasons, among which Farquhar was later to number "snobbishness" and "prejudice against Americans".[10]

3. Perhaps the main result of Farquhar's first period as Student Secretary was the growth of his own conviction that, as he told Mott, "my own work ought to be largely writing".[1] His experience with the Dewan of Mysore was not isolated. "Wherever I went", he wrote, "my books had prepared the way for me."[2]

At the same time he believed that the need for such literature was increasing. As an evangelist among students and the educated classes generally he wished to exercise the widest possible influence, and felt that this could best be done by means of literature. Lectures and addresses, though potentially valuable, were largely ineffective, for the reasons we have suggested above:[3] apathy, the force of resurgent Hinduism and the condemnation in some quarters of Christianity as un-Indian and denationalizing.[4] Only literature remained, it seemed.[5]

---

[7] Farquhar to Mott, 5.12.1907.

[8] In this Farquhar was over-optimistic. V. S. Azariah, whose dramatic appeal for "friends" stirred the 1910 Edinburgh conference so deeply, was himself a YMCA man. See World Missionary Conference, 1910: *History and Records* (IX), p. 315.

[9] YMCA Secretaries' Reports: J. N. Farquhar, 1907, p. 283 (YMCA Hist. Lib.). Hereinafter *Report 1907*.

[10] See Farquhar to Mott, 10.2.1910 (YMCA Hist. Lib.).

[1] Farquhar to Mott, 5.12.1907.

[2] *Ibid.*

[3] Above, p. 220 f.

[4] *Report 1907*, p. 286.

[5] *Ibid.*, p. 287.

Considerable difficulties however stood in the way of such work, of which by far the greatest was finding time to write. Most missionaries were simply unable, by reason of the many calls on their time, to write books. Not until after 1911 was Farquhar himself able to produce any large-scale work, for the selfsame reason. The plan to be followed, if and when literature could be produced, was however clear.

Such work must be in English, and must pass three severe tests: they [the books] must be thoroughly Christian, truly scholarly and genuinely sympathetic towards Indian thought.[6]

It is hardly necessary to point out that these three "tests" were those that had actuated Farquhar's previous work, and we shall see how he endeavoured to follow his own guiding principles in future, as well as finding other missionaries able and willing to follow them. A final question asked by Farquhar in his 1907 report deserves mention, before we pass on to consider something of the religious and political background of the period. "When", he asked, "will the Y.M.C.A. have a capable man set apart for literary work?"[7]

Religious Nationalism

Farquhar's first years as National Student Secretary were in no way notable for any lessening of political tension. On the contrary; the Indian political situation in 1907 and 1908 saw an intensification of the crisis begun in 1905. It was the Congress of 1907 at Surat which first confirmed the breach between moderate and extremist Indian nationalism; the extremists, led by B. G. Tilak and Aurobindo Ghose, were then able to declare themselves free from constitutional strictures, while Congress itself, deprived of its radical element, reverted to its earlier passivity.[8] In May 1907 another prominent nationalist, Lajpat Rai, was arrested on suspicion of being a revolutionary leader, an act which upset the nationalists

---

[6] *Ibid.*

[7] *Ibid.*

[8] For the constitutional aims of Congress after the 1908 split, see Besant, *How India Wrought for Freedom* (1915), p. 470. And yet the Congress of 1906 had been urged by Dadabhai Naoroji to "Agitate, agitate over the whole length and breadth of India ...". Lovett, *A History of the Indian Nationalist Movement* (1920), p. 67.

"in inverse proportion to their age".[9] This opened the way to overt acts of violence. The first shot was fired in December 1907: the first bomb was thrown early in 1908, and it seemed for a time as though India were threatened with a new Mutiny. This was not a purely political movement, however. It is a striking fact that the leaders of the extremist party of Indian nationalism—B. G. Tilak, B. C. Pal, Lajpat Rai and Aurobindo Ghose—were all in some sense religious leaders as well. Renascent Hinduism and Indian nationalism were henceforth complementary. As Farquhar wrote in 1908, "The two act and re-act on each other, as is inevitable. The Nationalist Movement tends to be Hindu; the Hindu revival stirs the fires of patriotism."[1] Here we shall be concerned with the religious aspect of the national movement, but it should be borne in mind that one "aspect" is not always easy to isolate from the complex phenomenon we call "religious nationalism".

Neo-Hinduism arose largely as a reaction against the Christian missions, and we have seen how, from the 1890's onward, it set itself up in direct opposition to Christianity.[2] But we have seen, too, how certain Hindu groups were prepared to imitate the missions in a number of respects.[3] Both these features of the situation were discussed in a debate precipitated in 1908 between Farquhar and certain nationalists.

In the May 1908 number of the *Contemporary Review* there appeared an article from Farquhar's pen on *Christianity in India*.[4] This article in many ways resembles his earlier pamphlet *The Future of Christianity in India* and his address to the 1907 Tokyo conference, of which it appears to be an expanded version. But while the optimism of the former pamphlet had been based on an analogy between the Indian missionary situation and the state of Christianity in the late Roman Empire, the optimism of *Christianity in India* was based on the thesis of the imminent collapse of Hinduism under the double pressure of modern life on the one hand and of the

---

[9] Rai, *Young India* (4th ed. 1927), p. 192.
[1] YMCA Secretaries' Reports: J. N. Farquhar, 1908, p. 211 (YMCA Hist. Lib.). Hereinafter *Report 1908*.
[2] Above, p. 144 f.
[3] Above, p. 196.
[4] It was shortly afterward reprinted separately, and it is the pagination of the offprint we use here. It is also interesting to note that a German translation of the original article, "Das Christentum in Indien", appeared in *AMZ* 35 (1908), pp. 465-90.

Christian mission on the other. Farquhar admitted the great intrinsic strength of Hinduism, derived from a "defensive armour" of conservatism:[5] an armour strong enough to withstand Buddhism, Jainism, Hellenism and even—to some extent—Islam. Hence, too, the slow progress of Christianity in India. But, says Farquhar, times are changing: the modern educated Hindu's chief concerns are for freedom, equality, social reform and education. Such concerns are incompatible with religious and social conservatism. And he concludes: "The minds of the educated classes have been forced open: *the protective armour of Hinduism has been pierced.*" (Farquhar's italics.)[6] Progress and change are henceforth inevitable, even if they bring the end of many old religious sanctions. The choice is plain: "... either the new morality or the old rule must go".[7] Farquhar was in no doubt that it was "the old rule" of Hinduism which, once questioned, was doomed to pass away. And since this state of affairs had been largely brought about by Protestant missionary efforts in education, doctrinal teaching and philanthropy, it was only to be expected that Protestant Christianity would in time take the place of Hinduism as the religion of India.

Farquhar's optimistic—some felt over-optimistic[8]—claim was not allowed to go unchallenged. A debate was begun in the Hindu periodical the *Indian World*,[9] in which certain leading Hindus and Brahmos stated clearly the reasons why they did not want to see Christianity as the religion of India, and were answered with equal clarity and firmness by Farquhar. We do not propose to give a full résumé of the debate here, since much of it is peripheral to our purpose;[1] the point at issue was the position of Christianity in

---

[5] *Christianity in India*, p. 7: "... the rigid adherence to every detail of traditional law and custom, and the uncompromising rejection of every new thing, whether good or bad".

[6] *Ibid.*, p. 12.

[7] *Ibid.*, p. 13.

[8] A YMCA colleague, F. W. Steinthal, called it "a brilliant, but perhaps too optimistic, article ..." *Edinburgh MS.*, Comm. I (MRL).

[9] Between May and September 1908.

[1] The original article appeared in the May 1908 number of the *Contemporary Review*; the May number of the *Indian World* (pp. 463 ff.) contained a summary of Farquhar's article (attributed to "Rev. J. N. Farquhar of the London Mission"!); it was attacked in the June 1908 *Indian World* by Lajpat Rai (pp. 485–93) and by B. K. Mullick (pp. 493–97). Farquhar answered in the June issue (pp. 61–68). Three further articles, to which I have not had access, appeared in the August number; and a further reply by Farquhar came in the September issue (pp. 283–91).

India, and not that of the missionary theories we are investigating in the missionary thought of the time.

One contribution is however of particular importance, since it comes from Lala Lajpat Rai, who since 1905 had emerged as one of the leaders of militant Indian nationalism—a new nationalism, closely linked with Hinduism. It is not possible in this context to provide a detailed history of this phase in Hindu thought, since that would lead us far beyond the bounds of our study; we must nevertheless pause to consider some of the main features of this new nationalism. A useful starting-point is provided by Lajpat Rai's article in the June 1908 number of the *Indian World*. Here we see the boundaries between nationalism and religion growing more and more indistinct, and one overall attitude to political and religious problems emerging. We shall see in due course that this was quite typical of the extremist nationalism of the day.

Not unnaturally, Rai denied warmly that the "defensive armour" of Hinduism had been pierced; on the contrary, he pointed out—not without justification—that "Hinduism has been nothing if not changing according to the needs of the times and adapting itself to the altered condition of things surrounding it".[2] It is this that has saved Hinduism so far, and it is this that will save Hinduism in future. But Hinduism has a solid core—what Rai calls "the pure monotheism of the Vedic times"[3]—of inspiration. Nevertheless the struggle with Western ideals is so "unequal in all its phases" that Hinduism has had to borrow Western methods in order to combat encroachments upon her territory.[4] A typically extravagant claim follows. Knowledge, says Rai, is the common property of man; when the Hindu borrows, he acknowledges. Not so the Christian.

Christianity may refuse to own that whatever truth there is in it existed in the world long before it was born and was freely and ungrudgingly taught to the world by the ancient Aryans; but the descendants of the latter ... have not lost that sense of honesty which distinguished their ancestors ...[5]

Rai's argument in the remainder of his article is that the West has brought industry to India, and with it all manner of social

----

[2] *Indian World* VII: 39 (June 1908), p. 489.
[3] *Ibid.*
[4] *Ibid.*, p. 490.
[5] *Ibid.*

and political diseases. These must be swept away: India must not be denationalized, but must remain Indian. "We will rather preserve the individuality of our own national genius than be saved at its cost."[6] And what is this "national genius"? In short, Hinduism. "We shall live and die as Hindus", writes Rai, and emphasizes once more that Farquhar's thesis is utterly mistaken.

Our learned critic is sadly mistaken if he thinks that Hindu India will ever be converted to Christianity. Certainly not, so long as there are tens of thousands in this land who will live and die for their faith.[7]

Here we see faith in Hinduism and faith in India so closely linked as to be practically indistinguishable. And its corollary, that Christianity, being Western and therefore denationalizing, could not conceivably be a fit and proper faith for India.[8] Nothing was more typical of this phase in the nationalist movement than these two ideas, expressed sometimes separately, sometimes in conjunction.

We have said that one of the primary causes of both the Indian nationalist movement and the Hindu Renaissance was the impact of Christianity on the mind of India. This must however be seen as part of a larger and deeper impact—of the Western mind, with its ideals of government, education and religion—on the mind of India. In religious matters there had been a deliberate effort made, extending over several generations, to *contrast* East and West; the religious nationalism of these years was in a sense a normal reaction brought about by the pressure of this antithesis. Faced with the claim of Christianity to be the absolute and universal religion, it became natural to advance the counter-claims of Hinduism. But again, as Christianity is to be seen as only part of the total impact of the West, so Neo-Hinduism is only part of the overall Indian reaction. But the Indian nationalism of the period was religious in essence: that fact must not be forgotten. McCully has pointed out that one of its main tenets was that the regeneration of India was dependent upon the restoration of Hindu culture.[9] This idea owed

---

[6] *Ibid.*, p. 492.

[7] *Ibid.*

[8] The roots of this view are to be traced back to Vivekānanda and the myth of the "spiritual" East and the "materialistic" West. Cf. Farquhar, *Modern Religious Movements in India* (1915), p. 204.

[9] In his book *English Education and the Origins of Indian Nationalism* (1940), pp. 253 ff.

its force to the conviction that the ancient Vedic culture was superior to that of the West[1]—though Vedic culture was currently in decline owing to the baneful influence of English education. It goes without saying that on this view Hinduism must be restored as the motive force and inspiration of the new India, and that Christianity—along with other Western ideals—must be finally rejected.

The leaders of Indian nationalism at this time—Tilak, Pal, Rai and Ghose—were all men who had been influenced by the Hindu revival. "It would not be incorrect", writes an Indian historian, "to state that their nationalism had taken large draught (*sic*) from the fountain of Hindu religion."[2] And Bengal was the centre of operations for three of the four.

What did these men do? Did they take their patriotism, and make of it a religion? Or did they allow their nationalism to become assimilated to their religion in such a way as to render the two virtually coextensive? We suggest that the latter alternative is the more correct. Lajpat Rai claimed that Hinduism was sufficiently flexible to withstand the attack of Christianity, and this flexibility is nowhere more in evidence than in the adjustment of Hindu thought which allowed Ghose to write

Nationalism is an *avatar* and cannot be slaim. Nationalism is a divinely-appointed *shakti* of the Eternal and must do its God-given work before it returns to the bosom of the Universal Energy from which it came.[3]

Or

The new religion of Nationalism is a creed indeed, a faith which already numbers its martyrs, which speaks through inspired voices, which looks beyond the present to a future promised by God, ... If there is to be a creed, this is the only possible creed for India.[4]

But before we examine the nationalism of one of this group, Aurobindo Ghose, we must note that the extremists of 1907/1908 were generally of two kinds. One we have already encountered: the Vedantist, deriving his religion historically from Rāmakrishṇa

---

[1] Nor was this a new view; it was clearly stated in the work of Dayānanda Sarasvatī, the founder of the Ārya Samāj. See Farquhar, *op. cit.*, pp. 111 ff.
[2] Raguvanshi, *Indian Nationalist Movement and Thought* (2nd ed. 1959), p. 113.
[3] Mukherjee and Mukherjee, *Sri Aurobindo's Political Thought 1893–1908* (1958), p. 58, n. 3A.
[4] *Ibid.*, p. 183.

and Vivekānanda, and a close student of the *Bhagavad Gītā*.[5] Nationalists of this type sought "to realise the old spiritual ideals of the race, not through monkish negations or mediaeval abstractions, but by the idealisation and spiritualisation of the concrete elements and actual relations of life".[6] The most extreme phalanx of this group comprised those who, in the words of Lajpat Rai, "worked for the salvation of their country with the bomb in one hand and the Bhagavat in the other".[7] B. G. Tilak was perhaps the foremost representative of this school of thought. We have noted his work in connexion with the Śivaji festival;[8] here it is sufficient to point out that in Tilak's view Śivaji "knew his Vedanta all right and also knew how to put that Vedanta to practical use".[9] Farquhar had already encountered the Vedantists, and his earlier books on the *Gītā* had been intended to undermine their historical foundations.

The second type of religious nationalist was the "mother-worshipper". This group was essentially Śaivite and polytheistic; the method they employed was to interpret the most popular of the Hindu goddesses as symbolic of the different types of national evolution: their centre was in Bengal. Their "prophet" was Bankim Chandra Chatterjee, a Bengali poet, author of the patriotic manifesto *Bande Mātaram* (Hail, Motherland!). Here we cannot do better than to quote Lajpat Rai.

Jagatdhatri—riding a lion which has the prostrate body of an elephant under its paw—represented the motherland in its early jungle-clearing stage. This is, says Bankim Chandra, the mother as she was. *Kali*, the grim goddess, dark and naked, bearing a garland of human heads around her neck—heads from which blood is dripping—and dancing on the prostrate form of Shiva, the god—this, says Bankim Chandra, is the mother as she is, dark, because ignorant of herself; the heads with dripping blood are those of her own children, destroyed by famine and pestilence; the jackals (foreign exploiters) licking their drippings are the symbol of desolation and decadence of social life, and the prostrate form of Shiva means that she is trampling her own God under her feet. *Durga*, the ten-headed goddess, armed with swords and spears in some hands, holding wheat-sheaves in some, offering coinage and peace with others, riding a lion, fighting with demons; with Sarasvati, or the goddess of Knowledge and Arts, supported by Ganapati,

---

[5] Above, pp. 194 ff.
[6] Raguvanshi, *op. cit.*, p. 203.
[7] *Young India*, p. 120.
[8] Above, p. 153 f.
[9] From a speech delivered in Marathi, on the occasion of the Śivaji Coronation Festival in Poona, 25.6.1907: *Speeches of Bal Gangadhar Tilak* (1918), p. 76.

the god of Wisdom, on her one side, and Lakshmi, the goddess of Wealth, protected by Kartikeya, the leader of the Heavenly army, on the other side—this, says Bankim Chandra, is the mother as she will be.[1]

This interpretation goes far towards explaining, among other things, the taking of the *swadeshi* vow before Kali in 1905.[2]

One Indian leader in which these two elements—Vedantism and mother-worship—were combined was Aurobindo Ghose (1872–1950).[3] Ghose, later more widely known as Sri Aurobindo, is one of the most interesting figures of the Indian national renaissance. His political thought I have discussed elsewhere;[4] here a brief mention must suffice. His chief contribution to the religious ground of the nationalist movement was made in the pages of the periodical press of Bengal—in *Yugantar, Bande Mataram, Karmayogin* and *Dharma*. His education in England and his Westernized family background had given him a command of the English language which few Indians could match, as well as making him a burning nationalist. Ghose was not a religious innovator: he took the religious life of the people as he found it, and turned it into a considerable force in the life of Bengal. Like Bankim Chandra Chatterjee and B. C. Pal he saw India personified in the great mother-goddess, Durga-Kali. This made of every act of worship a nationalist demonstration, and every worshipper a nationalist, whether consciously or unconsciously; nationalism, which had previously tended to be the prerogative of the educated classes, and particularly of the politicians, became in theory open to each and every Indian. Thus he reinterpreted the popular *Durga Pujah* festival[5] on nationalist lines, calling it a "national festival", and claiming that it could only be properly understood by the "patriot". In this he was doing for Bengal what Tilak had done for the Marathi country in the inauguration of

[1] Rai, *Young India*, p. 200 f.

[2] Above, p. 221.

[3] Many books have been written on Śri Aurobindo's philosophy and religious thought; few on his earlier political activities; see however Varma, *The Political Philosophy of Sri Aurobindo* (1960), Wolff, *Indiens Beitrag zum neuen Menschenbild* (1957), pp. 93–103, Mukherjee and Mukherjee, *op. cit.*, and Singh, *Sri Aurobindo: His Life and Religious Thought* (1962), pp. 1–5.

[4] Sharpe, "Sri Aurobindos politiska filosofi", in *SMT* 50: 3 (1962), pp. 151 ff.

[5] The great festival of the consort of Śiva (Durga, Kali, Shakti), worshipped as a deity in her own right in Bengal. Celebrated in September/October. The need, here as in the case of the Śivaji festival, was for a focus, a rallying-cry, a motto, a faith, independent of leaders whose freedom was always liable to be forefeit. In each case there was an element of local patriotism involved; but in each case the ultimate cause transcended local politics.

the Śivaji festival—and for more or less the same reasons. Though it is not easy to disentangle the religious and the political aspects of these popular manifestations of the national spirit, the cumulative effect was similar. Both helped the common people to join in the nationalist movement; both expressed the aims of nationalism in terms of Hinduism; both provided the aspirations of India with a popular focus and an opportunity for popular demonstration. And both, by implication, condemned Christianity as being foreign and therefore, as Bishop Neill has expressed it, "a western importation, a part of the exploitation of India by the West, and therefore not a fit home for the patriotic Indian".[6]

Thus in this period it became common for the educated Indian to accuse the missionary of being a representative of an un-Indian system, a belligerent, attacking time-honoured customs and institutions, traditions, memories and associations.[7] Christianity was part of Western civilization, and that civilization Ghose, and many others with him, despised as *māyā* (illusion); reality was the ancient Vedic, agrarian culture of India, a culture which the nationalists had set themselves to re-establish. "We in India fell under the influence of the foreigners' Maya which completely possessed our souls", said Ghose in 1908.[8] To dispel *māyā* there was needed suffering, but also positive principles, of which *swadeshi* and *swaraj*—both with political overtones—were the foremost. But, to quote Ghose once more, "If we are to organise Swaraj we must base it on the village".[9] Here politics, economics and religion combine for the restoration of the independence of India. Such was the complexity of Neo-Hinduism faced by the missionaries in these years. But Farquhar was convinced that the key was religious: politics and economics, though not to be ignored, were essentially secondary.[1] This being so, there were a number of good reasons why the old missionary method of marking the *contrast* between Christianity and Hinduism would have to be abandoned. Not only was it in-

---

[6] Neill, *Builders of the Indian Church* (1934), p. 113.

[7] So Prof. Har Dayal, quoted by Farquhar in *The Crown of Hinduism*, pp. 33 f., 43 ff.

[8] Sri Aurobindo, *Speeches* (1948), p. 44.

[9] *Ibid.*, p. 51.

[1] This has partly to do with Farquhar's background as a missionary, but probably, too, with his reading of B. J. Kidd, who had claimed that religion was in the last resort the decisive factor in human development. See above, p. 41 n. 9.

commensurate with what Farquhar felt to be the scientific approach and the Christian spirit; it was bound to alienate the Indian, since it called into question the worth of his national heritage. In a review from 1908 of Wilhelm Dilger's *Salvation in Hinduism and Christianity* and the O.M.C.'s *The Upanishads and the Christian Gospel*,[2] Farquhar attacked their method, the method of contrast, sharply, saying that "we believe we must get rid of it at all costs". His contention was once more that only the concept of "fulfilment" was adequate to meet the needs of the situation—"both Christian and scientific"—and at the same time able to do justice to the Indian national heritage, which, he held, was

too priceless a possession to be flung away and too closely intertwined with the vitals of the people to be got rid of ...[3]

During 1908 and 1909—years of intense religious and political activity in India—Farquhar was forced to concentrate while in India on local and organizational problems. On March 6, 1908, he took over the post of National General Secretary of the Indian Y.M.C.A.;[4] whether he did so willingly is open to some doubt, since it placed a further curb on his literary activities, but he seems to have been the only available man for the position, and in any case it was only a temporary measure. At all events, his writing was severely curtailed, and at least one scheme had to be laid aside for the time being. This was the production of a series of books on various aspects of Hinduism, to which Griswold, Hume, Macnicol and Hogg had been invited to contribute. But as Farquhar wrote to Mott, "... the very heavy work of this position has made it impossible for me to make any progress".[5] We shall however return to this topic.[6]

Yet his observation continued. Constantly travelling through India, he was in a position to note many details of the nationalist and religious situation, and in his reports conveyed his impressions of what he had seen. In general he was fully aware of the problems posed by the Hindu revival in its latest phase, but was nevertheless

---

[2] On Dilger, see above, p. 239 f.; on the original articles in the *Epiphany*, see above, p. 90 f.

[3] Review in *YMI* XIX: 8 (August 1908), p. 144.

[4] *Report 1908*, p. 210.

[5] J. N. Farquhar to J. R. Mott, 12.11.1908 (YMCA Hist. Lib.).

[6] Below, pp. 304 ff.

not discouraged.[7] A new openness to Christian teaching was, thought Farquhar, beginning to be manifested in India: missionaries were beginning to find their work less difficult than it had been at the time of the 1905 crisis. Most important, "The opportunity for the use of Christian literature nowadays is so great as to be beyond all description".[8]

At the same time Farquhar was more concerned than hitherto with the large-scale problems of the Christian world mission, mainly as a result of his contacts with Mott and the W.S.C.F. In August 1908 he wrote to Mott of the thoughts which had been passing through his mind, and concluded:

I need not go on to draw your attention to the large questions that are looming up, clearly or hazily, round the whole horizon. What I want to suggest is that you should write an article or series of articles on this huge subject, to call the attention of religious leaders everywhere to the immense questions involved, and perhaps also to suggest in outline a few strategic movements, which the Missions of the world ought to combine to carry out.[9]

Mott was of course fully aware of the need for "strategic movements". But he was not prepared at this stage to put his convictions into print, since another subject was engaging most of his attention—the subject of a World Missionary Conference. By 1908, after years of discussion and planning, it seemed that the proposed conference was well on the way to becoming a reality. The International Committee formed as a planning organ had met in Oxford in the previous month, July 1908, and among other things had appointed eight "Commissions" of some twenty members each to conduct the actual business of the conference, when it should take place.[1] The date had been fixed: Edinburgh, 1910. The scheme as such was first made public in October 1908.[2] At the same time plans were being made for the next W.S.C.F. conference, to be held in Oxford in 1909.

---

[7] *Report 1908*, p. 211: "Strangely enough this Hindu revival ... is yet a great help to our work; for it cannot defend modern Hinduism without leading men to think on the great problems and without introducing Christian ideas everywhere."

[8] *Ibid.*

[9] Farquhar to Mott, 1.8.1908 (YMCA Hist. Lib.).

[1] Gairdner, *"Edinburgh 1910"* (1910), p. 18 f.

[2] Mott, "A World Missionary Conference", in *The East and the West* VI (Oct. 1908), pp. 368–85.

The subject of "Edinburgh, 1910" is so important and its implications so far-reaching that it is best left to a separate chapter: accordingly we devote Chapter Nine to a detailed discussion of some of the conference material—in particular that connected with Commission IV (The Missionary Message in relation to Non-Christian Religions).

Oxford 1909

The historian of the W.S.C.F., describing the Oxford conference, suggests that social service was the main theme of its deliberations.[3] Although an emphasis on social issues was perhaps the most striking innovation at Oxford, it would be wrong to regard this conference solely from the "social" angle—as a forerunner of C.O.P.E.C. and no more. "The social problem" in fact occupies only 26 of the official report's 316 pages. That this was a sign of the times—a result of what Tatlow and Rouse have both called "the rise of the social consciousness"—cannot be denied; but at the same time it must be remembered that the conference was still largely run on traditional lines. Oxford, 1909, differed from Tokyo, 1907, in that it was a select conference of leaders, convened in order to discuss strategy and programme planning. Coming mid-way between Tokyo and Constantinople, 1911, it had more of the character of a private retreat than a public demonstration.

Farquhar's name appears three times in the conference report. He spoke twice, and—a significant indication of the esteem in which he was held in W.S.C.F. circles—contributed the essay on "The Oxford Conference" with which the official report begins (pp. 9–12). This essay need not detain us; Farquhar's two addresses, on the other hand, are of considerable interest and importance.

One primary concern of the W.S.C.F. leaders was to keep movements in different parts of the world in touch with one another: at all conferences "report lectures" were held, dealing with the latest developments and current problems on the respective fields. Farquhar's two lectures filled this type of function, though the first came under the leading of "Apologetics" and the second under "The Contribution of the Students of the West to the Building up of the Church in the East" (in the report).

---

[3] Rouse, *The World's Student Christian Federation*, p. 69.

We have already seen how "apologetics" had been introduced into the programme of the Tokyo conference.[4] Now, two years later, the Federation asked what effect, if any, this had had: "What Apologetic has been most Helpful in Leading Students into Faith in Christ?" was the theme of a series of three lectures drawing on experience from Germany, Italy and India.[5] Farquhar's lecture was entitled "Lessons from Experience in India".[6]

Farquhar's first point is worthy of special note, in view of subsequent confusion over the meaning and implications of the word "apologetics". He defines the word as having to do with a double-sided phenomenon: "one side is negative, meant to remove the hindrances which the old faith puts in the way of Christianity, the other positive, meant to build up faith in Christ".[7] Beginning with the negative aspect of apologetics—the removal of hindrances—Farquhar sketches by way of background the basic differences between the Hindu and the Christian view of life. He concludes that although Hinduism is "a very wonderful synthesis indeed", the true Hindu cannot without more ado become a Christian. "In order that Christ may be accepted, the Hindu mind has to be recreated."[8] Having made this important point, Farquhar goes on to discuss the methods of apologetics—of presenting the Gospel, in other words—so far practised by missionaries in India. For the traditional Evangelical attitude (1830–1860) he has little good to say; in the next period, however, from 1860 on, he is disposed to find promise of better things, particularly in the attitude of greater sympathy for India, and the frank acknowledgement of "good things in Hinduism".[9] The main point of his address follows: an explanation of his own method. Although there is nothing here that we have not already seen in his work in India, this is nevertheless a useful statement of principle—one of the earliest, as well as one of the clearest, we possess.

The method I refer to consists in setting forth Christianity as the fulfilment of all that is aimed at in Hinduism, as the satisfaction of the spiritual yearnings of her people, as the crown and climax of the crudest forms

[4] Above, p. 232 f.
[5] *Report of the Conference of the World's Student Christian Federation held at Oxford, England* (1909), pp. 65–78.
[6] *Ibid.*, pp. 68–75.
[7] *Ibid.*, p. 68.
[8] *Ibid.*, p. 70.
[9] *Ibid.*, p. 71.

of her worship as well as of those lofty spiritual movements which have
so often appeared in Hinduism but have always ended in weakness. This
new movement ... sets forth every part of Hinduism as springing from
some real religious instinct and having a value of its own, and thus gives
the religion the full credit for every fragment of moral and religious help
it contains; yet it sets Christ supreme over all, and proclaims Him to be
the consummator of religion. The theory thus satisfies the science of religion to the uttermost, while conserving the supremacy of Christ.[1]

This statement of principle Farquhar included as part of the
"negative" aspect of apologetics—which we recall implied the removal of hindrances to faith. His exposition of the "positive" aspect
is of less importance in this context (no criticism is of course implied
of its value in the Oxford context), but we may note that it is
fully representative of his basic evolutionist position. But at the
same time for Farquhar the object of missionary work was to win
men for Christ, and apologetics—however expressed—could only fill
a preparatory function. Once the preparation had been completed,
"the right way is to forget Hinduism altogether and present only
Christ".[2]

Later in the conference Farquhar spoke again, on "The Call from
India".[3] This address took the form of a presentation of the essentials of the Indian missionary situation, inevitably compressed
for a qualified audience, but clear throughout. His introduction is
drawn with bold strokes: the world is now one; the races of mankind
have become "almost a single community".[4] And a single community
must live a single life, and follow a single religion. In time "there
will not be many religions as there are today. There will be one
religion or none".[5] But which religion? We cannot be any doubt
as to Farquhar's own convictions; yet the final triumph of Christianity in which he so firmly believed could not, he felt, come
except as the result of conflict—"the supreme struggle of human
history".[6]

What of India in this struggle? Farquhar's appeal was first for
reconciliation between East and West, knowledge about the present

---

[1] *Ibid.*, p. 72.
[2] *Ibid.*, p. 74. Cf. above, pp. 206 ff.
[3] *Oxford Report*, pp. 187–99.
[4] *Ibid.*, p. 187.
[5] *Ibid.*, p. 189.
[6] *Ibid.*

upheaval in the East, and sympathy with the aspirations of the East. Then he called for Christian scholarship—tones we recognize from his reports:

We need a band of Christian scholars to set forth in clear perspective the relation which Christianity bears to the leading religions of Asia.[7]

Such scholars must know the religions of the world, but realize that all must eventually yield to Christ. And the only way in which such a conviction can be embodied in literature is "by setting forth Christianity as the crown and fulfilment of all the religions of the world".[8] This ideal is no less necessary for the missionary authorities at home, since they tend to lag behind in their appreciation of developments in missionary thought.

A parallel need is for "the restatement of Christian truth in forms suited to Asiatic apprehension".[9] The recognition of the deep differences between Eastern and Western psychology inevitably causes Western expressions of Christianity to be seen as relative. This applies particularly to Western formal theology—an obvious conclusion to a man of Farquhar's background. Hence: "Not until Christianity has assumed a real Indian dress will it be naturalized in India; and the same is true of China and Japan."[1] Such work is equally the concern of Indian Christians, missionaries and scholars in Europe. Secondary, yet indispensable needs are for unity in Christian work, for money and for men. The situation is grave, concluded Farquhar, and yet not impossible, if there be readiness to do the will of God. The need is thus for self-examination and devotion: the results will then follow.

Farquhar's lectures aroused no debate, as far as we can see, since the Oxford conference was not one at which any extended discussion was possible. As Farquhar himself wrote in his conference impressions, "We came together for business, transacted it, and separated".[2] But that they were favourably received by the majority of delegates seems likely, in view of the general climate of opinion among student movement leaders at this time.

Summing up, at Oxford we see the mature Farquhar expounding

---

[7] *Ibid.*, p. 192. Cf. below, p. 304 f.
[8] *Ibid.*, p. 193.
[9] *Ibid.*
[1] *Ibid.*
[2] *Ibid.*, p. 10.

his views for a select audience of student and missionary leaders. As yet he had written no large-scale work, but he had stated plainly the principles such work must follow. The anti-Christianity movement had reached its pre-War zenith: the thesis of the incompatibility of East and West in religion had been stated and widely accepted by Indians. For more than a decade Farquhar had been working, studying and observing on the frontier of the conflict, seeking to create a dialogue in its place. During these years his vision of the application of the science of religion, the evolutionary hypothesis and modern knowledge generally, to the missionary situation in India, had been clarifying. Yet Christ must not be compromised. His innermost conviction, which he asserted again and again, was that Christianity was destined, by fulfilling Hinduism, to replace that religion at the heart of India, without, however, destroying the genuine Indian cultural and religious heritage. But at the same time that replacement would not take place of itself. The Christian Churches and missionary societies would have to provide a body of consecrated scholars, ready, able and willing to penetrate to the depths of Hinduism, and to confront Hinduism with the Gospel of Christ. Their work must be sympathetic, accurate, scholarly and readable—for the sake of their own generation and for generations to come. Very little had as yet been done to put this scheme into operation, it is true, but the plan was prepared, if only the pressure of other work could be relaxed sufficiently to allow such books to be written.

Two more years were to elapse before Farquhar could be given the leisure he required to set his plan in motion, to write *The Crown of Hinduism* and to recruit a body of helpers. Now, as we turn to a consideration of those years, we see, first, how Farquhar himself continued to write to the best of his ability, and secondly, how his plans for a "new" Christian literature for India matured, how they were received by Mott, and how he was finally set free from student work in order to give his mind, and his time, to writing.

Literary Work before 1911

One of the most remarkable things about Farquhar's years as National Student Secretary, viewed in retrospect, was not that he failed to write any large book, but that he was in fact able to accomplish so much literary work—albeit on a small scale—amid the pressure of his other duties. *Christianity in India* we have already discussed: this appeared in 1908. In 1909 he published a revised version of his commentary on St. Matthew's Gospel, which he called *The College St. Matthew*; to Hastings' *Encyclopaedia of Religion and Ethics* he contributed an article (the first of several) on the Brāhma Samāj; and he sent answers to Commission I and IV of the Edinburgh conference. A series of articles in the *Young Men of India* under the general heading "Glimpses of Hinduism" extended throughout the period, though their appearance was somewhat irregular, owing to his frequent absences on tour. Reports of the Oxford conference from his pen appeared in the *Student World,* the *Young Men of India,* the *Bombay Guardian,* the *Christian Patriot* and the *Indian Witness.*[3] In 1910 came three important articles, two in the *Contemporary Review,* on "The Greatness of Hinduism" and "The Crown of Hinduism", and one in the *Student Movement,* on "Christ and the Religions of the World". And finally, in 1911, shortly before his release from responsibility for student work, appeared an elementary text-book on Hinduism, *A Primer of Hinduism.*

Not all these writings are of equal importance. The *ERE* article is purely historical and descriptive, and while it is an early proof of Farquhar's scholarly attainments, and of his powers of detailed observation, it is of no immediate significance for his missionary theories.[4] Again, the articles on "Glimpses of Hinduism" are brief popular accounts of various aspects of Indian religion; for the most part following the same plan as that later adopted in *A Primer of Hinduism* and *The Crown of Hinduism*— an objective exposition of some aspect of Hindu faith or life, followed sometimes (but not invariably) by a very brief Christian application.[5]

The College St. Matthew is a revised and simplified version of *The Crossbearer,* which we discussed in an earlier context.[6] The main outlines of the two books are virtually identical, but there are

---

[3] YMCA Secretaries' Reports: J. N. Farquhar, 1909, p. 265 (YMCA Hist. Lib.). Hereinafter *Report 1909.*

[4] Farquhar, "Brāhma Samāj", in *ERE* II (1909), pp. 813–24. The concept of "fulfilment" is however mentioned even here. The article ends: "Hinduism must die into Christianity, in order that the best her philosophers, saints and ascetics have longed and prayed for may live."

[5] So e.g. "The Bibles of India", in *YMI* XXI: 3 (March 1910), pp. 37–41; "The Hindu Conception of God and the World", in *YMI* XXI: 5 (May 1910), pp. 71–75.

[6] Above, pp. 165 ff.

differences of detail. Thus *The Crossbearer* was based on Farquhar's own revision of the AV text: *The College St. Matthew* on the RV text; the former book, being intended for private students, was more detailed than the new version, which was expressly designed for use in the class-room. There are also significant differences in the subject matter.

We may take as a convenient illustration the concept of fulfilment, which in its development fits in with what we have seen from Farquhar's other writings. We have noted that he began to make use of the concept in the pages of the *Inquirer* shortly after joining the Y.M.C.A. in 1902. Thus Farquhar's earlier commentary (1899–1900) on Matt. 5.17 ("I am not come to destroy, but to fulfil", AV) expressly limited the concept of fulfilment to the relationship of Christianity to Judaism, and said nothing whatever about Hinduism.[7] in 1909 it is perhaps not surprising to find the same passage expounded somewhat differently. Jesus, says Farquhar, came to lift every part of the old religion to completion—this is substantially what he was saying in 1900. But then he goes on:

This is the attitude of Jesus to all other religions also. Each contains a partial revelation of God's will, but each is incomplete; and He comes to fulfil them all. In each case Christianity seeks not to destroy but to take all that is right and raise it to perfection. Christianity is the full, final truth, towards which every religion has been straining.[8]

That this did not imply any weakening of Farquhar's Evangelical position—a point we have had occasion to stress on a number of occasions—is shown by the passages relevant to the death and resurrection of Christ. *The College St. Matthew* contains almost three times as much material on these two subjects as did the earlier work. But there is a change of emphasis nevertheless, coming from the revised climate of opinion with regard to apologetics: in short, Farquhar discusses more and asserts less. The abrupt dogmatic statements of the earlier book are gone; in their place we find closely-reasoned discussions of the significance of the doctrine in question for the individual. The basic standpoint is however unchanged: that Christ died on the cross to purchase forgiveness for all men,[9] and that the resurrection is evidence of death conquered

---

[7] Above, p. 166 n. 8.
[8] *The College St. Matthew*, p. 106 f.; cf. *The Crossbearer*, p. 71.
[9] *The College St. Matthew*, p. 170 f.

and sacrifice completed.[1] Farquhar does not attempt to gloss over the resurrection: indeed he writes, "The facts are so stubborn that no explanation except that given by the Apostles will explain them".[2] And further, "To believe in the Resurrection of Jesus is an act of faith of the purest, noblest and most fruitful type. From this faith has sprung the unconquerable moral and spiritual energy of the Christian Church".[3] Statements such as these on the basic points in the Evangelical creed might very easily be multiplied: their cumulative effect is to show that Farquhar was very far indeed from having been turned by his study of Hinduism from what he regarded as the essentials of Evangelical Christianity, however critical he might have been with regard to its accretions and traditional missionary attitudes.[4]

But meanwhile Farquhar was working steadily along the missiological lines he had himself laid down, taking every opportunity to widen and deepen his knowledge of Hinduism and to apply to it his conception of Christianity (as centring on the person of Christ). The idea of "Christ the fulfiller of Hinduism" was by now the ruling conception in his thought. But he had done no extended work along these lines since 1903.[5] It is of course true that he had expounded the *need* for such an approach, and that the religious and political developments of the intervening years had confirmed him in the conviction of its value in the Indian context, but the demands of his position as a Y.M.C.A. secretary hampered, for the time being, his own contribution. In 1910, the year of the Edinburgh conference,[6] he was however able to publish three articles in which the "fulfilment" idea was presented with renewed force.

The first two appeared in the June and July 1910 numbers of *The Contemporary Review,* a liberal journal with a wide circulation in the English-speaking world. In the first, "The Greatness of Hinduism", Farquhar began by laying down a philosophical justification of Hinduism as a religion. "Few people", he wrote, "realise how great Hinduism is."[7] Its greatness is to be found in its bold

---

[1] *Ibid.*, pp. 172 ff.
[2] *Ibid.*, p. 173.
[3] *Ibid.*, p. 174.
[4] Cf. above, pp. 165 ff.
[5] Above, pp. 198 ff.
[6] Below, pp. 272 ff.
[7] Farquhar, "The Greatness of Hinduism", in *CR* XCVII: 12 (June 1910), p. 647.

conception of God and the world, its organization, its asceticism, its quest for a spiritual faith, and its great variety. "Its appeal is almost as wide as human nature."[8] But Hinduism has encountered the West, has adopted certain of the West's methods, religious, political and material, and is now seeking a new ethos, ultimately incompatible with ancient Hindu ideals.[9] The cyclical Hindu conception of the world, ruled as it is by the doctrine of *karma,* has broken down under the forces working for progress; education has undermined Vedic and Brahmanic authority; the religious basis of caste has gone, and the institution is doomed; the new tendency towards monotheism has made polytheism and idolatry "vanishing simulacra in the mind of educated India".[1]

The second article, "The Crown of Hinduism" (not to be confused with the later book of the same name) is based on the conviction so often expressed in Farquhar's writings, that Christianity is destined to become the one religion of India. But not by destroying India's national heritage: for "no religion will ever captivate and satisfy the heart of India that does not enrich itself with these spiritual treasures, in order to use them for the health and help of India".[2] Only Christianity is in a position to be able to do this, since "Hinduism is a rudimentary faith, Christianity its culmination".[3] Farquhar goes on to show briefly how the chief items of Hindu belief and practice are severally fulfilled in Christianity. The evolutionary basis of Farquhar's thought, which was already in evidence in 1901,[4] is here expressly stated in his summing up, as he suggests that "Christianity is the evolutionary crown of Hinduism".[5] And he concludes:

Thus the New Testament will remain the focus of all revelation, the central sun in the light of which everything else must be read and estimated. But the greater books of Hinduism will form a sort of second Old Testament, set like stars around the sun; and the teaching of the old saints will be abundantly used by the Christian sons of India. Every Hindu belief, rite

---

[8] *Ibid.,* p. 655.
[9] This was to be one of the major contentions of his later book *The Crown of Hinduism* (1913); see below, pp. 333 ff.
[1] "The Greatness of Hinduism", p. 658.
[2] Farquhar, "The Crown of Hinduism", in *CR* XCVIII: 1 (July 1910), p. 57.
[3] *Ibid.,* p. 60.
[4] Above, pp. 167 ff.
[5] *Ibid.,* p. 67.

and institution will be seen to have been a germ, an adumbration, the full-blown flower and reality of which came with Christ.[6]

These two articles aroused widespread interest in India, being received, as Farquhar himself noted, "with a flood of commendation and criticism of every type".[7] Unfortunately such material is very difficult of access, but one series of articles singled out for special mention by Farquhar[8] was later reprinted in book form, providing a valuable indication of the reactions of an orthodox Hindu to the "fulfilment" doctrine. The series in question, the work of Professor K. Sundararaman, was originally published in *The Hindu,* and afterwards appeared under the title of *Mr. J. N. Farquhar on Hinduism and Christianity: A Criticism.*[9]

Sundararaman's criticism in many ways resembles that of Lajpat Rai, two years before,[1] though it is more detailed and less concerned with politics. His position is severely conservative: he takes his stand on the authority of the Vedas, the Upanishads and the *Bhagavad Gītā* as sources of religious faith;[2] he argues in favour of the caste system, claiming that "we (Hindus) have no reason for despondency regarding the future and no need to adopt violent measures of social transformation";[3] and he defends all forms of Hindu worship, including "idolatry".[4] It is, then, hardly surprising that he contradicts Farquhar at practically every point, and that, although he is prepared occasionally to compliment the missionary on his diligence, he never accepts his conclusions. He accuses Farquhar—quite mistakenly—of having only second or third hand knowledge of the Upanishads and the *Gītā;*[5] he claims that he has "completely failed to understand the place of images in Hinduism";[6] and Farquhar's classification of Hinduism as a national religion he calls "a huge blunder".[7] Such examples might be multiplied. On

---

[6] *Ibid.,* p. 68.
[7] YMCA Secretaries' Reports: J. N. Farquhar, 1910, p. 275 (YMCA Hist. Lib.).
[8] *Ibid.*
[9] Published in Madras in 1910. Two copies of this rare book were placed at my disposal simultaneously: one by the Government of India National Library in Calcutta, and one by Mrs. M. I. G. Dibben (Farquhar's own copy).
[1] Above, p. 246 f.
[2] Sundararaman, *op. cit.,* pp. xi f., 27.
[3] *Ibid.,* p. 47.
[4] *Ibid.,* pp. 54 ff.
[5] *Ibid.,* p. 21 f.
[6] *Ibid.,* p. 54.
[7] *Ibid.,* p. 16 f.

the credit side, Sundararaman on one occasion praises Farquhar's "historic insight" and "impartiality" (on a minor point),[8] and elsewhere even writes, in connexion with Farquhar's study of the caste system, that "To be a Christian of Christians and yet a Hindu of Hindus has been Mr. Farquhar's rare privilege and fortune".[9] But this seems to have been more an expression of conventional politeness than a genuine tribute. Otherwise his tone is polemical.

Comparing Farquhar's and Sundararaman's articles, one fact stands out with some clarity: that the two were arguing from dialectically impregnable positions. In other words, that neither was in the least susceptible to the arguments of the other, since their presuppositions were too different. Farquhar had admitted "the greatness of Hinduism", but it was a philosophical, abstract greatness, rather than a definite theological or empirical quality: his desire as a missionary and as a Christian was to see Hinduism transformed and in effect replaced by Christianity as the religion of India. And Sundararaman, while giving Farquhar some credit for impartiality, was concerned as a philosopher to defend his ancestral faith from the assaults of outsiders.[1] In such a situation, mere dialectics were of little use, and the attempt to reason away "hindrances to the acceptance of Christ" largely fruitless. Whatever the value of the apologetical method in the student situation (a question on which it is impossible to be too categorical), it evidently made little impression on a philosopher. It is instructive in this connexion to note that two scholars of such widely differing backgrounds and attainments as the Christian A. G. Hogg and the Hindu S. Radhakrishnan—both philosophers—were also suspicious of Farquhar's method, Hogg because he felt it to be condescending, rather than genuinely sympathetic to Hinduism,[2] and Radhakrishnan because to his mind it sounded "the imperialistic note that Christianity is the highest manifestation of the religious spirit" throughout.[3] Sundararaman's criticism was basically of this type.

Of greater significance for the history of the development of Farquhar's missionary theories was however a debate resulting from the third of the 1910 articles mentioned above, that in the *Student*

---

[8] *Ibid.*, p. 7, cf. pp. 35, 37 f.
[9] *Ibid.*, p. 45.
[1] For the reasons we have suggested above, pp. 247 ff.
[2] Below, p. 350 f.
[3] *East and West in Religion* (1933), p. 24.

Movement on "Christ and the Religions of the World". But the actual debate came later. The article in question was reprinted in 1912 in India, and those who challenged Farquhar's thesis did so on a basis of the article as reprinted, not the original. We shall therefore defer consideration of this debate until Chapter Ten.[4]

There remains *A Primer of Hinduism*.[5] This little book was written as a direct result of Mott's "mission-study policy",[6] and is an elementary text-book on the history and ethos of Hinduism. It is for the most part from the standpoint of objective historical scholarship, and presents a large amount of factual material in a highly concentrated form. The book is however not wholly dispassionate; it is a missionary text-book, designed to meet the need for a convenient modern account of the major forms and beliefs of Hinduism, for use in mission study and the training of missionaries. Thus some attention is paid, alongside the description of Hindu history and phenomena, to the problem of Hindu-Christian relations. Farquhar lays great stress on the non-moral character of Hindu beliefs and practices: Hinduism has suffered from the lack of "a limiting moral conception". "There was no definite conception in the Hindu mind as to what a god must be",[7] and hence morality, when it is found in modern Hinduism, is due to the impact of Christianity.[8] Dealing with modern developments in the religious picture of India, Farquhar makes extensive use of the material of earlier lectures and articles; thus, to take only one example, an outline of Chapter XI, "Period of Western Influence" is to be seen in his 1907 address to the Tokyo W.S.C.F. conference on "India and Christianity".[9] The final chapter, that dealing with the future of Hinduism, repeats the arguments of "Christianity in India" (1908) and his 1910 *Contemporary Review* articles. Farquhar concludes that "We may expect

---

[4] Below, pp. 309 ff.
[5] We use the second revised edition of 1914, the first of Farquhar's books to be published by arrangement with the Oxford University Press.
[6] Above, p. 235.
[7] *Primer*, p. 194.
[8] *Ibid.*, p. 197: "The modern Hindu who has drunk of Western thought in Indian or European universities ... maintains that Hindu morality has a solid spiritual base in Hindu philosophy; and from that starting-point man's moral relation to God and his complete responsibility to God may be clearly worked out. This is strange, if it be true; for it is certain no one attempted to find such things in Hindu philosophy until Christian thought appeared in India."
[9] *Tokyo Report*, pp. 37–45.

great developments within Hinduism, a stubborn and prolonged resistance from the central party, but an abundant victory for Christ in the end".[1] *A Primer of Hinduism* is nevertheless more a work of scholarship than an essay in missionary apologetics; the proportions were to be reversed two years later, in *The Crown of Hinduism,* a work towards which the *Primer* is to be seen as paving the way.

One of Farquhar's quarterly report letters from 1911 contains a series of reviews of the *Primer,* none of which are either dated or provided with source references.[2] The total impression is however one of favourable appreciation: one reviewer called it "a serious contribution to the study of Hinduism", despite its limitations; D. S. Cairns wrote that he was "looking forward to a wholesale *plagiarismus* from it with my class this winter"; and L. P. Larsen, "I am using your *Primer of Hinduism* with a class of young missionaries and find it most valuable as a text book. We have reason to be grateful to you."

This was only a small book, however, designed to meet a limited objective, and though Farquhar seems to have been satisfied with its reception, he was anxious to see literary work, particularly on the relations of Christianity and Hinduism, done on a much larger scale. We turn now to this wide question, before discussing the problem of Farquhar's own personal future as a scholar and author.

Recruitment of Writers

We have been concerned in our study so far with J. N. Farquhar's personal development as a leader of missionary thought—with his study of Hinduism and the patterns of his own literary work—and with the religious and political background against which this development is to be seen. But all this is preliminary. Many writers have stressed that Farquhar's contribution to the thought of the Church in India was twofold: not only did he write books embodying a new attitude to the cultural heritage of India; he was also responsible for recruiting a band of writers—European, American and Indian—who were prepared to join him in the task of providing scholarly, sympathetic Christian literature for India. The maturing

[1] *Primer*, p. 202.
[2] Farquhar collection.

of this process lies outside the scope of this study: the first works in the *Religious Quest of India* series and the *Heritage of India* series did not appear until 1915.[3] But we must note briefly the stages by which this plan came to fruition.

A vision of the potential scope of high-class literature in the work of Christian missions in India had been crystallizing in Farquhar's mind since at least the turn of the century. In his paper on *Great Religious Books*[4] he had said that "for the evangelization of India the production of a single great work, a book that would not only command respect, but would actually compel the attention of the people of this country, would be a thing of inestimable value".[5] And at the same time he had laid down strict standards for the writing of such a book, of which good workmanship and sympathy were the chief. These conditions he had elaborated in 1903:

A mere repetition of the old Christian formulas is useless. We want men who know Sanskrit, and understand Hinduism, who know something about the history of religions generally, and who are really trustworthy scientific students of the New Testament.[6]

His ideal he set out in more detail in the course of his 1909 report. The Church, he claimed, must rethink her intellectual position. The Christian position must be expounded—largely by writers—in such a way that the peoples of India shall see in Christ the fulfilment of their deepest religious instincts and loftiest aspirations. The relationship between Christianity and Hinduism must be stated so as to give the old religion its rightful place and yet secure for Christianity "undisputed supremacy". And further, the statement of Christianity must be Christian without being local, sectarian, or denominational; nothing less can suffice for "the naturalization of Christianity in the East".[7]

Returning to 1906, after a largely abortive attempt to form a Theological Circle in Calcutta,[8] Farquhar had come to the conclusion that his purposes would best be served by a Christian Society

---

[3] For details, see bibliography.
[4] Above, p. 170 f.
[5] *Great Religious Books* (s.a.), p. 58. Cf. above, p. 171.
[6] *Report 1903*, p. 109.
[7] *Report 1909*, p. 264.
[8] *Report 1904*, p. 156.

for the study of Hinduism and its relationship with Christianity. "Membership", he wrote, "I shall propose to restrict to a few men who will really work. We shall probably divide the field, and try to produce a series of reliable monographs on the subject."[9] The problem, however, was finding time for such work. We have noted that this had already caused Farquhar some concern, though he believed that the Y.M.C.A. might well be able to solve the problem by setting apart a man for literary work pure and simple.[1] Still, nothing concrete was done, despite Farquhar's constant emphasis on the need for literature, and despite the 1907 Calcutta conference.[2] His own earlier work had proved unexpectedly successful, but as he put in 1908, "This type of work ought now to be done by scores of writers in every part of India".[3]

At length, in November 1908, Farquhar wrote to Mott personally, lamenting that pressure of work as National General Secretary[4] was preventing him from making progress with a new literary enterprise which he and a number of other missionary scholars had decided upon.[5] They had been deeply impressed with the need for a clear, full statement of the relationship of Christianity to Hinduism,[6] and had planned a series of books on various aspects of Hinduism, which they hoped to publish within the next few years. Farquhar was to be responsible for a book on the religious literature of India; H. D. Griswold of Lahore was to write on the Rig Veda; R. A. Hume of Ahmednagar on the Upanishads; A. G. Hogg of the Madras Christian College on the Vedanta; and Nicol Macnicol of Poona on Indian theism. This was the first concrete indication of the coming *Religious Quest of India* series, thought the original conception came to be considerably modified later.[7]

Mott wrote in reply:

---

[9] *Report 1906,* p. 216.
[1] *Report 1907,* p. 287. Above, p. 243.
[2] Above, p. 240.
[3] *Report 1908,* p. 211.
[4] Above, p. 228.
[5] Farquhar to Mott, 12.11.1908 (YMCA Hist. Lib.).
[6] Cf. Farquhar's address at the Oxford WSCF conference, above, pp. 255 ff.
[7] The original plan was for five books: *The Religious Literature of India,* by Farquhar; *The Rigveda,* by H. D. Griswold; *The Upanishads,* by R. E. Hume; *The Vedanta,* by A. G. Hogg; and *Indian Theism,* by N. Macnicol (Farquhar to Mott, 12.11.1908). Four of the five were eventually published, Hogg being prevented by pressure of work from writing on the Vedanta.

I am deeply impressed by the outline of the list of works you are planning to bring out with reference to the relationship of Christianity to Hinduism. This will be not only a scholarly, but a statesmanlike service.[8]

But however scholarly and statesmanlike Farquhar's plans may have seemed in Mott's eyes, nothing could be done towards their realization by a man working in his spare time. That the work of the Y.M.C.A. secretaryship was absorbing most of Farquhar's energies cannot be gainsaid: travelling, organizing and routine administration were taking up so much of his time that his literary work had to be relegated to a subordinate position. It is true that he had accomplished much with the limited time at his disposal: we have seen something of the result. But two new questions were forcing themselves on his mind: Was he making the best use of his time? Was he the right man for the Student Secretaryship? These he raised with Mott early in 1910.

Release from Student Work: Constantinople 1911

By 1910 Farquhar was growing more and more dissatisfied with his work in the student department of the Indian Y.M.C.A. It was in many ways a repeat of what had happened in 1902. Then, as a teacher in a missionary college, he had been prevented by his classroom work from taking part in "active" evangelization among students; now pressure of administrative and organizational work was keeping him from writing.

In May 1910 he wrote in the course of a letter to Mott that his mind was now made up, and that he was convinced of his own unsuitability for student work. He was almost fifty years old, and one of the reasons prompting his decision may have been the wide gap between his own age and that of the men with whom he was dealing.[9] At all events, he requested either to be given a teaching post or to be appointed "literary secretary to the National Council"— which would imply the creating of a new position especially for

---

[8] Mott to Farquhar, 7.12.1908 (YMCA Hist. Lib.).
[9] Cf. *Report 1904*, p. 156: "I confess to being much more attracted myself by the visitation of older men, and so during the past few months I have called on a considerable number of the Brahmos and better-known Hindus of our locality."

him.[1] Mott replied, assuring Farquhar of his sympathy, and of "the most fairminded and conscientious treatment" of his request.[2] It seemed, however, that little could be done, at least for the time being.

Later in the year Mott received confirmation of Farquhar's request from Sherwood Eddy, at that time a National Secretary of the Indian Y.M.C.A., with his headquarters in Madras. Eddy wrote:

His [Farquhar's] heart is in literary work. Apart from correspondence he is doing practically nothing for the Student Movement in India and we deeply need a National Student Secretary. He is the most valuable asset in India for literary work and should be freed for that if we can find the right man for National Student Secretary ...[3]

Farquhar and Mott did not meet again until April, 1911, at the Constantinople conference of the W.S.C.F. Of what passed between them there we have no detailed knowledge, except that Mott promised to secure Farquhar's release from the Student Secretaryship at the earliest opportunity, and agreed to create the new appointment that Farquhar had suggested—the post of Literary Secretary to the Indian National Council of the Y.M.C.A. This post he was to fill until his final retirement from missionary work, in 1923. Under the terms of this appointment Farquhar was to spend six months of each year in India, travelling, lecturing and gathering material, and the remaining six months in England, writing.[4]

The Constantinople conference was in many ways one of the most important in the history of the W.S.C.F.; to attempt to discuss the reasons for this would, however, lead us far beyond the bounds of this study. In brief, apart from being "an adventure of faith even more than in the case of Tokyo", it marked a new phase in the ecumenical attitudes of the Federation, particularly with regard to the Orthodox Churches.[5] Farquhar's personal contribution to the

---

[1] Farquhar to Mott, 14.4.1910 (YMCA Hist. Lib.): "I must be put into *teaching* and *writing* or at least one of the two if I am to do my best, and not feel that I am bound in chains ... The most experienced missionaries in India want to have me write."

[2] Mott to Farquhar, 6.5.1910 (YMCA Hist. Lib.).

[3] Eddy to Mott, 5.11.1910 (YMCA Hist. Lib.).

[4] YMCA National Council Office, 19.10.1911, Minute 622: "It was recommended that at the request of the International Committee and Mr. Farquhar, we release with regret Mr. Farquhar after March next from the responsibility of the student work. It being understood that hereafter he will divide his time between England and India ..."

[5] Rouse, *The World's Student Christian Federation*, pp. 152–161.

conference was slight. As at Oxford, he contributed introductory "Impressions of the Conference",[6] and gave an address on "What Aspects of Christianity are Essential for Propagation to all Mankind?"[7] Neither give any fresh insight into his development as a missionary leader, though his devotional address shows clearly the character of the non-dogmatic, "living" Christianity which formed the basis of his missionary activity.[8]

The same note is found in his "impressions", where he wrote:

We are learning to believe more surely every day that we are really all one man in Christ Jesus. When we live the spiritual life with Him, we are one in spite of differences of creed, of ritual, or of Church government.[9]

But although this address, and his conference "impressions" show that Farquhar was by no means insensible to the probable importance of the Constantinople conference to the future development of the movement for Christian unity,[1] it is hardly too much to say that it was most significant to him personally as the second turning-point in his missionary career. As in 1902 John R. Mott had provided the way out of a difficult and hampering situation—an intervention for which Farquhar was, and continued to be, grateful: twelve years later he was to write to Mott to thank him yet again for his act of "emancipation" in Constantinople.[2] What this emancipation implied in terms of the production of Christian literature, and how Farquhar's ideas were thereby given wider currency, it will be our task to inquire in a future chapter. But before doing so, we must retrace our steps a little, to the Edinburgh conference of 1910.

---

[6] *Report of the Conference of the World's Student Christian Federation, Robert College Constantinople* (1911), pp. 13–16.

[7] *Ibid.*, pp. 79–89.

[8] *Ibid.*, p. 81: "The innermost heart of our religion is a living faith, not a theology. Where dogma and rule are uppermost, Christianity may live and grow, but it fails to produce the richest fruits of character, and it loses the power of leavening society. It is a question of emphasis. Theology and organization have a large value of their own, yet it is not these things, but living religion that produces Christianity's fruits."

[9] *Ibid.*, p. 15 f.

[1] On this subject generally, see Rouse and Neill (ed.), *A History of the Ecumenical Movement, 1517–1948* (1954), pp. 324 ff.

[2] Farquhar to Mott, 25.10.1923 (Farquhar collection): "My purpose in writing this letter is to express to you my very great gratitude for your act of emancipation in Constantinople, which enabled me to give my mind and energy to Christian literature in India." Cf. Mathews, *John R. Mott: World Citizen*, p. 350.

CHAPTER 9

Edinburgh 1910: A. G. Hogg, D. S. Cairns and the World Missionary Conference

ONE STRIKING feature of the Indian missionary debate, as it developed during the years before the first world war, is its apparent lack of any serious theological attempt to get to grips with the problems involved in the developing Christian–Hindu dialogue. We say "apparent" lack advisedly, because of the risks inherent in subjecting this period to post-Barthian judgment on what is, and what is not, "theology". But it will have been clear from our study thus far that the debate surrounding the "fulfilment" doctrine was not for the most part conducted in theological categories. For instance, Farquhar's arguments we have seen to have been derived from historical and evolutionary theory, and supported by the findings of the "science of religion"; his Indian opponents argued out from their distinctive premises, in which religious and nationalist arguments were inextricably mixed; and we shall see in our next chapter that those conservative missionaries who challenged his views in 1912 did so because of their traditional Evangelical position, in which a particular theory of Biblical inspiration and a particular interpretation of the Atonement were prominent.[1] This latter position is of course in a sense theological—or at least dogmatic—but its representatives had made no attempt at a theological reinterpretation of the Indian situation on a basis of all the available evidence.

This is perhaps understandable. While undue generalization is risky, it is true to say that the Indian missionary force of the first decade or so of the twentieth century was still being recruited along traditional lines. The Evangelical position (or its confessional equivalent in the case of Continental missions) was implicit in virtually all Protestant missionary bodies at that time, the Y.M.C.A. not excepted. Independent or "liberal" thought was likely to disqualify a

---

[1] For a discussion of the theological trend, see above, pp. 25 ff., and for the debate in question, see below, pp. 309 ff.

potential missionary from the start, and was looked upon with suspicion when it developed after a missionary had begun work in India.[2] Further, the majority of Protestant missionary workers came from Britain and America, where systematic and dogmatic theology was passing through a period of comparative neglect. Very few knew German, and most were thus isolated from all but second-hand knowledge of theological developments on the Continent. And in any case the pressure of work experienced by the ordinary missionary prevented him from devoting more than a fraction of his time to serious theological study.

One exception to this rule is however to be seen in the Scotsman A. G. Hogg, of the Madras Christian College, who came to India in 1903. Hogg had studied philosophy before taking his theological course; he had spent a period in Germany, and was familiar with the German schools; his intellectual capacity was outstanding; and he had had time to study and write, at least during his early years in India.[3]

The development of Hogg's theological thought is deserving of a separate detailed study, and we can do little more than indicate in this chapter the general lines on which such a study might be undertaken. What is of special interest for our purposes is his role in connexion with the 1910 Edinburgh World Missionary Conference, and the direct confrontation of his theory of "significant contrast" with Farquhar's "fulfilment" doctrine. In addition the close friendship of Hogg with Principal D. S. Cairns of the United Free Church College in Aberdeen led to a particular emphasis being placed on the idea of "redemption from this world" in volume IV of the conference report, as well as providing Commission IV with a significant body of material worked out on theological lines. Hogg's material also criticized sharply the "fulfilment" idea, at least in some of its aspects. We shall accordingly devote part of this present chapter

---

[2] Examples are to be seen in the cases of T. E. Slater and the London Missionary Society (above, p. 99) and L. P. Larsen and Det Danske Missionsselskab (above, p. 107).

[3] Hogg in fact published very little. His two most influential books, *Karma and Redemption* and *Christ's Message of the Kingdom*, appeared in 1909 and 1911 respectively. In 1922 appeared his Cunningham Lectures on *Redemption from this World*. Pressure of teaching and administration prevented him from writing any further large-scale work until after his retirement, when his important book *The Christian Message to the Hindu* appeared (1947). However, he wrote a fair number of articles, and left a quantity of manuscript sermons and letters (Hogg collection).

to an examination of this, the first cogent theological criticism of Farquhar's work.

To deal with these complex matters in the course of one single chapter is no easy undertaking. The fact remains, that these important lines of development came to a highly significant focus in and around the Edinburgh conference. Many correspondents submitted material in which they spoke with at least implicit approval of the idea of "fulfilment"; Hogg submitted a paper in which he subjected that same concept to sharp criticism; and Hogg and Cairns together were in process of working out a theological view which left distinct traces in the official report. These related and yet separate ideas must all be borne in mind throughout the present chapter.

First, however, we must discuss in general terms the significance of Edinburgh 1910 in the development of the missionary thought of the period.

The Edinburgh Conference

Much has been written during the last fifty years about the World Missionary Conference of 1910, its background, its origins, its findings and its impact.[4] Most commentators are agreed as to its place in the history of the Church in the twentieth century: for instance, Wilhelm Andersen writes that it is hardly possible to exaggerate its importance: "the achievement of Edinburgh is the pre-supposition of all the later world conferences ..."[5] Latourette calls the conference "one of the great landmarks in the history of the Church";[6] and Rouse characterizes it as "'possibly the most significant missionary event of the twentieth century".[7] Some historians regard it as having been the end of an epoch; others see in it the beginning of a new age in the history of the Church. Both views are of course substantially correct, for reasons we cannot discuss here.[8] But however the conference may be judged, it is clear, after rather more than fifty years, that it marks a watershed

---

[4] A comprehensive (though not exhaustive) bibliography will be found in the *Occasional Bulletin* of the Missionary Research Library XI: 5 (14.6.1960).

[5] Andersen, *Towards a Theology of Mission* (1955), p. 16.

[6] Rouse and Neill (ed.), *A History of the Ecumenical Movement, 1517–1948* (1954), p. 355.

[7] *The World's Student Christian Federation* (1948), p. 128.

[8] Hogg (W. R.), *Ecumenical Foundations* (1952), p. 98.

in missionary discussion. As A. J. Boyd has observed, the conference is perhaps best thought of as

the last word, the memorable and inspiring last word, of the Age of Missions, soon to be succeeded by the Age of the Missionary Church.[9]

But though there has been no lack of commentators on Edinburgh 1910, most historians have been content to treat the subject summarily, rather than in detail. Here there are certain facts which it would be well to bear in mind. The nine volumes of the conference report, though invaluable as the expression of the mind of the respective commissions, represent bodies of material *after* having undergone a process of co-ordination and systematization.[1] It is, then, possible that a study of the original manuscript material, as submitted to the commissions by working missionaries in various parts of the world, might well give results differing from those which have been enshrined in the reports. It is surprising, in view of the fact that so much of this manuscript material is in fact available to scholars, to find that so little work has been done along these lines. Even W. Richey Hogg, who is perhaps the one modern scholar who has subjected the World Missionary Conference to a thorough scrutiny, has been concerned mainly with its origins and background. He has evidently examined a good deal of the pre-Edinburgh manuscript material; but he seems not to have touched the material sent in by the correspondents. Hence his treatment of the work of the Commissions is cursory at best, and he makes no attempt to set the conference in its theological context.[2] This omis-

---

[9] Boyd, *Christian Encounter* (1961), p. 7 f.

[1] With the exception of World Missionary Conference 1910: *The History and Records of the Conference* (Vol. IX).

[2] See e.g. *Ecumenical Foundations*, pp. 115 ff. It must further be pointed out that a conference such as Edinburgh 1910 is not placed in its theological context merely by passing adverse judgment on "liberalism". The task is much more demanding than that. There have of course been numbers of such "theological" verdicts passed on Edinburgh 1910. The view of the Danish scholar Johannes Aagaard, that "everything that took place at this conference was characterized by a moderate (*afdæmpet*) liberalism" is an over-simplification ["Evangelium og religion. Opfyldelse eller ophævelse?" in *SMT* 52: 1 (1964), p. 30]. Aalholt, "Den liberale teologi i den internationale missionsbevægelse", in *NMT* 75: 1–2 (1964), pp. 12 ff., 85 ff., is guilty of a similar over-simplification, and a number of factual errors. And a judgment such as that of Baez-Camargo, in *Ecumenical Review* XVI: 3 (1964), p. 266, that "The corporate mind of *Edinburgh 1910* was still shrouded in the veil of Western and Victorian self-complacency and paternalism", is a caricature. None of these are really historical judgments, since none makes any attempt to place Edinburgh in *its own* context.

sion may have to do with the current lack of theological interest in the pre-1914 period; or it may be felt by some that it is still too early to attempt a re-evaluation of the whole of Edinburgh manuscript material. The fact remains, that the material is there, as yet virtually untouched.[3]

To proceed to the aims of Edinburgh 1910, the first public announcement of the character of the coming conference was made in 1908, in an article by J. R. Mott in *The East and the West*.[4] Mott first defined what was to be the purpose of the proposed meeting, as compared with earlier conferences in the same *genre*. Unlike the 1888 London conference and the 1900 New York "ecumenical" conference it was not to be "a great missionary demonstration for educational and inspirational purposes primarily", but a consultative assembly, or, as Mott put it, "a Conference for conference".[5] In terms of practical organization this meant that instead of the prolix addresses and discussions which had been a feature of most previous missionary conferences, the delegates to Edinburgh were to be presented with documents, drawn up in advance by experts on a basis of material sent in from the missionaries themselves. Thus it was hoped to have a large body of representative material from all the major mission fields available, giving a complete cross-section of contemporary missionary opinion on leading problems. To avoid confusion, the field had been divided, and eight "Commissions" appointed, each under a Chairman, who in his turn was to be served by a select international committee. It was the responsibility of the Chairman in each case to draft the report of his Commission.[6]

---

[3] Most of the material is in the Missionary Research Library, New York. See *Occasional Bulletin*, 14.6.1960, p. 7 f., and cf. bibliography.

[4] *The East and the West* VI (Oct. 1908), pp. 368–85. The article, entitled "A World Missionary Conference", was distributed as an offprint (pagination 1–15), and it is to that offprint we refer.

[5] *Ibid.*, p. 1.

[6] Thus in the case of Commission IV, the report was drafted by D. S. Cairns alone, and not by Cairns and Speer together, as Aalholt wrongly assumes (*NMT* 75: 1, p. 14). He has been led astray by a phrase in *IRM* XVIII: 71 (1929), in which Cairns speaks of "the evidence read by Dr Speer and myself ... for the Edinburgh conference of 1910" (p. 321). Speer was of course vice-chairman of Commission IV, and had to approve Cairns' draft (which he did wholeheartedly, as Cairns' letter to A. G. Hogg, 19.3.1910, makes clear), but his active role was limited to closing the public discussion on behalf of the Commission: see World Missionary Conference, 1910: *Report of Commission IV*, pp. 324 ff.

Perhaps the most striking thing about Mott's presentation of the fourth of these Commissions (that on the Christian message in relation to non-Christian religions) is the fact that the word "apologetic" occurs no less than four times in seventeen lines. Missionaries have had wide "apologetic" experiences; these experiences are to be studied by "apologetic" thinkers in the West, in correspondence with "apologetic" workers abroad; and the aim of the commission will be to call attention to the distinctive "apologetic" to be used in the various missionary situations.[7] The word is to be found nowhere else in Mott's account, and it is clearly the case that he was using it in the specific sense of the communication of the Gospel to adherents of non-Christian religions.[8] It has a twofold purpose: in Mott's words, ". . . to avoid unnecessary opposition and objection and to commend most strongly the Christian truth".[9] In other words, how was the Christian missionary to preach the Gospel without giving *unnecessary* offence to adherents of other religions, and at the same time without in any way compromising the claims of Christ? The crux of the matter lay in the missionary's attitude; hence the fifth question in the Commission IV questionnaire asked, "What attitude should the Christian preacher take toward the religion of the people among whom he labours?"

The questionnaire was sent to a select group of missionaries[1]—a fact which must be borne in mind when judging the representativeness or otherwise of the Commission's conclusions. Of the sixty-five missionaries working in the Hindu milieu (those with whom we are most closely concerned), eight only were representative of Continental societies, or of Continental origin; eleven were Indians. The remainder were either British or Americans.

---

[7] Mott, *A World Missionary Conference*, p. 5.

[8] Cf. above, p. 16 f.

[9] Mott, *ibid.* Cf. Farquhar's use of the word at the Oxford conference of 1909, above, p. 255 f., and Cairns' article "The Need for Apologists", in the *Student World* IV (April 1911), pp. 49–57.

[1] "These questions are being sent to a comparatively small number of missionary leaders through the world—persons chosen with great care by a representative committee after correspondence with the secretaries of the missionary societies in Great Britain, American and the Continent." Mott, open letter (undated), sent with the questionnaire (MRL).

The Commission IV Material: the Missionary Attitude towards Hinduism

The section of the official conference report devoted to the Christian message to the Hindu opens with the following words:

The replies, one and all, lay emphasis upon the necessity that the missionary to Hindus should possess, and not merely assume, *a sympathetic attitude towards India's most ancient religion*.[2]

It goes on to point to the correspondents' emphasis on study, and observes that a great deal of harm has been done in the past, particularly in India, by missionaries who have been so unwise as to fail in sympathy.[3]

Reading the manuscript answers, it is clear that this is a fair summary of the opinions of the correspondents. The report quotes a number of instances in support of the above statement;[4] it would not be difficult to find many more. But at the same time it must be recognized that, while all—or virtually all—urged the need for sympathy, not all did so for quite the same reasons. Some held that sympathy was necessary on account of the religious truth of Hinduism in some of its aspects. The first step was outlined by T. E. Slater, who stated that sympathy was a *sine qua non* for a right appreciation of Hinduism, since lack of sympathy inevitably leads to misinterpretation of any religion.[5] Nicol Macnicol went a step further, writing that the missionary must look upon Hinduism "as having been at some time or other a sincere attempt to find God, and learn His will, and still perhaps capable of being so used by an earnest spirit".[6] Bernard Lucas, an L.M.S. missionary, stressed the same point, that every religion has been an attempt to reach out towards the highest, and that no missionary "should forget this true signification".[7] It goes without saying that on this view an attempt

---

[2] *Report of Commission IV*, p. 171. Gairdner calles the Report as a whole "one of the most remarkable, perhaps the most remarkable, of a great series". *"Edinburgh 1910": An Account and Interpretation of the World Missionary Conference* (1910), p. 134, cf. p. 137.

[3] *Report of Commission IV*, p. 171.

[4] *Ibid.*, pp. 171 ff.

[5] *Ibid.*, p. 174. Cf. above, p. 207.

[6] Edinburgh manuscripts, preserved in the Missionary Research Library, New York (hereinafter *Edinburgh MS*). An incomplete copy of these same mss., used by Cairns, is in the library of Christ's College, Aberdeen.

[7] *Edinburgh MS*.

must be made to find, and use, the best that Hinduism has to offer as the starting-point of the Christian proclamation. But only as the starting-point. As Samuel Ambat of the Basel Mission expressed it, "Wherever we find rays of light in the non-Christian religions, we should unhesitatingly express our appreciation of them and do our best in order to lead our hearers from the external to the internal, from the shadow to the body itself".[8]

The words "fulfil" and "fulfilment" occur frequently in the missionaries' answers. R. A. Hume of Ahmednagar, an American Board missionary, described the Christian position as being "in accordance with Christ's attitude to the older dispensation to fulfil, i.e. to fill fuller, the best phases of what the people now accept".[9] One of the Indian correspondents, J. Lazarus, stressed that Christ must be presented as "the Divine Fulfiller of the longings and hopes of Hinduism" and that the Christian preacher must stress "the positive rather than the controversial, the comparative rather than the contrasting methods".[1] And another L.M.S. missionary, while not expressly using the word "fulfilment", advocated treating Hinduism as a preparation for Christianity, "regarding even its errors as a means being used by the Divine wisdom to lead men to see their need of the truth ...".[2]

But there were others who regarded such an approach as dangerous. A medical missionary, Mrs. Ferguson Davie of the S.P.G., urged care, particularly among Europeans, lest the spirit of sympathy should go too far: "We have to find what is good in their religion, but to show also what is better in Christianity."[3] Wilhelm Dilger of the Basel Mission was afraid that too close approximation to Indian thought, and particularly to Vedantism, might, if unchecked, give rise to a new Gnosticism.[4] The Bishop of Madras—whom we have already seen to have been an opponent of the philosophical approach to the Hindu[5]—stressed that the main object of the Christian preacher must be "to bring home to the hearts and consciences of the people the great differences between Christianity and their

---

[8] *Ibid.*
[9] *Ibid.*
[1] *Ibid.*
[2] *Ibid.*
[3] *Ibid.*
[4] *Edinburgh MS.* Cf. *Report of Commission IV*, p. 317 f.
[5] Above, p. 27 n. 5.

own religion, and not merely the points of contact between them".[6] And the only Swedish correspondent, J. Ruthquist of *Svenska Missionsförbundet,* was of the opinion that the Christian preacher should, as a rule, preach to the people "as if he knew of no other religion than the Christian one".[7]

This seems however to have been largely a matter of emphasis, as the report suggests.[8] The uncompromising claims of Evangelical Christianity were in no case weakened; but missionaries differed slightly as to the extent to which they felt sympathy for Hinduism to be justified. There seem in some cases to have been undertones of policy: to attack Hinduism is to destroy the preacher's chance of a hearing, and it is therefore a matter of practical expediency to adopt an attitude of sympathy. But these went unexpressed, as often as not: an amusing exception was the paper of Canon Nihal Singh, who stated bluntly that the Christian preacher "should try to show the futility and absurdity of these religions in a nice pleasant sort of way".[9] "Approach" was all-important: the reasons for adopting the attitude of sympathy less so. Most correspondents agreed with Farquhar's thesis, that Hinduism gave evidence of man's need of a Saviour, and was therefore to be treated with respect; and they agreed that it was unable to provide that Saviour. It is in this sense that the word "fulfilment" was used, when it was used.

Taken as a whole the correspondents' answers bear out the correctness of Farquhar's summary of the Indian situation at the Oxford conference of the preceding year: that many were prepared to treat Christ as the fulfilment of certain aspects of Hinduism—to speak of his fulfilling the best of Hindu thought and practice. But few had taken the further step of setting forth Christianity as the fulfilment, the crown and the climax of "the crudest forms of her worship as well as of those lofty spiritual movements which have so often appeared in Hinduism but have always ended in weakness".[1] This is to say that few shared Farquhar's evolutionary interpretation of the religious situation, and were prepared in consequence to express

---

[6] *Edinburgh MS.*
[7] *Ibid.*
[8] *Report of Commission IV,* p. 177.
[9] *Edinburgh MS.*
[1] Cf. the important statement in *Oxford Report* (1909), p. 71 f., quoted above, p. 255 f.

the relationship between Christianity and Hinduism in terms of the evolutionary postulate.

Farquhar's own paper reiterated the principles which we have noted so many times in our study thus far: in brief, that all religions are human, yet only one—Christianity—satisfies all the religious instincts and yet can be held by modern thinking man. He goes on:

> But if all religions are human, and yet man can in the long run hold only Christianity, clearly it must be, in some sense, *the climax of the religious development of the world* [our italics], the end and culmination of all religions. If all the great religious instincts, which have created the other faiths, find ultimate satisfaction in Christianity, then Christianity stands in a very definite relation to every other religion. It is the fulfilment and crown of each; and it is our privilege and duty to trace the lines of connection and lead the peoples up to the Christ.[2]

The consequences of this clearly evolutionist view—which others tended to accept irrespective of their ultimate origins—were worked out by Farquhar in five points: reverence for non-Christian religion; unwillingness to criticize—or praise—unduly; a scientific attitude when criticism and comparison is unavoidable; an eagerness to conserve all the really "religious" elements in the life of the people; and a preparedness to set forth Christ as the fulfilment of the peoples' old faiths. And he concluded:

> This method alone is true to the large facts of history and evolution; for many a crude rite and many a wild myth hide ideas which have later bloomed in beauty and borne fruit.[3]

Finally in this section we must note that many of those who took part in the discussions accompanying the presentation of the Commission IV report expressed substantially the same views as those we have noted in the correspondents' replies. G. E. Phillips of the L.M.S.[4] and Principal Mackichan of Bombay[5] both expressed

---

[2] *Edinburgh MS.*

[3] *Edinburgh MS.* For the continuation of this quotation, see *Report of Commission IV*, p. 173, para. 2.

[4] *Report of Commission IV*, p. 312.

[5] Principal Mackichan's contribution is doubly interesting in view of his later attack on *The Crown of Hinduism* (see below, p. 347 f.). On this occasion Mackichan said, "We have to tell the Indian that we sympathise with his struggle, and we sympathise with his failure, and that the Christ whom we preach to him brings to him the message which satisfies his longings and fulfils his desires. In this sense Christ is the fulfiller, not simply the supplementer of something that has been discovered and achieved, but one who fulfils the desire and the striving of the soul, and one who in the truest sense meets the soul's human need." *Report of Commission IV*, p. 320.

their approval of the "fulfilment" idea, in the restricted sense we have described. And no clearly critical voices were raised. But at the same time there was general insistence that none but Christ could serve to transform India. The existence of the sympathetic approach and the rejection of overt iconoclasm are in all cases taken for granted. A significant fact is however the absence of all mention of "evolutionary" fulfilment, in the sense advocated by Farquhar; it would seem that the conference as a whole was selective in its reception of Farquhar's views, accepting his conclusions in many cases, but without his personal scientific motivation.

Hogg and Cairns

The Commission IV report, particularly in its "General Conclusions"[6] is a document of considerable importance for the study of the history and theology of missions, and not least for the problems with which we have been concerned in this study. These "Conclusions" are the work of the Chairman of the Commission, Professor D. S. Cairns of Aberdeen, and bear the clear stamp of his personality. The circumstances surrounding the writing of this report are of particular interest, since they are bound up also with the contribution of A. G. Hogg to the Edinburgh conference as a whole, and with his criticism of Farquhar, which we have not as yet discussed.

D. M. Baillie has spoken of the "rich intellectual friendship" of Cairns and Hogg.[7] That this friendship affected both men's *later* production is an acknowledged fact, to which Baillie has also called attention.[8] But the process of mutual influence on the literary level began—a fact which Baillie does not point out—with the Edinburgh report. In order to understand something of the way in which this came about we must digress slightly, and give a brief resumé of the contacts between Cairns and the Hogg family.

In 1884 D. S. Cairns, then a twenty-two-year-old student, was compelled by ill-health to take a Mediterranean voyage. Before leaving Scotland he had been given an introduction to an American

---

[6] *Ibid.*, pp. 214 ff.

[7] Baillie (D. M.), Memoir of D. S. Cairns, prefixed to *David Cairns: An Autobiography* (1950), p. 25.

[8] *Ibid.*, p. 24 f.

missionary in Cairo (Dr. Lansing).[9] There he had met Dr. John Hogg, a Scottish Presbyterian missionary, at that time working in Assiut.[1] Cairns' physical collapse had coincided with a crisis of faith, and Hogg's influence helped to place his religious life on a firmer footing: he was later able to write that "Dr. Hogg's personality and character in particular made a deep impression on me ..."[2]. Cairns' stay in Egypt was short (less than six months in all), but important for his development as a Christian leader. John Hogg died three years later, in 1886, and his wife and eight children returned to Scotland, settling in Edinburgh.

Alfred George Hogg, John Hogg's son, was born in Egypt in 1874. On his return to Scotland he attended George Watson's college in Edinburgh, and later Edinburgh University, where he read philosophy under Professor Andrew Seth (later Andrew Seth Pringle Pattison), graduating M.A. in 1897. The Hogg family belonged to the Morningside United Presbyterian Church, where A. G. Hogg was received into full communion in 1889. In 1892 D. S. Cairns, having completed his theological training, was appointed for six months assistant to the minister of this church, Dr. Alexander Mair.[3] A. G. Hogg was a member of Cairns' Bible class, and a friendship sprang up between them—the "deep intellectual friendship" of which Baillie speaks. In 1897 Hogg entered the Theological Hall of the United Presbyterian Church, but broke off his studies after a year for further thought and study. In fact he seems to have passed through a crisis of faith similar to that experienced by Cairns; and in the event he was helped by an extensive correspondence—now unfortunately lost—with Cairns, on the subject of the personal and philosophical implications of the Christian faith.[4]

After completing his theological training at New College, Edinburgh (the United Presbyterian Church having joined with the

[9] *Ibid.*, p. 90.
[1] Hogg (Rena L.), *A Master-Builder on the Nile: Being a Record of the Life and Aims of John Hogg, D.D., Christian Missionary* (1914), pp. 266 ff.
[2] *David Cairns: An Autobiography*, p. 100. Cf. a passage in one of Cairns' letters to A. G. Hogg: "My mind went back to old days when your father's life so deeply influenced mine, and everything fell suddenly into unity, and I felt the wonder and delight of the Divine presence, and took courage." Cairns to Hogg, 25.8.1909 (Hogg collection).
[3] *Ibid.*, p. 139 f.
[4] For this and other details I am indebted to the late Mr L. A. Hogg of Edinburgh, who wrote a short memoir of his brother A. G. Hogg at the request of the present writer.

Free Church in the meantime to form the United Free Church of Scotland), Hogg was appointed in 1902 Professor of Mental and Moral Science in the Madras Christian College; while Cairns, after some years spent as a parish minister, became Professor of Dogmatics and Apologetics in the United Free Church College at Aberdeen in 1907.

A further fact of great significance is that both Cairns and Hogg had studied in Germany, although only for one term each: Cairns in Marburg, where he had attended the lectures of Herrmann, and Hogg in Halle under Titius.[5]

In later years both were to make ample public acknowledgment of the debt they owed each other in the realm of theological thought. So Hogg, in the Preface to his study-book *Christ's Message of the Kingdom* (dated July 5, 1911), wrote that compared with his fundamental debt to Cairns, "all others have been but incidents in the germination and growth of seeds which were planted by him ...".[6] A quotation from Cairns is printed on the title page of the same book. And Cairns in his turn included in the Preface of *The Faith that Rebels* (1928) an acknowledgment that Hogg's books *Christ's Message of the Kingdom* and *Redemption from this World* (1922) contain "the fullest and ablest statements of that idea [the teaching of Jesus on faith] known to me ...".[7] The significance of this statement will be clearer as we proceed.

Hogg's Attitude to Hinduism

Hogg, as we have said, came to India in 1903. We have also seen[8] that the early years of the twentieth century were noteworthy for

---

[5] This is however not the same thing as saying that both Cairns and Hogg were Ritschlians pure and simple. That Cairns and Speer were Ritschlians is assumed, somewhat uncritically, by Aalholt, *NMT* 75: 1, p. 14. Against this it would however be well to set Cairns' own evidence, from which it appears that he learned much from Ritschlianism without ever accepting it wholeheartedly as a system, particularly since it seemed to him to be defective on the subject of the Divinity of Christ: see *Autobiography*, p. 135. That he was impressed as a young man by Herrmann is undeniable (letter written from Marburg by Cairns to his Father, undated, in the possession of Prof. D. Cairns, Aberdeen); but full account must be taken of Cairns' distinctively Scottish background. Hogg had learnt much from Herrmann, Kaftan and Titius, but also from Kant, Hegel, Bergson, Croce and Pringle Pattison, and from Cairns himself; see *Redemption from this World* (1922), p. xi. See also Reid's article in the *Expository Times* LXXII: 10 (1961) on Hogg's *Christ's Message of the Kingdom*. More work needs to be done on this subject, and it is not a topic we can discuss further here.

[6] Preface, p. iv.   [7] Preface, p. 5.   [8] Above, pp. 194 ff.

a great increase in the popularity of Neo-Krishnaism in India. Most Christian observers were agreed that this was in some measure a reaction to the impact made upon Hinduism by the missionaries' presentation of Christ as Saviour. And we have noted that the missionary literature of the period tended to concentrate on the question "Christ or Krishna?" In *Gita and Gospel* (1903) Farquhar had applied the methods of historical criticism to the respective documents, the *Bhagavad Gītā* and the Synoptic Gospels. A. G. Hogg was also interested in this problem, and in a series of articles published in the *Madras Christian College Magazine* during 1904 and 1905 discussed the rival conceptions of *karma* and redemption from his own distinctive philosophical and theological standpoint.[9] A full comparison between *Gita and Gospel* and *Karma and Redemption* is however out of the question: the two differ too radically in conception and execution to make this possible. Where Farquhar was concerned with the historical reliability of the documents on which the respective parties based their allegiance, Hogg attempted to trace the philosophical validity of the basic concepts of Krishnaism and Christianity. And while Farquhar's ultimate object was to trace relationship, Hogg's was to work out areas of fundamental contrast.

One significant point in Hogg's interpretation of religion which must continually be borne in mind is the distinction he draws between "faith" and "beliefs". Faith *in* God is one thing; beliefs *about* God another, though the first invariably gives rise to the second. Faith is an inner trust and assurance; beliefs are the intellectual expressions of that assurance,[1] and may degenerate into superstition,[2] though at best they may be "the instruments of a living trust in God".[3] Both Christians and Hindus, maintained Hogg, have beliefs about God, and the religious conflict exists mainly on this level, though the common tendency is to confuse them with faith, and

---

[9] These articles were later republished in book form (in 1909); they were still in print as late as in 1923. We use the pagination of the 1923 impression. At the time of writing these articles Hogg hoped to make a distinctive contribution to missionary theology. In 1904 he wrote: "I have a vague dream that some day I might head a doctrinal new departure. I feel that if Christianity is to conquer India the old doctrines must go first and new ones—like the old and yet Indian in colour—must take their place." Hogg to D. S. Cairns, 27.11.1904 (Prof. D. Cairns). For his more mature view, see *The Christian Message to the Hindu*, p. 7.

[1] *Karma and Redemption*, p. v f.

[2] *Ibid.*, p. vii.

[3] *Edinburgh MS.*

to set them up as criteria of absolute truth.[4] But beliefs are capable
of modification, and indeed must be modified from time to time in
response to the changing patterns of intellectual and environmental
forces if faith is to be preserved inviolate.[5] Missionaries have often
been guilty of presenting Christianity on the intellectual level, as a
body of beliefs, rather than as a system of faith and life; hence
their comparative failure on certain levels.[6] What is necessary is
a presentation of Christianity *vis-à-vis* Hinduism in which beliefs
are subordinated to faith, and in which the differences of faith
which undoubtedly exist are to be summed up, not in terms of
conflicting beliefs, but "in one pre-eminent contrast of principle"—
such as that between the Hindu idea of *karma* and the Christian
idea of redemption.[7]

Hogg was far from being unsympathetically inclined towards
Hinduism as such, though he confessed that he found the beliefs
of even the higher Hinduism "strange and rather dismal". In fact
he claimed that one of his objects in writing *Karma and Redemption*
was to win greater understanding of, and sympathy for, the Hindu
point of view.[8] But he was not prepared either to overlook fundamental contrasts in matters of faith, or to make illegitimate com-
parisons between incompatibles.

The basic contrast which he found between *karma* and Christian
redemption he called a contrast "so fundamental ... that by its aid
many of the other outstanding differences can be explained".[9]
Briefly, the idea of *karma*, of mechanical retribution in the moral
and ethical spheres, he regarded as having led to atomistic uni-

---

[4] *Edinburgh MS:* "We must hold on to the beliefs to which we have attained
not as the absolute truth but as the nearest approximation known to us, and as
the necessary instrument (at present) of our living faith; we must offer them
to India in the form that seems best calculated to meet her need; we will argue
against Hindu beliefs because we regard them as less true than our own, and as,
therefore, incapable of leading men into the same degree of intelligent fellowship
with the Divine mind and will; but at the same time we shall view the Hindu
system of belief with the respect due to ideas which have proved themselves
capable of being the instruments of a living trust in God."

[5] *Ibid.:* "The missionary ... has no right to assume that his own beliefs are
the ultimate truth ... It has been only by modifying its beliefs in response to
the changes in the prevailing outlook upon life, that Christianity has been able
to preserve the identical quality of its faith—the identical attitude of trustful
surrender to a God who attends unmerited love and favour and summons men
to fellowship with himself in service of the good."

[6] Hogg, "All Things to All Men", in *HF* XVIII: 4 (April 1907), p. 136 f.

[7] *Ibid.*, cf. *Karma and Redemption*, p. 2.

[8] *Karma and Redemption*, p. vii.

[9] *Ibid.*, p. 18.

versalism on the one hand, and to ascetic rigorism in ethics on the other.[1] The goal of the Hindu philosophies is in every case escape from *karma*. *Karma* cannot be scientifically proved; it is contradicted by theories of evolution (one of the few contexts in which Hogg mentions the theory); it robs history of meaning, since the Hindu is forced to deny that one man's actions can affect the destiny of others.[2] And though ostensibly moral, it in fact works as a judicial system without a judge. From the Christian viewpoint, it "fits beautifully into a system which recognizes no purpose in life other than expiation, but there is no room for it in a universe the purpose of which is moral not judicial".[3] This is the crux, since in Hogg's view the question between Christian and Hindu is not whether God is a just or unjust administrator of justice, but whether the purpose of the present order is judicial or moral. Hogg has no hesitation in affirming the latter alternative. Christianity is a religion of mercy and grace, not a judicial system, and the whole Hindu-Christian question must be viewed in this light.

Further—though this is somewhat incidental to his main purpose—Hogg notes that non-Christian religions may be a finding as well as a seeking. We know of the actual corruptions of these religions, "but we also know that in their origins and in portions of their history there was a 'giving substance to things hoped for', and a 'proving of things not seen' ".[4] Revelation, though of the essence of Christianity, is not restricted to Christianity, since "God's dealings with men in all times and places have been governed by the effort to prepare the way for the perfect revelation of Himself in Christ".[5] Here Hogg and Farquhar stand on virtually the same ground: they differ, however, at the point of emphasis. To Farquhar, the *praeparatio* concept was capable of being elevated, in the evolutionary scheme, into a universally valid system of comparison and relationship; Hogg, on the other hand, was seeking a valid principle of contrast.

Hogg's approach to the problem of Christian-Hindu relations thus differed radically from that of Farquhar. Farquhar had expressed in the strongest terms his opinion that the method of "contrast"

---

[1] *Ibid.*, p. 25.
[2] *Ibid.*, pp. 38–40, cf. pp. 60, 63.
[3] *Ibid.*, p. 49.
[4] *Ibid.*, p. 76.
[5] *Ibid.*

should be discarded at all costs.[6] Hogg, it is true, was not concerned to draw up a list of superficial discrepancies between Hindu and Christian beliefs and practices; nor did he attempt to deny the existence of incidental assonances; his purpose was more fundamental: in his own words, he wished

to inquire whether, amid the many obvious contrasts between Hinduism and Christianity, it is possible to light upon one that is fundamental, and having found it, to penetrate to its secret source.[7]

A further hint as to the reason why this should have been so is provided in an article written by Hogg in 1907, in which he pointed out that Christianity *as a doctrinal system*—i.e. as a system of "beliefs"—consists of an answer, or a series of answers, to problems "which cannot be keenly felt save by those who have admitted the Christian attitude to life". To present such Christian ideas as sin, grace, forgiveness and redemption as the satisfaction of the spiritual hunger of those whose attitude is one of longing for release from the bonds of the *karma* system is of course possible:

But the interpretation is a forced one, a compromise of incompatible tendencies of thought and feeling which is unlikely to commend itself to such as approach Christianity from the outside.[8]

Christian theology may well appeal to those for whom moral and social problems are fundamental; but not to others. That is why the picture of Christ has made more impression upon India than has Christianity, since "Christian theology *presupposes* the new spiritual attitude; the presentation of Christ *produces* it".[9] But the presentation of Christ could not take place in a theological vacuum.

Hogg's Contributions to Commission IV

Hogg was unique in that he submitted *two* papers to Commission IV of the Edinburgh conference. Cairns, impressed by what he

---

[6] In the course of a review in *YMI* XIX: 8 (August 1908), Farquhar had written: "We frankly acknowledge that the method we condemn is traditional in Indian missions, and we might almost say hallowed by its use by the great men of the past. Yet we believe that we must get rid of it at all costs. The method is the method of *contrast*: in every point Christian teaching is contrasted with Hindu teaching, and its great superiority demonstrated" (p. 143 f.). See above, p. 251 f.

[7] *Karma and Redemption*, p. 2.

[8] *MCCM* VII: 5 (Nov. 1907), Notes of the month, p. 258.

[9] *Ibid.*, p. 259.

called the "massiveness and insight" of *Karma and Redemption,*
ordered copies for all the members of the sub-commission on Hinduism.[1] And then there was Hogg's paper in answer to the official
questionnaire, on which Cairns commented:

No correspondent has gone so deep into the heart of the speculative and
theological problem as you have done, and I am proud of you, my brother![2]

Both are quoted in the official report.[3]

Hogg's answer to the Commission IV questionnaire is long and
highly detailed, and in this context we can do little more than
point to his explicit criticism of Farquhar's "fulfilment" hypothesis.
Furthermore, a large part of the paper goes over the same theological
ground as that covered in *Karma and Redemption.* But Hogg discusses the question of "attitude" far more fully here than in his
earlier monograph, and it is in this context, rather than in the
paper's purely theological sections, that he criticizes the "fulfilment"
idea.

We have seen that the fulfilment hypothesis had several facets,
one of which was the fulfilment, or satisfaction, of Hindu religious
needs in Christianity. This idea Hogg felt to be of doubtful value in
the practical missionary situation:

I am persuaded [he wrote] that in the stratum of Indian life known to me
the attitude of the missionary who should ... profess to be the possessor of
that which India had been vainly seeking, would be felt as presumptuous.[4]

For the history of Hinduism cannot be regarded merely as the
pursuit of a vain quest; it has been a finding as well as a seeking.
And the converse is in some measure true also: that Christianity is
in practice often a seeking as well as a finding.

It is of course possible to draw attention to resemblances between
specific Christian and Hindu doctrines or beliefs,[5] but this was in
no way a solution of the problem of faith. The missionary

may use them profitably as texts to hang sermons upon; but Hinduism as
a religion sits very loosely to its doctrines; it is a mood, a social system,

---

[1] Cairns to Hogg, 5.7.1909 (Hogg collection).
[2] Cairns to Hogg, 1.7.1909 (Hogg collection).
[3] *Karma and Redemption* is quoted on p. 184 f., Hogg's paper on pp. 173, 193.
[4] *Edinburgh MS.*
[5] *Ibid.*

anything but a creed; and to make any permanent impression upon its elusive nature some more subtle form of attack is needed . . .[6]

This criticism extends to the comparative study of mysticism. If mystical thought expressed the *real* essence of the Christian Gospel, thought Hogg, then a case might well be made out for treating some forms of Hindu mysticism as the fulfilment of Christian mysticism, and not *vice versa*. And since in his view mysticism certainly was of the essence of the higher Hinduism, and particularly of the Vedanta, wherein lies the relevance of claiming Christianity as its fulfilment?

The direct presentation of Christianity as the fulfilment of Hinduism, though apparently acknowledging that Hinduism has been at least a partial finding, is therefore open to serious objection. "Outside of the region of vague abstractions", asked Hogg, "what does it mean?" Christian *doctrines* do not fulfil Hindu doctrines; nor do Christian *rites* fulfil Hindu rites. Christian "ideals of practice" do not seem *to the Hindu* to be better than his own, however they may seem to the Christian; and if the Christian claims to have found in his own religion a deeper and more lasting satisfaction of his own religious needs than that experienced by the Hindu, it is obvious that such an assertion is incapable of either proof or disproof.

But the idea of fulfilment may perhaps have some justification in practice, since

it has proved possible, in actual experience, to awaken in some Hindus a sense of want, which their own religion has proved unable to satisfy and for which they have found satisfaction only in Christianity.[7]

In this sense Hogg is prepared to accept the idea of fulfilment; but only in this sense. He rejects outright the suggestion that "Christianity is a fulfilment pointed to by the typical undisturbed Hindu consciousness", pointing out that Christianity is *the solution of a religious problem which the typical Hindu does not feel, the answer to questions he has never asked,* but which can be induced in him, under certain conditions. If the Hindu religious mind can be thrown out of equilibrium in some way, then it may be argued that

---

[6] *Ibid.*
[7] *Ibid.*

the Christian message provides the resolution of the difficulties thereby induced.

The question is, how this is to be accomplished, and it is this which occupies the greater part of the remainder of Hogg's paper —and incidentally of his later publications.[8] Since we shall return to the problem in Chapter Eleven,[9] it will suffice here to point out that he touches upon the question of "telling the historical story of Jesus", only to reject it as impracticable.[1]

Now our gospel is not a mere chronicle but an interpreted history—an interpreted Jesus, a Christ. The New Testament narratives themselves set us the example of presenting not a mere Jesus but the Christ. We must, therefore, present Jesus to India in terms of our own interpretation of Him.[2]

It will be clear that at this point Hogg and Farquhar are occupying distinct and in some measure incompatible positions, since Farquhar's ideal was the presentation of "mere Christianity", separate from every form of local, temporal or denominational accretion.[3] It is, then, not surprising that Hogg was led to recognize that the logical consequence of his view was the transmission of "a comprehensive system of Christian theology"—an alternative for which Farquhar's undogmatic view left no room.

These were telling criticisms. There is no evidence that Farquhar ever read Hogg's paper, or that his later development was in any way affected by Hogg's comments. But that they provide a remarkable anticipation of later theological criticism of the "fulfilment" school cannot well be doubted. We shall however return to the subject of Hogg's views in a later context. Now we must turn to another aspect of Hogg's influence on the official findings of the Edinburgh conference. This is purely theological, and has little direct bearing on his attitude to the "fulfilment" doctrine. Never-

---

[8] See the series of articles, "The God that must needs be Christ Jesus", in *IRM* VI (1917), pp. 62–73, 221–32, 383–94 and 521–33. Cf. also *The Christian Message to the Hindu* (1947), which follows substantially the same pattern, though with significant modifications, particularly in respect of the doctrine of the Church (pp. 43 ff.).

[9] Cf. below, pp. 350 ff.

[1] *Edinburgh MS.*

[2] *Edinburgh MS.* Another writer who challenged the assumptions of the age on this point was P. T. Forsyth. His lecture on "The Religion of Jesus and the Gospel of Christ" in *The Person and Place of Jesus Christ* (1909, 6th ed. 1948), pp. 35 ff., offers interesting parallels.

[3] Cf. Farquhar's statement quoted below, p. 341.

theless it is of importance for our understanding of the theological nature of his criticisms. It may be summed up in the phrase "redemption from this world", and is again deserving of more detailed treatment than we can give it in this context.

Redemption from this World

We have previously noted that Hogg had studied for a short time in Germany, and that he was familiar with current developments in German theology, among which "Ritschlianism" was the most outstanding. In 1909 he published in the *Madras Christian College Magazine* two critical articles on the theology of Julius Kaftan,[4] in which he took up to discussion Kaftan's thesis that redemption *from the world*—as distinct from redemption from the guilt and power of sin—is the leading and fundamental thought in Christianity.

Kaftan had emphasized Jesus' Messianic consciousness, his Messiahship in present fact, and the fact of his being the Messiah of Jewish Apocalyptic, whose establishment was to be the work of God, not man. Thus the Kingdom of God, in Kaftan's view, had arrived, without thereby having ceased to be a thing of the future. It was present, but not manifest, attainable inwardly, but not in fact.[5]

Hogg suggested that this was an unnecessarily complex solution.[6] He could not accept the view that Jesus had come upon the human scene separately from the Kingdom of God, and that though the Messiah had arrived, the Kingdom had not.[7] What of Jesus' miracles and the answer to John's messengers in Lk. 7.19–23? Kaftan had

---

[4] Hogg, "Christianity as Emancipation from this World", in *MCCM* IX: 1–2 (July–August 1909), later published separately. It is the offprint which we use, and its pagination to which we refer. We cannot here go into the subject of Kaftan's theology, but an account of his view of the Kingdom of God will be found in Bohlin, *Den kristna gudsrikestanken under 1800-talet och i nutiden* (1928), pp. 163 ff.

[5] On this subject generally, see Cairns, *Christianity in the Modern World* (2nd ed. 1907), pp. 165 ff.

[6] There appears to be a further connexion with Cairns here. In the preface to his study-book *Christ's Message of the Kingdom* (1911), which deals with this theme, Hogg writes, "For initiation into this distinctive standpoint I am indebted to my friend Prof. D. S. Cairns; and, compared with this fundamental obligation, all others have been but incidents in the germination and growth of seeds which were planted by him three years ago during certain memorable but all too brief conversations" (p. iv). For a concise statement of Cairns' view of the Kingdom at this time, see *Christianity in the Modern World*, pp. 29 ff.

[7] Hogg, *Christianity as Emancipation*, p. 7.

evidently missed the significance of Jesus' supernatural works: the Kingdom, with its redemption from *all* evil, had indeed arrived. Here we must quote:

The Kingdom, as well as the Messiah, had arrived. It was there, both in inner fact and outer manifestation. But in outer manifestation it was present only sporadically, *because of the rare occurrence of the faith necessary to its effectiveness* [our italics]. Therefore, Jesus could speak of the Kingdom sometimes as present, sometimes as future. It was there already in the sense of being fully availabe. It was not yet there in the sense of being fully availed of.[8]

This knowledge—that faith, if present in sufficient strength, was able to overcome both moral and physical evil—Hogg (and Cairns with him[9]) believed to have been an integral part of Apostolic Christianity: but he was equally certain, for a variety of reasons,[1] that traditional Protestantism had neglected it to its great loss.

The missionary significance of this view Hogg was sure was immeasurable, since it offered a true means of emancipation to a race (the Hindus) inherently preoccupied with the problem of release from the bonds of *karma*.[2] In this sense the Gospel becomes something resembling a new Vedanta, and is thus capable of being presented to the Hindu in terms which he has some likelihood of being able to understand.

According to the old Vedanta, through human insight the universe becomes Brahman. According to the new, through human faith the universe becomes the plastic instrument of a Father ... According to the old Vedanta, for each man the consummation can be reached through his own attainment of insight. According to the new it can be reached only through the faith of all.[3]

Cairns had for some time been engaged upon these same problems when Hogg's articles reached him.[4] He hailed them as "masterly", and commented: "I cannot say with what pleasure I see a powerful and independent mind driving a road through thickets that have made my progress so toilsome and so slow."[5] The idea that the realization of the Kingdom is in very great measure brought about

---

[8] *Ibid.*, p. 8.
[9] Cf. n. 9 above. See also Cairns, *The Faith that Rebels* (1928), p. 92 f.
[1] Hogg, *op. cit.*, p. 14 f.
[2] *Ibid.*, p. 2.
[3] *Ibid.*, p. 28.
[4] Cairns to Hogg, 25.8.1909 (Hogg collection).
[5] Cairns to Hogg, 25.8.1909.

by the response of man's faith to God's initiative in Christ, and that the whole is bound up with the doctrine of the Holy Spirit, was henceforth to occupy a great deal of both Cairns' and Hogg's thought and energy; both were to publish books on the subject.[6]

The immediate problem, however, was to make this interpretation of faith known to as many theologians as possible.[7] If this could be incorporated in some way into the findings of the Edinburgh conference, then much might be gained: such was Cairns' view. And in the event, it came to occupy a prominent position in the Commission IV report.

Cairns' "General Conclusions"

We are now perhaps in a position to evaluate the "General Conclusions" of the Commission IV report, at least in so far as they are concerned with the Indian material.[8] We have seen that a number of strands have gone into the making of the report, of which the two most important are the material sent in by the correspondents and the theological position worked out by Cairns and Hogg together. As far as the first of these is concerned it is sufficient to point out that Cairns once more attested at the end of the report "the practically universal testimony that the true attitude of the Christian missionary should be one of true understanding and, as far as possible, of sympathy", and noted that "the merely iconoclastic attitude" had been universally condemned as both unwise and unjust.[9] This is said, it would be well to note, without explicit or im-

---

[6] Hogg, *Christ's Message of the Kingdom* (1911) and *Redemption from this World* (1922); Cairns, *The Faith that Rebels* (1928).

[7] This is most clearly seen in Cairns' letters (Hogg's have for the most part not been preserved). Cairns at least believed that the workings of Divine Providence were to be seen in his and Hogg's wrestling with the problems of the Kingdom and of miracle. In 1909 he wrote that "we must strengthen one another for the sake of the generations that are coming after us along these ancient highways that have so long been lost and covered with the jungle. Vexilla regis prodeunt!" (Cairns to Hogg, 25.8.1909). And in 1910: "So the light spreads. But what we want is a practical demonstration" (19.3.1910). This "practical demonstration" was to be the General Conclusions of the Commission IV Report (below). In effect, this recall to a sense of the "supernatural" in Christianity was a considerable reaction against much of the thought of the period— a factor which modern commentators on Edinburgh 1910 have overlooked altogether.

[8] *Report of Commission IV*, pp. 224 ff. Cf. Gairdner, "*Edinburgh 1910*", pp. 151 ff.

[9] *Report of Commission IV*, p. 267.

plicit advocacy of any particular theory of the relationship of Christianity and non-Christian religions, least of all one *based* on the findings of "comparative religion".[1] Science, historical criticism and the comparative study of religions have "deeply stirred" Christian intelligence:[2] but the solution of the problems raised is to be found elsewhere—in Cairns' words: "What is needed is a living faith, and a living faith demands a living theology."[3] This may perhaps be taken as a criticism, perhaps inspired by Hogg, of a view such as that of Farquhar: that the conditions which have defined the problem also offer its solution.

Cairns was uncertain as to how much of his and Hogg's view of Christianity as "redemption from this world" it would be possible to incorporate into his report. Hogg's earlier contribution to the conference *News Sheet,* in which he had claimed that Christian power was limited only by the extent of men's faith, not by the extent of God's willingness, and that the Kingdom would come "whenever men learned faith", had called forth a mild protest from the editor.[4] Cairns was nevertheless eager to incorporate as much of this view as possible into the report, and wrote to Hogg:

I chafe under the need for reticence ... Still I could not hold my peace when it came to writing that Draft. It is not, of course, anything like all that I would like to say, but is drawn up in part with a view to getting through our most composite committee.[5]

In fact, of the "most composite committee" only Johannes Warneck objected to the extent of the passage in question, not to the principle expressed.[6] Speer, Garvie, Mullins, Mrs. Romanes, Canon

[1] That this was substantially Farquhar's position will be clear.
[2] *Report of Commission IV,* p. 245.
[3] *Ibid.,* p. 218.
[4] Hogg, "A New Year Message from India", in *World Missionary Conference News Sheet* (Jan. 1910), pp. 71–75. The editor commented: "Many may not be disposed to agree with all of Mr. Hogg's statements, nor even with his general standpoint ... [but] the article will have completely served its purpose if it leads those interested in the Conference to devote much thought and prayer in the coming months to the fundamental question, whether there are not available in God resources far beyond those of which our feeble faith lays hold" (p. 80).
[5] Cairns to Hogg, 19.3.1910 (Hogg collection).
[6] Cairns to Hogg, 19.3.1910: "I had a criticism of my Draft Report, generally approving, from Johs. Warneck. He had been greatly interested by 'Karma' (*Karma and Redemption*) which had been sent him as one of our committee, called my attention to it and wondered why I had not quoted it! ... Warneck on the whole approves, but would like the crucial section to be shorter." In a later letter Warneck wrote, "I am very glad to have received now all the drafts concerning Commission IV. I hope that both missionary work and theology will

Robinson and Simon were all prepared to let it stand; while it is not known how Andrews, Macnicol and Farquhar, to whom Cairns sent copies, reacted.[7]

The "crucial section" which Warneck wanted shortening is evidently pp. 249–267 in the report, where Cairns makes a plea for a return to "radical supernaturalism", and for a view of Christianity in which the aspect of redemption from the evil world is given due prominence. He also lays stress on the unchanging grace of God, and on its conditional nature, saying that

while God remains unchanging in His grace, the Church has failed to comply with the primal conditions of its reception ... and so [faith] has lost the expectancy which is the condition of all spiritual achievement.[8]

The resources of God are available to the Church, if they can only be availed of in faith—such was Cairns' and Hogg's conviction, and such was the view which was expressed in the Commission IV report.

It would of course have been more than desirable to have discussed these profound questions in exhaustive detail. This is, however, perhaps not the most suitable place for such a study. We have noted the extent of A. G. Hogg's contribution to the Edinburgh material and Cairns' report, and we have noted his express criticisms of the "fulfilment" theory with which we are most closely concerned here. And we have attempted to sketch some of the features of Hogg's

---

have great advantage from the important material gathered by our Commission. I agree with all the drafts I have read." Warneck to Cairns, 13.5.1910 (Prof. D. Cairns). For a more detailed account of Warneck's reactions to Hogg's book, see his review "Karma und Erlösung", in *AMZ* 37 (1910), pp. 209–19, in which he describes Hogg's effort as "äusserst beachtenswert". Warneck also wrote at length on the message of Commission IV, in two articles, "Die missionarische Botschaft in Auseinandersetzung mit den nichtchristlichen Religionen", in *AMZ* 37 (1910), pp. 521–35, 573–90. In a further article, "Edinburg—eine Rechtfertigung der freien Theologie?" in *AMZ* 38 (1911), pp. 489–501, he defended the conference from the accusation of fostering a rootless theological liberalism, stressing that although the *form* of the Gospel message may not have been expressed in confessional terms, "... von einer Reduktion unseres biblischen Evangeliums hat niemand gesprochen" (p. 501).

[7] Farquhar's reaction may however be gauged from his comment on the reprinted "General Conclusions": "The best introduction to the whole subject ... Dr. Cairns' masterly summing-up ..." in *A Bibliography for Missionary Students*, ed. Weitbrecht (1913), p. 84. Note also his comment on *Karma and Redemption*: "This is a most original piece of thinking ..." in *A Primer of Hinduism* (2nd ed. 1914), p. 214.

[8] *Report of Commission IV*, p. 260.

theological position, as they gave rise to his criticism. The full significance of these elements will be more fully apparent when the time comes to consider Farquhar's book *The Crown of Hinduism,* and the various contributions and comments to which its publication gave rise.[9]

---

[9] Below, pp. 329 ff.

CHAPTER 10

Christian Literature for India

ON OCTOBER 19, 1911 the American National Council of the Y.M.C.A. ratified, at the request of the International Committee, J. N. Farquhar's release from responsibility for the student work of the Indian Y.M.C.A., thus bringing to completion the line of action suggested by Farquhar himself, and supported by Mott and Eddy.[1] This was very much a step in the dark for the International Committee, a step the justification of which depended very largely on the correctness of Farquhar's analysis of the Indian situation, and of course on his capacities as a writer. The Association in India had not previously had a Secretary who could assume full responsibility for the co-ordination of literary effort; the task had been largely left in the hands of the literature societies and the enterprise of individual authors. But Mott and his committee were prepared to make Farquhar Literary Secretary nevertheless.

Under the terms of his new appointment, Farquhar was to divide his time equally between India and England. He chose to make his home in Oxford, where he would have access to the library of the Indian Institute, and where he could keep in touch with the latest developments in oriental scholarship.[2] And while in India he would be able to lecture, meet inquirers, gather material and help the team of writers he hoped to be able to recruit from among the ranks of Western missionaries and Indian Christians alike.[3]

That this arrangement was a considerable improvement—from Farquhar's own point of view—cannot be doubted, despite the travelling involved. For instance, in 1911 Farquhar spent eight and a half months in India: for two and a half months he was on tour in various parts of India; four weeks were taken up by conferences; and of his remaining time in Calcutta not more than one quarter (at a

---

[1] Cf. above, p. 269 f.
[2] This was his home for half of each year until he moved to Manchester in 1923.
[3] On the employment of Indian writers, see below, p. 305.

generous estimate) had been available for literary work.[4] Between October 1, 1911 and March 16, 1912 (the date on which his responsibility for the student work formally ended) his time in India was divided between (i) the work of the secretary of the student department, (ii) addresses to educated Hindus and personal work among them, (iii) teaching in the Y.M.C.A. training school for Indian secretaries, (iv) literary work, and (v) starting other people to write.[5] From April 3, 1912 to September 30, 1912 he was in Oxford, where he was able to spend practically the whole time studying and writing.[6] It is probably true to say that never since coming to India in 1891 had he been able to devote such a long period of time to undisturbed literary work as he did in the summer of 1912. He was understandably grateful, and wrote to the International Committee expressing his thanks, and assuring them that despite the great freedom he now enjoyed, he was in no danger of wasting time.

I believe ... my inexpressible desire to serve the cause of Christ by means of my pen is sufficient to keep me from misusing in any particular the unusual liberty which I now enjoy. I can assure the Committee that I have worked as hard this summer as ever I did at any time.[7]

The Need for Literature

We have traced the course, in our investigation so far, of Farquhar's conviction that Christian literature was peculiarly fitted as an instrument of the Gospel in the Indian situation of the time. And we have attempted to show why this was so.[8] In his 1912 report he outlined once more the reasons why this conviction was still central in his thought. There is nothing really new in this report: merely a further confirmation of the trends which had been apparent for some years. In the first place, the missionary situation in India was in Farquhar's view a crisis situation, brought about by the

---

[4] YMCA Secretaries' Reports, J. N. Farquhar 1911, p. 306 (YMCA Hist. Lib.).
[5] YMCA Secretaries' Reports, J. N. Farquhar 1912, p. 404 (YMCA Hist. Lib.). Hereinafter *Report 1912*.
[6] *Report 1912*, p. 405. He also made a large number of new contacts, among them Baron von Hügel and the "Cumnor group" around Lily Dougall, under whose auspices a conference on "Christian Apologetics in India" was held in October 1919 (minutes in Farquhar collection). Among his correspondents in these and later years were von Hügel and Rudolf Otto. Little of this correspondence has however been preserved.
[7] *Report 1912*, p. 405 f.
[8] Cf. above, pp. 219 ff.

steady growth of missionary work over the past years, the gradual
increase in the Christian population of India and a corresponding
gradual decline in Hinduism as a religious force.[9] Two results could
be discerned: first an even more emphatic, though temporarily less
militant, nationalism;[1] and secondly, an increased tendency on the
part of Hindus to attack Christianity and everything connected with
it—an attack conducted both in the press and in the lecture room.
"Christianity is being condemned", wrote Farquhar, "not as being
untrue, but as a destroying and denationalizing force."[2] This tendency had been present throughout the period, as we have seen.[3]

But although attacks on Christianity, and on the missionary force,
were becoming more frequent and more violent,[4] many Hindus were
still prepared, in Farquhar's view, to listen to what the missionary
had to say. "Hence a certain type of man attends Christian meetings ... to glean what religious help he can from the missionary"—
without, however, having any intention of becoming a Christian.[5]
The task of the missionary must therefore be twofold: to convince
the Hindu that he must become a Christian, and at the same time
to make it plain that "the religion of Christ is not destructive and
anti-national".[6]

Christian literature, written with these considerations in mind,
could, Farquhar felt, fill a double function. It could speak direct
to the Hindu, showing him that the Christian Gospel was not, as
he tended to suppose, inextricably bound up with Western imperialism and therefore an enemy of the Indian religious and
cultural heritage. And it could provide guidance for the missionary,
laying down the lines on which his preaching and teaching might
profitably be carried out. The overall need was thus for a restatement of the Christian position, embodying primarily a fresh statement of the Christian attitude to the non-Christian faiths of the

[9] For an elaboration of this last point, see above, pp. 244 ff.
[1] Many of the nationalist leaders, notably B. G. Tilak, were in detention;
Curzon had been replaced by Lord Minto as Viceroy; in 1911 the Partition of
Bengal was revoked. Lajpat Rai wrote: "The year 1911 was perhaps the dullest
year from the revolutionary point of view." *Young India* (4th ed. 1927), p. 195.
[2] *Report 1912*, p. 406.
[3] Above, pp. 242, 247, 251.
[4] In the words of Har Dayal, the missionary "is the arch enemy, who appears
in many guises, the great foe of whatever bears the name of Hindu, the ever-
watchful, ever-active, irreconcileable destroyer ..." Quoted by Farquhar (*Report
1912*, p. 406) as "a sample of the denunciation we are favoured with nowadays".
[5] *Report 1912*, p. 406.
[6] *Ibid.*, p. 407.

world, and Hinduism in particular. Farquhar had in fact spent 1911 and 1912 in the preparation of a book on precisely these lines, to embody the results of his studies and his experience over the years, and to be called *The Crown of Hinduism*.

By this time Farquhar's views on the need for Christian literature in India, and on the form that that literature ought ideally to take, had awakened a response in missionary circles, both inside and outside India. The growing use of the concept of "fulfilment" to describe the relationship of Christianity to Hinduism we have discussed in connexion with the 1910 Edinburgh conference: in 1911 came further confirmation from D. S. Cairns of Aberdeen, who had been Chairman of Commission IV (that on the Missionary Message in relation to non-Christian faiths). In an article published in the January, 1911 number of the *Student World*,[7] Cairns called for Christian "apologists". The ambiguity of the word "apologetics"— a subject which we have already had occasion to discuss—was fully recognized by Cairns on this occasion: in fact he frankly described it as a term "of quite remarkable infelicity".[8] But he went on to point out that the thing was not necessarily to be equated with the name; apologetics was not "a mere barrister science devoted to the proving of foregone conclusions",[9] but rather a means by which faith and knowledge together might be brought to bear on a situation of much complexity and difficulty for the Church. There is, wrote Cairns, the utmost need for Christian apologists of a specific kind, apologists drawn not from the missionary body primarily, but from the indigenous churches,

men whose knowledge and understanding of the inner life and genius of the religion of their own peoples on the one hand and of the Christian faith on the other, will enable them to present Christ to their own countrymen as the Fulfiller of every need which their own religion reveals and which it has been unable to satisfy . . .[1]

Eclecticism is no solution. If Christian apologetics is to be true to the genius of its own faith, it must hold fast to "the absoluteness of

---

[7] Cairns, "The Need for Apologists", in the *Student World* IV (April 1911), pp. 49–57.
[8] *Ibid.*, p. 50.
[9] *Ibid.*
[1] *Ibid.*, p. 52.

the Christian religion".[2] But this is not to say that all non-Christian religions are mere falsehood, since all demonstrate the existence of human need. Thus the apologist must both penetrate to the inner meaning of the religion he is trying to supplant, and learn to understand the genius and spirit of Christianity, "the absolute religion".[3] This was fully in accordance with Farquhar's double emphasis on the absoluteness of Christianity and of the fulfilment of non-Christian needs and insights in the Christian revelation, without, however, going so far as Farquhar had done in the use of the evolutionary hypothesis as a working method. Cairns' emphasis was on Christ as "the Fulfiller of all that is noble and true in the time hallowed faith".[4]

The rejection of religious eclecticism was also the main point of a lecture delivered by Farquhar to the Edinburgh Continuation Committee Conference (Bengal Section) meeting in Calcutta in December 1912. He pointed out that, while it may be possible in some cases to make use of Hindu *practice* in the work of the Christian church,[5] it is utterly out of the question to take up any element of Hindu religious *thought*. "There can be no eclecticism in India", said Farquhar.

Strength and life depend on complete faithfulness to Christ. This is particularly clear in the case of Hinduism; for the genius of the religion is so different from the essential character of Christianity that *to introduce any Hindu doctrine into the Church of Christ would be to pour poison into it.*[6]

Six "Continuation Committee Conferences"[7] were held at various centres in India between November 18 and December 18, 1912, followed by an "India National Conference" at Calcutta, December 18–21, 1912. Common to all of them was an emphasis on the need

---

[2] *Ibid.*, p. 54.
[3] *Ibid.*, p. 56.
[4] *Ibid.*, p. 55.
[5] "Thus the mode of worship which arose in the *bhakti* sects, and is still used in the Brāhma Samāj in prayer meetings—when people squat on the ground, and by means of prayer and singing stir each other to great spiritual exaltation— may be required to make Christian worship truly indigenous and really effective to the Indian heart." Farquhar, *Syncretism or Eclecticism?* (Lecture delivered before Continuation Committee Conference, Bengal, in YMCA Hist. Lib.).
[6] *Ibid.* Our italics.
[7] For full details, see Mott (ed.), *The Continuation Committee Conferences in Asia 1912–1913* (1913).

for good Christian literature, both in the vernaculars and in English. A syllabus of questions had been sent out in advance, including three on Christian literature,[8] and the answers given show a remarkable measure of agreement. The Madras Conference was "fully convinced that the place of Christian literature in the missionary enterprise is growing steadily in importance";[9] the Allahabad Conference further recommended that "controversial literature" should be made "more generous and sympathetic in tone";[1] and at Lahore it was felt that mission boards and tract and book societies should set apart men and women as writers, translators and editors;[2] summing up, the India National Conference stated (one recognizes Farquhar's hand in the formulation of this clause) that:

Through the progress of education the literacy of the people of India is steadily rising; the Indian mind, awakened to the thought and intellectual methods of the West, needs new literature of every type for its nourishment; the chief religious sects are scattering wide their literature, much of it distinctly antichristian; and the Indian Church, daily growing in numbers and intelligence, requires an abundant supply of fresh, healthy and varied reading.[3]

An Interim Literature Committee was set up, with Farquhar as Convener, and C. F. Andrews, Nicol Macnicol and H. A. Popley among its members (two out of twelve were Indians). It thus might fairly be said that the need for Christian literature was universally recognized by Protestant missionaries in India by the end of 1912. The problem remained, however: who was to write it, and what form was it to take?

---

[8] They were as follows: 1. In this area what Christian literature is most urgently needed: (1) for Christians? (2) for the educated non-Christians? (3) for the less educated non-Christians? 2. What can be done to raise up able Christian writers, both among Christian [Indians] and among the missionaries? To what extent would setting apart men for specified pieces of work for a limited time meet the case? 3. What can be done to ensure a wider and more effective use of the best literature already in existence? *Ibid.*, p. 473.

[9] *Ibid.*, p. 35.

[1] *Ibid.*, p. 78.

[2] *Ibid.*, p. 94.

[3] *Ibid.*, p. 134 f. Cf. YMCA Scretaries' Reports, J. N. Farquhar, 1913, p. 530 (YMCA Hist. Lib.): "Dr. Mott's Continuation Conferences in India last cold season registered a great advance in Christian unity and co-operation. There is one point of connection with my own work. Every Conference laid great stress on the need for a new Christian literature, scholarly, sympathetic, enthusiastically Christian. It was a great encouragement to have ideas, which I have been endeavouring to propagate for several years, so widely accepted."

The Source of the New Literature

In Chapter Eight we saw how Farquhar had first conceived, and first brought to Mott's attention, his plan for a group of Christian scholars able and willing to help in writing books on the relationship of Christianity and Hinduism; this we may assume to have been a contributory factor in his release for literary work. After 1911 he was able to concentrate more fully on the recruiting of writers. In 1912 he was able to write that "There is a group of missionaries who have banded themselves together to produce literature ...; and I have been chosen to lead the group."[4] Though he mentions no names in this particular context, it is clear that he is referring to substantially the same group as that originally formed for this purpose,[5] though it was later widened substantially, as a list of later publications shows.[6]

By 1914 he was able to inform Mott that he had planned several series of books, of which the most noteworthy were "The Quest of India Series", "The Indian Religious Life Series" and "The Heritage of India Series". In the same context he wrote that he had done his utmost to start Y.M.C.A. men in study and writing.[7] But although he was still in the service of the Y.M.C.A., he was less concerned to see the Y.M.C.A.'s influence extended by means of literature than to provide a worthy Christian literature supported by, and intended for, the Indian Church as such. In this it was imperative that Indian Christians should play as large a part as possible in the production of literature. A. J. Appasamy has criticized Farquhar for relying too exclusively on European and American writers in his literary enterprise, claiming that "Dr. Farquhar had certain rigid standards of scholarship and unconsciously came to believe that they could be reached only by European writers".[8] We can of course know nothing of Farquhar's unconscious processes, but it seems clear that Farquhar drew no distinction in theory between European and Indian writers. In 1915, again writing to Mott, he expressed his ideal in these words:

---

[4] *Report 1912*, p. 407.
[5] Above, p. 268.
[6] See e.g. authors of *Quest* and *Heritage* series in bibliography.
[7] Farquhar to Mott, 4.4.1914 (YMCA Hist. Lib.).
[8] Appasamy, "Dr. J. N. Farquhar", in *YMI* XLI: 9 (Sept. 1929), p. 688.

I am endeavouring to lead a great group of *missionaries and Indian Christians* [our italics] to write Christian literature of the highest type. I do my best to get them to produce scholarly work which can be trusted, to use the experience they have of the people in interpreting the religions of India, to regard all these strange faiths with the sympathy which characterizes the best scholars, and to set the life and teaching of Christ alongside of all.[9]

By 1920 he had fifteen Indian Christians in his team;[1] in 1921 the number had risen to seventeen, and one Singhalese.[2] Nevertheless, by 1923, when Farquhar left India, only *one* Indian (F. Kingsbury) had contributed to the *Heritage* series,[3] and none to the other major series. One is forced to conclude, in the absence of positive evidence, that Farquhar was unable to accept such work as Indian Christians were able to complete in English; and one suspects that most of the Indian writers concerned failed to complete the tasks they were set. At the same time, Farquhar's standards were undeniably rigorous.

The Characteristics of the New Literature

It may be of value at this stage in our study to sum up once more the chief characteristics of the Christian literature that Farquhar wished to see written in India. These were three in number: (a) accuracy, (b) sympathy and (c) uncompromising faithfulness to Christ.

(a) We have seen throughout our investigation that Farquhar's standards of scholarship were high. His own work was characterized by painstaking attention to detail, and by an emphasis on the best scholarly thought of his day. (That scholarly fashions have since

---

[9] Farquhar to Mott, 22.6.1915 (YMCA Hist. Lib.).

[1] Farquhar to J. W. Lyon, 26.10.1920 (YMCA Hist. Lib.).

[2] Farquhar to E. C. Jenkins, 7.5.1921 (YMCA Hist. Lib.). In 1922, Farquhar told a missionary conference that, "given two writers of equal capacity, one a missionary and one an Indian Christian, the Indian Christian will be of far more value than the missionary." "Christian Literature in Modern India", in *IW* 5.7.1922, p. 435, reprinted in Sharpe, *J. N. Farquhar: A Memoir* (1963), p. 132. It must however be pointed out that after the first world war Farquhar's attention had turned more and more to the production of Christian literature in the *vernaculars*, and it was in this field he wished to recruit Indian writers rather than missionaries. Cf. Farquhar, *Some Thoughts on Christian Vernacular Literature* (1922), p. 9: "We ought to form our plans most carefully, so as to secure the best possible results, eagerly anticipating an early day when no American or European shall dream of writing vernacular Christian literature."

[3] Kingsbury and Phillips, *Hymns of the Tamil Saivite Saints* (1921).

undergone far-reaching changes is of course irrelevant in this context: Farquhar cannot be criticized for not having been born fifty years later.) As early as in 1901 he had expressed his belief that the "Science of Religion" contained "boundless possibilities" for the Christian preacher and writer, but at the same time he stressed that it would have to be studied "in no amateurish way, but seriously, laboriously, continuously".[4] The historical method he accepted fully, both in its application to Christianity and to the non-Christian religions.[5] And the evolutionary hypothesis he had called a "Master Idea" for the understanding of history.[6] Farquhar's own early books had begun to show how these principles might be applied to the work of Christian missions in India: in *Gita and Gospel* and *The Age and Origin of the Gita,* he had applied the methods of historical scholarship, as then understood, to the study of the *Bhagavad Gītā,* with some measure of success.[7] In 1903 he was therefore able to call for well-informed helpers in the developing dialogue of religions:

We want men who know Sanskrit, and understand Hinduism, who know something about the history of religions generally, and who are really trustworthy scientific students of the New Testament.[8]

This demand he had elaborated in 1905 in his paper on *Missionary Study of Hinduism;* here he provided an outline of the practical measures which might be taken by the missionary in order to gain an adequate knowledge of Hinduism, with a short bibliography. Once more he stressed that "There is need for study, for far more study than has ever yet been given to this subject ..."[9] Exhortations of this kind recur frequently in Farquhar's reports, letters and articles between 1905 and 1912: to mention them all in this context would however serve no useful purpose. It is sufficient to note the

---

[4] "The Science of Religion as an Aid to Apologetics", in *HF* XII (Oct. 1901), p. 369.
[5] *Criticism and Christianity* (1901), p. 2: "Historical science can unveil the past: everything connected with the past is in consequence fascinated by it (*sic*). The deeper the interests involved, the more imperious is the need for full and free investigation."
[6] *Ibid.*
[7] Above, pp. 98 ff.
[8] *Report 1903,* p. 109.
[9] *Missionary Study of Hinduism* (1905), p. 14.

fact of his constant emphasis on study and accuracy, and on the historical method as the only adequate scientific approach.[1]

He was no less concerned as Literary Secretary that books written and published by Christian writers should reach the highest standards, "equal to the best work done by Oriental scholars".[2] For two reasons: first because, as a painstaking scholar himself, he could not tolerate inferior work in others; and secondly because he felt—and continued to feel—that only the best was good enough to win the attention of India.[3] These standards he endeavoured to apply to his own written work: sections of *The Crown of Hinduism* and virtually the whole of *Modern Religious Movements in India* and *An Outline of the Religious Literature of India* are the fruits of independent historical research. And many books in the series which he edited after 1912 are noteworthy for the same scholarly accuracy. Much they contain has since been superseded, but that is incidental to the point at issue.

(b) Although Farquhar regarded accurate scholarship as a prime necessity for the Christian writer in India, sympathy was no less important. It is scarcely necessary at this stage to point to the radical reorientation in the Christian attitude to Hinduism which had come about since the 1880's—a reorientation in which Miller, Slater, Kellett and Farquhar himself had played a large part. Again we may take *Missionary Study of Hinduism* as a convenient early example of Farquhar's views. "All our study of Hinduism", he had written, "and everything we write and say on the subject should be sympathetic."[4] Unsympathetic denunciation of Hinduism he believed to have done "incalculable harm" to the Christian cause, leading to a false estimation of Hinduism itself, and alienating Hindu listeners and readers. And he was prepared to criticize books written on traditional lines, in which *contrast* was made a basis of study, very sharply indeed: Dilger's prize essay on *Salvation in Hinduism and Christianity* was a case in point.[5] The reasons for this attitude we have had occasion to discuss in detail, and there is no need to repeat

---

[1] A. J. Appasamy, whose interests lie elsewhere, has criticized Farquhar's attachment to the historical method in *YMI* (Sept. 1929), p. 686 f.

[2] *Report 1912*, p. 407.

[3] Cf. Farquhar, "Christian Literature in Modern India", in *IW*, 5.7.1922, pp. 435 ff.

[4] *Missionary Study of Hinduism*, p. 5. In the original these words were printed in capitals.

[5] Above, p. 251 f.

them in full here. We might however sum up by saying that Farquhar had felt the full force of the Indian nationalists' claims to have a genuine indigenous cultural heritage, and was anxious that the missionary force as a whole should not underestimate that claim, whether through prejudice, ignorance or throughtlessness.[6] Hence his demand for sympathetic treatment of Hinduism—for sympathy called forth by the demands of justice, charity and prudence. The private prospectus of *The Heritage of India* series, issued in 1913 or 1914, included this statement of policy:

The treatment must be sympathetic throughout. The attitude of writers must be that of the great Western scholars who have written on these subjects. Our aim must be, while frankly acknowledging a great deal that is unhealthy in the work of the past, to seek out and set forth the best, so that it may be known, enjoyed and used.[7]

(c) The third characteristic of Farquhar's Christian literature ideal is again one which needs little or no explanation at this stage. Expressed at its most concise, as in his 1912 report, it is this:

We [the group of Christian authors of whom Farquhar was the leader] remain altogether loyal to Christ and His Gospel. Nothing else we believe can solve the problems of India.[8]

More explicitly, it involved the insistence on a largely traditional Protestant Evangelical Christianity, centred on the person and work of Christ, as the final, absolute and universal religion—without, however, denying some validity to the non-Christian religions as being partial, incomplete glimpses of truth, awaiting their consummation in Christ. Eclecticism, syncretism and compromise on the one hand, and religious bigotry on the other, he rejected altogether.

By 1912, then, the way seemed to lie open for the production of a body of scholarly Christian literature for the use of the Church in India—literature embodying the basic attitude of sympathy towards the Indian cultural and religious heritage of India that Farquhar had been advocating for the past ten years. Farquhar himself had been given an appointment which permitted him to spend the

---

[6] *YMI* XIX: 8 (August 1908), p. 144: "... the national inheritance is too priceless a possession to be flung away and too closely intertwined with the vitals of the people to be got rid of ..."

[7] Undated prospectus in YMCA Hist. Lib.

[8] *Report 1912*, p. 407.

greater part of his time in writing; a group of scholars, acknowledging Farquhar as their leader, had been formed, and was in process of being augmented; the Edinburgh Continuation Conferences had ratified Farquhar's policy. But this was not the whole picture. Farquhar and his immediate associates, calling themselves, in H. A. Walter's phrase, "progressive conservatives",[9] were offering one solution of the problem of the Christian attitude to Hinduism—recognition of the legitimacy of the quests of Hinduism, coupled with a consistent refusal to moderate or adapt the claims of Christ for the allegiance of India. This position was however challenged from two quarters: by the conservative Evangelicals, to whom the sympathetic approach to Hinduism was suspect *a priori*, particularly when it involved the evolutionary hypothesis; and by the liberals (properly so-called), to whom the attitudes of even the "progressive" conservatives appeared narrow and inadequate.

The Challenge of the Conservative Approach

The basic missionary attitude of the conservative Evangelicals we have already had occasion to describe.[1] On this view, the non-Christian religions (in this case Hinduism) were interpreted as being of the Evil One, hopeless corruptions of primeval revelation, to be attacked, destroyed and replaced by Biblical Christianity. This approach, which was traditional in Indian missions, and practically universal up to the turn of the century, has never been wholly abandoned, and in the years before 1914 was very far indeed from having been superseded by the more sympathetic approach of the "fulfilment" school. (That the Edinburgh material conveys a different impression is to be explained on the simple grounds that Mott's Commission IV questionnaire was sent only to a select group of missionaries, and not to the missionary force as a whole.) A debate

---

[9] H. A. Walter was the YMCA's expert on Islam [Latourette, *World Service* (1957), p. 122]. Writing to Farquhar in connexion with the case of C. F. Andrews (below, p. 327), he asked: "What do you make of all this? The beaten track of progressive conservatism seems safest, does it not? We can be scholarly and accurate and sympathetic, without running so far to meet the enemy that we lose our bearings—and our distinctive message. I think your own books are a standard example of the true Christ-like method and position." Quoted by Farquhar in a letter to Mott, 4.6.1914 (YMCA Hist. Lib.).

[1] Above, Ch. 1.

carried on in the pages of the Methodist journal the *Indian Witness* in 1912 gives evidence of a far wider range of opinion than is shown by the Edinburgh material. It is also interesting as providing a direct criticism of Farquhar's concept of "fulfilment".

The immediate cause of "the *Indian Witness* debate" was an article which Farquhar had published two years earlier (June 1910) in the *Student Movement,* the organ of the British Student Christian Movement.[2] In order to get a clearer perspective of the course of the debate we must first draw attention to certain salient features of the article in question.

Farquhar's thesis in this article, which he entitled "Christ and the Religions of the World" was familiar: that the accepted, orthodox missionary attitude—that Christianity is true and every other religious system false—was no longer tenable, in face of (a) the practical contact between the Christian and non-Christian religions and (b) the study of the science of religion, which had placed Christianity, in some sense at least, on the same footing as other religions. Writing for an educated British public, Farquhar had argued on an expressly evolutionist basis, and had expounded the theory that all forms of religion occupy relative positions on an ascending ladder of development, with Christianity on the topmost pinnacle. Religious phenomena, being varying forms of expression of a basic human religious instinct, differ only in degree, not in kind.

The term "fulfilment" came into use in this article on several occasions, and it is important once more to note that Farquhar meant two distinct things when he used this term: both must be kept in mind. (i) The religious phenomena of Christianity are universal religious phenomena on the highest level of their development. The corresponding Hindu phenomena, of which there are many, are lower on the evolutionary scale, and are therefore "fulfilled" by the former in the course of the process of evolution: "The Hindu image points forward to Christ, the image of the invisible God."[3] (ii) Man's basic religious instincts are satisfied, i.e. they reach fulfilment, only in Christianity, although all religions provide partial answers to the questions raised by the unsatisfied instinct. As we have seen, this was very far indeed from being the first occasion on which Farquhar

---

[2] Farquhar, "Christ and the Religions of the World", in the *Student Movement* (June 1910), pp. 195 ff.

[3] *Ibid.*, p. 197.

had used the fulfilment hypothesis; but seldom had he expressed its evolutionary basis so plainly as on this occasion.[4]

The reasons for this are fairly clear. Farquhar was writing for the student reading public, whose views might reasonably be supposed to be more advanced than those of missionaries and Church leaders. Students were unlikely to be shocked by the mention of the word "evolution". Further, it was aimed at preventing, if possible, a younger generation (including many potential missionaries) from entertaining mistaken ideas on the nature of the non-Christian religions. It was thus intended to act as a guide to those who found themselves in difficulties over the question of Christian-Hindu relations, to indicate to students the existence of a practical method of apologetics in a non-Christian milieu, and to provide a safeguard against syncretism—or rather, to indicate how syncretism might in theory be avoided.

Before going on to the debate proper, we shall quote three short passages from Farquhar's original article: against these the shafts of Farquhar's critics were largely directed, and around them the battle was mainly fought. The first concerns the basic religious instincts of mankind.

If we seriously believe that religion is a permanent element in human life, we shall be driven to conclude that there is a certain legitimacy in every form that religion has taken anywhere. Every religious belief, rite and institution must contain within itself something that comes from our common religious sensibility. Thus every detail of every religion has, as it were, a right of existence, and is significant.[5]

The second passage concerns the evolutionary basis of the fulfilment hypothesis,

Christ's own declaration, "I came not to destroy but to fulfil", has cleared up for us completely all our difficulties with regard to the Old Testament ... We recognize the whole history to be a religious evolution which finds its perfect consummation in the life, death, resurrection and teaching of Jesus Christ ... Can it be that Christ Himself was thinking of pagan faiths as well as Judaism, when he said, "I came not to destroy, but to fulfil?" ... Few have gone so far as to say that Christ is in detail, or even in general, the fulfilment of the gross worship, law, literature and morals of paganism. Yet is not that the right way to look at these religions? ... If

---

[4] See however above, pp. 168, 205, 255 f., 281.
[5] *Ibid.*, p. 195.

Christ has given us the final religion, clearly all our religious instincts will find their satisfaction in Christianity ... If Christ is able to satisfy all the religious needs of the human heart, then all the elements of pagan religions, since they spring from these needs, will be found reproduced in perfect form, completely fulfilled, consummated in Christ.[6]

And the third passage sums up the article as a whole, and is perhaps the most advanced public statement of his views on the evolutionary relationship of Christianity to Hinduism that Farquhar had so far made.

Christianity stands related to Hinduism as no other religion does. The correspondence point by point is most remarkable; only everything appears at a higher state of evolution: multiplicity gives place to unity, the natural and material to the spiritual, the particular to the universal, the mythical to the historical, the racial to the human, philosophy to simplicity, the privilege of the philosopher becoming the birthright of the coolie.

It is the belief of the writer that the application of the principle of fulfilment to all other religions will show that these stand related to Christianity in the same way that Hinduism. They are early, rudimentary, undeveloped. Christianity is the evolutionary crown of all.[7]

On March 12, 1912, the *Indian Witness* contained an editorial pointing out that Farquhar had begun "a new series of articles" in *Progress* on the relationship of Christianity to the non-Christian religions, a series in which he defined the "new attitude", and took up the "old theory"—"only to lay it aside as incredible".[8] These *Progress* articles were in fact the original *Student Movement* article, divided into two parts and reprinted; the editor of the *Indian Witness*, whilst not expressly condemning Farquhar's thesis, carried the process of dilution one step further by printing only selections from the first of these two articles. It need hardly be said that the result was a distortion of the original article: the passages which the editor communicated to his readers included little beyond the passages which we have already quoted, without any attempt being made to set them in their context. The debate was thus conducted from the first on a basis of reprinted—and distorted—reprints.

Contributions to the debate were not immediately forthcoming. The first attack on Farquhar's principles did not appear until April 9, and was not a direct result of the article. It was in fact

---

[6] *Ibid.*, p. 196.
[7] *Ibid.*
[8] *IW*, 12.3.1912, editorial.

another reprint, again from the pages of the *Student Movement,* of an article by a C.M.S. missionary, the Rev. A. W. Davies, of St. John's College, Agra, entitled "The 'New Thought' and the Missionary Message".[9]

Davies considered that the new emphasis on the positive relationship between Christianity and Hinduism was responsible for a distinct weakening of the missionary message, or at least that it tended to exercise such an influence. "Sympathy for everything Indian may easily result", he wrote, "in vagueness and uncertainty in regard to our message, and a loss of true evangelistic zeal."[1] If the nature of this danger were not seen and recognized, missionary enthusiasm might well weaken; the missionary message, too, would tend to lose "all real conviction and aggressive force".[2] Davies believed that all such missionaries as subscribed to the "new" views were becoming much too polite, and ready to give far too much credit to India and things Indian: in addition, he accused them of rationalism and of laxity in questions relating to individual conversion.

These warnings were couched in very general terms; Davies had however expressly identified Farquhar as the principal figure in the "fulfilment" movement, and had referred to Farquhar's "Christ and the Religions of the World" in the process.[3] The extent to which he suspected every tendency in the direction of Indianization is perhaps most clearly seen in the categorical statement with which he counter-attacked Farquhar and his sympathizers. Western theology, he claimed, being the fruit of enormous experience, and the foundation on which Protestant missions in India were trying to build, was too precious to be thrown away without a second thought. In fact, "Today we do not need less Western Theology but more".[4] In other words, any attempt to incorporate Indian elements into the theology of the Christian Church in India, or to take up a sympathetic attitude to the positive aspects of Hindu belief and Indian culture generally, is both unneccessary and dangerous, and therefore to be discouraged.

---

[9] Davies, "The 'New Thought' and the Missionary Message", in the *Student Movement* (March 1912), pp. 128 ff., reprinted in *IW*, 9.4.1912, pp. 287 ff.

[1] *Ibid.*, p. 128.

[2] *Ibid.*, p. 129.

[3] Other leading figures mentioned included C. F. Andrews and S. K. Rudra, Principal of St. Stephens' College, Delhi.

[4] Davies, *op. cit.*, p. 131.

The first contemporary contributions to the debate were both firmly negative. The first came from a Baptist missionary, the Rev. Arthur Jewson of Calcutta,[5] a personal acquaintance of Farquhar's, but a man who nevertheless proved to be completely out of sympathy with everything that Farquhar was trying to do. Though he claimed to admire Farquhar personally, he regarded his theories as "enervating, corrosive error". Jewson, on a basis of what the *Indian Witness* had published, had come to the conclusion that Farquhar was defending idolatry, and idolatry could not be tolerated under any circumstances. The idea that religious instincts may conceivably be satisfied in more than one way, he found intensely repugnant. This too was idolatry, which he characterized as "an illegitimate and wrong expression of the God-implanted religious sensibility". He concluded with a great flourish:

On behalf of the God who by idolatry has been insulted and dethroned, and of men who by idolatry have been befooled, and robbed and degraded, I raise a whole hearted protest against the teaching that "there is a certain legitimacy in every form that religion has taken anywhere".[6]

The second article, which bore the title "Farquhar's Fallacies", was by Dr. William Huntly,[7] also of Agra, a Scottish medical missionary working under the auspices of the Edinburgh Medical Missionary Society. Huntly, a strict conservative, took precisely the same line as Jewson: that of immoderate denunciation. Farquhar, in Huntly's opinion, had aimed at conciliating the Hindu mind towards Christianity "by becoming an apologist and defendant of Hinduism and paganism in general". Judgment having been passed, Huntly continued his attack on two fronts: he attacked the idea that a non-Christian satisfaction of religious instincts can be legitimate under any circumstances; and he attacked the concept of religious evolution as such. The former he regarded as encouraging idolatry, grossness and immorality; the latter he flatly denied as subversive of all true faith.[8] Huntly renewed his criticisms on several further occa-

---

[5] Jewson, "The New Attitude", in *IW*, 9.4.1912, p. 299.
[6] *Ibid.*
[7] Huntly, "Farquhar's Fallacies", in *IW*, 16.4.1912, p. 306 f.
[8] Huntly's articles consist primarily of polemic against what he believed Farquhar to have said: "Mr. Farquhar aims at conciliating the Hindu mind towards Christianity by becoming an apologist and defendant of Hinduism and paganism in general" (*ibid.*, p. 306).

sions, in an extended series which he called "Studies in Idolatry". The series however contains little of either interest or value.[9]

After the publication of these articles, in which Farquhar had been exposed to attack without even having been adequately quoted, the Editor of the *Indian Witness* placed the debate on a somewhat firmer footing by reprinting the second part of Farquhar's article *verbatim*.[1] This set at least the third of the above quotations in its context, and gave Farquhar's reasons for writing as he had done. Contributions to the debate were thereafter plentiful. The Editor himself began by quoting extracts from some of the letters and articles which he had received, though without naming the sources of his quotations. All appeared to agree as to the importance of the subject, but all held Farquhar's solution to be an illegitimate one. One condemned Farquhar's views as being at variance with the Pauline doctrine of regeneration; another stated categorically that "Mr. Farquhar's articles have no place in the teaching of Christian missionaries, and are no aid to the evangelization of the world"; a third proclaimed his own lack of sympathy with bigotry, but his equal lack of sympathy with "the people who can talk of degrading superstitions as leading up by evolution to Christ".[2] The Editor himself carefully refrained from expressing an opinion, but the tone of the examples quoted suggests in which direction his sympathies lay.

Farquhar was out of India at the time of the debate, and made no direct contribution. And only one other missionary, Nicol Macnicol of Poona, wrote in complete defence of Farquhar's articles.[3] Macnicol pointed out that Huntly and Davies were not looking at the same things in Hinduism as was Farquhar, and that in any case their reactions had evidently been wholly different. "What the former see fills them with indignation and disgust, while what the latter sees produces in him respect and sympathy with compassion ... The one sees only the fall; the other nobility in the very greatness of the fall."[4] At the same time he criticized both Davies and Huntly,

---

[9] The series began in the 28.5.1912 number of *IW*.

[1] *IW*, 16.4.1912, pp. 307 ff.

[2] An Irish missionary, unnamed, quoted in *IW*, 7.5.1912.

[3] Macnicol, "The Missionary Message and the Non-Christian Religions", in *IW*, 14.5.1912, p. 388. Even so, the defence was more of Farquhar's *approach* than his detailed method. Macnicol never made the same wide use of the evolutionary hypothesis as did Farquhar.

[4] *Ibid.*

the one for lack of sympathy with the errors of Hinduism and the other for unjust and unworthy accusations aimed at Farquhar personally. Macnicol ended by making a plea for sympathy and understanding, and called for a final rejection of polemics in missionary work. "The note of denunciation", he asserted, "is not the note of the Gospel."[5]

This was in fact the only article in the entire course of the debate which offered unqualified support to Farquhar, though J. M. Macphail of the Church of Scotland Santal Mission wrote a letter expressing his conviction that Farquhar's thesis was essentially that of Paul at Athens, and that Farquhar's message could be summed up in the text, "Whom therefore ye ignorantly worship, him declare I unto you".[6] Macphail also asked whether it was fair to judge Hinduism only by its lowest, and Christianity only by its highest, manifestations—a criticism which could be applied with equal justification to conservative Evangelical missionaries of all periods, at least before 1914.

It is quite out of the question to try and summarize in this context all the articles which were published in the columns of the *Indian Witness* in 1912, condemning Farquhar's theories. Instead we shall concentrate on the main features of their criticism. The first of these was, naturally enough, the doctrine of evolution in general, and religious evolution in particular. Almost all contributors took exception to the idea of Christianity as the "evolutionary crown" of Hinduism. For obvious reasons. It seemed to suggest that Hinduism, if left to itself, would eventually evolve into Christianity; the category of redemption was minimized; the authority of the Bible was called in question; the moral claims of the Gospel were seemingly placed on a par with the immoralities of popular Hinduism; in short, "degrading superstitions" could not reasonably be regarded as having any evolutionary connexion with the truth of the Gospel as it had been revealed in Christ. The very idea of evolution suggested a mechanical process: what, then, was to become of the sovereignty of God?

It was on these lines that a Canadian Presbyterian, Dr. J. Fraser Campbell, defended the Evangelical position, with its associated

---

[5] *Ibid.*
[6] MacPhail, "St. Paul at Athens", in *IW*, 14.5.1912, p. 389.

denunciatory and iconoclastic view;[7] it was, he wrote, "not so wildly absurd as some conclusions to which he [Farquhar] now invites us". These conclusions could only be explained, thought Campbell, by ignorance of the level to which popular Hinduism had sunk (the implication of course being that Farquhar had spent so much of his time among students and educated Hindus generally that he had no adequate conception of the situation of Hinduism outside these circles), and by a too thoroughgoing reliance upon evolution as the explanation of all the problems of religion. Campbell saw in the evolutionary hypothesis a reduction of religion to natural categories— and a refusal to accept the category of revelation—and felt that such was bound to be followed by grave consequences, since it buttressed the faith of educated Indians in Hinduism. And on the more practical level, ". . . it is such ideas as he sets forth that . . . are lessening self-sacrificial giving for Missions".

Another aspect of the basic conflict was to be seen in the contribution of the American Brenton T. Badley (later Bishop) of the Methodist Episcopal Church, who claimed that idolatry was no part of religious evolution, but a perversion, the author and consummator of which was the devil. We have seen[8] that traditional Evangelical theology divided existence sharply into the realm of God, light and life, and the realm of Satan, darkness and death; some knowledge of God there had been, but the Fall had perverted that knowledge beyond recognition; from the world, ruled by the Evil One, to the Kingdom of God there was only one path—the atoning death of Jesus Christ. The religious world of popular Hinduism, summed up in the word "idolatry", was commonly identified with the prince of darkness; and on this basis it seemed little short of blasphemy to postulate a direct organic connexion with Christianity. It is always possible, maintained Badley, to be sympathetic and loving towards pagans, but never towards paganism. There must be no compromise whatsoever, since "every religion, in every point where it differs from Christianity, is wrong, not requiring development but eradication".[9]

This same attitude—that Christianity must be presented as an absolute contrast to all other forms of religion—was advocated by

---

[7] Campbell, "The New Attitude", in *IW*, 21.5.1912, p. 408.

[8] Above, pp. 25 ff.

[9] Badley, "Does the Hindu Image Point Forward to Christ?" in *IW*, 4.6.1912, p. 447 f.

several of the contributors to the debate. For example, Dr. George P. Taylor of the Presbyterian Church of Ireland denied that there could be any real contact between Christianity and Hinduism, and quoted the example of Paul in Ephesus. Christ did not *fulfil* Aphrodite, claimed Taylor: he came *instead*. Thus what is needed in the Indian situation is a "real, radical change" from Hinduism to Christianity, involving complete rejection of all that has been associated with the past; "a mere furbishing up will not avail. Instead of the thorn shall come up the fir tree—*instead, instead*".[1] The absolute contrast motif was summed up by Dr. J. J. Lucas, an American Presbyterian, in an appeal to remember the preaching of the cross.[2] The very life of the Church, he wrote, "depends upon her refusal to recognize any other Gospel than that of Christ on the Cross ... The love of the Church for Christ must be exclusive. She cannot join in the praises of the hero-gods and goddesses of the sacred books of India."[3] Similar views were expressed by Dr. G. W. Brown, also an American Presbyterian,[4] A. E. Collier of the Baptist Missionary Society,[5] and A. E. Maclean of the Church of Scotland Santal Mission, who also echoed Campbell's judgment, that the higher Hinduism of the books and philosophies was very far indeed from being the Hinduism of the people of India as a whole.[6]

But not all missionaries who contributed to the debate were wholly unfavourable to Farquhar's views. As in the Edinburgh material,[7] a number were prepared to allow that there might well be points of contact between the highest and best in Hinduism and Christianity, though at the same time they were aware of the risks involved in applying the evolutionist view too fully, and felt that Farquhar had gone too far along these lines. Moderation was urged by a British Baptist, I. G. Dann, who recognized that the impression of Hinduism gained by a man of Farquhar's background must inevitably differ from that obtained by a missionary working on the frontiers.[8] In the circumstances, wrote Dann, it may well be

---

[1] Taylor, "Fulfilment or Antithesis: Which?" in *IW*, 14.5.1912, p. 387 f. Quotation from p. 388; the italics are Taylor's.

[2] Lucas, "Our Attitude to Non-Christian Religions", in *IW*, 14.5.1912, p. 388 f.

[3] *Ibid.*

[4] Brown, "The Modern View of Christianity and its Relations to Other Religions", in *IW*, 28.5.1912, p. 428.

[5] *IW*, 28.5.1912.

[6] *IW*, 18.6.1912.

[7] Above, pp. 278 ff.

[8] Dann, "Methods of Study", in *IW*, 14.5.1912, p. 389.

legitimate to say that Christ fulfils the best in Hinduism; it is no less necessary to say that he destroys the worst.[9] J. C. Knight Anstey, a Wesleyan Methodist working in a mass-movement area in Hyderabad, also emphasized the need for care, particularly in the application of results and theories derived from the science of religion and evolutionism.[1] He pointed out that the science of religion was still a young science, with very few assured results available. The evolutionary hypothesis, too, was far from being a self-evident fact. He therefore thought Farquhar's conclusions too radical and insufficiently supported by evidence, and appealed for an empirical attitude based on close acquaintance with the men who were to be brought to Christ.

An attitude which, judging from the Edinburgh material and the later progress of thought in India, was typical of that held by a fair proportion of Protestant missionaries in India, was expressed by J. Ireland Hasler of the Baptist Missionary Society.[2] Hasler was cautious, and, while not prepared either to contradict Farquhar categorically or to lend him unqualified support, was generally favourable. His conclusion is worth quoting, expressing as it does what must have been a common attitude in these years.

I shall await with interest the advice and opinion of others [he wrote], but the more one considers the subject, the more one feels that in the shaping of one's message there will necessarily be more of the influence of the spirit and attitude which Mr. Farquhar has in his paper expounded in a perhaps too extreme and one sided a way than in the denunciatory attitude that formerly occupied so large a place.[3]

The stumbling-block to the general acceptance of Farquhar's thesis was, it need hardly be said, the doctrine of evolution. This is illustrated most strikingly in a paper submitted by Dr. J. P. Jones of the American Board and the South India United Church.[4] It is clear from this paper that Jones was fully convinced of the need for sympathy in all dealings with Hindus; that he believed Christ to be the fulfiller of "every spiritual yearning" in the hearts of the

---

[9] This point was also made by Prof. J. R. Banerjea (the only Indian contributor to the debate), in an article, "Mr. J. N. Farquhar on 'Christ and the Religions of the World' ", in *IW*, 28.5.1912, p. 429.

[1] Anstey, "Mr. Farquhar's Zeal for the Kingdom", in *IW*, 21.5.1912, pp. 405 ff.

[2] *IW*, 21.5.1912, p. 408 f.

[3] *Ibid.*, p. 409.

[4] Author of *India's Problem: Krishna or Christ?* (1903).

people of India; and that he felt there to be "fundamental assonances" in Christianity and Hinduism.[5] Nevertheless Jones was
unable to accept the idea that Christ may be regarded as the fulfiller of *all* religion, i.e. that all religions stand in the same fundamental relationship of evolution toward Christianity. He rejected
the "old attitude", without being able to go so far as Farquhar in
his advocacy of the new. His rejection of the attitude of iconoclasm
was in fact expressed in the strongest terms:

The old attitude has become impossible; it is repugnant to modern light,
sentiment and thought. It is not in harmony with enlightened Christian
principles. The missionary who holds to the old view that Hinduism is
of the evil one ... needs to find anew his bearings both towards his own
faith and to the religions which have dominated millions for milenniums.[6]

But being unable to accept the theory of religious evolution, he
was forced to dissent from Farquhar's view that there is legitimacy
in all forms of religion.[7] It is interesting that an identical argument
was later advanced by Principal Mackichan in criticism of *The
Crown of Hinduism*,[8] and it was this form of reasoning, rather than
Farquhar's, which was ultimately to survive (always allowing for
the fact that Farquhar himself laid rather less stress on the evolutionary basis of his thought after this date).[9]

One final article calls for comment, before we leave the *Indian
Witness* debate. This was by K. J. Saunders, a C.M.S. missionary
working in Ceylon.[1] Saunders was not unknown to Farquhar. In
1909 his scholarship in the field of Buddhism had come to Farquhar's
notice, and he had written to Mott, suggesting that he might possibly
be useful to the Y.M.C.A., and calling him "a very promising young
missionary ... whom we must watch".[2] Two years later he had called
him "a fine scholar and a writer of promise", and had written:
"As far as I know, there is no missionary in India, Burma and

---

[5] It is interesting to note that in the previous year Jones had put forward
a plea for "A National Church for the Indian Christians"; cf. Sundkler, *Church
of South India* (1954), p. 86.

[6] Jones, "The Modern Missionary Attitude", in *IW*, 21.5.1912, p. 409.

[7] This criticism we have already noted in connexion with the Edinburgh
material, above, pp. 279 ff.

[8] Below, p. 347 f.

[9] Below, pp. 335 f., 353 f.

[1] Saunders, "The so-called New Attitude: A Few Platitudes for the Laity",
in *IW*, 2.7.1912, p. 525 f.

[2] Farquhar to Mott, 17.11.1909 (YMCA Hist. Lib.).

Ceylon who promises so well as a student of Buddhism and also as a writer."[3] Saunders had already contributed a series of articles to the Y.M.C.A. periodical the *Young Men of India*. He was later to be taken on to the Y.M.C.A. staff as an expert on Buddhism,[4] though in the long run he came to adopt a theological position unacceptable to Farquhar.[5]

On this particular occasion, Saunders attempted to summarize the position reached by the *Indian Witness* debate thus far. He entitled his article "The So-called New Attitude: A Few Platitudes for the Laity", and revealed both an overall attitude of sympathy towards Farquhar and his aims, and a recognition that Farquhar's statement might perhaps call for modification. He enumerated six possible attitudes which the missionary *might* adopt in the face of the non-Christian religions. Four he dismissed; the two remaining, which he regarded as having been sanctioned by the "new attitude" were (i) a compromise between the merciless condemnation of the past and indiscriminate appreciation, and (ii) outward ignoring of these religions, combined, however, with a real adaptation of the Gospel to suit the minds and hearts of their adherents, and a real knowledge of their strength and weaknesses.[6] Both these attitudes, claimed Saunders, were as old as St. Paul. Why, then, label them "new", and why treat them as dangerous heresy?

He felt that Farquhar had overstepped the mark in some of his more categorical statements, had taken too much for granted, and had unwittingly given many conservative missionaries the wrong impression of what he was trying to do. "Mr. Farquhar is a reformer, and reformers are doomed to exaggerate." But Saunders was on the side of the reformers. He stated his case moderately and carefully, taking exception to any form of indiscriminate condemnation, and formulating his own positive convictions in these words:

---

[3] Farquhar to Mott, 21.6.1911 (YMCA Hist. Lib.).

[4] Saunders was the third member of the YMCA triumvirate, whose other members were Farquhar (Hinduism) and H. A. Walter (Islam). See Walter, "Some Possibilities before Our Movement in India", in *FM* XXI: 4 (July–August 1914), pp. 1–4.

[5] Below, p. 328.

[6] There were, felt Saunders, real weaknesses to be taken into account. He wrote ("The So-called New Attitude", p. 525): "If Mr. Farquhar would apply the test he proposes and would bring every part of Hinduism before 'the searching of the Spirit of Christ', he would surely find that while it is true that Hinduism has been the most passionate search for God, it has also been the most terribly perverted of all religions ..."

Personally I believe that our best attitude will be a loving and thoughtful presentation of a positive Gospel: uncompromising but not antagonistic; and our presentation must issue from profound knowledge of the subconscious mind of India and from that insight which sympathy with and reverence for all that is lovely and of good report can give.[7]

For Saunders, the crux of the matter was to be found in the "attitude" of the missionary. Whether or not a new attitude might imply the revision of theological axioms he does not discuss.

Despite the cross-section of missionary opinion given by this debate, and the value of the contributions we have discussed in complementing the material submitted by the Edinburgh correspondents, it is difficult to suppress a feeling of dissatisfaction with the debate as such. In the first place, Farquhar's original article was written for a reading public different in almost every way from that among whom the *Indian Witness* circulated; nor was it ever reprinted in full. Further, its repeated references to the evolutionary hypothesis, touching a notorious sore spot among conservative Evangelicals, aroused such indignation that many were in no position to be able to assess the objective worth of Farquhar's argument as a whole. None placed the problem in its political and social setting. One contributor (Hasler) recognized that it was not a change in the *nature* of the missionary message that was being advocated, but only a change of *attitude*; many failed to penetrate so far. Rightwing extremists either thought that Farquhar was advocating idolatry, which they traditionally associated with the Evil One; or they felt that by introducing the idea of evolution into a Christian argument Farquhar was subverting the whole of the Evangelical faith. Moderates, such as J. P. Jones and Saunders, accepted Farquhar's conclusions without necessarily accepting the whole course of his reasoning; but their contributions are brief, and in no way touch the heart of the problem. Further, it is unfortunate that Farquhar made no personal contribution to the debate: nor do we know what were his reactions.

The principal importance of the *Indian Witness* debate is to be seen in its complementary nature over against the Edinburgh Commission IV discussions. The Edinburgh papers had been forwarded to an élite group among missionaries, few of whom were represented

---

[7] *Ibid.*, p. 526.

in this debate. It is perhaps not too much to see in the *Indian Witness* debate something of the reactions of the rank-and-file missionary of the Protestant societies to the concept of "fulfilment".

The Challenge of the Liberal Approach

The right wing of Evangelical missionary opinion in India was, as we have seen, suspicious of what it felt to be the unwarrantable liberties taken with the Gospel message by a man in Farquhar's position. The left wing was also dissatisfied, though less vociferous. In fact the years before 1914 saw only the first beginnings of what was to become, in the years between the wars, a widespread and powerful movement, leading to an attitude of what Edwyn Bevan was to call "a warm-hearted but muddle-headed comprehensiveness blurring vital distinctions".[8] Nevertheless it must be mentioned at this stage, though it was as yet far from systematic, and involved several distinct impulses.

The first of these was perhaps the contact of the missionary movement with certain aspects of Hinduism. The insistence of Rāmakṛishṇa and Vivekānanda that all religions are of equal value as pathways to the one God, and the eclecticism of such movements as the Brāhma Samāj and the Theosophical Society were not without a certain superficial attraction. Contact with pious and cultured Hindus caused some missionaries to ask what was the point of attempting to press for their conversion.[9] The writings of for example Max Müller and Paul Deussen, as well as strengthening Hindus in their ancestral faith, laid great stress on the heights already attained by Hinduism, and were not without their effect on the missionary body. Secondly, the Hindu revival was producing forms of religion far different from the traditional Hinduism of the older missionary text-books; while the vehemence of the Hindu defenders was of a force sufficient to throw some missionaries off balance. And thirdly, there had for some years been elements in the Christian situation

[8] Review in *IRM* XIX: 75 (July 1930), p. 447. Cf. Neill, *A History of Christian Missions* (1964), pp. 454 ff.

[9] This was in a sense C. F. Andrews' later attitude, particularly after 1914. Before his first visit to South Africa in that year he was content to work in a Christian college, though deeply concerned with the problem of creating true understanding between East and West. In 1914, however, he wrote to Tagore: "I am still the restless Englishman ... But, but, is there not a more excellent way, a way of *being* rather than *doing*." Quoted by Chaturvedi and Sykes, *Charles Freer Andrews* (1949), p. 101. On Andrews, see further below, p. 327.

which tended in the direction of compromise. Before the turn of the century the World's Parliament of Religions in Chicago had borne witness—enigmatic and confused, but attractive to a certain type of mind—to the underlying unity and validity of all religion. And in England R. J. Campbell had more recently begun to propagate, with eloquence and charm, his "New Theology". This calls for special mention.

It is common knowledge that the period around the turn of the century in Britain was notable for a decline of dogmatic theology, a "drift into theological nihilism".[1] In 1907 the Rev. R. J. Campbell, then minister of the City Temple in London, published his book *The New Theology*, which was expressly designed as a counterblast to traditional Reformed theology. Campbell's "theology" was expressed in terms of divine immanence in nature and in man; he called it "the gospel of the humanity of God and the divinity of Man".[2] It attempted to banish supernaturalism, and the idea of God as transcendent, and substituted an immanent aestheticism, a gospel of self-realization in which the old categories of "sin" and "salvation" were virtually abandoned. Although it aroused a great furore in England, it was not to be expected that such an un-Evangelical interpretation of Christianity would arouse much response on the Indian mission-field. Nevertheless it did have a champion in the Rev. E. P. Rice (1873–1936) of the London Missionary Society.[3]

In an article in the *Harvest Field* for 1908 Rice suggested that missionaries ought to pay more attention to the well-known fact that Hindus, while they were often ready to accept Christ, often fought shy of organized Christianity.[4] This was no new realization; the question of over-Westernization in the Christian Church in India had been raised before, most recently by Rice's colleague Bernard Lucas, in his book *The Empire of Christ* (1907).[5] Rice—and

---

[1] Grant, *Free Churchmanship in England 1870–1940* (s.a.), p. 114, cf. pp. 115 ff.
[2] Quoted by Grant, *op. cit.*, p. 135.
[3] A missionary in Bangalore, employed at this time chiefly on the revision of the Kanarese Bible.
[4] Rice, "The New Theology and Mission Work", in *HF* XIX: 10 (Oct. 1908), pp. 364 ff.
[5] Lucas' *The Empire of Christ*, "a study of the missionary enterprise in the light of modern religious thought", is a stimulating but not altogether satisfactory attempt to break free from traditional restraints in the field of Indian missions, based on a reinterpretation of Christianity as a "realized ideal" rather than a system of theology. Lucas later expanded this thesis in his book *Christ for India* (1910), which we cannot however discuss in this context.

to some extent Lucas—claimed that what was wanted was a new theology, and not merely a refurbishment of the old.[6] Rice's new theology was in fact "the New Theology"—"the Inductive Method applied to the facts of religion". The historical basis of Christianity would have to be subordinated to the "spiritual": the "historical Jesus" (though still to be reverenced as a teacher) to "the Sempiternal Spiritual Christ". The incarnation, he claimed, could no longer be viewed as an isolated historical event, but a spiritual process, "dating from the creation of man, extending through all history, and finding its crown in Jesus".[7] This latter phrase must be noted: the similarity of Rice's and Farquhar's phraseology is otherwise not marked, but there may well have been an incipient source of misunderstanding here.

Rice was of course criticized, though not by Farquhar.[8] And in 1912 he was once more to become the centre of a controversy, this time between the London Missionary Society and the British and Foreign Bible Society, who considered him a heretic.[9]

The years between 1908 and 1912–13 were otherwise not noteworthy for any really widespread attempt on the part of left-wing missionaries (who in any case lacked common ground) to influence missionary opinion as a whole. In 1913 and 1914, however, there took place two separate episodes with which Farquhar was at least indirectly concerned, and which served to underline his previously-expressed conviction that to preach eclecticism and compromise would be the most serious disservice that could be done to the Christian cause in India.[1]

The first of these had to do with the demand (later to become widespread) that the Old Testament should be excluded from Chris-

---

[6] Rice, *op. cit.*, p. 367. Cf. Lucas, *The Empire of Christ*, p. 26: "If the missionary enterprise cannot be re-stated in terms which are in agreement with our altered religious thought and feeling, its glory has departed and its very existence is imperilled."

[7] Rice, *op. cit.*, p. 374 f.

[8] See Thompson, "The New Theology—A Criticism", in *HF* XIX: 10 (Oct. 1908), p. 384: "The New Theology as a method is identified with caricature, superficiality and clamour. It is not Induction, but Induction marred by egoism." Lucas came to Rice's defence in *HF* XIX: 11 (Nov. 1908), p. 433 f.; see also Slater, "Modern Theology and Missionary Enterprise", in *ibid.*, pp. 403–13.

[9] An extensive correspondence on this subject is in the LMS Archives. See *Minutes of LMS Eastern Committee*, 14.11.1911, § 14, Rice to R. W. Thompson, 27.12.1911, Thompson to Rice, 26.1.1912, *Minutes of a Meeting of the South India D.C. of the LMS held at Bellary*, 10–24.1.1912, *Minutes of the LMS Eastern Committee*, 15.4.1913, § 14, etc.

[1] Above, p. 302.

tian worship in India, and replaced by suitable selections from the Hindu scriptures. What, it was argued, was the point of making Indian Christians read the Old Testament, when there was such a vast difference between Semitic and Indian ways of thought, and when it was in any case coming to be widely accepted that the Hindu scriptures contained a genuine *praeparatio evangelica*? As the Australian Methodist J. W. Burton had put it in 1909:

Should we be wrong in allowing the more evolved races to place *their* Old Testament where we place the Jewish? If God has spoken in divers manners through the prophets of the human race and has not left Himself without witness, can we be wrong in allowing the Hindu his Isaiah who tells of the "Coming One"?[2]

Shortly before the publication of *The Crown of Hinduism* in 1913 a similar proposal had been put forward by the Rev. R. G. Milburn of Bishop's College, Calcutta, who had suggested that Vedantist writings should take the place of the O.T. in the Indian Church.[3] Farquhar wrote in reply that while he was in sympathy with Milburn's general aims, he could not accept his solution, since there was a vast difference between the Christian and Hindu scriptures. It might be possible, he felt, to visualize "the clearer expression and fuller illustration of certain aspects of Christ's teaching by the Indian mind"; and much study must be directed to that end. But:

To me the development of the Hindu faith seems to be an unceasing struggle to reach that which the Vedānta does not contain, rather than a fuller and clearer expression of its inner spirit. It is in this sense, I believe, that all Hinduism points to Christ ...[4]

In other words, for Farquhar there could be no question of Hinduism *supplementing* Christianity. When he spoke of the "fulfilment" of Hinduism in Christianity this was not merely another way of saying that Hinduism *as it is* may be of service to the Christian cause. Hinduism, being shot through and through with inadequate conceptions of God, man and the universe, must die into Christianity if its genuine quests are to be attained and its genuine insights preserved. To admit Hindu scriptures into the Church would be a

---

[2] Burton, "Christian Missions as Affected by Liberal Theology", in *HF* XX: 2 (Feb. 1909), p. 71.

[3] Milburn, "Christian Vedantism", in *Ind. Interp.* VII: 4 (Jan. 1913); see also Macnicol's comment on p. 151 f.

[4] Letter in *Ind. Interp.* VIII: 1 (April 1913), p. 26 f.

first step towards admitting Hindu doctrine, and this could not be permitted.[5]

The second of these episodes concerns C. F. Andrews. It seems not too much to say that great concern was caused to Farquhar and his colleagues at this time by "the Andrews school of compromise", as H. A. Walter called it.[6] The crux here was that Andrews and his closest followers (among whom may be mentioned Pearson and Stokes), inspired by a burning desire to be utterly fair to all things Indian, and a desire to make atonement for the mistakes and injustices of the West *vis-à-vis* the Indian people, had come to occupy a position in which passive evangelism took precedence over active. Andrews *credo* in these years was Johannine—that Christ is "the Eternal Word, the Light and Life of all mankind", and that there is an "experience of Christ-life outside the Church of the baptized". The phrase "missions to the heathen" he had come to regard as "positively repellant".[7] Consequently he had long rejected all thought of Christian "proselytism", and in 1914 took the further decisive step of resigning his Anglican Orders and joining Rabindranath Tagore in his school at Bolpur, Bengal.[8] Of the sincerity of his reasons for doing so there can be no question: devoted, pious, passionate in his attachments, Andrews was undoubtedly actuated by the highest motives, feeling that he could exercise a more pervasive influence from a position outside the Christian missions.

Farquhar's reaction was however one of great disappointment. To Mott he wrote, "I have been greatly grieved over the matter ... I think he is grievously mistaken ... I hope that within a few months he will see the impossibility of doing any serious service where he is, and revert; but this is but a hope."[9] Nicol Macnicol,

---

[5] Cf. above, p. 302. In 1930 A. J. Appasamy published *Temple Bells: Readings from Hindu Religions Literature* for the use of Indian Christians; not, however, for use in public worship.

[6] Letter from H. A. Walter to J. N. Farquhar, quoted above, p. 309 n. 9.

[7] Andrews, "A Missionary's Experience", in *Ind. Interp.* IV: 3 (Oct. 1909), p. 102.

[8] The standard biography, Chaturvedi and Sykes, *Charles Freer Andrews* (1949), has no satisfactory account of how this took place. See however *ibid.*, pp. 89 ff., 323 f.

[9] Farquhar to Mott, 4.6.1914 (YMCA Hist. Lib.). Farquhar's reaction was also conditioned by the fact that only a few months earlier he had published *The Crown of Hinduism*, in the writing of which he had been helped by Andrews (Preface, p. 4). To Farquhar this was an abrupt and unexpected defection from what he held to be the true missionary position.

too, was disturbed at this growing trend. Commenting on a proposed "Congress of Liberal Religions" (to which Andrews was to be the Christian delegate), he drew attention to "a spirit abroad today which is not so much a spirit that denies as a spirit that refuses to affirm with any conviction", and suggested that, so far from being a sign of spiritual maturity, "much that boasts itself as religious 'breadth' and tolerance is due to nothing better than intellectual sloth and narrowness of conviction".[1]

That this was also Farquhar's settled opinion was later to be shown by a further episode, that of K. J. Saunders,[2] who came in the years between the wars to adopt an equivocal attitude to Buddhism. Though this lies outside our present period, Farquhar's conclusion is significant—that "all scholars recognize clearly that those people who accept the theory that all religions are practically the same are frightfully loose as scholars".[3]

Farquhar's position, then, was one mid-way between the "conservative Evangelical" and "liberal" extremes of missionary opinion. This cannot be emphasized too highly, particularly in view of the tendency to ascribe to Farquhar the paternity of later "liberal" attitudes.[4] Farquhar called himself a "liberal evangelical" or "progressive conservative", and it is in this distinctive combination of "progressive" and "conservative" elements that his contribution to missionary thought consists. We must bear this in mind now, as we turn to a consideration of *The Crown of Hinduism*.

---

[1] *Ind. Interp.* IX: 2 (July 1914), p. 39;; cf. Robertson, "Eclecticism and Compromise", in *ibid.*, pp. 41–49.

[2] Above, p. 320 f.

[3] Farquhar to F. V. Slack, 15.2.1923 (YMCA Hist. Lib.). A fuller account will be found in Sharpe, *J. N. Farquhar: A Memoir*, pp. 85–88.

[4] See e.g. Immanuel, *The Influence of Hinduism on Indian Christians* (1950), p. 133: "The followers of Farquhar, nicknamed 'universalists' by their opponents, used to contend that Christ came to dot the 'i's and cross the 't's of every religion ..."

CHAPTER II

The Crown of Hinduism

IN OUR Introduction we quoted E. C. Dewick as saying that Farquhar's book *The Crown of Hinduism* "marked a definite milestone in the history of missionary thought and ideals in India".[1] He was referring to the "new attitude" of sympathy towards Hinduism, which in this book received its first really systematic exposition, and which by the end of the 1920's had become "almost the norm of the missionary point of view".[2] But *The Crown of Hinduism*, published in 1913—by which time Farquhar was fifty-two years old and had been in India for twenty-two years—is not to be viewed, and indeed cannot be understood, in isolation.

There are at least three aspects in which the book may be viewed. First, as an experiment in missionary apologetics, the summing-up of Farquhar's career as a missionary apologist, the end product of the long process we have attempted to describe in this study. Secondly, as a statement of the Christian attitude to Hinduism in the context of the missionary situation as it was immediately prior to the outbreak of the first world war. And thirdly, as one of the sources for the missionary thought of a later period.

An Experiment in Missionary Apologetics

In a sense, *The Crown of Hinduism* contains nothing new; nothing, that is, which is not to be found in Farquhar's earlier written work. The whole intellectual foundation on which this book is based was in evidence as much as twelve years earlier, in the pamphlets published for "the Thinking Men of Calcutta".[3] The principle of taking the Hindu evidence and subjecting it to the tests of history

---

[1] Dewick, "Dr. J. N. Farquhar", in *YMI* XLI: 10 (Oct. 1929), p. 753. Cf. above, p. 10.

[2] *Ibid.* See also Boyd, *Christian Encounter* (1961), p. 74, quoted below, p. 358.

[3] *Christ and the Gospels* and *Criticism and Christianity* (both 1901), which we have discussed above, pp. 167 ff.

and practical worth had been applied ten years before to the *Bhagavad Gītā*.[4] The use of the concept of "fulfilment" to describe the relationship between Christianity and Hinduism is to be found throughout the whole of Farquhar's literary production, from 1902 on.[5] Even the title was not new: in 1910 Farquhar had published an article on "The Crown of Hinduism" in the *Contemporary Review*.[6] Nor was the missionary situation which produced the book new; its main features, as we have tried to show, had been developing gradually since the 1870's at least.

The newness and experimental quality of *The Crown of Hinduism* lies not in its plan, nor its pattern, nor even the basic thought by which it is inspired, but in its execution. For in it Farquhar was trying to do what he had not been able to do before, and what no other missionary had attempted during the past decade, to write a book in which all the main features of Hinduism—as a religion and as a social system—were confronted with the Christian message. To find a similar attempt we must go back to the turn of the century, to T. E. Slater's *The Higher Hinduism in its Relation to Christianity*—a work with which *The Crown of Hinduism* has a number of marked affinities, but which Farquhar does not mention having used.[7]

The main features of Hinduism which Farquhar discusses may be enumerated. After a historical survey of Indo-Aryan religion, Farquhar considers in turn the Hindu family, the doctrine of *karma*, the caste system, Vedānta, asceticism, image-worship, the great sects, the doctrine of incarnation, and "the religious organism". In each case the distinctive elements of the Hindu system are outlined historically, and in their contemporary application; after which they are placed over against the Christian message, as Farquhar understood it. The scheme is an ambitious one, but even so there are omissions from the Hindu material, as Farquhar himself pointed out.[8]

The opening sentence of the book indicates its object: "to discover and state as clearly as possible what relation subsists between Hin-

---

[4] In e.g. *Gita and Gospel* (1903), above, pp. 198 ff.
[5] For earlier statements on the concept of "fulfilment", see above, pp. 189 f., 255 f.
[6] Above, p. 262.
[7] On Slater, see above, pp. 94 ff.; for Farquhar's judgment that Slater's book was "on the right lines", see *Missionary Study of Hinduism* (1905), p. 14.
[8] *The Crown of Hinduism* (1913), p. 3. Hereinafter abbreviated to *Crown*.

duism and Christianity".[9] It is scarcely necessary at this stage to point out how the need for such a statement had exercised Farquhar's mind during the years since joining the Y.M.C.A. We may recall only that the whole of the missionary situation *vis-à-vis* the educated classes since the late 1870's had been such as to make the need for some such statement imperative. The reasons for this are summarized by Farquhar in his Introduction; we have discussed them elsewhere. We may perhaps sum up by saying that historical criticism and the "science of religion" working from within the missions, and the growing force of the Hindu revival working from without, had modified the traditional Evangelical attitude towards Hinduism. The more sensitive among the missionaries were no longer prepared to dismiss Hinduism as the work of the Evil One; some "light", some "truth" there undoubtedly was in it, however it may have come there; and it was the duty of the missionary to seek for this light and truth, and use it in his preaching. And then there was the further inescapable fact that educated Hindus were no longer willing either to listen to, or to read books written by, missionaries whose line was one of denunciation. This process had been going on, as we have said, since the 1870's; Slater had spoken of it in 1876;[1] in 1913 Farquhar could write that, even should a missionary be unwise enough to want to polemize against Hinduism, "he would not dare to do it; for no educated audience would stand it".[2] But he could also note with satisfaction that "that is now almost altogether a thing of the past".[3] In general, though, there was a growing tendency to condemn Christianity, not as being untrue, but as being un-Indian, a "denationalizing" force; such criticisms as these were most noticeable among the educated classes.

The emphasis on the educated classes is worthy of close attention. We have attempted to trace the course of the Christian higher educational enterprise up to the turn of the century, and have noted that Christian, Hindu and secular centres of higher education, working on Western lines, had by the early years of the twentieth century created an intellectual aristocracy, at least partly Westernized (though frequently critical of the West), and often at least partly disassociated

---

[9] *Crown, loc. cit.*
[1] Above, p. 101.
[2] *Crown,* p. 35.
[3] *Ibid.*

from its traditional background. A great proportion of the Protestant missionary effort before 1914 was channelled into the attempt to reach this class. Farquhar, as a college teacher, Y.M.C.A. secretary and writer, was concerned only with this class and its problems. Of village work and the mass movements he had no direct experience.[4] What this meant for his interpretation of Hinduism is clear on almost every page of *The Crown of Hinduism*. One of his main arguments is not unlike that of Alexander Duff, that to bring a man into the "atmosphere" of Western education was to lay the axe to the roots of his traditional religion: "The thought of the West creates a new climate which is fatal to Hinduism."[5] But this climate was as yet felt only by the few, in the colleges primarily, but also in books and in the press; the problems of the many, the illiterate masses, were not his concern at this time.

Thus when Farquhar speaks of Hinduism, it is commonly either the Hinduism of the classical canonical scriptures, or Hinduism as modified by the impact of the West, that he means. Time and time again he returns to the argument that the educated classes have begun to call for reform; have indeed begun to impose reforms of their own accord; but in so doing have departed from their traditional religious basis. There is no alternative but to replace this discarded basis by a new, Christianity, for social reform must be based on religion, and what the educated *élite* has done, the masses can and must do.

Farquhar's argument, then, was directed towards representatives of a Hinduism that had already begun to feel the force of religious and secular pressures which were not felt as long as the original structure was retained. But was this tantamount to saying that the religious structure as such had in fact been undermined, and might be expected to collapse at any moment? Such was in fact Farquhar's belief, and that of many (though not all) of his contemporaries, as we have already had occasion to point out.[6] In *The Crown of Hin-*

---

[4] This is not to say that he had no knowledge of its problems, or of the vernaculars; it is merely that his field of service was elsewhere; cf. Farquhar, *Some Thoughts on Christian Vernacular Literature* (Lecture delivered on 4.12.1922), pp. 3-5.

[5] *Crown*, p. 42. Cf. above, pp. 63 ff.

[6] This is seen especially clearly in his article *Christianity in India* (1908), which we have discussed above, p. 244 f. An analogy was frequently drawn between the situation in India and that in the late Roman Empire; see e.g. Farquhar, *The Future of Christianity in India* (1904), and Ewing, "Christianity in India and in

duism he reiterates his conviction that Hinduism is indeed in process of decay; for example, the beliefs at the root of family worship are passing away: "... the forces of the new time have created an atmosphere in which these beliefs cannot live".[7] These "forces" include Christianity, but are wider than Christianity: "... disbelief of these things is bound to spread. No one can now stay the progress of Western education in India."[8] Similarly with the beliefs forming the foundation of the theory of *karma* and transmigration: new thought from the West "is stirring the educated class and rousing them to action; and, in consequence, the old transmigration ideas are everywhere being ousted from their places".[9] And in respect of asceticism: "The spirit of the West has come in and revolutionized the mind and the environment of the educated man. In consequence, the more faithful the ascetic is to the ancient ideal, the more hopeless and useless he appears to the modern man."[1]

So we see that Farquhar's appeal was to the educated classes. It was primarily the Western education given to these young men that had, in Farquhar's view, undermined the foundations of their traditional faith. But these were the men with whom the future of India lay—the men whose political activities were so much a feature of the years after 1905, who were so scandalized by the words and works of Lord Curzon, and who, given the choice between Christ and Kṛishṇa, were choosing Kṛishṇa, because he was Indian, *swadeshi*. These were the "patriots" to whom Farquhar turned, again and again, to ask: "Given these postulates, this evidence, in this situation, what will the Indian patriot do?" Again, this is not new. One of the features of the Indian situation of the period under discussion to which we have tried to draw attention has been the growth of the nationalist movement. Here it would be well to emphasize once more that there was the closest of connexions be-

---

the Roman Empire—An Analogy", in *MCCM* IV: 5 (Nov. 1904), pp. 225 ff. On the "decline" of Hinduism, see e.g. Mott, *The Decisive Hour of Christian Missions* (1910), pp. 62, 65, and Oldham, *The World and the Gospel* (1916), p. 101. Others were more cautious; in 1908 Nicol Macnicol asked whether the "new life" which some had seen in Hinduism would be "a new Hinduism or a further phase in the unwearied life of Christianity", Review in *Ind. Interp.* II: 4 (Jan. 1908), p. 196. Most were convinced, however, that India's religious ferment was a direct result of the work of the Christian missions.

[7] *Crown*, p. 115.
[8] *Crown*, p. 116.
[9] *Crown*, p. 151.
[1] *Crown*, p. 276.

tween the nationalist movement and the Hindu revival, at least in some of its forms, and that the "Indian patriot" was not infrequently in the forefront of Neo-Hinduism.[2] There were those among the missionaries who had begun to call in question the sincerity of some of these "patriots", wondering whether personal convictions were not being subordinated to political opportunism.[3] But Farquhar never took the fact of nationalism and Neo-Hinduism anything but seriously, and one of the objects of *The Crown of Hinduism* was to attempt to turn the energies of the nationalists into new channels, since he was convinced that Hinduism could never provide a ground of belief for the India of the future; for some ground there must be. Here we find one of the basic factors conditioning the "fulfilment" hypothesis.

Farquhar was convinced that no society could subsist without a religious foundation. "For the purpose of creating a living social order", he wrote, "a living religion is needed. It alone provides moral conceptions of strength and reach sufficient to lay hold of man's conscience and intellect and to compel him to live in society in accordance with them."[4] And then he went on to make a statement which, perhaps more than any other, marks the date of his book as pre-1914: "No lasting society has ever yet been formed on a secular basis."[5] But this is by the way. For the purposes of Farquhar's argument the point was made: disturb the religious foundations of Hindu society by rendering its basic beliefs incredible, and there remain three alternatives: either to turn one's back on progress and retreat into Hindu obscurantism; or to ignore the religious basis of society altogether; or to find some new foundation capable of bearing up the new structure imposed by the new age. To Farquhar the first of these was unthinkable; the second not even feasible; leaving the third, the Christian, alternative:

Christ ... provides the necessary religious foundations for a society characterized by equality, freedom, and strict justice. Social evolution all over the world is steadily tending in the direction of these Christian ideals, and the needs of modern men will inevitably increase the rate of the movement.

---

[2] This applies both to the leaders of the movement, such as B. G. Tilak and Aurobindo Ghose, and to its followers; cf. above, pp. 243 ff.

[3] This was the view of Farquhar's YMCA colleague F. W. Steinthal, expressed in an article "The Religious Aspect of the National Movement", in the *Indian World* VII: 38 (May 1908), p. 396.

[4] *Crown*, p. 191.

[5] *Ibid.*

Universal intercourse necessarily demands a universal society, complete social liberty, and a social morality of depth and strength sufficient to bear the unparalleled strain of the new state of affairs. Nothing but a conception of human brotherhood which contains within itself these liberties and obligations is equal to the creative task. Thus Christian society is the evolutionary goal of all living forms of society and of all the social unrest and agitation of our day.[6]

But when Farquhar spoke of Christian society as the "evolutionary goal" of all other forms of society, Hindu society included, it must not be imagined that he envisaged an automatic process in which Hindu society, or any other society, would simply develop into Christian society of its own accord. *For Farquhar the process of evolution, social or religious, was inseparable from the exercise of choice.* In other words, an individual (or a nation) reaches a higher evolutionary level when that level has been presented to him, and when he has made an active descision to embrace it.

The understanding of this principle is vital to the understanding of the whole of Farquhar's missionary thought. Much misunderstanding was—and still is— caused by the tacit assumption that to speak of "evolution" was always to postulate a mechanical process, in which things happened because they would happen, in which the laws of cause and effect were all in all, and in which the crown rights of the Redeemer and the freewill of man went for nothing. But this was not so in Farquhar's case. Development was as much a matter of the will as of outward circumstances, and to pass from a lower evolutionary stage was a conscious step, not an unconscious movement.

Leaving on one side for the moment the question of the relations of religion and society, and concentrating on the central question of religion, Farquhar held that religion was of value to a people only so long as it was the highest they knew. For obvious reasons; if religion be *the* creative force in human life, it cannot lead men from behind. And he went on: "When most of the leading ideas

---

[6] *Crown*, p. 202. The question of "social evolution" bulked large in the thought of the late 19th and early 20th centuries. An influential book was Kidd's *Social Evolution* (1894), cf. above, p. 41 n. 9. In the field of missions, it had been taken up by J. S. Dennis, in *Christian Missions and Social Progress* (1897), who spoke of the missionary enterprise as "the story of social evolution with Christianity introduced as a factor ... the adjustment of society to its higher spiritual and supernatural environment" (I, p. 51). Cf. Mathews (S.), "Missions and the Social Gospel", in *IRM* III (1914), pp. 432–46.

of a religion have become incredible to its people, they may continue to observe its ancient practices, but clearly it cannot exercise the old influence over their minds and hearts."[7] What then is to be done? Clearly a Hindu who has been brought into contact with the constellation of Christianity and Western civilization has been introduced to something "higher"; Christianity may said to be "the highest he knows"; and it is therefore his duty, for his own sake and for the sake of his nation, to *choose* Christianity. For, as Farquhar makes abundantly clear, the Christian message as he knows it is there for the taking; becoming a Christian is a matter of "utter sincerity", of "turning", of "acceptance", of "straightforward obedience"; it is a "pose of the soul", an "attitude".[8] The non-Christian (in this case the Hindu), having encountered Christianity, and having reached some measure of conviction, "if he fail to confess Christ publicly ... if he continue to bow down to idols; his old faith, however valuable it may have been to him formerly, can never be for him a door into fellowship with God again; for he has turned his back upon the highest, and has made the great refusal".[9]

This gives us a basis on which to understand the meaning of "fulfilment" as used by Farquhar in this and other contexts. We may expand slightly.

First, as Farquhar himself pointed out repeatedly, "fulfilment" means "replacement". In the evolutionary scheme as he understood it, a "lower" stage does not merely *develop into* a "higher": it is *replaced by* a "higher", in a conscious choice of will. The ultimate criterion was, as we shall see, empirical: the "higher" religion is to be judged primarily by its practical manifestations in the life of the individual and society. This implies that the old, once recognized to be imperfect, must be abandoned. In this case the Hindu, faced by the challenge of the Gospel of Christ, once he recognizes it as superior (by the superiority of its practical results), must abandon Hinduism. Otherwise he is impeding the work of God. Continues Farquhar: "This dying to all that impedes the work of God includes for the Hindu a dying to Hinduism, which is no easy or pleasant duty ... Hinduism must die in order to live. It must die

---

[7] *Crown*, p. 32.
[8] *Crown*, p. 27.
[9] *Crown*, p. 28.

into Christianity."[1] Only thus can its truths be realized and its quests reach fruition.

The second and third senses in which Farquhar uses the concept of "fulfilment" in *The Crown of Hinduism* have to do with these "truths" and "quests".

The recognition of "truths" enshrined in the non-Christian religious systems was no new one. In fact we have seen it to have formed a more or less consistent feature of the missionary thought of the late nineteenth and early twentieth centuries. These "truths" may have been looked upon, as Monier-Williams looked upon them, as fragments of primeval revelation retained in the human heart since the Fall.[2] Or as Max Müller believed, as evidence of the working of the Spirit of God on the mind of man everywhere and in all ages.[3] The point is that by the time *The Crown of Hinduism* was written, few doubted that these "truths", "flashes of light", "insights" existed, and that it was the plain duty of the missionary to take and use them in the presentation of his own message.[4] In the Edinburgh material we noted that many missionaries made precisely this point, that the Christian preacher must recognize the presence of these truths, and might profitably present Christ as "fulfilling" them, i.e. bringing them to completion in "the truth";[5] at the same time there was considerable hesitancy as to whether Christ could be said to "fulfil" anything else. In the Edinburgh material and in the *Indian Witness* debate there were those who said that, although Christ fulfilled the best in the non-Christian religion, he also destroyed the worst.[6] The difficulty was, where the line between the "best" and the "worst" was to be drawn.

Farquhar's approach was slightly different—but not so different as some imagined. For while he was in no way blind to the corruption of much that went by the name of Hinduism, and recognized that it must be removed, he was still able to discern a "quest" behind it. In addition it must be remembered that it was against his avowed principles to confront Hinduism at its worst with Chris-

---

[1] Cf. above, p. 259 n. 4.
[2] Above, p. 51.
[3] Above, p. 45.
[4] The "elementary Christian conceptions" "... ought to be eagerly searched for by the missionary as a basis for his own superstructure", Monier-Williams, *Modern India and the Indians* (4th ed. 1887), p. 234.
[5] Above, pp. 236 ff., 278 ff.
[6] Above, pp. 279 f., 319.

tianity at its best, and to indulge in polemics for its own sake.[7]
As an example of the way in which this was worked out in practice
we may take the question of idolatry. In the course of the *Indian
Witness* debate a correspondent had accused Farquhar of trying to
conciliate the Hindu by becoming an advocate of idolatry.[8] A quotation such as this, taken out of context, might well give the same
impression: "The use of idols is thus completely justified in the
case of men who really believe in them. If each image is a living
god, then every detail of the worship is not only natural but right;
and we have no difficulty in understanding how men and women
lavish their affection upon idols."[9] But the reason for this judgment must be understood. As Farquhar put it, the reason why
idolatry has played such a large part in Hindu history is the fact
that it "ministers to some of the most powerful and most valuable
of our religious instincts".[1] Nevertheless—and here we return to the
theme of the decay of Hinduism under the impact of Western
education—"idolatry is dying among educated Hindus", and it will
soon be the responsibility of Hindu leaders to "seek to destroy the
practice among the common people", since "the degrading superstition of idolatry" is one of the chief hindrances to the progress of
India. And he sums up: "The clear-sighted patriot will do his utmost
to wean the simple Hindu villager from idols."[2]

But how was idolatry to be removed? For Farquhar it was evident
that the existence of idolatry—and indeed of the whole Hindu
religious system—was evidence of the existence of a series of complex
religious needs. Deprive these needs of their legitimate satisfaction,
and they are bound to seek an illegitimate; without Christ, idolatry
is inevitable. And conversely, if idolatry be removed, something
must be found to replace it, for there can be no vacuum. "We must
find a spiritual force as vivid and real as idolatry, and as fully
charged with religious emotion, a spiritual dynamic which will
render idols obsolete by appealing as successfully as they do, and
yet in healthy spiritual fashion, to the religious imagination and

---

[7] Farquhar's earlier reports occasionally provide glimpses of a less sympathetic
attitude; so e.g. in the case of the Kalighat meeting of the *swadeshi* movement in
1905, above, p. 221.

[8] Huntly, "Farquhar's Fallacies", in *IW*, 16.4.1912, p. 306.

[9] *Crown*, p. 341.

[1] *Ibid.*

[2] *Crown*, p. 342.

feeling."[3] The "spiritual force" was Christ, "fulfilling" idolatry by satisfying the needs which had called it into being.

So we see that by "fulfilment" Farquhar meant three distinct and yet related processes. First, Hinduism is "fulfilled" by being replaced by Christianity: "fulfilment" therefore means "replacement". Secondly, the "truths" in Hinduism are "fulfilled" by reappearing in a "higher" form in Christianity. And thirdly, Christ "fulfils" the "quests" of Hinduism, by providing an answer to its questions, a resolution of its problems, a goal for its religious strivings; in this third sense there need be no recourse to postulated "truths", since a genuine quest can reach an illegitimate goal and an adequate question receive a wholly wrong answer. All three senses were used, sometimes separately, sometimes in conjunction, by Farquhar in *The Crown of Hinduism*.

When we say that Farquhar put forward Christ as the true satisfaction of the Hindu's quests and needs, we come once more to the vexed question of the nature of Farquhar's Christian faith and Christian theology. Christ, he claimed, was the satisfaction of the spiritual hunger of the idolater; but he also stated that his book was written in order to show "that *Christianity* is the Crown of Hinduism". What, then, was the relationship between Christ and Christianity; and how could Christianity be set forth as the fulfilment of something so foreign as Hinduism? These questions we must now consider briefly.

Once more we find that we are faced not so much with a new interpretation of the Christian faith, thought out by Farquhar in face of the demands of a new book, as with the application of a previously-held conviction. Many of the features of the Christian faith as they are expounded in *The Crown of Hinduism* we have previously noted in connexion with Farquhar's commentaries on the Gospel of Matthew.[4] And once more we must stress that Farquhar was never trained as a theologian, and that *The Crown of Hinduism* must not be regarded as a treatise in systematic theology. Farquhar was however brought up and worked in a definite tradition, the tradition extending from the Evangelical Union through the Nonconformity of Fairbairn to the Congregational and Y.M.C.A. missionary

---

[3] *Crown*, p. 342 f.
[4] Above, pp. 165 f., 259 ff.

enterprise of the early twentieth century. And this situation was not impervious to what Grant has called "the transfer of interest from doctrine to apologetics and ethics and, indeed, the widespread repudiation of any kind of dogmatic theology".[5]

The Christianity of *The Crown of Hinduism* is the Christianity of the missionary apologist rather than the dogmatic theologian. It is conditioned by the whole climate of opinion of its period, and attempts to present Christianity in a way acceptable to its readers, partly for practical reasons,[6] and partly as a result of the theological presuppositions of its writer, which were real and to some extent systematic, though limited in their scope. The key—or rather one of the keys—to its understanding is to be found in Farquhar's use of the historical method, in which the influence of Harnack is also to be seen.[7]

In 1901 Farquhar had published a pamphlet on the subject of Christ and the Gospels, in which he had concluded that the real need of the age was to turn to the figure of Jesus, the historical Jesus as he seemed to have been revealed by the scholarship of the time. "Will you not try to see the real Jesus?" he had asked. "Will you not study the Gospels, and try to understand the secret of this extraordinary influence?"[8] His commentaries on the Gospel of Matthew were written with this same end in view, to bring men face to face with the Jesus who was such a topic of interest and

---

[5] Grant, *Free Churchmanship in England 1870–1940* (s.a.). It is also interesting to note that Grant reckons the emergence of the "social gospel" as another of the factors influencing the situation of the time in the British Free Churches. This has clear parallels with the situation in India.

[6] The teaching of Jesus, and particularly the Sermon on the Mount, had long exercised a marked attraction in India. This is particularly noticeable in the Edinburgh material, where correspondents repeatedly asserted that the Sermon on the Mount was the most powerful attractive force in evangelistic work.

[7] In 1901 Farquhar had called Harnack "the greatest Biblical scholar in Germany, perhaps in the world, to-day", *Christ and the Gospels*, p. 13. Cf. *idem*, *The Future of Christianity in India*, pp. 20 ff., *Crown*, p. 426 f. Richardson, *The Bible in the Age of Science* (1961), p. 87, writes that in Harnack's view, Christianity "was still a 'positive historical religion'; it was in fact 'the religion of Jesus', which consisted essentially in two affirmations, the Fatherhood of God and the Brotherhood of Man"; and further, that according to Harnack, "the earliest 'Christianity' was essentially a theology without a Christology; and so we reach the classic Liberal Protestant distinction between the pure 'religion of Jesus' and the 'religion about Jesus' with which St Paul and the Hellenizers quickly obscured it". There can be no doubt that here we have one of the primary sources of Farquhar's view of Christianity.

[8] *Christ and the Gospels*, p. 27.

discussion in the India of his day.[9] Like Miller and Andrews (to name only two examples),[1] Farquhar firmly believed that what was needed was a return to the "simple" teaching of Jesus as the normative basis of Christianity. Hence the statement of policy controlling the exposition of *The Crown of Hinduism* reads:

... in setting forth Christianity as the Crown of Hinduism, we shall restrict ourselves to Christ Himself, drawing our evidence only from His own life and teaching, and from those parts of the Old Testament which He accepted without alteration. If we use a sentence here and there from the Apostles, we do so only to further illustrate the meaning of Christ.[2]

And it may be well to have Farquhar's explanation of what he meant by "Christianity":

When we say that Christianity is the Crown of Hinduism, we do not mean Christianity as it is lived in any nation, nor Christianity as it is defined and elaborated in detail in the creed, preaching, liturgy, and discipline of any single church, but Christianity as it springs living and creative from Christ Himself.[3]

His starting-point is really the doctrine of the Fatherhood of God, the "relation of Father and child", subsisting between God and man—every man—irrespective of nation or even of religion.[4] Given a certain attitude of mind, it is "possible for our Father to enter into personal fellowship with His child"[5]—and this law "applies to men in every religion".[6]

But God in Christianity is moral, and God's Fatherhood is a moral Fatherhood. Here there is a fundamental contrast between Hinduism and Christianity, for the Indian moral theory, as interpreted by Farquhar, stands apart from God, and is therefore no more than a "mechanical, automatic system",[7] while the supreme God of the system (Brahman) is non-moral, and therefore neither a Father nor a suitable foundation on which to build a moral

---

[9] *The Crossbearer* (1900), p. v.

[1] Chetty, *William Miller* (1924), p. 52; Andrews, "A Missionary's Experience", in *Ind. Interp.* IV: 3 (Oct. 1909), p. 111, in which he spoke of his "passionate longing to return to the simplicity of the primitive Gospel".

[2] *Crown*, p. 64.

[3] *Crown*, p. 58.

[4] *Crown*, p. 119: "The central message of Christianity is the Fatherhood of God."

[5] *Crown*, p. 27.

[6] *Ibid.*

[7] *Crown*, p. 152.

society. Christianity, on the other hand, is based on the ethical righteousness of God, as shown forth in the life of the historical Jesus, who "exhibited in character and life the moral ideal at its very height" and who was therefore "also the revelation of God".[8]

This is the meaning of revelation, as Farquhar understood it: that God is ethical, and that Jesus shows forth the ethical and moral concern of the Godhead in human life, and thereby becomes an example for men.

When we say that God is ethical, we mean that He Himself conforms to the standard which He bids us live by; but no religion, except Judaism and Christianity, has had the courage to say this frankly. It is the message of the Old Testament. It receives concrete expression in the character of Jesus, who, being the revelation of the Father, the express image of the righteous God, is also the example for men.[9]

Whether this is tantamount to calling Christ divine is a question which Farquhar does not discuss. He does however state that Christ was human: that is, belonging to the whole human race, "and the riches that are in Him can be set forth only by the united efforts of the whole human race".[1] He was a teacher of "the spiritual principles which are necessary for our human life"; not a lawgiver, for "there is no law in the New Testament"; instead he conveyed to his disciples and, through them, to his followers in all ages "His own principles and the divine freedom of sons of God".[2]

The question of the work of Christ Farquhar treats in accordance with the same basic moral-ethical view. If the teaching and life of Jesus were "the healthiest and holiest influences of the time",[3] no less can be said about his death, which was something capable of exercising "influence".[4] Christ's "method" being self-sacrifice, it follows that the crucifixion "is only the final exhibition before all the world of what had been going on in the life of Jesus from the beginning",[5] a final demonstration of the principle of self-giving love which, by its very radicality, was capable of commanding human allegiance. The resurrection is scarcely mentioned in Farquhar's

---

[8] *Crown*, p. 437.
[9] *Ibid*.
[1] *Crown*, p. 63.
[2] *Crown*, p. 58 f.
[3] *Crown*, p. 45.
[4] *Crown*, p. 292.
[5] *Crown*, p. 433.

exposition of Christianity. He states in passing that after the crucifixion "the disciples were overwhelmed with despair. But His resurrection brought Him back to them; and the meaning of the Cross began to dawn on them."[6] But it is evident that the resurrection occupied only a subordinate place in Farquhar's thought.[7] It is also surprising to find so little explicit mention of the Kingdom of God in the Christian passages of *The Crown of Hinduism*. The omission is however more apparent than real. There can be no doubt that Farquhar regarded the Kingdom of God as the ultimate goal of the teaching of Jesus, and in some sense as the goal of the "social evolution" on which so much of his argument is based. The Indian nation needs a new basis (such was his argument), in its families, in its religious practices and in its wider human relationships: a basis of complete social equality, full social freedom and real justice in social relations. This basis is in effect the Kingdom of God:

... a new age is dawning. We see Jesus already crowned with many crowns; but we do not yet see all things put under Him. But in this new age on which we have entered His Kingdom will continue to extend rapidly ...[8]

For Farquhar, religion and social issues were inseparable: religion *is* in a sense what religion *does*; in fact one of the texts he uses might well be placed as a motto over the book as a whole: "By their fruits ye shall know them" (Matt. 7.16). Religion and conduct; discipleship and ethics; personal conviction and social seriousness—these are inseparables. What is needed in order to determine the relationship between religions is therefore "a calculus for determining the *practical* value of each religion"; the need is for "a clear statement of the *practical* relationship of Christianity to the other great religions".[9] The matters in which Christianity differs from other religions are "of supreme *practical* value and significance for the life of man".[1]

An interesting supplementary illustration of this element in Far-

---

[6] *Crown*, p. 349.

[7] Farquhar never actually called in question the *fact* of the resurrection of Christ. He did however tend to remove it from the sphere of objective reality to the sphere of moral apprehension. "To believe in the Resurrection of Jesus is an act of faith of the purest, noblest and most fruitful type", *The College St. Matthew* (1912), p. 174.

[8] *Crown*, p. 63.

[9] *Crown*, p. 15.

[1] *Crown*, p. 31.

quhar's thought is provided by a series of lectures, *The Approach of Christ to Modern India,* delivered by Farquhar in India while working on *The Crown of Hinduism.*[2] In these lectures Christ is represented as a social reformer and servant, a man, teaching and healing the soul. This is a conscious adaptation of the Christian message to the needs of modern India: again we find emphasis placed on the typically Indian concerns, reform, the overcoming of poverty, the uplift of the depressed classes, and the like. In fact Farquhar advises his hearers to "run through the Gospels as you would run through any modern text-book", marking those passages having a bearing on social service and social reform.[3] And after having described Christ the working man, Christ the patriot, Christ the hero-saint ("precisely the type of leading spirit Hindus need to-day")[4] and Christ the teacher and healer, Farquhar concludes:

It is surely true ... that the considerations urged afford sufficient reason for believing that the thoughtful study of His life and teaching cannot but be of large practical value to the India of our day. In these circumstances what will the true Indian patriot do?[5]

Summing up, this we have found in *The Crown of Hinduism*: an overriding emphasis on the humanity of Christ, on the moral basis of the message he proclaimed, and on the exemplary value of his life and death in self-sacrifice; a large stress on the practical basis of religion, motivated, no doubt, partly by apologetical considerations. To this may be added the view of conversion as "an act of will, in which the man surrenders himself completely, gives up the citadel of his being to Christ, that henceforward he may obey Christ in all things".[6] As we have already pointed out, acceptance by God depends on a man's "utter sincerity, the turning of his whole soul towards the light, the frank acceptance of truth into his heart ...".[7] Having been shown the highest, the Hindu must accept Christ or make "the great refusal".[8] That man is capable of such an act of will is because he is made in the image of God, "fit for the immediate, personal, spiritual intercourse of a son with his Heavenly Father"—

---

[2] Cf. also his lecture on *Civic Virtues,* delivered in the Government College, Lahore, in December 1912.

[3] *The Approach of Christ to Modern India* (1913), p. 21.

[4] *Ibid.,* p. 28.

[5] *Ibid.,* p. 47.

[6] *Crown,* p. 282.

[7] *Crown,* p. 27.

[8] *Crown,* p. 28.

a possibility open to every man, woman and child, irrespective of background.[9]

It must however be pointed out that there is a great deal which is *not* to be found in *The Crown of Hinduism*. There is no treatment of the question of sin and its effects on man's relationship with his Creator; no real treatment of the themes of atonement, forgiveness, reconciliation and salvation; the work of Christ is subordinated to the life and teaching of Christ; there is no eschatology; no mention of the Church as "the communion of saints", even where it might seem most motivated, in the chapter on "The Religious Organism" (Ch. XI). And while it is no part of our purpose to pass theological judgment on the Christianity put forward by Farquhar as "the Crown of Hinduism", a comparison with, for example, the theological writings of Farquhar's fellow-Congregationalist and fellow-Aberdonian P. T. Forsyth would reveal Farquhar occupying most of the positions against which Forsyth was polemizing most energetically when he wrote that "undogmatic Christianity is foreign, false and fatal to any church".[1]

Comment and Debate

The second aspect in which *The Crown of Hinduism* may be considered is as an expression of contemporary missionary opinion on the subject of Christian-Hindu relations. The book had a mixed reception, and we may take the debate attending its publication as an indication of the climate of missionary opinion on the subject of Christian-Hindu relations as it was at the outbreak of the first world war.

We have already had occasion to discuss the reaction of other schools of missionary thought to the basic ideas of *The Crown of Hinduism*, and in particular to the concept of "fulfilment". Objections were, as we have seen, forthcoming from a number of different directions; as far as the Protestant missionary force was concerned, there were three basic sources of criticism. First, from the

---

[9] *Crown*, p. 120.

[1] Forsyth, *The Person and Place of Jesus Christ* (1909, 6th ed. 1948), p. 30. The essentials of Forsyth's position will be found in this and two other books, *The Cruciality of the Cross* (1909, 4th imp. 1957), and *The Work of Christ* (1910, 6th imp. 1958). On Forsyth's theology, see most recently Hunter, *Teaching and Preaching the New Testament* (1963), pp. 131 ff.

conservative Evangelical missionaries, who objected to the use of the term "evolution", and to the bringing of the findings of "comparative religion" to bear on missionary matters. Here, too, there was still a tendency, conditioned by the situation in which many missionaries were working, to judge Hinduism by its lowest manifestations, and to be impatient of its higher forms, which were believed to be something other than the religion of the mass of the people. This reaction was most clearly marked in the *Indian Witness* debate of 1912. Secondly, there was a tendency—though still no more than a tendency—to relativize the Christian message, or at least to call for a rethinking of the whole of the missionary enterprise over against Hinduism. One expression of this is to be seen in the school of thought around C. F. Andrews, another in the group of which typical representatives were E. P. Rice and Bernard Lucas of the L.M.S. Here the reaction against theological and dogmatic thinking was carried to considerable extremes. And thirdly, there was the isolated criticism put forward by A. G. Hogg in the Edinburgh material—a theological and philosophical criticism in which the concept of "fulfilment" was called in question as being vague, abstract and inadequate.

The reception given to *The Crown of Hinduism* reflected in some measure all of these divergent positions, though the second (that which we have called "the liberal approach") put forward little explicit criticism. But at the same time it seems that those who actively criticized the book were in the minority. One reason is perhaps the fact that the *Indian Witness* debate had taken place comparatively recently, and the conservative missionaries had no really new criticisms to make.[2] And the liberal approach was as yet more marked outside the missions than inside.[3] Those who, like Lucas, were calling for a transformation of missionary methods,[4] found in *The Crown of Hinduism* little real support, since the book was written not to advocate new methods but to stress the need for a new *attitude*; its purpose was rather one of justification of the existing missionary enterprise in face of changed conditions, and this was widely accepted, being warmly welcomed by the

---

[2] On the *Indian Witness* debate, see above, pp. 309 ff.

[3] *Crown*, pp. 20 ff.

[4] Expressed in his books *The Empire of Christ* (1907) and *Our Task in India* (1914). Cf. above, p. 324 f.

majority. We must however examine briefly some of the dissenting opinions, as put forward by a conservative (Mackichan) and by Hogg, after which we shall look at the reactions of some of Farquhar's associates, and the course of the later debate aroused primarily by Mackichan's criticism.

1. *Conservative criticism*

We have said that the *Indian Witness* debate blunted the force of the conservative Evangelical missionaries' criticism of *The Crown of Hinduism*. Criticism was however forthcoming from substantially this direction. An article in the *International Review of Missions,* by Principal D. Mackichan of Wilson College, Bombay (United Free Church of Scotland), took up to discussion the fundamental idea of "Christ the fulfiller of Hinduism", and dissented sharply, not so much from Farquhar's findings, as from the argument behind them.

Mackichan's attitude to Farquhar's work seems at first sight ambiguous. At the Edinburgh conference of 1910 he had shown himself to be largely in sympathy with the religious strivings of Hinduism, and had even spoken of Christ as the one "who fulfils the desire and the striving of the soul, one who in the truest sense meets the soul's human need".[5] It will be clear that this view was in line with Farquhar's own opinions.[6] Nevertheless Mackichan's article took the form of a sharp attack, less (or so he claimed) on the views of individuals than on "a mental attitude which has scarcely passed ... into the region of definite conclusion".[7] This was the mental attitude of the "fulfilment" school, of which Farquhar was the leader. Mackichan claimed not to be an iconoclast (a claim borne out by his Edinburgh address), but at the same time he was opposed to what he called "facile adaptation". This he believed to be the fault of the "fulfilment" school: that they had postulated an evolutionary connexion between Christianity and religious beliefs and practices having nothing whatever in common with the moral and ethical Gospel. Hindu beliefs, he argued, being based on abstract metaphysical speculation, could not possible lead to genuine spirituality,

---

[5] World Missionary Conference, 1910: *Report of Commission IV*, p. 320.

[6] Above, pp. 200, 281, 311 f.

[7] Mackichan, "A Present-day Phase of Missionary Theology", in *IRM* III (1914), pp. 243–254. The quotation is from p. 243.

which is ethical in origin and manifestation.[8] Sympathy with the religious needs revealed in Hinduism is one thing; placing Christianity in some form of positive evolutionary relationship to Hinduism another. The first Mackichan could admit: the second he rejected outright. The "motto" of the "fulfilment" school (Matt. 5.17), claimed Mackichan, refers only to the partial revelation contained in Judaism; it has nothing to do with Hinduism, or with any other non-Christian religion, none of which can be regarded as "steps in a development that finds its culmination in the religion of Jesus Christ".[9] The very title of Farquhar's book jars, because "the crown" is Christianity. This Mackichan held to be irrelevant and contradictory. Christ, he stressed, is *not* the "crown" of Hinduism; such a claim misrepresents the Christian message and is misleading to the mind of India. And the method he considered to be no more than a sign of immaturity and impatience in those who had accepted it.

In effect, Mackichan's criticism provides further evidence of that attitude which we have already noted in the Edinburgh material and in the *Indian Witness* debate, and which Farquhar had taken up in 1909 as a separate stage in the development of Christian apologetics in India—a stage he wanted to see superseded.[1] It might perhaps be characterized as a willingness to try and see the best in Hinduism, to pick out the truth in Hinduism, to sympathize with the quests of Hinduism, but to go no further. The necessity of a sympathetic approach to Hinduism; a conviction of the unconditional superiority (particularly in the ethical and moral spheres) of Christianity over Hinduism; the awareness that replacement of Hinduism by Christianity was the goal of missionary work: on all these points Mackichan and Farquhar shared substantially the same position. But the use of the term "evolution" was a different matter. The evolutionary position was anathema to the conservative Evangelical mind *a priori*: hence Mackichan's attack.

This was the only severe criticism from this direction at this stage, though slighter criticisms were forthcoming from a number of other directions. Thus the S.P.G. journal *The East and the West,* while

---

[8] *Ibid.,* p. 250.
[9] *Ibid.,* p. 248.
[1] *Report of the Conference of the World's Student Christian Federation held at Oxford, England* (1909), p. 71.

stating that the book would almost certainly appeal to a wider circle of readers than Slater's *Higher Hinduism*,[2] suggested that the optimistic character of the book as a whole was due to the fact that Farquhar had had little contact with popular Hinduism, since his work had lain chiefly among "Indian students and the more cultured representatives of Hinduism".[3] The inference was one previously made by conservatives, that closer contact with the earthy realities of Hindu life on another level might well have modified Farquhar's opinions on a number of points.

Continental critics had little to say about *The Crown of Hinduism*. The shadow of war was already spreading over Europe by the time the book came out, and the theological dialogue, already slight, was on the verge of being broken off altogether. Johannes Warneck, whom we have already seen to have been a defender of the Edinburgh findings,[4] was generally appreciative, though not prepared to accept Farquhar's application of the concept of "fulfilment".[5] And a writer (E.H.) in the Basel Mission's *Evangelisches Missions-Magazin*, while pointing out that Farquhar seemed not to be acquainted with the German literature on the subject, acknowledged that "Als Handbuch für die Auseinandersetzung mit gebildeten Hindu kann Farquhars Buch ausgezeichnete Dienste tun";[6] in two later articles the same writer discussed the whole question of the Christian approach to the Hindu, without however making any direct comment on Farquhar's book.[7] It is scarcely surprising that so little comment was forthcoming from this direction; since the climate of theological opinion in the confessional missions differed so widely from that of the British and American "liberals" and "liberal evangelicals", a meaningful exchange of ideas was difficult.

In Scandinavia, contact was rather better, though still subject to wide divergencies. A writer (K.L.) in *Svensk Missionstidskrift* felt that Farquhar's judgment on "idolatry" was capable of being mis-

---

[2] Above, p. 103.
[3] *The East and the West* XI: 44 (Oct. 1913), p. 469.
[4] Above, p. 295 f.
[5] *AMZ* 41 (1914), p. 361 f.
[6] *EMM* 57 N.F. (1913), p. 480.
[7] E. H., "Die Ueberwindung des Hinduismus durch das Evangelium", in *EMM* 58 N.F. (1914), pp. 294 ff., 340 ff. These articles stressed the "scandal" of the Cross as the only true basis of missionary preaching, but also emphasized the missionary's need to acquire a thorough knowledge of Hinduism, and to make the best possible use of his knowledge. "Können wir nicht aufbauen, so können wir ein anderes, wir können *anknüpfen*; und das *müssen* wir tun" (p. 340).

interpreted,[8] but also called Farquhar's approach in general "the only way both to understand Hinduism and to be understood by its adherents".[9]

2. A. G. Hogg's criticism

At Edinburgh, we saw how A. G. Hogg, on the basis of a consistent and distinctive theological position, had criticized the concept of "fulfilment", advocating instead an effort to reach "selective contrast" or, as he later expressed it "a challenging relevancy", aimed at penetrating to the essentials of the Christian and Hindu positions respectively.[1] Hogg published two reviews of *The Crown of Hinduism,* one in the *Madras Christian College Magazine* and the other in the *International Review of Missions,* in which he renewed his earlier criticism, and in so doing provided what was really the only contemporary theological criticism of Farquhar's book.[2]

Hogg's review in the Madras journal is subdued in tone, and one cannot escape the feeling of latent criticism even here. The idea of Christianity as "the Crown of Hinduism", wrote Hogg, is not "flung at the reader's head as a foregone conclusion".[3] Instead it is based on scholarly historical analysis. Nor is it to be ruled out as incredible *a priori.* It might perhaps have deserved such treatment, had Farquhar postulated "the formulated theology of Christendom" as the crown of Hinduism. But what he puts forward is not this, but "Christ and His profound simple message as found in the Gospels".[4] Hogg concludes that Farquhar's answer has no right to be pronounced absurd, and recommends all who are looking elsewhere than to Christ for the solution of India's problems at least to read Farquhar's argument and judge of its worth for themselves.

We have already seen that Hogg was critical of the idea of "fulfilment".[5] But on this occasion, writing for a general public, he was evidently not disposed to bring the full force of his criticism

---

[8] The passage to which the reviewer is referring is that on p. 341 in *The Crown of Hinduism*: "The use of idols is thus completely justified in the case of men who really believe in them."

[9] *SMT* 1: 6 (1913), p. 284: "... i det stora hela måste man ge författaren rätt. Detta är nog den enda vägen både att förstå hinduismen och blifva förstådd af dess anhängare."

[1] Above, pp. 284 ff.

[2] *MCCM* XIII: 8 (Feb. 1914), p. 423 f.; *IRM* III (1914), pp. 171 ff.

[3] *MCCM, loc. cit.*

[4] *Ibid.*

[5] Cf. above, p. 289.

to bear on *The Crown of Hinduism*. In the *International Review of Missions,* however, he repeated something of his former criticism.

Hogg first confirmed that his view of Farquhar's book was very far indeed from being wholly negative. Indeed it was "a distinguished book ... a book to be depended on; its impressive argument rests on a solid basis".[6] But having said this, he went on to give his opinion that "Mr. Farquhar does not seem to be at his best in theology".[7] The point was, as at Edinburgh, the idea of "fulfilment": what exactly is "fulfilled" by what? Does the "fulfilment" hypothesis in fact provide the basis for missionary work in India that Farquhar claimed? Hogg's view was that it did not.

He was prepared to allow that Farquhar had proved that the impact of Christ upon India had brought her to the point at which none but Christ could satisfy her need. But this was not the whole of Farquhar's view. And the idea of "fulfilment", as formulated by Farquhar, was in Hogg's view of little practical value: "... the claim that Christ is the crown of Hinduism is little more than a debating-point".[8] For if the theory be pressed, then it must be admitted, first, that in practice Christ leaves out a great deal of the content of Hinduism, and secondly, that he "fulfils" a great deal that was never in Hinduism; on this view, "Mr. Farquhar's tracing out of the aspect of fulfilment sometimes seems far-fetched".[9] Hogg went on to say that what Christ directly fulfils is *not* Hinduism, but a sense of need; and once that need has begun to be felt, India is no longer altogether Hindu. And he concluded:

In the first place, if Mr. Farquhar is right in his claim, then India ought always to have been hungry for Christ. But the reason why mission work is so slow of success is that we have first to be used to make India hungry for Christ before we can be used to give Christ to her. In the second place, we think that the message, "You need Christ now", is really more telling than "Christ fulfils your old religion". The latter message can hardly be freed from condescension.[1]

The full implications of this criticism are very far-reaching indeed, touching as they do the very heart of the problem of communica-

---

[6] *IRM* (1914), p. 171.

[7] *Ibid.*, p. 172.

[8] *Ibid.*

[9] *Ibid.*

[1] The charge of "condescension" was later levelled at Farquhar's work by Kraemer, in *Religion and the Christian Faith* (1956), p. 215. Cf. also Radhakrishnan, *East and West in Religion* (1933), p. 24.

tion. Hogg was later to work out his own theory in a series of articles in the *International Review of Missions*, and thirty years later in a group of lectures published as *The Christian Message to the Hindu*.[2] These articles and lectures, which have not received the attention they deserve from missionary scholars, cannot however be considered in this context. The development of Hogg's missionary thought, from *Karma and Redemption* to *The Christian Message to the Hindu*, together with his work in connexion with the conferences of 1910, 1928 and 1938, would provide a fruitful field of specialist study.

3. *Other missionary comment*

So far in this section we have been concerned only with criticism of *The Crown of Hinduism* from those occupying theological positions different from that held by Farquhar himself. There was, however, a warm and positive response from his immediate fellow-workers in India, those who shared more or less the same presuppositions and who were placed in substantially the same apologetical position.

K. J. Saunders, whom we have seen to have been an authority on Buddhism,[3] wrote congratulating Farquhar on the publication of his book, and calling it "the greatest bit of apologetic I know".[4] Garfield Williams, of the Church of England St. John's College in Agra, wrote: "It is a long way the finest thing I have read in the way of missionary apologetics. In my opinion it stands absolutely in a class by itself."[5] Rather surprisingly, the *Indian Interpreter*, which for some years had been following an almost identical line under the guidance of Nicol Macnicol, engaged a reviewer (V. A. Sukhtankar) who could only comment that "the crown of Hinduism [in Farquhar's book] is Christianity—and Christianity of a pretty orthodox type".[6] It seems likely that Sukhtankar was himself a Hindu: at all events he concentrated in his review almost entirely on the Hindu material. But one of the leading Hindu newspapers in

[2] Hogg, "The God that must needs be Christ Jesus", in *IRM* VI (1917), pp. 62–73, 221–32, 383–94 and 521–33; *idem*, *The Christian Message to the Hindu* (1947). Cf. above, p. 291 n. 8.

[3] Above, p. 320 f.

[4] Quoted by Farquhar in a letter to J. R. Mott, 15.3.1914 (YMCA Hist. Lib.).

[5] Garfield Williams to Farquhar, 22.3.1914 (YMCA Hist. Lib.).

[6] *Ind. Interp.* VIII: 4 (Jan. 1914), p. 171.

India, which had long had a reputation for being unsympathetic towards Christian missions, said that no one could read the book without feeling that Christianity would probably influence the religious life of India more than the writer had thought possible.[7]

In Britain, a writer in the *Aberdeen Free Press* (very possibly D. S. Cairns) gave *The Crown of Hinduism* an excellent review, saying that it would place Farquhar in the front rank of writers on religion, and especially on the religions of India, and concluded: "... this is an important work, deserving careful study".[8] And the *Student Movement* reviewer (Canon Waller of the C.M.S.), wrote: "The call is for a constructive study of religion, and it is because Mr. Farquhar has given us this in his 'Crown of Hinduism' that we hail his book as marking an epoch in the study."[9]

4. Debate, 1914–1915

Principal Mackichan's article in criticism of *The Crown of Hinduism*, which we have considered above,[1] called forth a debate, covering some of the ground already covered by the *Indian Witness* debate, though this time in a more representative forum. The discussion, though it began in the *International Review of Missions*, continued in the *Harvest Field*, in a review of Farquhar's book by W. E. Tomlinson. Tomlinson's position was much the same as Mackichan's. He was largely positive, but was reluctant to accept the "fulfilment" hypothesis in its entirety. He also offered a partial defence of the iconoclastic attitude, claiming that "a work of destruction must needs first be done before Christ can be set forth as the fulfilment of India's desire to see God".[2]

In 1912, Farquhar had been unable to take any active part in the *Indian Witness* debate. Now, however, he was given the opportunity of answering some of his critics, principally Mackichan, in the *International Review of Missions*. In his answer he discussed the principles on which *The Crown of Hinduism* had been based.

---

[7] Quoted in Farquhar's Quarterly Report Letter, dated 27.12.1913 (Farquhar collection).

[8] Large sections of this review, which is mainly a summary of the argument of the book, are copied *verbatim* in Farquhar's Report for 1913, p. 527 f. (YMCA Hist. Lib.). No indication of author is given.

[9] Appended by Farquhar to his letter to Mott, 15.3.1914. E. H. M. Waller later became Bishop of Tinnevelly (1914–23) and Madras (1923–41).

[1] Above, p. 347 f.

[2] Review in *HF* XXXIV: 1 (Jan. 1914), p. 11.

He was most concerned to stress the urgency of finding an adequate way of stating the relationship of Christianity to Hinduism. "The time has come", he wrote, "when the Christian Church must set the finest scholarship and the most penetrating thought she controls to the solution of the problem of the relation in which Christianity stands to Hinduism."[3]

On the subject of the term "fulfilment", Farquhar pointed out significantly that it was not merely a matter of an inadequate synonym for "evolution". The idea contained in the Gospel account is rather that men are brought by Jesus to the final truth of God; and only in this light are they able to see the imperfections of their own religions, and to find in him their completion.[4] The crux is empirical: the coming of Christianity to India has done much to show up the weaknesses of Hinduism, but has also provided a standard by which its better parts are to be judged. Farquhar was concerned to stress that not every element in the old religion neces-sarily reappears in the new. To those who argued that it was better not to discuss the "best" in Hinduism in the presence of Hindus he answered that obscurantism of this kind was of no value to the Christian cause: truth was of more importance. "The last thing Hindus wish us to say is that it is necessary to give up Hinduism and accept Christianity; and that is the very foundation of the principle of fulfilment."[5]

This bears out what we have been saying about the concept of "fulfilment" implying "replacement": the replacement of Hinduism by Christianity.[6] Not the replacement of the Christian Gospel, as Farquhar knew it. It had seemed to some that he was advocating a new message, whereas his intention was more to create a new *attitude* in the mind of the missionary. He held fast to his view that theories of Christian-Hindu relations, whatever their provenance, were un-conditionally to be kept in the background of missionary work: they were under no circumstances to be used in preaching. At most they could provide an intellectual foundation with the help of which the missionary might shape his message:

---

[3] Farquhar, "The Relation of Christianity to Hinduism", in *IRM* III (1914), pp. 417–31. The quotation is from p. 419.
[4] *Ibid.*, p. 427: "When Jesus used the term fulfilment, he did not mean that the Jews, if left to themselves, would have reached His teaching in the ordinary course of evolution ..."
[5] *Ibid.*, p. 428.
[6] Above, p. 336.

The movement to relate Christianity to Hinduism [he wrote] is an intellectual necessity, necessary for the missionary himself, for all who are interested in the missionary movement, for the inquiring Hindu, and for the intelligent convert. No one proposes to use it instead of the Gospel. The idea is seldom if ever used in religious addresses to Hindus.[7]

Farquhar concluded his article by declining to set up his own work as the touch-stone by which the new movement in missionary thought was to be judged. He was very conscious of being a pioneer, he wrote, and the meagreness or apparent fancifulness of his results ought not to be used to condemn the theory as such.[8]

Further comment was soon forthcoming, though no new ground was broken. The Editor of the *Harvest Field* (H. Gulliford), wrote a leading article in which he called in question the validity of Farquhar's position.[9] Gulliford was prepared, like Mackichan, to allow that Christ might be called the "fulfiller" of the best aspects of Hinduism, but not of the practices of popular Hinduism.[1] Christ may "fulfil" needs; but Gulliford was convinced that Hinduism manifestly failed to meet any need whatever. Judaism could be "fulfilled" because Judaism, though incomplete, was ethically sound; Hinduism is essentially unsound, and therefore the only relationship permissible is one of contrast.

Bernard Lucas, who, as we have seen, had already shown himself critical of traditional missionary methods, and is to be reckoned as belonging to the left wing of missionary opinion in India at the time,[2] took up the debate in Farquhar's favour in the following number of the *Harvest Field*. Lucas disagreed completely with the reasons given by both Mackichan and Gulliford for the refusal to accept the idea of "fulfilment". Their argument that the validity of the concept was limited to the relationship of Christianity and Judaism, Lucas regarded as being in absolute conflict with any true exegesis of Matt. 5.17.[3] He went further, accusing Farquhar's critics of entirely misinterpreting "those who adopt the words of Christ

---

[7] *IRM* (1914), p. 429.

[8] *Ibid.*, p. 430.

[9] *HF* XXXIV: 10 (Oct. 1914), pp. 364 ff.

[1] *Ibid.*, p. 364: "We thoroughly believe in applying the principle of 'fulfilment' as far as it can legitimately be employed, and there is ample scope for its application if knowledge and wisdom are exercised." But—"... in what we regard as the essentials of Hinduism ... Jesus Christ has neither part nor lot" (p. 368 f.).

[2] Above, p. 324 f.

[3] Lucas, "Not to Destroy, but to Fulfil", in *HF* XXXIV: 11 (Nov. 1914), p. 424.

as the motto of their school of thought".[4] At the same time, he was insistent that Christianity *as a system* did not fulfil Hinduism *as a system*.[5] "Systems" must be eliminated from the argument altogether. *Christianity,* claimed Lucas, is not yet the fulfilment of Hinduism, and it is premature to try and represent it as though it were. Just as the Gospels precede the Epistles (*sic*) the preaching of the Gospel in India must precede the presentation of "theological Christianity" to the Indian mind.[6] This retreat from theological Christianity is, as we have seen, a typical feature of the period; it is to be seen to a large extent in Farquhar himself, in C. F. Andrews,[7] and in others; among its critics was A. G. Hogg.[8]

In reply to Lucas a German missionary, Christoph Wohlenberg of the Schleswig-Holstein Evangelical Lutheran Missionary Society, stressed that what was wanted was a correct exegesis of Matt. 5.17; Lucas' interpretation he rejected.[9] Lucas answered that the whole text and context were of immeasurably greater importance than the correct linguistic interpretation of the verb *plērōmai,* since words do not necessarily carry the same meaning every time they occur, and asked whether Wohlenberg had ever heard of progressive revelation?[1] Another criticism of Lucas, this time by Gulliford, was that he had not attempted to define what he meant by "Hinduism". Lucas answered that Hinduism was "the religion of the Hindus, as it has been developed and nurtured by the Hindu Scriptures".[2] Gulliford was naturally unable to accept such a vague definition, and concluded that his differences with Lucas were so fundamental that further discussion was a waste of time.[3]

---

[4] *Ibid.,* p. 425.

[5] *Ibid.* This same observation was made by Hogg, but for different reasons.

[6] *Ibid.,* p. 427. Lucas had previously distinguished between "Christianity" and "Christian theology", writing that "We are bound to give the one, we are prohibited from imposing the other. To bestow the one is to evangelize in the truest sense; to impose the other is to proselytize in the worst sense." *The Empire of Christ* (1907), p. 71. Cf. *idem, Our Task in India* (1914), p. 120: "We must no more endow the Indian Church with our theology than with our money."

[7] In Andrews' case there was also a marked retreat from his earlier Anglican ecclesiology. For a summary of Andrews' later view, see his book *The Sermon on the Mount* (1942).

[8] Above, p. 291.

[9] *HF* XXXIV: 12 (Dec. 1914), p. 456.

[1] *HF* XXXV: 2 (Feb. 1915), p. 64.

[2] *Ibid.,* p. 67.

[3] *Ibid.,* p. 70: "Our difference with Mr. Lucas is fundamental. We do not place the revelation contained in the Hebrew and Christian Scriptures on the same plane as that contained in 'the Hindu Scriptures', as that term is generally

This was to all intents and purposes the end of the public debate, apart from two slight contributions to the *Harvest Field* in which it was concluded that the whole question was doctrinaire,[4] and a final letter from Farquhar.[5]

Farquhar pointed out once more that while it was a primary duty of the missionary to study Hinduism, it should be a matter of policy to "say nothing about it" in ordinary preaching and teaching.[6] But—and this was of the essence of the apologetical situation—it is not always possible to avoid mentioning it. Direct attacks are made by non-Christians; serious inquirers come to the missionary for guidance; men on the point of baptism wonder what attitude to take towards the religion they are on the point of leaving; and the missionary himself may be in doubt as to what attitude to adopt.[7]

Sympathy, he went on to say, is not enough; some theory of relationship there must be; and *The Crown of Hinduism*, with its concept of "Christianity the fulfilment of Hinduism", was an attempt to provide guidance for those who required it. Criticism of his views, he stressed, had so far been almost entirely negative; no alternative theory had been suggested. And he concluded:

I have no desire to represent the Fulfilment hypothesis as a revelation from heaven or as a postulate of reason. It is to my mind merely the best hypothesis which has yet been suggested, a hypothesis to be tried and tested by all the relevant facts. I have read with interest all that has been said in criticism of it, and have found much of it helpful. The more light that can be thrown on the question from experience the better.[8]

Here we bring to a close our account of the development of Farquhar's missionary thought. There remains only to say a few words about the course of events after this date.

---

accepted, nor do we regard 'the religion of the Hindus', as commonly practised, likely to lead them to a knowledge of the true God and Jesus Christ whom He has sent. Discussion therefore is impossible."

[4] Editorial, and Tomlinson, "An Evangelistic Experiment", in *HF* XXXV: 4 (April 1915), particularly p. 126 f.

[5] Letter dated 3.6.1915, in *HF* XXXV: 8 (August 1915), pp. 315–17.

[6] This was not the first time Farquhar had made this observation; cf. *Missionary Study of Hinduism* (1905), p. 3: "Let us realize that, while every Missionary ought to study Hinduism as much as he possibly can, yet in ninety-nine hundredths of his work he ought to keep his knowledge strictly in the background."

[7] Farquhar, letter 3.6.1915, *HF* (August 1915), p. 315 f.

[8] *Ibid.*, p. 317.

After 1914

What we might call the "effect" of the attitude expounded in *The Crown of Hinduism* is not a subject we can go into here, but what it was may perhaps be gauged from the words of A. J. Boyd, that the concept of "fulfilment" came to be widely accepted, and "became for a time almost the accepted orthodoxy for large numbers of thoughtful Christians, both Asian and Western",[9] but that "it was often ambiguously stated, and needed both clarification and criticism".[1]

There is little real ambiguity in Farquhar's use of the term, either in *The Crown of Hinduism* or in his earlier work, provided that we keep in mind its various facets, and in particular the cardinal point that fulfilment involved replacement, and took place by the active exercise of the human will in passing from one religion to another, in which the needs expressed in the former could be fully satisfied. But this is far from saying that all those who in later years took up the motto did so in full awareness of all its implications. That semantic confusion was likely must be admitted. The *word* "fulfilment" admits of many interpretations, and has indeed been used in a number of different ways since Farquhar's day.[2] Thus when we read in a book by an Indian Christian that the followers of Farquhar were nicknamed "universalists" by their opponents, and "used to contend that Christ came to dot the 'i's and cross the 't's of every religion",[3] we suspect that a large measure of misunderstanding had come to be associated with the use of the word in Indian missions after the war. But Farquhar's position must not be confused with that extreme liberal position which later came to be expressed in the "laymen's report" *Re-thinking Missions* (1932).

There remains, therefore, a considerable work of historical examination to be carried out on the literature and debates of the post-war period, with a view to tracing the later use of the concept of "fulfilment", the attitudes it presupposed, and the theology on which it was built, in the Indian context. *The Crown of Hinduism* we have described as "an experiment in apologetics"—an experiment carried on in the series of books, notably *The Religious Quest of*

[9] Boyd, *Christian Encounter* (1961), p. 74.

[1] *Ibid.*

[2] See e.g. Hebert, *Liturgy and Society* (1935, paperback ed. 1961), pp. 45 ff., Zaehner, *At Sundry Times* (1958), pp. 173, 180.

[3] Immanuel, *The Influence of Hinduism on Indian Christians* (1950), p. 133.

India series, edited by Farquhar during the remainder of his time in India. These, too, made wide use of the concept and exercised wide influence, but belong rather to the post-war than to the pre-war period. This later period we have however not felt able to consider in this present work, for a number of reasons.

First, because of the distinct change in the climate of opinion in India which came about during and after the first world war, particularly in respect of the nationalist movement and its religious affiliations. Secondly, because of the far-reaching changes which took place in Protestant Christian theology and missionary practice during the same period: the emergence of a new Evangelical theology on the Continent, and to some extent also in the English-speaking world; the growing participation of Continental theologians in the international missionary debate, with a consequent break-up of what was previously a fairly homogeneous body of opinion, dominated by British and American influence; and the reorientation in the thought of some of the international missionary leaders which took place after the war—Mott, Eddy and Oldham were three notable examples. To this must be added, thirdly, the changing emphasis in Indian missions—from evangelism on an individualist basis to the establishment of an Indian Church; from the Western missionary to the Indian theologian and churchman; from the atomistic evangelization of educated Indians to the establishment of the local church in the Indian community. And in the Y.M.C.A., from Western to Indian leadership, from evangelism to social service. Of scarcely less importance was, fourthly, the change which came about in the matter of the study of the religions of the world. The concept of religious evolution, and with it the idea of "comparative religion", were discarded and replaced by the more accurate "history of religions" and "phenomenology of religion". This was to call most seriously in question the entire foundation of the work of a whole generation of scholars, inside as well as outside the missions, and to place the problems with which they had wrestled in an entirely new light.

The task of historical inquiry must however be continued: only when it has been done will there be available an overall picture of the course taken by Christian apologetics and Christian evangelism in the Hindu context between the wars. It will involve an examination of the factors we have mentioned above, as reflected in books, articles, letters and reports of Western missionaries. It will also involve an examination of emergent Indian theology, as written in English (for example by the Chakkarai-Chenchiah-Appasamy group), and, ideally, in the leading vernaculars as well. It will call for a thorough consideration of the changing face of Hinduism, and how Christian observers set about studying and interpreting its many phenomena; and of the reactions of Indian Christians and missionaries to the religious aspects of the nationalist movement in its post-war guise. There will be many names calling for consideration: Farquhar himself, whose Indian missionary career did not come to an end until 1923; A. G. Hogg, who remained in India until the beginning of 1939; Macnicol, Larsen and Andrews, whom we have mentioned here. And others who belong to the inter-war period: Stanley Jones, W. S. Urquhart, John McKenzie, J. C. Winslow, H. W. Schomerus, E. C. Dewick, H. A. Popley, Karl Hartenstein—to name only a few. The international leaders, notably Mott, Oldham and William Paton, must be considered. And the question of Farquhar's continued influence must be reckoned with throughout.

We have seen that Farquhar's emphasis was threefold. He insisted that the missionary, in his attitude to Hinduism, must show sympathy first of all; secondly, that all his work on Hinduism, or any other non-Christian religion, must be scientifically accurate; and thirdly, that he must be uncompromising in his loyalty to Christ.

The first two of his requirements—sympathy and accuracy—have ever since Farquhar's day be recognized as essentials. It is the third—loyalty to Christ—which has given rise to difficulties. What exactly is meant by "loyalty" in this context? Farquhar, attempting as he did to come to terms with missionary problems as he understood them, the problems of the India of his day, answered this question as a historian, as a *Religionsgeschichtlicher,* as a man convinced of the claims of the social conscience, or—in later terms—as a "liberal" (Farquhar would have said "liberal evangelical"). The task now is for missionary scholars to lay bare the thought of a later age on these large questions. But while this is done, and while Farquhar's influence persists, it would be well to remember that although he claimed that Christ was "the Crown of the faith of India",[4] he also wrote that

Hinduism must die into Christianity, in order that the best her philosophers, saints and ascetics have longed and prayed for may live.[5]

---

[4] *Crown*, p. 458.
[5] Farquhar, "Brāhma Samāj", in *ERE* II (1909), p. 824.

Abbreviations

AMZ	Allgemeine Missions-Zeitschrift
CMI	Church Missionary Intelligencer
CMR	Church Missionary Review
CR	Contemporary Review
EB	Encyclopaedia Britannica
EMM	Evangelisches Missions-Magazin
ERE	Encyclopaedia of Religion and Ethics
FM	Foreign Mail
HF	Harvest Field
IRM	International Review of Missions
IW	Indian Witness
MCCM	Madras Christian College Magazine
MH	Missionary Herald
NCCR	National Christian Council Review
NMT	Nordisk Missions-Tidsskrift
SMT	Svensk Missionstidskrift
YMI	Young Men of India

Names of other journals, etc., are either shortened or given in full.

Bibliography

A. Unpublished Sources

1. *The Farquhar collection* (lent by Mrs. M. I. G. Dibben, Sutton-in-Ashfield, England)

J. N. Farquhar's own copies of his books, pamphlets, offprints and proof sheets. Some annotated.
Personal diary and notebook, 1907.
Loose pages from Quarterly Report Letter, 1911.
Letters from and to Baron F. von Hügel, 1921.
Letter to Mott, 1923.
Letters and papers relative to appointment to the Chair of Comparative Religion: Manchester, 1923.
Letters and papers relative to award of Aberdeen D.D., 1926.
Letters and papers relative to Wilde Lectureship, Oxford, 1927.
Papers relative to Electorship to Boden Chair of Sanskrit, Oxford, 1928.
Manchester lecture notes in comparative religion, 1928–1929.
Letters of condolence to Mrs. E. N. M. Farquhar on J. N. Farquhar's death, 1929.
Obituary notices, 1929.

2. *The Hogg collection* (lent by Mrs. L. A. Hogg, Edinburgh, Scotland)

A. G. Hogg's own copies of books, pamphlets, offprints and articles.
Letters to A. G. Hogg from D. S. Cairns, 1909–1920.
Madras Christian College lecture notes, undated.
Bible class notes, undated.
Miscellaneous correspondence, 1938–1945.
Manuscript sermons, mostly from period after 1939.

3. *Professor David Cairns, Aberdeen*

Letter from D. S. Cairns to his father, the Rev. D. Cairns, 1890.
Letters from A. G. Hogg to D. S. Cairns, 1904–1905.
Letter from H. R. Mackintosh to D. S. Cairns, 1909.
Letter from J. Warneck to D. S. Cairns, 1910.

4. *The Archives of the London Missionary Society*

a. T. E. SLATER

Letters to Foreign Secretary of the LMS, in *Letters Received, S. India, Tamil*, Boxes 15 (1870–1874), 16 (1875–1880) and 17 (1881–1885).

b. J. N. Farquhar

Candidature papers and letters, in *Candidates' Papers,* Box 5 (1796–1899), Du-Fr, No. 909.

Letters to Foreign Secretary of the LMS and others, in *Letters Received, N. India, Bengal,* Boxes 16 (1889–1892), 17 (1893–1895), 18 (1896–1898), 19 (1899–1900) and 20 (1901–103).

Letters from Foreign Secretary of the LMS, in *Eastern Outgoing Letters,* Boxes 30 to 43 inclusive (July 4, 1890 – Dec. 5, 1902).

c. E. P. Rice and B. Lucas

Letters to Foreign Secretary of the LMS, in *Letters Received, S. India, Canarese,* Boxes 23 (1905–1907), 24 (1908–1911) and 25 (1912–1915).

Letters from Foreign Secretary of the LMS, in *Eastern Outgoing Letters,* Box 54 (Feb. 17, 1911 – April 4, 1912).

d. General

Committee Minutes, India, Box 5, Books 10 (July 8, 1895 – Nov. 13, 1899) and 11 (Jan. 8, 1900 – July 10, 1905); Box 6, Book 13 (Jan. 11, 1910 – Jan. 13, 1914).

India Odds, Box 13.

Candidates' Papers, Box 20 (rejected candidates), Envelopes 49 and 50 [E. Evans].

5. *The Y.M.C.A. Historical Library, New York*

Annual Reports of Secretaries, sent to the International Committee. [These are contained in bound volumes of typescript, arranged chronologically and alphabetically, not by field.]

Reports consulted: J. N. Farquhar, 1902–1914.
　　　　　　　　　G. W. Sarvis, 1902.
　　　　　　　　　F. W. Steinthal, 1907.

Letters:　J. Campbell White to J. R. Mott, 1902.
　　　　　J. Campbell White, circular letter, 1902.
　　　　　J. N. Farquhar to Mott, 1902–1915.
　　　　　Farquhar to J. L. Macpherson (Toronto), 1904.
　　　　　Farquhar to F. J. Nichols, 1920.
　　　　　Farquhar to J. W. Lyon, 1920.
　　　　　Farquhar to E. C. Jenkins, 1921.
　　　　　Farquhar to F. V. Slack, 1923.

Copies of Letters:
　　　　　Mott to Farquhar, 1903–1910.
　　　　　G. S. Eddy to Mott, 1910.
　　　　　Garfield Williams to Farquhar, 1914.

Copy of an Address given to J. N. Farquhar at a reception given in his honour by the Prime Minister of the Mysore State, 1907.

Notes on the National Secretaries' Conference held in Yokohama, 1907.
Y.M.C.A. National Council Office Minutes, 1911.
Private Prospectus of the *Heritage of India* Series, undated.

6. *The Missionary Research Library, New York*

Manuscript answers sent in by missionary correspondents to Commissions I and IV of the World Missionary Conference, Edinburgh 1910. Stored alphabetically, cataloguing proceeding.
Copies of covering letters sent to correspondents with original questionnaires.

7. *Christ's College Library, Aberdeen*

Three bound volumes of typed copies of the manuscript answers sent in by missionary correspondents to Commission IV of the World Missionary Conference, Edinburgh 1910. Formerly the property of Principal D. S. Cairns. Volume on Islam and one of the two volumes on India missing. (Made available by Professor D. Cairns.)

8. *New College Library, Edinburgh*

Unpublished Ph.D. theses, presented in Edinburgh University:
DAVIS, W. B. *A Study of Missionary Policy and Methods in Bengal from 1793 to 1905* (1942).
KIRSCH, C. E. *The Theology of James Morison.* With Special Reference to his Theories of the Atonement (1939).
LOOS, A. W. *The Theology of A. M. Fairbairn* (1939).

9. *Archives of the Cambridge Mission to Delhi, London*

Folder entitled "Correspondence re Appointment of Prof. Rudra as Principal, 1907". Contains letters and memoranda by Bishop G. A. Lefroy, S. S. Allnutt, H. C. Carlyon, W. S. Kelly, F. J. Western and C. F. Andrews.

10. *Mansfield College Library, Oxford*

Correspondence on "Unevangelized Heathen, Everlasting Torments and Church Missions", between H. Shepheard and C. C. Lowndes (1866).

B. Literature

1. *General Works*

AAGAARD, J. "Evangelium og religion. Opfyldelse eller ophævelse?" in *SMT* 52 (1964), pp. 27 ff.
AALHOLT, P. "Den liberale teologi i den internationale missionsbevægelse", in *NMT* 75 (1964), pp. 11 ff., 85 ff.
ADAMSON, W. *The Life of the Rev. James Morison, D.D.* London 1898.
ALLEN, E. L. *Christianity among the Religions.* London 1961.

ANDERSEN, W. *Towards a Theology of Mission.* (IMC Research Pamphlet No. 2.) London 1955.

ANDREWS, C. F. "The Religious Basis of a National Movement", in the *Epiphany,* 17.8.1907, p. 125 f.

—— "A Missionary's Experience", in *Ind. Interp.* IV (1909), pp. 101 ff.

—— *The Renaissance in India.* London 1912.

—— *The Sermon on the Mount.* London 1942.

ANSTEY, J. C. K. "Mr. Farquhar's Zeal for the Kingdom", in *IW,* 21.5.1912, pp. 405 ff.

APPASAMY, A. J. "Dr. J. N. Farquhar", in *YMI* XLI (1929), pp. 684 ff.

AZARIAH, V. S. "Living Forces behind Mass Movements", in *IRM* XVIII (1929), pp. 509 ff.

—— *India and the Christian Movement.* Madras 1936.

BADLEY, B. H. *The Spiritual Possibilities of the Heathen.* Calcutta 1889.

—— "Does the Hindu Image point forward to Christ?" in *IW,* 4.6.1912, p. 447 f.

BALFOUR, E. (ed.). *Cyclopaedia of India.* 3rd ed. London 1885.

BANERJEA, J. R. "Mr. J. N. Farquhar on 'Christ and the Religions of the World' ", in *IW,* 28.5.1912, p. 429.

BANERJEA, K. M. *The Relation between Christianity and Hinduism.* (Oxford Mission Occasional Papers No. 1.) Calcutta s.a.

BARBER, B. R. "Mr. Mott's Visit to Calcutta", in *FM* IX: 2 (1902), pp. 27 ff.

BARROWS, J. S. (ed.). *World's Parliament of Religions I–II.* New York 1893.

BEACH, H. P. *A Geography and Atlas of Protestant Missions.* New York 1901.

—— *India and Christian Opportunity.* New York 1904.

BEARCE, G. D. *British Attitudes towards India 1784–1858.* Oxford 1961.

BERNARD, C. E. *A Christian University for India.* Madras 1889.

BESANT, A. *How India Wrought for Freedom.* The Story of the National Congress told from Official Records. Madras 1915.

BHAGAWAT, R. R. "Hindrances to the Spread of Christianity", in *Ind. Interp.* II (1907), pp. 17 ff.

BINDSLEV, C. *L. P. Larsen.* Hans Liv og Gerning. København 1945.

BODELSEN, C. A. *Studies in Mid-Victorian Imperialism.* København & London 1924.

BOHLIN, T. *Den kristna gudsrikestanken under 1800-talet och i nutiden.* Lund 1928.

BOSE, S. C. *The Hindoos as they are.* Calcutta 1883.

BOYD, A. J. *Christian Encounter.* Edinburgh 1961.

BRAUER, J. C. *Protestantism in America.* Philadelphia 1953.

BROWN, G. W. "The Modern View of Christianity and its Relations to Other Religions", in *IW,* 28.5.1912, p. 428.

BUCHAN, J. *Lord Minto.* A Memoir. London 1924.

BURTON, J. W. "Christian Missions as Affected by Liberal Theology", in *HF* XX (1909), pp. 66 ff.

CAIRNS, D. S. *Christianity in the Modern World.* 2nd ed. London 1907.

—— "The Need for Apologists", in the *Student World* IV (1911), pp. 49 ff.

—— *Life and Times of Alexander Robertson MacEwen, D.D.* London 1925.

—— *The Faith that Rebels.* A Re-examination of the Miracles of Jesus. London 1928.

—— "The Christian Message. A Comparison of Thought in 1910 and in 1928", in *IRM* XVIII (1929), pp. 321 ff.

[CAIRNS, D. S.] *David Cairns: An Autobiography.* Some Recollections of a Long Life, and Selected Letters, Edited by his Son and Daughter, with a Memoir by Professor D. M. Baillie. London 1950.

CALDWELL, R. *The Relation of Christianity to Hinduism.* London 1874.

[CALDWELL, R.] *Bishop Caldwell on Krishna and the Bhagavad Gita.* Madras 1894.

CAMPBELL, J. F. "The New Attitude", in *IW*, 21.5.1912, p. 408.

CAMPBELL, J. McLEOD. *The Nature of the Atonement and its Relation to Remission of Sins and Eternal Life.* Edinburgh 1856.

CARPENTER, S. C. *Church and People 1789–1889.* London 1933.

CHANDLER, J. S. *Seventy-five Years in the Madura Mission.* Madras s.a.

CHATTERJEE, A. & BURN, R. *British Contributions to Indian Studies.* London 1943.

CHATTERTON, E. *The Story of Fifty Years' Mission Work in Chhota Nagpur.* London 1901.

CHATURVEDI, B. & SYKES, M. *Charles Freer Andrews.* A Narrative. London 1949.

CHETTY, O. K. *William Miller.* Madras 1924.

CHIROL, V. *Indian Unrest.* London 1910.

COUPLAND, R. *The Indian Problem 1833–1935.* (Report on the Constitutional Problem in India, Part I.) London 1942.

CROOKE, W. *Religion and Folklore in Northern India.* 3rd ed. London 1926.

CROSS, F. L. *The Oxford Dictionary of the Christian Church.* Oxford 1957.

CUMMING, J. (ed.). *Political India 1832–1932.* A Co-operative Survey of a Century. London 1932.

[CURZON, Lord] *Lord Curzon in India.* Being a Selection from his Speeches as Viceroy and Governor-General of India, 1898–1905. London 1906.

DALTON, L. *The Story of the Oxford Mission to Calcutta.* London 1947.

DANN, I. G. "Methods of Study", in *IW*, 14.5.1912, p. 389.

DASGUPTA, H. N. *The Indian National Congress I–II.* Calcutta 1946.

DATTA, S. K. *The Desire of India.* London 1908.

—— "Causes of the Expansion or Retrogression of Religions in India", in *IRM* III (1914), pp. 649 ff.

DAVIES, A. W. "The 'New Thought' and the Missionary Message", in *IW*, 9.4.1912, pp. 287 ff.

DENNIS, J. S. *Christian Missions and Social Progress.* A Sociological Study of Foreign Missions. I–III. Edinburgh & London 1897.

DEWICK, E. C. "Dr. J. N. Farquhar: An Appreciation", in *YMI* XLI (1929), pp. 751 ff.

— *The Gospel and Other Faiths.* London 1948.

— *The Christian Attitude to Other Religions.* Cambridge 1953.

DIEHL, C. G. *Instrument and Purpose.* Studies on Rites and Rituals in South India. Lund 1956.

— *Kristendomens möte med religionerna.* Lund 1961.

DIGBY, W. *"Prosperous" British India: A Revelation from Official Records.* London 1901.

DILGER, W. *Die Erlösung des Menschen nach Hinduismus und Christentum.* Basel 1902.

— *Krischna oder Christus?* Eine religionsgeschichtliche Parallele. Basel 1904.

— *Probleme der Missionsarbeit im heutigen Indien.* Basel 1909.

DODWELL, H. H. (ed.). *The Cambridge History of India VI.* The Indian Empire 1858–1918. Cambridge 1932.

DUFF, A. *India and Indian Missions,* including Sketches of the Gigantic System of Hinduism. Edinburgh 1839.

— *Missionary Addresses.* Edinburgh 1850.

DUNBAR, G. *A History of India* from the Earliest Times to the Present Day I–II. 3rd ed. London 1943.

DUTT, R. *The Economic History of British India.* London 1902.

EBRIGHT, D. F. *The National Missionary Society of India 1905–1942.* An Expression of Movement towards Indigenization within the Indian Christian Community. Chicago 1944.

EDDY, G. S. "The Evangelization of India by Indians", in *FM* XIII: 3 (1906), pp. 16 ff.

— *India Awakening.* New York 1911.

— *The Students of Asia.* London 1917.

— *Pathfinders of the World Missionary Crusade.* New York 1945.

EDWARDS, T. R. "Face to Face with Hinduism", in *MH* VII (1905), pp. 488 ff., 533 ff.

ELLIOTT-BINNS, L. E. *Religion in the Victorian Era.* London 1936.

— *English Thought 1860–1900: The Theological Aspect.* London 1956.

ELMORE, W. T. *Dravidian Gods in Modern Hinduism.* New York 1925.

ESTBORN, S. *Indiens nydaning och kristendomen.* Stockholm 1945.

[Evangelical Union] *Report of the Proceedings of the Evangelical Union,* at its second annual meeting, held in Falkirk, June 16th–20th, 1845. Falkirk 1845.

— *The Worthies of the Evangelical Union.* Being the Lives and Labours of Deceased Evangelical Union Ministers. Glasgow 1883.

— *Jubilee Conference Memorial Volume,* issued by the Evangelical Union Conference 1892. Glasgow 1892.

EWING, A. H. "Christianity in India and in the Roman Empire—an Analogy", in *MCCM* IV (1904), pp. 225 ff.

FAIRBAIRN, A. M. *The Place of Christ in Modern Theology*. London 1893.
—— *The Philosophy of the Christian Religion*. London 1902.
—— *Catholicism, Roman and Anglican*. London 1903.
FARQUHAR, J. N. *The Higher Education of Christians in Bengal*. Reprinted from the *Indian Evangelical Review*, April 1896.
—— *The Crossbearer*. Being Extracts from the Gospel according to St. Matthew, Translated, Analysed and Explained in a Brief Commentary. Calcutta 1900.
—— *Christ and the Gospels*. A Letter to the Thinking Men of Calcutta. Calcutta 1901.
—— *Criticism and Christianity*. A Letter to the Thinking Men of Calcutta and Bengal. Calcutta 1901.
—— "The Science of Religion as an Aid to Apologetics", in *HF* XII (1901), pp. 369 ff.
—— *Great Religious Books*. Source unknown.
—— "The Church and Biblical Criticism", in *East and West* I (1902), pp. 1313 ff.
—— [ALEXANDER, Neil] *Gita and Gospel*. Calcutta 1903.
—— *Permanent Lessons of the Gita*. Madras 1903.
—— *The Future of Christianity in India*. (Pice Pamphlets No. I.) Madras 1904.
—— *The Age and Origin of the Gita*. (Pice Pamphlets No. III.) Madras 1904.
—— "Missionary Study of Hinduism", in *HF* XVI (1905), pp. 166 ff.
—— *Old Stalwarts of Bow Bazaar*. Calcutta 1904.
—— "A National Missionary Society for India", in *HF* XVII (1906), pp. 60 ff.
—— "Calcutta—Then and Now", in *FM* XIII: 5 (1906), pp. 17 ff.
—— "Education in India and Japan", in *MCCM* (1907), pp. 231 ff.
—— *Christianity in India*. Reprint from the *Contemporary Review*. Madras 1908. German translation in *AMZ* 35 (1908), pp. 465 ff.
—— *The Sermon on the Mount edited for Bible Circles*. Calcutta 1908.
—— "The Influence of India on Japan", in the *Hindustan Review* XVII (1908), pp. 329 ff.
—— "Christianity in India", in the *Indian World* VIII (1908), pp. 61 ff.
—— "The most Fruitful Apologetic Methods among Hindu Students", in the *Student World* I (1908), pp. 60 ff.
—— *The College St. Matthew*. The Text in the Revised Version with Introduction and Commentary. Madras 1909.
—— "Brāhma Samāj", in *ERE* II (1909), pp. 813 ff.
—— "The Bibles of India", in *YMI* XXI (1910), pp. 38 ff.
—— "The Hindu Conception of God and the World", in *YMI* XXI (1910), pp. 71 ff.
—— "Field Training for Missionaries", in *HF* XXI (1910), pp. 166 ff.
—— "Christ and the Religions of the World", in the *Student Movement* XII (1910), pp. 195 ff.

—— "The Greatness of Hinduism", in *CR* XCVII (1910), pp. 647 ff.

—— "The Crown of Hinduism", in *CR* XCVIII (1910), pp. 56 ff.

—— *Syncretism or Eclecticism?* Lecture given at the Edinburgh Continuation Committee Conference, Bengal. Calcutta 1912.

—— *Civic Virtues.* Lahore 1912.

—— *The Approach of Christ to Modern India.* Calcutta 1913.

—— *The Crown of Hinduism.* Oxford 1913.

—— "The Relation of Christianity to Hinduism", in *IRM* III (1914), pp. 417 ff.

—— *A Primer of Hinduism.* 2nd ed. Oxford 1914.

—— *Modern Religious Movements in India.* New York 1915.

—— *An Outline of the Religious Literature of India.* Oxford 1920.

—— *Some Thoughts on Christian Vernacular Literature.* Calcutta 1922.

—— "Christian Literature in Modern India", in *IW*, 5.7.1922, pp. 435 ff.

—— *Hinduism, its Content and Value.* Calcutta s.a.

FENGER, J. F. *History of the Tranquebar Mission.* Madras 1906.

FERGUSON, F. *A History of the Evangelical Union* from its Origin to the Present Time. Glasgow 1876.

FINDLAY, G. G. & HOLDSWORTH, W. W. *The History of the Wesleyan Methodist Missionary Society V.* London 1924.

FIRTH, C. B. *An Introduction to Indian Church History.* (The Christian Students' Library No. 23.) Madras 1961.

FISHER, G. M. *John R. Mott, Architect of Co-operation and Unity.* New York 1952.

FLEMING, J. R. *A History of the Church in Scotland 1843–1874.* Edinburgh 1927.

FLEMING, D. J. (ed.). *International Survey of the Young Men's and Young Women's Christian Associations.* New York 1932.

FORSYTH, P. T. *The Person and Place of Jesus Christ.* 6th ed. London 1948.

—— *The Cruciality of the Cross.* 4th imp. London 1957.

—— *The Work of Christ.* 6th imp. London 1958.

GAIRDNER, W. H. T. *"Edinburgh 1910".* An Account and Interpretation of the World Missionary Conference. Edinburgh 1910.

GARDNER, C. E. *Life of Father Goreh.* London 1900.

GHOSE, A. [Śri AUROBINDO] *Speeches.* Calcutta 1948.

GHOSE, A. K. "Japanese Polity", in *East and West* IV (1905), pp. 866 ff.

GLOVER, T. R. *The Jesus of History.* London 1907.

GLOVER, W. B. *Evangelical Nonconformists and Higher Criticism in the Nineteenth Century.* London 1954.

GOODALL, N. *A History of the London Missionary Society 1895–1945.* London 1954.

GOPAL, R. *Lokamanya Tilak.* A Biography. Bombay 1956.

GOPAL, S. *The Viceroyalty of Lord Ripon, 1880–1884.* London 1953.

GOREH, N. *Theism and Christianity I–II.* (Oxford Mission Occasional Papers Nos. 6 and 7.) Calcutta 1882.

GRAHAM, C. *Azariah of Dornakal.* London 1946.

GRANT, C. *Observations on the State of Society among the Asiatic Subjects of Great Britain.* London 1792.

GRANT, J. W. *Free Churchmanship in England 1870–1940.* With Special Reference to Congregationalism. London s.a.

GRIFFITHS, P. *The British Impact on India.* London 1952.

—— *Modern India.* London 1957.

GUPTA, U. K. "The Christ-Ideal in the Brahmo Samaj", in *East and West* I (1902), pp. 1434 ff.

"E.H." "Die Ueberwindung des Hinduismus durch das Evangelium", in *EMM* 58 (1914), pp. 294 ff., 340 ff.

HARGREAVES, R. *Red Sun Rising.* The Siege of Port Arthur. London 1962.

HARTENSTEIN, K. *Was hat die Theologie Karl Barths der Mission zu sagen?* 2 Aufl. München 1928.

HAYWARD, E. E. "Impressions of India", in *MH* X (1907), pp. 83 ff.

HEBERT, A. G. *Liturgy and Society.* The Function of the Church in the Modern World. Paperback ed. London 1961.

HINDEN, R. *Empire and After.* A Study of British Imperial Attitudes. London 1949.

HODGE, J. Z. *Bishop Azariah of Dornakal.* Madras 1946.

HOGG, A. G. *The Christian Interpretation of Mediation.* (Papers on the Great Truths of Christianity No. 10.) Madras 1904.

—— "All Things to All Men", in *HF* XVIII (1907), pp. 134 ff.

—— *Karma and Redemption.* An Essay toward the Interpretation of Hinduism and the Re-statement of Christianity. Madras 1909.

—— *Christianity as Emancipation from This World I–II.* Reprinted from *MCCM* IX (1909). Madras 1909.

—— "A New Year Message from India", in *World Missionary Conference News Sheet* (Jan. 1910).

—— *Christ's Message of the Kingdom.* Madras 1911.

—— "The God that must needs be Christ Jesus" I–IV, in *IRM* VI (1917), pp. 62 ff., 221 ff., 383 ff., 521 ff.

—— *Redemption from This World,* or the Supernatural in Christianity. Edinburgh 1922.

—— *The Christian Message to the Hindu.* Being the Duff Missionary Lectures for 1945 on the Challenge of the Gospel in India. London 1947.

HOGG, R. L. *A Master-builder on the Nile.* Being a Record of the Life and Aims of John Hogg, D.D., Christian Missionary. New York 1914.

HOGG, W. R. *Ecumenical Foundations.* A History of the International Missionary Council and its Nineteenth-Century Background. New York 1952.

HONDA, Y. "Some Results of the Federation Conference in Japan", in the *Student World* I (1908), pp. 4 ff.

HOPKINS, C. H. *History of the Y.M.C.A. in North America.* New York 1951.

HOWELLS, G. "Short Papers on Non-Christian Religions", in *MH* IX (1906), pp. 15 f., 55 f., 75 f., 111 f., 139 f., 181 f., 218 f., 247 ff., 282 ff.

HUNTER, A. M. *Teaching and Preaching the New Testament*. London 1963.

HUNTLY, W. "Farquhar's Fallacies", in *IW*, 16.4.1912, p. 306 f.

HUTTON, J. H. *Caste in India*. London 1946.

HYNDMAN, H. M. *The Awakening of Asia*. New York 1919.

IMMANUEL, R. D. *The Influence of Hinduism on Indian Christians*. Jabalpur 1950.

[Indian Empire] *The Indian Empire Reader*. Designed to show the progress of India under British rule, with the work yet to be done to make the country prosperous and happy. 2nd ed. Madras 1898.

JAMES, E. O. *Comparative Religion*. An Introductory and Historical Study. London 1938.

JAMES, H. R. *Education and Statesmanship in India 1797–1910*. London 1911.

JEWSON, A. "The New Attitude", in *IW*, 9.4.1912, p. 299.

JHAVERI, K. M. "Krishna, the Hindu Ideal", in *East and West* I (1902), pp. 657 ff.

JOB, G. V. and others. *Rethinking Christianity in India*. Madras 1938.

JONES, J. P. *India's Problem: Krishna or Christ?* London 1903.

—— "The Modern Missionary Attitude", in *IW*, 28.5.1912, p. 427.

KARANDIKAR, S. L. *Lokamanya Bal Gangadhar Tilak*. The Hercules and Prometheus of Modern India. Bombay 1957.

KELLETT, F. W. *Christ the Fulfilment of Hinduism*. (Papers for Thoughtful Hindus No. 10.) Madras 1896.

KENNET, C. E. *The Catechetical School of Alexandria*. Its Lessons to the Missionary Clergy of India. (Oxford Mission Occasional Papers No. 3.) Calcutta s.a.

KIDD, B. J. *Social Evolution*. London 1894.

—— *Principles of Western Civilization*. London 1902.

KNOWLES, D. *Lord Macaulay 1800–1859*. Cambridge 1960.

KRAEMER, H. "Christianity and Secularism", in *IRM* XIX (1930), pp. 195 ff.

—— *De Outmoeting van het Christendom en de Wereldsgodsdiensten*. 's-Gravenhage 1936.

—— *The Christian Message in a Non-Christian World*. London 1938.

—— *Religion and the Christian Faith*. London 1956.

—— *World Cultures and World Religions*. London 1960.

KRÄMER, A. *Christus und Christentum im Denken des modernen Hinduismus*. Bonn 1958.

LARSEN, L. P. "The Fact of Christ", in *MCCM* I (1902), pp. 640 ff.

—— "The Interest of Mystical Christianity to Missionaries", in *HF* XVI (1905), pp. 3 ff., 53 ff.

—— "Kristendom och folkkaraktären i Indien", in *Nutida Missionsupp-gifter,* pp. 101 ff. Uppsala 1906.

—— *Hindu-Aandsliv og Kristendommen.* København 1907.

—— *Religion och Kristendomen.* (Sveriges kristliga studentrörelses skrift-serie 35.) Uppsala 1913.

LATOURETTE, K. S. *A History of the Expansion of Christianity I–VII.* London 1938–1945.

—— *World Service.* A History of the World Service of the American Y.M.C.A. New York 1957.

LAZARUS, J. "The Future Religion of India", in *MCCM* VI (1907), pp. 449 ff.

LEFROY, G. A. *Christ the Goal of India.* (CMD Occasional Papers No. 15.) Cambridge 1889.

LINDSAY, A. D. and others. (ed.). *Report of the Commission on Christian Higher Education in India.* An Enquiry into the Place of the Christian College in Modern India. London 1931.

LLOYD, R. *The Church of England in the Twentieth Century I.* London 1946.

LONGRIDGE, G. & HUTTON, W. H. *A History of the Oxford Mission to Calcutta.* London 1910.

LOVETT, R. *The History of the London Missionary Society 1795–1895 I–II.* London 1899.

LOVETT, V. *A History of the Indian Nationalist Movement.* London 1920.

LUCAS, B. *The Empire of Christ.* Being a Study of the Missionary Enterprise in the Light of Modern Religious Thought. London 1907.

—— *Christ for India.* Being a Presentation of the Christian Message to the Religious Thought of India. London 1910.

—— *Our Task in India.* Shall we Proselytise Hindus or Evangelise India? London 1914.

—— "Not to Destroy, but to Fulfil", in *HF* XXXIV (1914), pp. 421 ff., 451 ff.

LUCAS, J. J. "Our Attitude to Non-Christian Religions", in *IW,* 14.5.1912, p. 388 f.

McCORKEL, R. J. (ed.). *Voices from the Younger Churches.* New York 1939.

McCULLY, B. T. *English Education and the Origins of Indian Nationalism.* New York 1940.

McGAVRAN, D. A. *The Bridges of God.* A Study in the Strategy of Missions. London 1955.

MACKICHAN, D. "A Present-day Phase of Missionary Theology", in *IRM* III (1914), pp. 243 ff.

McNEILL, J. T. *The History and Character of Calvinism.* New York 1954.

MACNICOL, N. "The Missionary Message and the Non-Christian Religions", in *IW,* 14.5.1912, p. 388.

—— *The Making of Modern India.* London 1924.

—— "Dr. J. N. Farquhar", in *YMI* XLI (1929), pp. 681 ff., and *NCCR* XLIX (1929), pp. 449 ff.

—— *India in the Dark Wood*. London 1930.

MACPHAIL, J. M. "St. Paul at Athens", in *IW*, 14.5.1912, p. 389.

[Mansfield] *Mansfield College, Oxford*. Its Origin and Opening, October 14–16, 1889. London 1890.

MANSHARDT, C. *Christianity in a Changing India*. An Introduction to the Study of Missions. Calcutta 1933.

MASANI, R. P. *Britain in India*. An Account of British Rule in the Indian Subcontinent. Bombay 1960.

MATHEWS, B. *Dr. Ralph Wardlaw Thompson*. London 1917.

—— *John R. Mott: World Citizen*. New York 1934.

MATHEWS, S. "Missions and the Social Gospel", in *IRM* III (1914), pp. 432 ff.

MATHIESON, W. L. *Church and Reform in Scotland*. A History from 1797 to 1843. Glasgow 1916.

MAURICE, F. *The Life of Frederick Denison Maurice I–II*. London 1884.

MAURICE, F. D. *On the Religions of the World*. 3rd ed. London 1852.

MAYHEW, A. *The Education of India*. A Study of British Educational Policy in India, 1835–1920, and of its Bearing on National Life and Problems in India today. London 1926.

—— *Christianity and the Government of India*. An Examination of the Christian Forces at work in the Government of India and of the Mutual Relations of the British Government and Christian Missions, 1600–1920. London 1929.

MAYNARD, J. D. "The Relation of Missions to Caste", in *HF* XVII (1906), pp. 447 ff.

MERSEY, Viscount. *The Viceroys and Governors-General of India 1757–1947*. London 1949.

MESTON, W. *Aspects of Indian Educational Policy*. Madras 1922.

MILBURN, R. G. "Christian Vedantism", in *Ind. Interp.* VII (1913), pp. 154 ff.

MILLER, W. *Indian Missions and How to View Them*. Edinburgh 1878.

—— *Educational Agencies in India*. Madras 1893.

—— *The Madras Christian College*. A Short Account of its History and Influence. Edinburgh 1905.

[Missionary] *Report of the General Missionary Conference, held at Allahabad 1872–1873*.

—— *The Missionary Conference: South India and Ceylon 1879 I–II*. Madras 1880.

—— *Report of the Centenary Conference on the Protestant Missions of the World, London 1888 I–II*. London 1888.

—— *Report of the Fourth Decennial Indian Missionary Conference held in Madras, December 11th–18th 1902*. Madras 1903.

MONIER-WILLIAMS, M. *The Study of Sanskrit in Relation to Missionary*

Work in India. An Inaugural Lecture Delivered before the University of Oxford on April 19, 1861. London 1861.
— *Indian Wisdom*. London 1875.
— *Hinduism*. London 1877.
— *Religious Thought and Life in India*. London 1885.
— *Modern India and the Indians*. 4th ed. London 1887.
— *Brahmanism and Hinduism*. London 1887.
— *The Bible and the Sacred Books of the East*. London 1887.
MONK, F. F. *A History of St. Stephen's College, Delhi*. Calcutta 1935.
MONTGOMERY, H. H. (ed.). *Mankind and the Church*. Being an Attempt to Estimate the Responsibilities of the Great Races to the Fulness of the Church of God. By Seven Bishops. London 1907.
MOODY, W. R. *D. L. Moody*. New York 1930.
MORAES, F. *Jawaharlal Nehru*. A Biography. New York 1957.
MORISON, J. & RUTHERFORD, A. C. *Evangelical Union*. Its Origin, and a Statement of its Principles. Glasgow 1845.
MORRIS, H. *The Life of John Murdoch*. London 1906.
MOSES, D. G. "Apologetical Literature since Farquhar", in *NCCR* LXXXIII (1963), pp. 276 ff.
MOTT, J. R. "The Christian Ministry in Relation to the Non-Christian World", in *The Report of the British Theological Students' Conference, held at Birmingham, April 12–16, 1898*, pp. 45 ff. London 1898.
— *The Decisive Hour of Christian Missions*. London 1910.
— "A World Missionary Conference", in *The East and the West* VI (1908), pp. 368 ff.
— (ed.). *The Continuation Committee Conferences in Asia 1912–1913*. A Brief Account of the Conferences together with their Findings and Lists of Members. New York 1913.
— (ed.). *Evangelism for the World Today* as Interpreted by Christian Leaders Throughout the World. New York 1938.
MOULTON, J. H. *Religions and Religion*. London 1911.
MUIR, J. *A Brief Account of our Lord's Life and Doctrines*. Calcutta 1848.
— *An Essay on Conciliation*. Calcutta 1849.
— *A Short Life of the Apostle Paul*. Calcutta 1850.
— *An Examination of Religions I–II*. Mirzapore 1852 (I), Calcutta 1854 (II).
MUKERJI, D. P. *Modern Indian Culture*. 2nd ed. Bombay 1948.
MUKERJI, N. G. *Missionary Colleges*. (Oxford Mission Association Paper No. 14.) Calcutta 1889.
— "The Presentation of Christianity to Hindus", in *Ind. Interp.* IV (1909), pp. 33 ff.
MUKHERJEE, H. & U. *Sri Aurobindo's Political Thought 1893–1908*. Calcutta 1958.
MÜLLER, F. M. *Chips from a German Workshop I–IV*. London 1867–1875.
— *Lectures on the Origins of Religion*. London 1882.
— *Biographical Essays*. New York 1884.

—— *India, What can it Teach Us?* London 1892.

—— *Last Essays I–II.* London 1901.

—— *Introduction to the Science of Religion.* (Collected Works XIV.) London 1909.

[MÜLLER] *The Life and Letters of the Rt. Hon. Friedrich Max Müller, Edited by his Wife I–II.* London 1902.

MULLICK, B. K. "Christianity in India", in the *Indian World* VII (1908), pp. 493 ff.

MURDOCH, J. *The Indian Student's Manual.* Madras 1887.

—— *A Religious History of India for Educated Hindus.* Madras 1900.

MURRAY, J. L. *The Organization of Mission Study among Students.* New York 1908.

MYLNE, L. G. *Missions to Hindus.* A Contribution to the Study of Missionary Methods. London 1908.

NAOROJI, D. *Poverty and un-British Rule in India.* London 1901.

[National] *The First Ten Years of the National Missionary Society 1905–1916.* Salem s.a.

NEILL, S. C. *Builders of the Indian Church.* Present Problems in the Light of the Past. London 1934.

—— *Men of Unity.* London 1960.

—— *A History of Christian Missions.* (The Pelican History of the Church: 6.) London 1964.

NISH, I. H. *Young Men's Christian Association of Calcutta 1857–1957.* Calcutta 1957.

OLDHAM, J. H. *The World and the Gospel.* London 1916.

O'MALLEY, L. S. S. (ed.). *Modern India and the West.* London 1941.

O'NEILL, S. W. *Brahmoism—Is it for or against Christianity?* (Oxford Mission Occasional Papers No. 2.) Calcutta s.a.

[Oxford] *India and Oxford.* Fifty Years of the Oxford Mission to Calcutta. London 1933.

PAL, B. C. *Nationality and Empire.* Calcutta 1916.

PANIKKAR, K. M. *Asia and Western Dominance.* A Survey of the Vasco Da Gama Epoch of Asian History 1498–1945. 2nd imp. London 1954.

—— *A Survey of Indian History.* 3rd ed. Bombay 1960.

PASCOE, C. F. *Two Hundred Years of the S.P.G. 1701–1900 I–II.* London 1901.

PATON, W. *Alexander Duff, Pioneer of Missionary Education.* London 1923.

PAUL, K. T. *The British Connection with India.* London 1927.

PHILIPS, C. H. and others (ed.). *Select Documents on the History of India and Pakistan IV.* The Evolution of India and Pakistan, 1858 to 1947. London 1962.

PICKETT, J. W. *Christian Mass Movements in India.* New York 1933.

POPLEY, H. A. *K. T. Paul, Christian Leader.* Calcutta 1938.

PURANI, A. B. *Sri Aurobindo in England*. Pondicherry 1956.

QUICK, O. C. *Liberalism, Modernism and Tradition*. London 1922.

RADHAKRISHNAN, S. *East and West in Religion*. London 1933.

RAGUVANSHI, V. P. S. *Indian Nationalist Movement and Thought*. 2nd ed. Agra 1959.

RAI, L. "Christianity and Hinduism", in the *Indian World* VII (1908), pp. 485 ff.

—— *Young India*. An Interpretation and a History of the Nationalist Movement from Within. 4th imp. Lahore 1927.

RAICHUR, S. R. S. *Religion in Public Education in India*. Mysore s.a.

REID, J. K. S. "Under-estimated Theological Books: A. G. Hogg's 'Christ's Message of the Kingdom'", in the *Expository Times* LXXII (1961), pp. 300 ff.

RICE, E. P. "The New Theology and Mission Work", in *HF* XIX (1908), pp. 364 ff.

RICHARDSON, A. *Christian Apologetics*. London 1947.

—— *The Bible in the Age of Science*. London 1961.

RICHTER, J. *Indische Missionsgeschichte*. 2 Aufl. Gütersloh 1924.

—— *Evangelische Missionskunde I–II*. 2 Aufl. Leipzig 1927.

ROBERTSON, A. "Eclecticism and Compromise", in *Ind. Interp.* IX (1914), pp. 41 ff.

ROBSON, J. *The Science of Religion and Christian Missions*. Glasgow 1876.

—— *Hinduism and Christianity*. 3rd ed. Edinburgh 1905.

RONALDSHAY, The Earl of. *The Life of Lord Curzon*. Being the Authorised Biography of George Nathaniel Marquess Curzon of Kedleston, K. G. I–III. London 1928.

ROUSE, R. *The World's Student Christian Federation*. London 1948.

ROUSE, R. & NEILL, S. C. (ed.). *A History of the Ecumenical Movement, 1517–1948*. London 1954.

ROUTLEY, E. *Hymns and Human Life*. London 1952.

ROWJI, R. B. "A Petition on behalf of the Rural Poor of India to H. E. Lord Curzon", in *East and West* I (1901), pp. 265 ff.

SANDEGREN, H. *Kast och Kristendom i Sydindien*. Stockholm 1921.

—— *Kristen och Hindu*. Stockholm 1934.

ŚARMA, D. S. *Studies in the Renaissance of Hinduism in the Nineteenth and Twentieth Centuries*. Benares 1944.

SAUNDERS, K. J. "The So-called New Attitude: A Few Platitudes for the Laity", in *IW*, 2.7.1912, p. 525 f.

SCHOMERUS, H. W. *Religionernas Kamp*. (Translation of *Das Geistesleben der nichtchristlichen Völker und das Christentum*.) Uppsala 1921.

—— *Kan Kristendomen erövra Indien?* (Translation from author's MS.) Stockholm 1923.

—— *Indien und das Christentum I–III*. Halle & Berlin 1931–1933.

SELBIE, W. B. *The Life of Andrew Martin Fairbairn*. London 1914.
—— *Congregationalism*. London 1927.
—— *Fifty Years at Oxford*. (Reprinted from the *Congregational Quarterly*.) London 1936.
SEN, K. C. *An Appeal to Young India*. Madras 1897.
SEN, P. A. N. *Memoir of the Revd. Canon W. E. S. Holland*. London 1951.
SHARMA, I. D. "Western Ideas and Indian Religious Renaissance", in the *East and West Review* XXVIII (1962), pp. 50 ff.
SHARPE, E. J. "Ett missionens dilemma", in *SMT* 48 (1960), pp. 244 ff.
—— "John Nicol Farquhar", in *Association Men* XIII: 8 (1961).
—— "Sri Aurobindos politiska filosofi", in *SMT* 50 (1962), pp. 151 ff.
—— *J. N. Farquhar: A Memoir*. Calcutta 1963.
—— "George Sherwood Eddy 1872–1963", in *SMT* 51 (1963), pp. 173 ff.
SHAY, T. L. *The Legacy of the Lokamanya*. The Political Philosophy of Bal Gangadhar Tilak. Bombay 1956.
SHEDD, C. P. (ed.). *History of the World's Alliance of Young Men's Christian Associations*. London 1955.
SHUKLA, B. D. *A History of the Indian Liberal Party*. Allahabad 1960.
SINGH, H. J. *Sri Aurobindo: His Life and Religious Thought*. Bangalore 1962.
SJÖLINDER, R. *Presbyterian Reunion in Scotland 1907–1921*. (Acta Universitatis Upsaliensis: Studia Historico-Ecclesiastica Upsaliensia 4.) Uppsala 1962.
SLATER, T. E. *Report of Work among the Educated Classes, Madras, in connection with the London Missionary Society*. Madras 1876.
—— *God Revealed*. An Outline of Christian Truth. Madras 1876.
—— *The Philosophy of Missions*. A Present-day Plea. London 1882.
—— *The Higher Hinduism in Relation to Christianity*. 2nd ed. London 1903.
—— *Missions and Sociology*. London 1908.
—— "Modern Theology and Missionary Enterprise", in *HF* XIX (1908), pp. 403 ff.
SMITH, G. *The Life of Alexander Duff*. 3rd ed. London 1899.
SMITH, W. M. *An Annotated Bibliography of D. L. Moody*. Chicago 1948.
SPEER, R. E. *Missionary Principles and Practice*. A Discussion of Christian Missions and Some Criticisms upon them. New York 1902.
—— *Missions and Modern History*. A Study of the Missionary Aspects of Some Great Movements of the Nineteenth Century. New York 1904.
—— *Christianity and the Nations*. (The Duff Lectures 1910.) New York 1910.
—— *Studies of Missionary Leadership*. (The Smyth Lectures 1913.) Philadelphia 1914.
STEINTHAL, F. W. "National Character in Making", in *FM* XIII: 4 (1906), pp. 22 ff.
—— "The Religious Aspect of the National Movement", in the *Indian World* VII (1908), pp. 395 ff.

378

STOCK, E. *The History of the Church Missionary Society I–III.* London 1899. *IV.* London 1916.

[Student Volunteer Movement] *Report of the Third International Convention of the Student Volunteer Movement.* New York 1898.

—— *The Student Volunteer Movement after Twenty-Five Years 1886–1911.* New York 1912.

SUNDARARAMAN, K. *Mr. J. N. Farquhar on Hinduism and Christianity— A Criticism.* Madras 1910.

SUNDKLER, B. G. M. *Church of South India.* The Movement towards Union 1900–1947. London 1954.

SWAVELY, C. H. (ed.). *The Lutheran Enterprise in India.* Madras 1952.

SWEET, W. W. *The Story of Religions in America.* 6th ed. New York 1930.

—— *The American Churches: An Interpretation.* New York 1948.

TAGORE, R. *Nationalism.* London 1918.

TATLOW, T. *The Story of the Student Christian Movement of Great Britain and Ireland.* London 1933.

TAYLOR, G. P. "Fulfilment or Antithesis: Which?" in *IW*, 14.5.1912, p. 387 f.

THOMAS, P. *Christians and Christianity in India and Pakistan.* A General Survey on the Progress of Christianity in India from Apostolic Times to the Present Day. London 1954.

THOMPSON, E. W. "The New Theology—A Criticism", in *HF* XIX (1908), pp. 379 ff.

[TILAK] *Speeches of Bal Gangadhar Tilak.* Madras 1918.

TOMLINSON, W. E. "An Evangelistic Experiment", in *HF* XXXV (1915), pp. 126 ff.

TREVELYAN, G. O. *The Life and Letters of Lord Macaulay.* London 1908.

TYSON, G. W. *The Bengal Chamber of Commerce and Industry 1853–1953.* Calcutta 1953.

VARMA, V. P. *The Political Philosophy of Sri Aurobindo.* London 1960.

WALTER, H. A. "Some Possibilities before our Movement in India", in *FM* XXI: 4 (1914), pp. 1 ff.

WARNECK, J. "Die missionarische Botschaft in Auseinandersetzung mit den nichtchristlichen Religionen" I–II, in *AMZ* 37 (1910), pp. 521 ff., 573 ff.

—— "Edinburg – eine Rechtfertigung der freien Theologie?" in *AMZ* 38 (1911), pp. 489 ff.

WEBB, C. C. J. *A Study of Religious Thought in England from 1850.* (The Olaus Petri Lectures 1932.) Oxford 1933.

WEITBRECHT, H. U. (ed.). *A Bibliography for Missionary Students.* London 1913.

WESTCOTT, A. *Life and Letters of Brooke Foss Westcott I–II.* London 1903.

WESTCOTT, B. F. *Christus Consummator.* Some Aspects of the Work and Person of Christ in Relation to Modern Thought. London 1886.

—— *Christian Aspects of Life.* London 1897.

WESTERN, F. J. *The Early History of the Cambridge Mission to Delhi* (cyclostyled). London 1950.

WESTMAN, K. B. "Missionens uppgift i Indien", in *Religion och Bibel* IV (1945), pp. 22 ff.

WESTMAN, K. B. & VON SICARD, H. *Den kristna missionens historia.* Stockholm 1960.

WHITE, J. C. "Seven Years in Calcutta", in *FM* VII: 3 (1900), pp. 5 ff.

WHITEHEAD, H. "The New Movement in India and the Old Gospel", in *The East and the West* IX (1911), pp. 1 ff.

—— *The Village Gods of South India.* 2nd ed. Madras 1921.

—— *Indian Problems in Religion, Education, Politics.* London 1924.

WIDENGREN, G. "Evolutionism and the Problem of the Origin of Religion", in *Ethnos* 10 (1945), pp. 57 ff.

—— *Religionens Ursprung.* Stockholm 1946.

WILDER, R. P. *An Appeal for India.* Calcutta 1896.

—— "The Indian National Union of Young Men's Christian Associations", in *FM* IX: 3 (1902), pp. 17 ff.

WILDER BRAISTED, R. *In This Generation: The Story of Robert P. Wilder.* New York 1941.

WILLEY, B. *More Nineteenth Century Studies.* A Group of Honest Doubters. London 1956.

WILLIAMS, C. *Lord Macaulay.* (Reprinted in *The Image of the City,* ed. RIDLER, A.) London 1958.

WINDISCH, E. *Die altindischen Religionsurkunden und die christliche Mission.* Leipzig 1897.

WOLFF, O. *Indiens Beitrag zum neuen Menschenbild.* Hamburg 1957.

WOODGATE, M. V. *Father Benson: Founder of the Cowley Fathers.* London 1953.

WOODRUFF, P. *The Men who Ruled India.* I – The Founders, II – The Guardians. London 1953.

[World] World Missionary Conference, 1910. *Report of Commission I, Report of Commission III, Report of Commission IV, The History and Records of the Conference (IX).* Edinburgh 1910.

[World's] *Report of the Conference of the World's Student Christian Federation held at Eisenach, Germany, July 13–17, 1898.*

—— *Zeist, Holland, May 3–7, 1905.*

—— *Tokyo, Japan, April 3–7, 1907.*

—— *Robert College, Constantinople, April 24–28, 1911.*

YOUNG, R. *The Success of Christian Missions.* London 1890.

ZAEHNER, R. C. *At Sundry Times.* An Essay in the Comparison of Religions. London 1958.

2. Official Printed Reports

The Church Missionary Society.
The London Missionary Society.
The Wesleyan Methodist Missionary Society.
The Church of Scotland Mission.
The United Free Church of Scotland Mission.

3. Books Edited by J. N. Farquhar 1915–1923 [not used in this study]

a. The Religious Quest of India Series (in chronological order).

MACNICOL, N. *Indian Theism,* 1915.
STEVENSON, Margaret. *The Heart of Jainism.* 1915.
MOULTON, J. H. *The Treasure of the Magi.* 1917.
CAVE, S. *Redemption Hindu and Christian.* 1919.
STEVENSON, Margaret. *The Rites of the Twice-born.* 1920.
MCKENZIE, J. *Hindu Ethics.* 1923.

b. The Heritage of India Series (in chronological order).

SAUNDERS, K. J. *The Heart of Buddhism.* 1915.
MACPHAIL, J. M. *Asoka.* 1917.
BROWN, P. *Indian Painting.* 1918.
RICE, E. P. *Kanarese Literature.* 1918.
KEITH, A. B. *The Samkhya System.* 1918.
MACNICOL, N. *Psalms of Maratha Saints.* 1920.
KEAY, F. E. *A History of Hindi Literature.* 1920.
KEITH, A. B. *The Karma Mimamsa.* 1921.
KINGSBURY, F. & PHILLIPS, G. E. *Hymns of the Tamil Saivite Saints.* 1921.
THOMPSON, E. J. *Rabindranath Tagore.* 1921.
POPLEY, H. A. *The Music of India.* 1921.
MACDONELL, A. A. *Hymns from the Rigveda.* 1922.
BROWN, C. J. *The Coins of India.* 1922.
THOMPSON, E. J. *Bengali Religious Hymns, Sakta.* 1923.
MACNICOL, M. *Poems by Indian Women.* 1923.
KEITH, A. B. *Classical Sanskrit Literature.* 1923.

c. The Religious Life of India Series (in chronological order).

WHITEHEAD, H. *The Village Gods of South India.* 1916.
WALTER, H. A. *The Ahmadiya Movement.* 1918.
BRIGGS, G. W. *The Chamars.* 1920.
UNDERHILL, M. M. *The Hindu Religious Year.* 1922.

4. Newspapers and Periodicals

Aberdeen Free Press, The. 1913.
Allgemeine Missions-Zeitschrift. 1908–1914.
Association Men. 1961.

Biblical Repository, The. 1860.
British Weekly, The. 1912.
Church Missionary Intelligencer, The. 1855–58, 1880–1905.
Church Missionary Review, The. 1906–09.
Contemporary Review, The. 1910.
East and the West, The. 1904–14.
East and West. 1902–05.
East and West Review, The. 1962.
Epiphany, The. 1890–1911.
Ethnos. 1945.
Evangelisches Missions-Magazin. 1913–14.
Expository Times, The. 1961.
Foreign Mail. 1900–14.
Harvest Field, The. 1901–15.
Hindu, The. 1937.
Hindustan Review, The. 1908.
Indian Interpreter, The. 1907–14.
Indian Witness, The. 1912, 1922.
Indian World, The. 1908.
Inquirer, The. 1902–08.
International Review of Missions, The. 1912–64.
Madras Christian College Magazine, The. 1902–14.
Manchester Guardian, The. 1929.
Missionary Herald, The. 1900–11.
National Christian Council Review. 1929, 1963.
Nordisk Missions-Tidsskrift. 1964.
Observer, The. 1929.
Scotsman, The. 1929.
Statesman, The. 1929.
Student Movement, The. 1910.
Student World, The. 1908–14.
Svensk Missionstidskrift. 1913, 1960–64.
Times, The. 1929.
Young Men of India, Burma and Ceylon, The. 1910, 1929.

5. *Other Works of Reference*

Dictionary of National Biography (1885 ff.).
Encyclopaedia Britannica (1911 and 1963 eds.).
Encyclopaedia of Religion and Ethics, ed. HASTINGS (1908 ff.).

Index of Personal Names

HIEBERT LIBRARY

3 6877 00039 0319

DATE DUE

DE 20'91			
JA17'94			
MY22'92			
DE18'92			

BV   33627
3269
.F23   Sharpe, Eric J.
S53   Not to destroy but to
1965   fulfil.

HIEBERT LIBRARY
Fresno Pacific College - M. B. Seminary
Fresno, Calif 93702

DEMCO